W9-BRI-931
Parc de la Villette
JULES JOFFRIN
MARCADET POISSONNIERS
MARX DORMOY
CRIMEE
JOINVILLE
Canal de l'Ourcq
Flandre
LAMARCK CAULAINCOURT
Basilique du Sacré Cœur
Bd Barbès
CHATEAU ROUGE
Rue Marx Dormoy
RIQUET
Rue de
Jaurès
PORTE DE PANTIN
OURCQ
Bassin d. l. Villette
Av Jean
18E
BARBES
LA CHAPELLE
STALINGRAD
LAUMIERE
19E
ABBESSES
Bd de Rochechouart
Bd de la Chapelle
BARBES ROCHECHOUART
ANVERS
JAURES
LOUIS BLANC
DANUBE
GARE DU NORD
Rue du Faubourg St Denis
BOLIVAR
Parc des Buttes Chaumont
MAIRIE DES LILAS
Rue des Martyrs
St Martin
CHATEAU LANDON
Canal St Martin
BOTZARIS
PRE ST GERVAIS
Rue de Paris
Bd Sérurier
9E
POISSONNIERE
Bd de
SAINT QUENTIN
Rue de Strasbourg
GARE DE L'EST
Faubourg
COLONEL FABIEN
BUTTES CHAUMONT
CADET
PLACE DES FETES
PORTE DES LILAS
ELETIER
GARE DE L'EST
JOURDAIN
TELEGRAPHE
10E
Rue du Magenta
PYRENEES
Bd Montmartre
CHATEAU D'EAU
Bd de Strasbourg
BELLEVILLE
Bd Mortier
GRANDS BOULEVARDS
Bd Poissonnière
Bd de Bonne Nouvelle
BONNE NOUVELLE
JACQUES BONSERGENT
Parc de Belleville
Rue de Ménilmontant
ST FARGEAU
Av Gambetta
La Bourse
STRASBOURG ST DENIS
GONCOURT
BOURSE
SENTIER
Bd St Martin
COURONNES
PELLEPORT
2E
REPUBLIQUE
20E
RÉAUMUR SEBASTOPOL
ARTS ET METIERS
TEMPLE
Rue St Martin
Bd du Temple
MENILMONTANT
GALLIENI
Rue Montmartre
Rue Turbigo
Rue Réaumur
PARMENTIER
OBERKAMPF
Av de la République
Rue Belgrand
GAMBETTA
E. MARCEL
Bd Sébastopol
Rue du Temple
ST MAUR
PORTE DE BAGNOLET
Av de la République
LES HALLES
Forum
Centre National d'Art et de Culture G. Pompidou
Rue Beaubourg
3E
FILLES DU CALVAIRE
ST AMBROISE
PERE LACHAISE
Cimetière du Père Lachaise
CHATELET LES HALLES
RAMBUTEAU
ST SEBASTIEN FROISSART
RICHARD LENOIR
11E
LOUVRE RIVOLI
Rue de Rivoli
Rue du Renard
Bd Beaumarchais
Rue Richard Lenoir
Bd Voltaire
VOLTAIRE
PONT NEUF
CHATELET
PHILIPPE AUGUSTE
Conciergerie Ste Chapelle
HOTEL DE VILLE
CHEMIN VERT
BREGUET SABIN
ALEXANDRE DUMAS
Place de la Réunion
Hôtel de Ville
ST PAUL
Place de Vosges
RICHARD LENOIR
REUNION
Quai des Gr. Augustins
Bd du Palais
CITE
Rue de la Cité
Quai de l'Hôtel de Ville
PONT MARIE
Rue St Antoine
CHARONNE
PORTE DE MONTREUIL
ST MICHEL
Notre-Dame
ST MICHEL NOTRE DAME
Quai des Célestins
BASTILLE
MARAICHERS
ODEON
4E
BOULETS MONTREUIL
CLUNY SORBONNE
MAUBERT
SULLY MORLAND
Opéra Bastille
Rue du Faubourg St Antoine
AVRON
BUZENVAL
Bd Davout
Quai de la Tournelle
Bd St Germain
MAUBERT MUTUALITE
Bd Morland
Quai Henri IV
Bd Bourdon
Bd de la Bastille
LEDRU ROLLIN
FAIDHERBE CHALIGNY
ALIGRE
Place d'Aligre
NATION
Cours de Vincennes
PORTE DE VINCENNES
Bd St Michel
Rue St Jacques
L'Institut du Monde Arabe
Sorbonne
Quai St Bernard
Bd Diderot
REUILLY DIDEROT
CARDINAL LEMOINE
Panthéon
QUAI DE LA RAPEE
GARE DE LYON
LUXEMBOURG
JUSSIEU
Place de la Contrescarpe
Jardin des Plantes
GARE DE LYON
MONTGALLET
PICPUS
Quai de la Rapée
5E
PLACE MONGE
Musée National d'Histoire Naturelle
GARE D'AUSTERLITZ
Av Daumesnil
12E
BEL AIR
Rue Mouffetard
Bd de l'Hôpital
Quai d'Austerlitz
BERCY
DAUMESNIL
Bd Soult
PORT ROYAL
CENSIER DAUBENTON
Bd de Bercy
Palais Omnisports de Paris-Bercy
GARE DE PARIS-BERCY
DUGOMMIER
Bd de Port Royal
Bd St Marcel
ST MARCEL
QUAI DE LA GARE
Quai de la Gare
MICHEL BIZOT
Le Parc de Bercy
LES GOBELINS
CAMPO FORMIO
Seine
Quai de Bercy
PORTE D'OREE
CHEVALERET
Rue Auriol
Quai F. Mauriac
Bibliothèque Nationale de France-F. Mitterrand
Av des Gobelins
JACQUES
Bd Vincent
NATIONALE
Bois de Vincennes
Bd Poniatowski
GLACIERE
PLACE D'ITALIE
13E
PORTE DE CHARENTON
CORVISART
AUGUSTE BLANQUI
BIBLIOTHEQUE

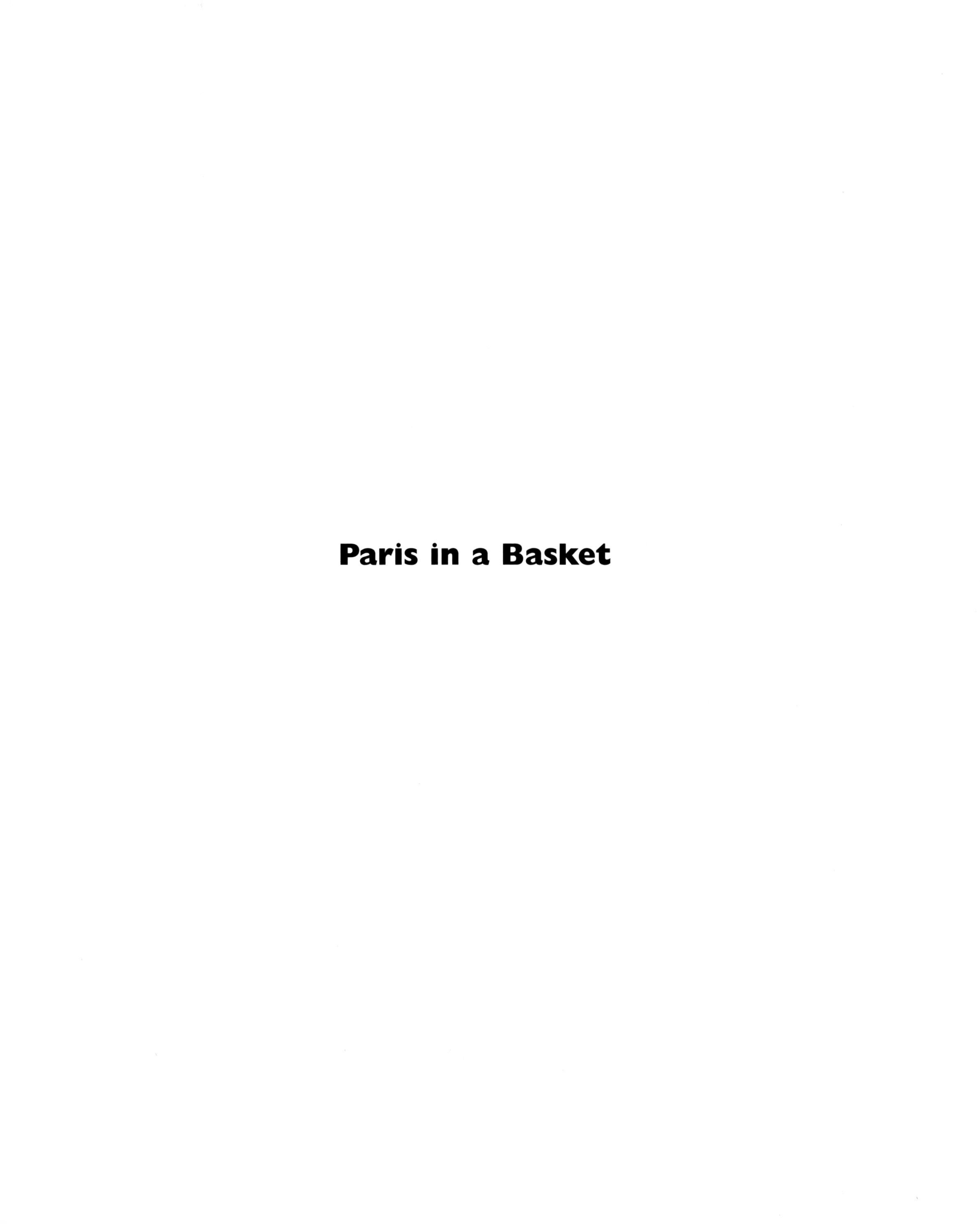

Paris in a Basket

This book would not have been possible without the help and support of our friends and families.
In particular, we would like to thank:
Aurore Besson, Paul Bocuse, Kevin Caldwell, Yves Clerc, Alain Cirelli, Roberto Dutesco, Duccio Ermenegildo, Ben Gdalewicz, Ellen Kaplowitz, Ulli and Ellen Kurtinat, Philippe Levy, Rita Alix Meyer, Anthony and Cayetana Meyer, François Mouriès, Brian Nakauchi, Eric Philippe, Babou, and Editha Poniatowski, Cynthia Rosenfeld, Elisabeth Slama, Alejandro, and Sheila Smith, Ellen Sugarman, Gottfried Tollmann, Elizabeth Will, Brigitte Willisch, and Johannes Zilkens.

Our deepest gratitude to Laura Capsoni and Christoph Radl for their time, creativity, and generosity in helping us complete our project.

We appreciate the technical expertise and enthusiasm of
Camilla Invernizzi, Roberto Gennari, Pia Scavia Sophia Wellmans, and Olaf Wipperfurth; the contributions made by:
Marie Christine and Jean Marie Allemoz - Caves Pétrissans; Isabelle Bantegny - Hediard; Gilles Bauduin - FNAC;
Pascal Bensidoun; Alice Bouteille - Fauchon; Caviar Kaspia; Carol Chretiennot - Café de Flore; Terri de Vito;
Marie-Héléne Passemier - Nicolas; Michel-Jacques Perrochon - Brasserie Lipp; and Pierre Tellier;
as well as the impromptu cooperation of: François Bastchera, Bruno Cigoi, Marie-France de Chabaneix,
Contesse Lucienne von Doz, Catherine Lacipiére, Penta Swanson, Mario Sampaio, and Michel Trousselle.

Finally, we would like to thank all of the vendors at the markets
who shared their know-how and joie de vivre making our work so enjoyable and enriching.
Among the many, special thanks to: Jean and Lucette Allain, Abdelrani and Laurence Benkritly, Edouard Boghossian, Annie Boulanger, André Camboulas, George Capitano-Courtot, Claude Ceccaldi, Madeleine and Basil Chauvel, Claudine and Jean Claude Crié, Nicole Denoit, Michel Felten, Christian Gardy, Henri-Jean Giboulot, Ginette Leconte, Monique and Daniel Letard, Jean-Marie Loren, Jacky Lorenzo, Dominique Martino, Laurence and Pascal Miolane, Raymond Neveux, Madame Ndongo, Philippe Perrete, Ibu Tall, and Joël Thiébault.

For my always inspiring and inspired mother, Rita Alix Meyer.

•

For my parents, Alejandro and Sheila Smith, in loving memory
of my sister, Maruca.

Bonner Straße 126, D-50968 Cologne

Publishing and art direction: Peter Feierabend
Project managment: Miriam Rodriguez Startz
Editing: Burke Barrett
Design: Laura Capsoni & Christoph Radl, R.A.D.L. Inc., New York
Production: Oliver Benecke
Reproduction: Omnia Scanners, Milan
Printing and binding: Mladinska knjiga tiskarna d.d., Ljubljana

Printed in Slovenia
ISBN 3-8290-4624-3

10 9 8 7 6 5 4 3 2 1

NICOLLE AIMEE MEYER & AMANDA PILAR SMITH

Paris in a Basket

MARKETS – THE FOOD AND THE PEOPLE

FOREWORD BY PAUL BOCUSE

KÖNEMANN

CONTENTS

Foreword by Paul Bocuse • *9*

Introduction • *12*

Ier - IVe ARRONDISSEMENTS • THE BELLY OF PARIS • *Les Halles* • *16*

Ve ARRONDISSEMENT • LITERARY LEGUMES • *The Maubert Market* • *38*

VIe ARRONDISSEMENT • THE GREENS OF SAINT GERMAIN • *The Raspail Organic Market* • *60*

VIIe ARRONDISSEMENT • IN THE SHADOW OF THE EIFFEL TOWER • *The Saxe-Breteuil Market* • *82*

VIIIe ARRONDISSEMENT • A LA MADELEINE • *The Aguesseau Market* • *104*

IXe - Xe ARRONDISSEMENTS • SLIM PICKINGS • *The Saint Quentin Market* • *120*

XIe ARRONDISSEMENT • STORMING THE BASTILLE • *The Richard Lenoir Market* • *134*

XIIe ARRONDISSEMENT • THE NOTRE DAME OF MARKETS • *The Aligre Market* • *158*

XIIIe ARRONDISSEMENT • A DAY IN THE COUNTRY • *The Auguste Blanqui Market* • *178*

XIVe ARRONDISSEMENT • A HIDDEN GEM • *The Montrouge Market* • *198*

XVe ARRONDISSEMENT • TO MARKET! TO MARKET! • *The Saint Charles Market* • *216*

XVIe ARRONDISSEMENT • FARMERS FOR THE HAUTE COUTURE • *The Président Wilson Market* • *236*

XVIIe ARRONDISSEMENT • A RAILROAD TO GREENER PASTURES • *The Batignolles Organic Market* • *260*

XVIIIe ARRONDISSEMENT • PARIS PAS CHER • *The Barbès Market* • *278*

XIXe ARRONDISSEMENT • THE MELTING POT • *The Joinville Market* • *296*

XXe ARRONDISSEMENT • VIVE LA FRANCE • *The Réunion Market* • *314*

Market Schedule • *338*

Market Addresses • *340*

Fish, Cheese, and Meat Charts • *342*

Cooking Glossary • *347*

Glossary • *348*

Addresses • *350*

Bibliography • *351*

MARKET RECIPES

APPETIZERS

ARTICHAUDS A L'ANCHOIADE • Artichoke Anchoiade • 58
SOUFFLE AUX FLEURS DE COURGETTE • Squash Flower Soufflé • 79
TAPENADE • Olive Caviar • 90
TARTE AU CHEVRE • Zucchini and Fresh Chèvre Tart • 101
DOLMA • 103
TERRINE DE FOIE GRAS • Foie Gras • 118
TERRINE DE LAPIN ET CONFITURE D'OIGNONS • Rabbit Pâté with Onion Jam • 195
POMMES DE TERRE AU CANTAL • Pan Gratinéed Potatoes • 197
RACLETTE AU MONT D'OR • Creamy Mont d'Or Raclette • 209
PISSALADIERE • Onion Tart • 232
FLEURS DE COURGETTE A L'ITALIENNE • Crispy Fried Zucchini Flowers • 255
CREPES AU SARRASIN • Sweet or Salty Buckwheat Crêpes • 275
CAVIAR D'AUBERGINE • Eggplant Caviar • 293
PASTILLA MAROCCAINE AU PIGEON • Moroccan Pigeon Pastilla • 294
CHAMPIGNONS DE PARIS FOURRES AUX ESCARGOTS • Escargot Stuffed Mushroom Caps • 305

SOUPS

SOUPE A L'OIGNON ET AU XERES • Onion Soup with Sherry • 37
SOUPE AUX MARRONS • Creamy Chestnut Soup • 196
VICHYSSOISE D'AVOCAT • Avocado Vichyssoise • 293

SALADS

SALADE DE MACHE ET DE BETTERAVE • Parisian Beet and Lambs Lettuce Salad • 79
SALADE DE COQUILLES ST JACQUES AU MONBAZILLAC • Scallop Salad with Monbazillac Vinaigrette • 117
SALADE DE POULPES ET DE POMMES DE TERRE • Mediterranean Octopus and Potato Salad • 155
SALADE AUX HERBES • Summer Herb Salad • 277

FISH AND SHELLFISH

HUITRES A LA NAGE • Oysters in a Riesling and Cream Broth • 57
SARDINES FRAICHES PRINTANIERES • Marinated Sardines with Spring Vegetables • 132
DORADE AU FENOUIL • Fennel Baked Sea Bream • 156
RAIE A LA VINAIGRETTE TIEDE • Skate with Warm Caper and Olive Vinaigrette • 176
BRUSCHETTA AUX PETONCLES • Bay Scallop Bruschetta • 232
TIMBALE DE CRABE ET RATATOUILLE • Ratatouille and Crab Timbale • 256
PAVE DE SAUMON A LA SALADE DE LENTILLES • Poached Salmon with "Puy" Lentils • 275
FRITURE D'EPERLAN • Two-Minute Fish Fry • 311
MOULES MARINIERES • Mussels Steamed with Shallots and Wine • 333
BRANDADE DE MORUE • Southern Style Codfish and Potato Purée • 334

POULTRY

LAPIN AU CALVADOS • Normandy-Style Rabbit Stew • 58
COQ AU VIN • Burgundy-Style Chicken Stew • 131
YASSA DE POULET • Spicy Lime Yassa Chicken • 155
MAGRET DE CANARD AU PORTO • Seared Magret of Duck in a Sweet Port Sauce • 175
PINTADE AU CHOU • Guinea Hen and Crinkly Cabbage • 196
CHAPON AU CHAMPAGNE • Capon with Champagne and Truffles • 214
CAILLES AUX FIGUES FRAICHES • Roasted Quails with Fresh Figs • 235
CANARD AUX CERISES • Cherry Roast Duck • 312
POULET AU RIESLING • Alsatian Style Chicken • 312

MEAT

POT AU FEU • Savory Bouillon Beef Pot • 35
ONGLET A L' ECHALOTE • Seared Steak in a Shallot and Wine Sauce • 80
PALETTE DE PORC FERMIER AU FOUR • Thyme Roasted Pork Shoulder • 101
CHEVREUIL AUX PRUNEAUX • Venison Chops in a Prune and Cognac Sauce • 117
ROGNONS DE VEAU A LA CREME • Veal Kidneys in a Cognac Cream Sauce • 131
AGNEAU AUX HARICOTS BLANCS • Lamb and White Bean Ragout • 175
ROTI DE VEAU AUX CAROTTES DOUCES • Veal Roast with Sweet Carrots • 256
BŒUF BOURGUIGNON • Beef Stew Simmered in Burgundy Wine • 258
TAGINE D'AGNEAU AUX CITRONS CONFITS • Tagine of Lamb, Olives, and Salt-Cured Lemons • 294
HACHIS PARMENTIER • Oven-Baked Meat and Potato Mash • 333

DESSERTS

MOUSSE AU CHOCOLAT • Classic Chocolate Mousse • 37
SOUFFLE AUX FRAMBOISES • Raspberry Soufflé • 80
GATEAU AUX AMANDES ET AU CHOCOLAT • Almond and Chocolate Cake • 103
MADELEINES • 118
SORBET DE KIWI • Kiwi Sorbet • 133
GATEAU AU FROMAGE BLANC • Fresh Farmer's Cheese Cake • 156
TARTE AUX MIRABELLES • Yellow Plum Tart • 176
COMPOTE DE FRUITS SECS • Stewed Fruits in White Wine • 197
GATEAU AUX POMMES • Warm Butter Apple Ring • 214
CREME CARAMEL • 235
TARTE AU CITRON • Lemon Curd Tart • 258
GATEAU A L'ORANGE • Glazed Orange and Cointreau Pound Cake • 277
COINGS POCHES AU CASSIS • Autumn Quince Poached in Cassis • 313
CLAFOUTI AUX CERISES • Cherry Clafouti • 334

COUNT / SIZE

Take hold of your basket and follow our two guides Nicolle Aimée Meyer and Amanda Pilar Smith, who invite you on one of the most original tours of Paris: that of the markets, neighborhood by neighborhood.

Forget the noise and bustle of the city and dive into a world of charming banter, where each of your senses is enticed by a wide variety of aromas and colors as well as voices both local and exotic. This is clearly a most engaging atmosphere, where you always sense the pulse of the city.

Maraîchers and local producers from the countryside call out to each other and squabble for the privilege of serving you. Here you can choose the choicest products–and it's certainly all right to haggle and sample the goods on offer, as long as you ask nicely. And these are just some of the bonuses of the markets. Put aside any shopping lists and routines and allow yourself to be tempted by the seasonal offerings while keeping an ear out for the vendors' suggestions and secret family recipes.

Take advantage of these exceptional places: a blending of cultures, tastes, and ideas, where everyone amicably meets and chats, all the time focusing on the simple pursuit of taking home the best. In order to get the best, be sure to set your alarm, as the most gorgeous displays are unveiled before 9 o'clock. Around this time you will have the chance to choose fresh produce that has been picked as recently as the night before, or, when weather permits, that very morning! As motivation, early risers can indulge in a *petit café* and croissant or buttered baguette at a local bistro before heading to the market.

For those of you who do not own an alarm clock and arrive a bit later, an early apéritif or glass of white wine accompanied by a few oysters or slivers of *saucisson* await you at the bar of these same bistros. This will fortify you for venturing into the market or to one of the many specialty food shops suggested in this book, to gather the provisions for your next meal.

Above all, do not forget to give a word of encouragement to the vendors when you find quality products. They value your opinion and it helps them to keep their stand and forge ahead in their continuing fight against industrialized products.

For those of you for whom it has become a "religion" to eat organic, here you will find some very precious addresses.
And remember, depending on the location of the market, diverse offerings such as clothing, shoes, hardware, birdseed, and so on can be found.

No matter what market you attend, you will be spoilt for choice by merchants whose creed is *joie de vivre* and you will come away feeling in the best of spirits. If, in addition, you happen upon a ray of sunshine, the bliss will certainly be complete!

When you return home, removing all of the marvelous products from your by now heavy basket, you will think of our two authors who completed this book for all those who enjoy good eating. Congratulations Nicolle Aimée and Amanda Pilar, we are enchanted. Thanks to this unforgettable promenade, we will soon be able to sit down to a meal, happy in mind and spirit.

Paul Bocuse

Paul Bocuse

POMMES DE TERRE

DERALE DES MARCHES
nfiance à notre adhérent
TUIT Jean-Pierre
97

INTRODUCTION

Imagine walking through the beautiful city of Paris, past the Eiffel Tower and the Louvre, sitting down at a sunny café terrace for a frothy *café au lait* then continuing on to luscious Notre Dame and suddenly stumbling onto a quaint square filled with titilating sights and smells: pyramids of succulent fruits, stacks of cheeses, rows of fresh pâtés, the wafting aroma of roasting chickens, bursts of peonies, and choreographed displays of sleek fish shimmering on beds of crushed ice. Or emerging from the métro in a sleepy part of town to find a whole stretch of pavement taken over by a riot of colorful canopies: hundreds of people making their way along a narrow aisle picking and choosing from a sea of produce with the cries of the vendors ringing through the morning air. Paris' open-air food markets are the city's best kept secret.

Having an open-air market at our doorstep triggered our curiosity; we wondered if we were just very fortunate or if the rest of Paris was able to profit from such a luxury. We soon could be seen pedaling to every corner of the city on our bicycles, equipped with cameras and note pads. What started as a hobby soon developed into a passion and the basis of this book. Anyone living in Paris is aware of their own local market but few would be savvy to the magnitude and diversity of this undertaking. We never imagined that there were as many as 62 of these roving markets, mobilizing an army of over 20,000 vendors, making Paris one of the best food-distributed capitals of the world. Guiding you from market to market, *Paris in a Basket* will open the doors to the city, its history, and its culinary customs.

A tradition that was established as far back as the 5th century when hawkers trafficked their wares on the square of Notre Dame, markets continue to be an important part of each Parisian's everyday life. Every evening along busy boulevards and tree-lined squares, iron poles are snapped into the pavement, canopies are unrolled, and the skeleton of the market is assembled awaiting the arrival of the vendors and their produce. Come rain or shine, by 6 a.m. the following morning, vendors who drive in from their farms or from the wholesale market, Rungis, can be seen setting up their trestle tables and unloading their many specialties. Tables are covered, backdrops are put up, lights are strung, displays are lovingly assembled, prices are chalked onto blackboards, and scales are adjusted. By 8 a.m. the first shoppers trickle into the aisles, equipped with baskets and caddies, to snatch up the freshest salads, the tastiest cuts of meat, the best catch of the day, and the choicest fruit.

Through the course of the morning the markets burst into life: customers line up at their favorite stands, neighbors share snippets of gossip, vendors hurriedly meet orders and offer tastings, pan handlers stake out strategic spots, dogs sniff under the tables for a little treat, babies in carriages blissfully teethe on a crust of baguette, and children peer over the sides of the displays, eye-to-eye with sugary tarts or savory hams. Time flies, and by 1 p.m. the crowds begin to thin, shoppers make their way home with heavy baskets and bulging plastic bags, and the stands are slowly dismantled. The vendors take a moment's rest for a cigarette and a chat, the remaining produce vanishes back into the refrigerated trucks, and towering stacks of empty crates and cardboard boxes tumble into the gutter. Dressed in green work frocks and armed with fluorescent green brooms, the city's clean-up crew tackles the mounds of debris while pigeons scavenge for the last morsels. By 3 p.m. the stretch returns to its original state without a hint of all the commotion that has just occured.

Markets are a living entity and they reflect the local color of each neighborhood giving you an insight into day-to-day life. The city is divided into 20 neighborhoods called "arrondissements", that start at the center of Paris and spiral around in the form of a snail ending at the easternmost section. Each of these arrondissements has its own character and history and in many cases its own culture. We have organized the book in the same manner as the city is planned. With each chapter you will discover a new arrondissement and our favorite of its markets, which we have chosen on the basis of its atmosphere and offerings. When there is more than one market in an arrondissement, which is often, you will find a brief description of each within the chapter as well as a table at the end of the book which lists the ratings and exact locations–you can use this as a guide. Here you will also find a complete list of all the shops and restaurants mentioned in the book as well as contact information for persons with (*) by their name.

We focus mainly on open-air markets due to their unique and festive atmosphere. Like a country fair, these markets transform bare strips of pavement into lively venues. Every season brings new colors and tastes, weekends invite a mélange of shoppers, entertainers serenade the crowds, and hectic city life seems to disappear behind the abundant displays and cheerful bantering of the vendors. Sweet-smelling melons, rows of freshly baked breads, and buckets of olives magically transport you to a sunny square in Provence–or bustling crowds, fragrant spices, and resonating cries might lead you through the packed aisles of a Moroccan *souk*. Often the backdrop of the markets are just as breathtaking as the displays themselves, and what a treat it is to look up from a bunch of radishes and see the Eiffel Tower or golden Genie de la Bastille hovering above.
Open-air markets are held only two or three times a week at any given location and open only in the morning hours (8 a.m. to 1 p.m.). Vendors pay yearly dues at one, two, or more of these markets where they set up on a regular basis, so as to establish a clientele. Covered markets and street markets are also reviewed in this book but given much less importance. Covered markets are food halls with individual stalls; street markets are pedestrian areas where shops open up their displays onto the sidewalk. They are open all day, every day of the week, except for the sacred lunch hour and the sacred Monday!

Delving into the market life and understanding the customs that surround it shows you another facet of this magnificent city. Through our tour of Paris we have stumbled upon restaurants and hidden nooks and crannies, visited all of the monuments and sights, and have spent many hours chatting with the vendors we present to you along with their secrets and know-how. All were enthusiastic about our project and many gave us their family recipes, which we prepared in our humble kitchen on two electric burners and a counter-top oven. Though some may seem quite sophisticated, they are foolproof and surprisingly easy to make.

Whether you spend the morning dallying away on a sunny marketplace, curling up on your sofa for an afternoon of reading, or preparing one of these recipes for a quiet tête-a-tête, we hope that through *Paris in a Basket* you will experience the same joy as we did, discovering Paris' colorful market life and traveling to the heart and soul of this magical city.

This symbol indicates a brief description of the other markets that are located in each arrondissement.

40F

25 Fr

Cachés par une primevère,

Une caille, un merle

sifleur,

Buvaient tous deux au

même verre

Dans une belladone

en fleur.

Victor Hugo

20

Ier-IVe ARRONDISSEMENTS

Traffic reigns in the heart of Paris: exasperated drivers nervously drum their fingers on dashboards, noisy vespas zigzag through a sea of cars, and throngs of pedestrians crowd narrow sidewalks. The area encompassing the first four arrondissements is one of the most congested and visited sections of the city. The conglomeration of monuments, ancient relics, museums, squares, shops, churches, department stores, and a massive commuter train station squeezed into this central part of town is mind-boggling. In addition to being home to the medieval streets and buildings of the Marais, the palace and gardens of the Louvre, the Gothic towers and spires of Notre Dame, and the superb buildings of Place Vendôme, for many centuries the heart of the city was also the site of the largest wholesale market in the world, Les Halles. Independent from the goings-on in the rest of the *quartier*, the "citizens" of Les Halles worked 24-hour days to assure the distribution of food to every corner of Paris. It is said that the commotion one finds here now was multiplied threefold—traffic then included trucks, horses, wagons, baskets, and cartons blocking the way. When Les Halles was closed down at the end of the 1960s and replaced by an antiseptic shopping mall, it was feared that the life would be drained from the area. This has not been the case. Even if the heart of the city no longer beats to the mesmerizing non-stop rhythm of Les Halles, this district remains one of the most vibrant in the city.

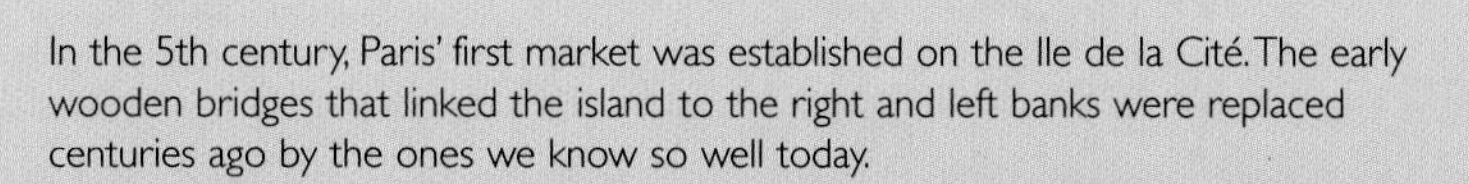
In the 5th century, Paris' first market was established on the Ile de la Cité. The early wooden bridges that linked the island to the right and left banks were replaced centuries ago by the ones we know so well today.

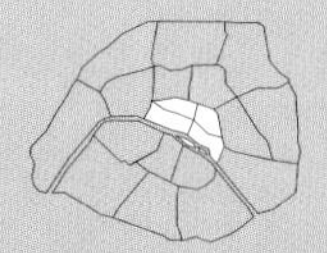

THE BELLY OF PARIS
Les Halles

For centuries, the first four arrondissements of Paris were the center of food distribution for the city. Up until 1968, the largest wholesale market of the world, Les Halles, thrived in the heart of the first arrondissement and numerous street and roving markets filled the neighborhood. Since as far back as the 3rd century BC, when the Celts founded Paris, tremendous energy has been dedicated to supplying food to the city. Then, Paris was but a small island in the middle of the River Seine, called "Lutecia"; its inhabitants, called the *Parissii*, subsisted on the bounty of the river and her fluvial trade. Hawkers would roam the streets of what is now Paris' Ile de la Cité, selling their goods from carts and baskets.

Then, as now, each vendor had his specialty. Whether they trafficked in oysters, fruits, mustard, cheeses, or fish, they would start their tour at daybreak, crying out to the inhabitants of the town. Not until the 5th century is there mention of an actual marketplace, Marché Palu beside the cathedral of Notre Dame. By then, the city had become a rich, industrious trading center with 20 churches and a growing population of approximately 15,000. Marché Palu and other smaller markets on the island offered a place where fishermen and hunters sold their catch, farmers unloaded their harvest of wheat and vegetables, and merchants from as far as the Middle East and the British Isles retailed various luxury goods.

By the end of the 1500s, the parameters of the small island had become too restrictive for the growing population. Wooden bridges were built connecting the island to the mainland, and vendors would crowd on them to hawk their wares. Here the first *tripière* of Paris set up cauldrons from which to sell piping-hot tripe stew to the *Parissii*, establishing the tradition of selling cooked food at the markets. Eventually, Marché Palu was relocated. Some of the merchants transferred to Place Maubert on the left bank, while others settled on the right bank at the new Place de la Grève. Today Place de la Grève is the square in front of Paris' town hall, Hotel de Ville. The market adopted the name of that square and remained there for centuries. Marché de la Grève became the city's largest market.

In 1137, King Louis Le Gros purchased a stretch of land to the north of the city with the intent of creating a new economic hub and containing the burgeoning market. Marché de la Grève was transferred to its new location and renamed "Les Champeaux" because of the surrounding fields (*champs*). The site was chosen for several reasons: its proximity to the main thoroughfare, Rue Saint Denis, through which the royal processions entered the city en route to Notre Dame; its relative proximity to the river banks, allowing merchants to bring their goods via boat; but also its distance from the river, protecting it from seasonal flooding. In order to assure a steady supply of wheat, which had become a staple for the French, a wheat warehouse was built at the market. In the early years, Les Champeaux accommodated mostly weavers, tanners, metal workers, haberdashers, and potters; smaller food markets remained in the city center, closer to the river and its inhabitants.

Left: A view of the crowds in front of Les Halles, the largest wholesale market of the world, which thrived in the heart of Paris (circa 1939). Above: Mustard and vinegar vendors were among the many who roamed the streets hawking their much-coveted wares.

Following in his grandfather's footsteps, Philippe Auguste developed Les Champeaux, adding two halls in 1183 to house a popular trade fair. This increased the importance of the market, from which he collected fees and taxes. With the intention of attracting people to the area, and building a center of trade and commerce, he gave orders to construct new shops and houses. He urbanized the area, then erected a new city wall which integrated Les Champeaux into the city limits. Butchers established new quarters, fishermen brought their daily catches, and farmers sold fresh produce. By the end of the 13th century, six new halls had been built. It attracted most of the city's 200,000 dwellers in search of furs, cloth, leather, mirrors, and costume jewelry, which were so in vogue at the height of the Middle Ages. Also, people came to buy pots, baskets, wine, salt, and of course fresh food. In the following years, there was not much development of the market, as Paris suffered the

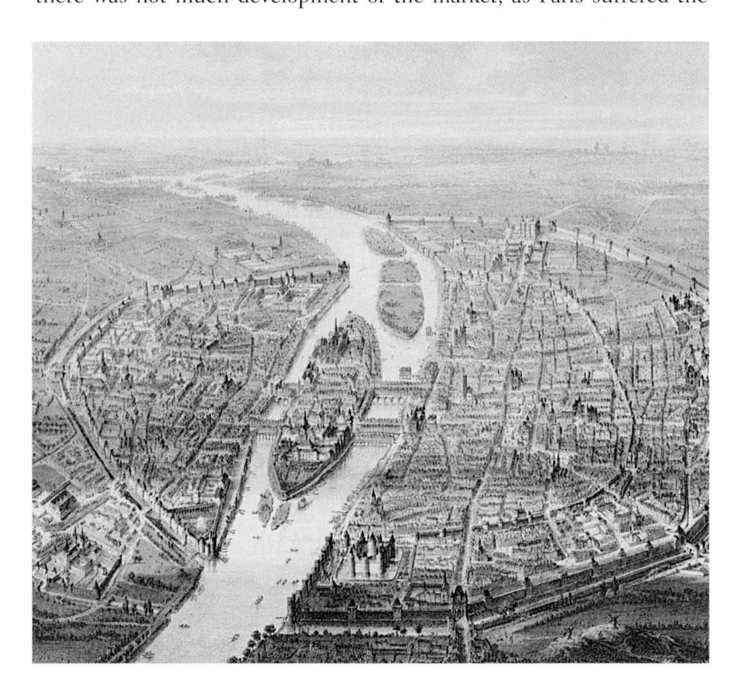

dual plight of the Plague and the Hundred Years' War. These tragedies starting in the mid-14th century reduced the town's population by almost one half.

By the middle of the 16th century, Paris had fully recovered. The city grew towards the north, encompassing the market, whose site had become a large section of the city center. Henry II, the reigning king, decided to enlarge Les Champeaux to accommodate the vendors who were setting up pell-mell outside the halls. New food halls were erected. Streets leading to the market were named after the produce sold, for example, "Rue de la Fromagerie." Les Champeaux was finally established as the central wholesale and retail food market of Paris. Over the years, the popular market acquired the name "Les Halles", from the verb *aller* (to go)—this was where everyone went and continued to go for the following four centuries.

The speed with which Les Halles grew was remarkable. It soon became a village, with its own culture and rhythm within the city, often referred to as the "belly" of Paris. In 1811, Napoleon III, recognizing the importance of the market, proclaimed *"Je veux que Les Halles soient Le Louvre du peuple!"* ("I want Les Halles to be the Louvre of the people!") Although it took 36 years, in 1847, he fulfilled his promise: Les Halles was razed and rebuilt to become the most modern and largest wholesale market of the world. He commissioned the architect Victor Baltard to design twelve pavilions made of iron and glass with underground cellars

and cold rooms, as well as sophisticated aeration systems, gas lighting, and an exceptional water distribution and sewer system. This megalopolis became the food capital of the world, with thousands of people living, eating, and working off the market's trade. Les Halles evolved into a separate entity that functioned according to its own rules; those who experienced it over the years knew the marketplace to be one of the true marvels of Paris.

The pavilions of Les Halles were lined up in pairs, forming a 450,000-square-foot hub of activity from Rue du Louvre to the famous Rue Saint Denis. It was a spectacular sight. Imagine the lofty glass structures with gaping entrances through which a steady stream of vendors and shoppers surged. In front of the pavilions, on every inch of sidewalk, even blocking the entrances, were towering stacks of fruit, vegetables, and flowers. Vendors hawked their wares, somehow managing to shout above the din of the honking delivery trucks. Hurried shoppers dashed about to buy the best produce as it emptied from crates, trucks, and trolleys at breakneck speed. Each hall was designated for a specific product: you would enter the *charcuterie* pavilion, followed by the poultry and game pavilion, then the beef, the vegetables, and the flowers; on the way back, the freshwater fish pavilion; then saltwater fish; butter, egg, and cheese; and finally the pavilion dedicated solely to oysters.

Les Halles grew to such proportions that it was said that a person could easily be working at one end of the market for years without ever having set foot at the other end. It was not uncommon for a driver arriving with a 20-ton truck at the wrong place to have to search for someone who could advise him where to go. The only people who knew every inch of the market were the *forts des Halles,* the police force within the pandemonium. The union of the *forts* was reinstated by Napoleon III in the early-19th century. By 1952, they counted 710 members, each of whom had been initiated to his rank only after having lifted a basket heaped with 450 pounds (204 kilograms) of stone and carrying it on his back clear across the hall. The *forts* were graced with badges; enormous floppy hats resembling mushroom caps; and absolute authority over the goings-on in and around Les Halles. They were indispensable to the market not only as keepers of the peace, but also as human forklifts. Their main role, aided by a slew of hired helpers known as *renforts*, was to load and unload the millions of crates, baskets, and carcasses that traveled through the market from dusk to dawn. Their only rivals in strength and power were the butchers, who were capable of carrying with ease whole sides of beef, weighing as much as 650 pounds (295 kilograms). The butchers were the wealthiest merchants of the lot, as meat was the most expensive commodity sold at Les Halles. Between *les forts* and *les bouchers*, any commotion was quickly settled. Officially, the city police came daily to check that no cheating took place and that the crates of produce held exactly what was listed. The city police were clad in long blue capes which, at the beginning of their rounds, would hang straight to the ground. But as the hours accumulated, so did their girth—it was customary to hand out a cheese, a chicken, a sausage, or a kilogram of apples to *les pelerines*, as they were commonly called. They tucked these "gifts" in the inside pockets of their capes and upon returning to the headquarters shared the booty with the troops.

Each hall was a world of its own: different hours, selling techniques, and habits coincided with the needs of the suppliers, the buyers, and

Above: Les Halles took up a large section of the central part of Paris with twelve glass and iron pavilions that attracted vendors and shoppers from all over the city and surrounding areas.
Following page: The many people that accumulated outside the pavilions often hired carriers known as *renforts* to accompany them to their vehicles (circa 1910).

HEL

the vendors. The first commodity sold was flowers, from 5 to 9 in the evening. The fishmongers, known as *chasse-marée*, had been commuting from the Normandy and Brittany coasts on their carriages and pushcarts since the Middle Ages; near midnight, they would arrive and display their catches in advance of the 2 a.m. auction. Around 4 a.m., the butchers and poultry vendors began unloading trucks that arrived during the night; then they cut, plucked, and gutted their merchandise in cellars furnished with marble tables and faucets; they stored their products in second-floor basement cold rooms, or began selling them at dawn. The *maraîchers* picked their garden fresh vegetables at day break, then traveled from the neighboring suburbs of the city to begin selling their produce by 9 a.m..This was no small operation. Les Halles was a 24-hour-a-day whirlwind of activity whose comings and goings infected all of the neighboring streets, boulevards, and alleys. This market could compete with any modern-day wholesale market. At its peak, the traffic reached 1.7 million tons of food per year. One million pigs, 700,000 cows, 900,000 sheep, 36,000 tons of butter, 300 million eggs, and 575,000 tons of vegetables made their way to the plates and bellies of Paris.

Attracted by its uncontrollable and continuous pace, characters from every walk of life came here to sell and buy produce, dine on hearty onion soup at the crack of dawn, earn a few francs for a bed and a meal, or disappear unnoticed into the sea of people. The streets were lined

with informal hotels where workers would collapse during the day or share an evening with one of the many prostitutes who contributed to the ambiance of the neighborhood. At Les Halles, everyone worked hard at every hour of the day and night, and the oldest profession in the world prospered in the flow of cash, alcohol, and incessant commotion. In the 1900s, a full ten percent of the female population of Paris was dutifully employed in this line of work. The adjacent Rue St. Denis still remains their main strip. Dominique Loï, who grew up in the neighborhood and owns the store Comptoir de la Gastronomie on the nearby Rue Montmartre, described it as follows: "One day when I was about eight years old, I was walking with my father, a local butcher, and I asked him who those young ladies standing on the streets were. He told me they were the secretaries of all of the merchants. This seemed perfectly logical to me considering the masses of people who, like my father, worked here. Of course, years later, I understood what 'secretary' actually meant."

Besides being home to the market, the neighborhood developed into a financially important part of town. Banks, newspapers, and the stock

Clockwise from left: Young helpers, circa 1900; the strongmen known as Les Forts sporting their famous hats, 1958; a fishmonger showing off her display, circa 1900; hard-working butchers, 1920; an apple vendor amidst the crowd, 1908; vendors at the cheese pavilion, circa 1900; an early morning coffee break, 1900; late-night delivery, 1938;.

market established themselves here, bringing considerable money and power to the *quartier*. Oddly enough, the merchants remained autonomous, which aided in the success of Les Halles. Most transactions and negotiations took place at the local cafés and bistros. These served as offices for the vendors. Wine flowed at every hour of the day, and one could always find warmth, the all-important telephone, and of course a hot meal and drink. *Financiers* would organize midnight transactions, closing loan deals with a handshake, following an unwritten code of conduct that anyone who spent a few hours at Les Halles could comprehend. Male or female, one had to be strong and streetwise in order to survive here. On the surface, it appeared to be a convivial place; but the rhythm was so intense, and the crowd so thick, that one always had to be on guard.

The bistros and cafés surrounding Les Halles had very recognizable names such as Le Chien qui Fume (The Smoking Dog), Le Cochon à L'Oreille (The Pig Grabbed by the Ear), and Au Pied de Cochon (The Pig's Trotter). Each establishment had a corresponding logo, which allowed the army of illiterate who worked at Les Halles to find their employers where they said they would be, busy negotiating over a drink.

As well as being centers of commerce, the bistros and cafés provided a spot for the riffraff to slip in unnoticed and a place for a lonely soul to find solace in the dark hours. Additionally, at the end of the night, workers who were often paid with 400 grams of meat, called *le gobet*, would bring it here to be grilled for a franc or two or exchanged for a steaming plate of *bœuf bourguignon* or *pot au feu*. To top it all off, wealthy night owls dressed in fancy frocks and glittering jewels could be found trampling through the sawdust-strewn floors in the wee hours, elbow to elbow with the fishmonger who just sold his last crate of sardines, the *maraîchère* on her way to unload a basket of watercress, or the butcher having his "mid-morning" shot of Calvados in a blood-bespattered work coat. This juxtaposition prompted the expression, *"Les visons aiment la sciure."* (Minks adore sawdust).

For decades, the idea of transferring the wholesale market to the suburbs was debated. Finally, in 1968, there were several compelling reasons for the move. The beautiful metal and glass umbrellas conceived by Baltard, so innovative at the time of their construction, no longer met updated sanitation regulations. The cold storage rooms in the basements of the food halls were antiquated in comparison with modern refrigeration techniques. The center of Paris was congested by the continuous to-and-fro of delivery trucks. Hundreds of thousands of rats infested the area. The government was also interested in gaining control of this important industry that up until then had eluded them. To the dismay of the Parisians, the whole structure and functioning of the market had become impractical. By transferring the market to a new location, handpicked and administered by the government, control was now possible. From 1969 to 1970, the market was transported to the southern suburbs and christened "Rungis." The worn pavilions in the center of Paris were demolished. Few merchants from Les Halles had the means to transfer their businesses to the new market, deciding instead to retire or find work elsewhere. By comparison, Rungis is a tame and clinical version of what was once the lifeblood of the city.

A few survivors of Les Halles who keep shop in the surrounding streets have managed to make do. But the face of the 2nd arrondissement has radically changed. Where meat hooks once strained under the weight of carcasses, trendy dresses now adorn the walls, as most of the businesses have been replaced by fashion boutiques. In the early morning hours only a few pigeons and straggling club-goers can still be seen wandering the streets, as the cafés and bistros have curbed their late-night hours, and the streets have been cleaned up. The gap left by the demolition of the pavilions has been filled by an underground shopping mall, a public garden, and the entrance to Paris' largest métro and suburban express train station for speeding commuters away to the surrounding suburbs.

A few remnants from the time of Les Halles have survived, such as the 24-hour bistros Le Pied de Cochon and Le Tambour. Here you can have a good onion soup, a tray of fresh oysters, and a steaming copper pot of *poule au pot*. If you are wandering about at the crack of dawn and want to stop for a coffee and *tartine*, go over to Le Cochon à l'Oreille and gaze sleepily at the hand-painted tiles depicting the neighborhood at the turn of the century.

Fortunately, the spirit, culture, and passion of Les Halles are alive and well at the 62 open-air markets and 12 covered markets that grace every corner of the city. These bountiful bazaars continue to make Paris the best supplied and fastest distributed food capital in the world. They also offer a wonderful way to visit Paris, discover its neighborhoods, and appreciate its many culinary wonders.

From left: The mixed late-night crowd at one of Les Halles' brasseries, 1960; a boy "checking out" a prostitute along Rue St Denis, 1952; working through the night, 1950; warming up with a *ballon de rouge* at the bar before returning to work, circa 1950; Les Halles at the crack of dawn, 1950; cheese vendors taking a cigarette break on top of the merchandise, circa 1950.

OYSTERS

SAUCE MIGNONETTE

Sauce Mignonette always accompanies a tray of oysters in France. It is made with finely chopped shallots, red wine vinegar, and crushed black pepper. Place this in a ramekin with a small spoon and allow your guests to help themselves.

One cannot help but associate Paris with oysters: trays of cracked ice and beds of seaweed decked with delicious briny oysters on the half shell. Here they are enjoyed with a squeeze of lemon or a touch of Sauce Mignonette, and a twist of pepper—or, for the purist, simply gulped down nature.

The Greeks and Romans prized the virtues of oysters and cultivated them along the coasts of Gaul. Though the fad dwindled during the Middle Ages, the oyster was back in the limelight in the 17th century, and Parisians consumed them in great numbers. In fact, they loved the little bivalves so much that they severely depleted the natural resources, until a decree limiting their harvesting was established to ensure their survival. They arrived, sealed tight in their shells or already shucked, from the shores of Brittany and Normandy. Oysters were frequently savored cooked, as refrigeration was nonexistent in those days and transportation was slow. For this reason, a law was passed in 1752 forbidding their sale during the warmest months of the year. Hence the adage that one should only eat oysters during months containing the letter "R". The rule is no longer strictly valid, as refrigeration has improved; however, the spring and summer months do coincide with the oyster's reproduction phase, which causes a milky, slightly acrid flavor that does not appeal to everyone. Really, it is only a matter of preference—what could be better than a terrace, une douzaine, and a bottle of chilled Sancerre on a warm summer day?

In France alone, 136,000 tons of this 100-million-year-old, gender-switching mollusk are devoured each year. Peak season is during the festive months of December and January.

Over the centuries, oysters have been cultivated and crossbred to achieve quite a number of varieties; among the most treasured are the Gillardeau, Belon, and Marennes d'Oléron. The species fall into two general categories: plats (flat and shallow shelled) and creuses (ellongated and deep shelled). Sub-categories are determined by size, depending on the amount of time the oysters spend fattening up in claires (oyster beds). Starting as miniscule "spats", the animals need to grow for two to three years before becoming full-fledged oysters. They are then transferred to the claires, where they are placed in plastic nets and closely monitored. The environment here determines their character. For example, the Marenne variety feast on microscopic plankton which give them their renowned limpid green tinge. The geographic specifics of each coastline, as well as precise cultivation methods, define the delicious characteristics of each region's harvest.

Some ostreiculteurs (oyster farmers) go so far as to train their oysters to keep their shells tight before reaching market. They do this by raising the nets containing the oysters above water level for several hours a day. This teaches them to keep their mouths shut so as not to lose their precious water. As a result, the yield can stay alive tightly packed in wooden crates for as long as three weeks! (Of course, refrigeration is still a must.)

RUNGIS

The wholesale market Rungis, which replaced the famous Les Halles in 1969, is located a short drive south of the city, near Paris' domestic Orly airport. A village in its own right, Rungis sprawls over 200 hectares, which is more or less equivalent to the circumference of the Principality of Monaco (though without the casinos or polished Rolls-Royces!).

Here, a battery of orange-lit toll gates let in a steady flow of freight trucks, vans, and cars. They zip off in a glaring stream of headlights, rumbling along the wide thoroughfares towards the various food halls. Even though this is a very modern and well-thought-out wholesale market, priding itself to be the largest in the world, at peak hours long trailer trucks block the way, backing up to the gaping entrances to load and unload; fork lifts weave their way through and buyers pull up their vehicles, circling the pavilions. Each commodity is allocated to its own hall, whose doors open consecutively: at 3 a.m., fish and shellfish; at 5 a.m., meat, poultry, game, tripe, and delicacies; at 6 a.m., cut flowers and potted plants; and at 7 a.m., cheese, dairy, fruit, vegetables, and the produce of the *maraîchers*.

The minute the fish-and-oyster pavilion opens, buyers rush into the brightly lit, football-stadium-sized hall to stake their claim on the best catch of the day. A total of 63 wholesalers spread out over the entire floor: box-after-box, crate-after-crate, sack-after-sack of *saint pierre*, *rouget*, salmon, turbot, sturgeon, squid, giant tuna, lobster, crab, mussels, oysters, and clams, to name but a fraction of the selection. White workfrocks and rubber boots are the dress code, covering layer upon layer of clothing to ward off the biting cold. The buyers, having made their selections, line up at individual cashier booths, while helpers load their purchases onto trolleys. This scenario is repeated in the different pavilions. After the initial rush, many of the wholesalers take a moment's rest, warming up at the numerous cafés that often resemble stock-exchange trading floors with everyone milling around and boisterously shouting across the bar counters to one another.

The overall atmosphere here is friendly, no matter into which pavilion you wander. We stopped to talk to Monsieur Pescheur from the tripe hall, who is an old-timer from Les Halles. He and his son, aided by several *tripiers*, were working away at huge quivering livers, as a line of massive pale-white calf heads peered down at them from a row of stainless-steel meat hooks. Although the sight of so much blood and wobbling body parts was quite impressive, Monsieur Pescheur insisted that this was nothing in comparison to what one encountered at the former wholesale market, Les Halles. Rungis might lack the phenomenal fascination that Les Halles once generated, but the working conditions are excellent, and the new location facilitates business.

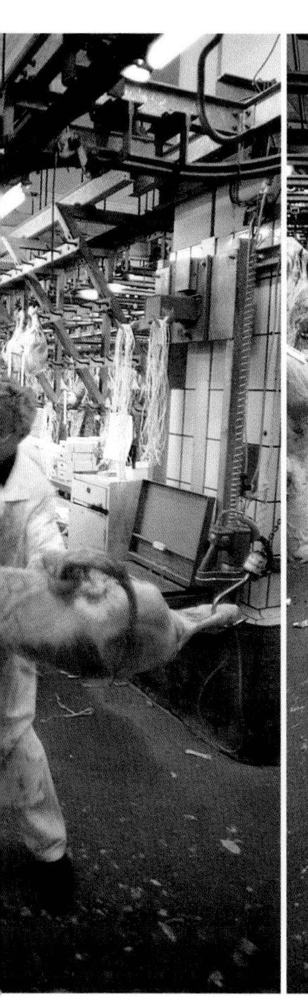

Today's functional Rungis makes sense; consider some staggering numbers: over 22,000 buyers pass daily through the toll gates, generating 390.3 billion francs in 1997. Through the same gates pass the following items each year: 92,000 tons of fresh and saltwater fish and shellfish; 372,000 tons of meat (poultry and game included); 1,000,000 tons of fruit and vegetables; 125,500 tons of delicacies, *foie gras*, smoked salmon, hams, and preserved goods; 191,000 tons of cheese and dairy products; 35,900,000 bunches of cut flowers; and 18,900,000 potted plants. The goods are dispersed throughout the different halls, accounting for approximately 50% of the food and flowers sold in Paris and its surrounding suburbs. The market's transactions are so significant that 20 banks have opened up branches within the premises to directly handle the business. There is even an incinerator on the grounds, which burns all of the non-recyclable packaging; the by-product is most of the warm water and heating for the whole of Rungis. To complete the amenities are 30 cafés and restaurants scattered in and around the different pavilions, a ten-story administration building, a newspaper stand, and a first-aid center, all of which cater to the army of 12,000 wholesalers, employees, and the flow of buyers.

Above: In a matter of minutes a whole beef carcass is expertly quartered and digitally weighed for sale at Rungis. Right: Tripe butchers at the spotless tripe pavilion in the early morning hours.

MARCHANDS DES QUATRE-SAISONS

Fruit and vegetable vendors have been around since the Middle Ages, when they wandered through the streets of Paris pushing their carts piled high with fresh produce, which they purchased from the surrounding farms. Known as *marchands des quatre-saisons,* the vendors would tap a wooden disk attached to their belts with a mallet in order to call attention to their seasonal offerings.

Their trade was exhausting as well as risky, considering all of the perishable items they stocked. So to protect against spoilage, the marchands conjured up methods of preservation: peaches and plums were cushioned on beds of dried moss; grapes were gently packed in layers of ashes and sealed tight in wooden barrels. This actually worked—the grapes would keep their freshness all winter long, simply needing to be dunked in a little wine to bring them back to life.

In 1638, when it was declared that these vendors were required also to carry eggs, butter, and fresh cheese, they used the same techniques to lengthen the life of dairy products; this may be the origin of the goat cheese rolled in ashes that one commonly finds at the market today. Over the centuries, the vendors reverted to selling only fruit and vegetables. Not all that long ago, you could still buy a salad or a bouquet of herbs from the few survivors who set up at the Marché d'Aligre and along the market street Rue Montorgueil.

Today, the only *marchand des quatre-saisons* left is Marcel Viard, who sells flowers in the evenings, at the Seine-Buci street market, in the 6th arrondissement, as he has been doing since 1952. If you have a chance, go by one day, and he will tell you of the times when he was one of many coloring the streets of Paris.

LE PILORI

During the reign of King Louis IX, an octagonal platform called "Le Pilori" was built in the middle of the marketplace Les Halles. On the ground floor of this structure resided an executioner; above him, under a wooden-peaked roof, prisoners were confined, their necks and wrists clamped in the iron vice of a stock. This medieval method of punishment was intended for pimps, blasphemers, petty thieves, and merchants who cheated by using fake weights to sell their goods. They were left at the mercy of the market-goers, who were allowed to pelt them with mud and rotten produce as the platform rotated throughout the day. For three consecutive market days, the culprits endured their plight, their only comfort being a stale crust of bread and gulp of water come nightfall.

RUE MONTORGEUIL

The streetmarket Rue Montorgeuil is a vestige of the time when the 2nd arrondissement was the "Belly of Paris," housing the world's largest wholesale market, Les Halles. Starting at the Forum des Halles and continuing up to Rue Réamur, this pedestrian street is bustling with cafés and food shops that pour out onto the paved lane. At number 13, Les Vergers St. Eustache carries an assortment of perfect fruit and vegetables; and it is said to supply many famous hotels and restaurants, including the Ritz. You will always find a basket of delicate raspberries, mangoes, and peaches; baby zucchinis and eggplants; and a rare assortment of mushrooms, no matter what the season.

A few doors up, an exotic display will tempt you into a *souk*-like shop overflowing with mounds of fragrant spices, burlap bags packed with every grain imaginable, and vats of tempting olives. Across the way, at number 38, you will find one of Paris's oldest landmark restaurants. L'Escargot, founded in 1875, is a shrine to the past. Though its reputation of being the snail-eaters mecca has been somewhat tarnished, it is still worth a detour.

Crossing Rue Etienne Marcel, you will come to the busier half of the market street, where there are numerous butcher shops, bakeries, and the reputed pastry shop Strohrer, which was originally opened by the pastry chef of King Louis XV in 1730. A large fishmonger with tanks of lobsters and crabs, several cheese shops, wine shops, and of all things the headquarters of the socialist party fill the remaining storefronts.

ENFANTS ROUGE

The only existing market in the heart of the city is in the 3rd arrondissement, at the northern tip of the picturesque Marais. A few blocks away from the busy Place de la Republique on Rue de Bretagne stands Paris' oldest covered market. Enfant Rouges derived its name when a handful of vendors set up next to a hospital and orphanage; in the mid-1500s, the mission housed the countless lost children who roamed the streets of Paris and dressed them from head to toe in red. Enfants Rouge expanded into a full-fledged covered market in 1777, when the mission was abandoned. Having been condemned in 1994, thanks to the efforts of president Chirac and the locals, the Enfants Rouges market is undergoing a complete restoration and was scheduled to reopen by now. Meanwhile, a provisional market sets up twice a week in front of the 3rd arrondissement's town hall.

Le Restaurateur

André Camboulas is the owner of one of Paris' landmark cafés built at the turn of the century near the site of the former wholesale market, Les Halles, where merchants would come at all hours of the day and night to warm up with a *coup de rouge* or piping hot bowl of soup before returning to hawk their wares in the hurly-burly of the market. He is a dynamic character with a fluffy mustache that curls up generously at the ends and gets caught in every sip of coffee. After 50 years of market and café life, he has acquired a boisterous personality and a voice that soars effortlessly above the din of clinking wine glasses.

André first came into contact with Les Halles at the very young age of eight, when he would take any opportunity to accompany his father who, after the war, had scraped together his meager savings and transformed a baby carriage into a makeshift butcher stand. Equipped with a scale, a few knives, a cutting board, and a wax cloth upon which to display the various cuts they would head off together at the crack of dawn, to the main market of the city. Having come from a family of survivors, as his fathers parents had been *chiffonniers*, this resourcefulness came as no surprise. Soon enough, André could also be seen scampering through the pavilions, giving a hand here and there, standing guard over stacks of purchases, relaying messages from one vendor to the other, and unloading crates of produce. By the age of 18 he was living the crazy hours of the wholesale market and taking any job he could get his hands on.

In 1975 a longtime dream came true and he was able to buy Le Cochon à l'Oreille, a small bistro on Rue Montmartre, decorated with beautiful vintage tiles depicting scenes from Les Halles. Even though the wholesale market had by then been moved, André wanted to keep the atmosphere of the place intact and had these words inscribed on the wall:

"Le ventre de Paris a pu emigré, mais son coeur reste la."
The belly of Paris (Les Halles) has gone but its heart remains.

Remaining faithful to the past, not only does he buy all his supplies from the surviving merchants in the *quartier*, but also strews sawdust on the floors, offers hearty classic French dishes like *lentilles aux lardons* and *pot au feu*, and opens his doors at four in the morning for the pre-dawn crowd to enjoy.

Together with his wife, Catherine, André owns the bistros Le Cochon à l'Oreille and Le Tambour.

MARKET RECIPES

POT AU FEU
Savory Bouillon Beef Pot

Pot au feu is often confused with *bœuf gros-sel* as they both have the same ingredients and are practically made the same way. The only difference is that when cooking *pot au feu*, the meat is placed in cold stock; with *bœuf gros-sel*, the meat is plunged into boiling stock. We chose to prepare the former, as we were told by Jean Camboulas that the only way to have genuine *bœuf gros-sel* was with meat directly from the abattoir (which is virtually impossible in modern days). Both are served in their stock with a variety of winter vegetables and eaten sprinkled with coarse sea salt, a dab of strong Dijon mustard, and crunchy *cornichons*. Traditionally, *pot au feu* is served in four courses: first the marrow is spread on a warm piece of toasted country-style bread and sprinkled with sea salt; then a bowl of bouillon is served to whet the appetite; followed by a large terrine filled with the meat and vegetables, for everyone to serve themselves as many times as they want; and the finale of the meal is another bowl of the clear bouillon, to cleanse the palate. It is not really worth making *pot au feu* just for two—a convivial table of eight or more is much more appropriate for this festive dish; and the leftovers are delicious reheated the next day or used to make a tasty *hachis parmentier*. Do not fret about the many cooking hours required—most of this is simmering time, and there is nothing nicer than the delicious aroma wafting from the kitchen!

30 minutes 8 hours

For the stock:
2 lbs (1 kg) beef bones, veal knuckle, and marrow bones
2 onions
4 carrots
2 leeks (greens only)
2 celery stalks
A few parsley sprigs
Salt (1 tsp per quart of water)
1 garlic clove
1 bay leaf

For the boiled beef:
8 lbs (4 kg) tip steak, short ribs, pot roast, shank, or a mix of several
4 carrots
4 leek greens
1 bouquet garni
1/4 tsp black peppercorns
4 marrow bones
3 onions
2 garlic cloves

For the vegetable garnish:
8 small turnips
8 carrots
8 leek whites
1 crinkly-leaved green cabbage (optional)

To make the stock: (Note: it is best to make the stock the day before, as it needs several hours to cook and cool)
1. Place the bones and onions in a baking dish, and bake in a hot oven for 1/2 hour. Let them brown nicely, as this will release all the flavors from the bones and lend a dark, rich color to the stock. **2.** Place the bones, vegetables, and spices in a large soup pot with enough cold water to generously cover. Tie the leek greens in a bundle together with the celery and parsley, and add to the pot. Add 1 teaspoon of salt per quart of water, and bring to a boil. Skim, reduce the heat to medium, and let simmer for 3 to 4 hours, skimming when necessary. You may need to add a bit more water if the stock reduces too much—the ingredients should remain covered. Cool, and chill overnight.

To make the *pot au feu*:
1. Remove the hardened fat from the surface of the cold stock, and pour it into a large pot. Tie the different meats into bundles, so that they hold their shape during cooking. Clean the carrots and leeks, and tie the leek greens into a bundle. Tie the *bouquet garni* and peppercorns in a cheesecloth. **2.** Place all the ingredients into the stock. If there is not enough stock to cover the meat, marrow bones, and vegetables, generously add water. **3.** Bring to a simmer over medium heat. Cook at a slow simmer for 3 hours, partially covered, skimming occasionally.

To make the vegetable garnish:
1. In the meantime, clean and peel the vegetable garnish, halve the turnips, and tie the white part of the leeks into two bundles. If you are using the cabbage, quarter and blanch it. **2.** At the final hour of cooking, discard the soup vegetables and replace with the garnish vegetables. Check the seasoning, and add more salt if necessary. If any meat is done at this point (very tender when poked with a skewer), it can be removed and returned to the pot to warm up at the last minute. Cook for 1 more hour.

To serve:
Remove the strings from the meat and vegetables. Arrange the meat on a serving dish, surrounded by the vegetable garnish. Strain the *bouillon* into a soup terrine, and remove any excess fat with a ladle. The meat can be carved directly at the table, and served in flat soup bowls with a portion of vegetables and a ladle of *bouillon*. **Serves 6 to 8.**

Rustic, coarse, full-bodied reds: Minervois, Fronsac, Moulis

SOUPE A L'OIGNON ET AU XERES
Onion Soup with Sherry

This simple dish brings one back to Paris in a flash. It still is possible to find a tasty onion soup, oozing with cheese, at the old bistros that line what used to be the old market place of Les Halles; and it seems that this restorative remedy for long cold nights has followed the wholesale market and is available at the bistros of Rungis as well. The trick to this recipe is the stock—make a good beef or chicken stock ahead of time, and you won't be sorry. (If you don't have time, buy it canned.)

15 minutes 45 minutes

4 tbs butter
6 to 8 onions thinly sliced
8 cups homemade beef or chicken stock
1 cup (250 g) grated emmentaler, gruyère or *comté* cheese
4 large slices toasted baguette
Salt and fresh ground pepper, to taste
A shot of sherry (optional)

4 individual, ovenproof soup terrines

1. Melt butter in a large casserole, add onions, and cook covered over low heat for 30 minutes, stirring every once in a while. **2.** Meanwhile, heat the stock, grate the cheese, toast the bread, and get the bowls ready. **3.** Once the onions are translucent and slightly caramelized, add the stock, and allow to cook covered for 15 minutes. Season to taste. Optionally, add a shot of sherry before serving. **4.** Stir the soup, and ladle into the four bowls. Place one piece of toast on top of each bowl, and cover generously with cheese. (You may find you want more cheese than the recipe calls for.) **5.** Place on a baking dish under the broiler until the cheese melts, bubbles, and is golden. Remove from oven, place bowl on a small plate, and serve immediately. **Serves 4.**

Crisp, citrusy whites: Sancerre, Pouilly Fumé

MOUSSE AU CHOCOLAT
Classic Chocolate Mousse

Use the best quality chocolate for this recipe: 70% cocoa content. *Mousse au chocolat* is usually served in the same bowl that it was made in and passed around the table for the guests to indulge themselves with a large spoonful—or two!

20 minutes 2 hours

5 oz (140 g) dark bittersweet chocolate (70%)
5 tbs sweet butter
3 egg yolks
3 tbs sugar
5 egg whites
1 pinch salt
Whipped cream, to garnish

1. Melt the chocolate with the butter in a double boiler. Remove from heat, and set aside. **2.** Pour the melted chocolate into a large bowl, and set aside. In a separate bowl, whisk the egg yolks together with the sugar until frothy and light. Add the egg mixture to the chocolate, and stir gently. **3.** In another large bowl, beat the egg whites with a pinch of salt. Whisk until firm but be careful not to over-beat them as the texture will become gritty. **4.** Delicately fold half the egg whites into the chocolate mixture. When well mixed, add the remaining whites; and fold until completely integrated. Try not to over-mix, as the *mousse* should remain airy and fluffy. Pour gently into a large serving bowl or into individual ramekins, and place in the refrigerator until it sets, approximately 2 hours. **Serves 6.**

Sweet whites: Maury, Banyuls

Résidence
HOTEL
GALERIE
Atalante

Depending on what side you enter the 5th arrondissement, you will either be trampled by droves of tourists on Place Saint Michel or get sidetracked in an antiquarian bookshop at the foot of the Panthéon. One of the oldest neighborhoods of the city, "Saint Michel," as the 5th is commonly called, is one of the main attractions for many visitors coming to Paris. Fortunately, the invasion has never managed to topple the authentic side of the *quartier*. Behind the brassy souvenir shops and postcard kiosks lining Boulevard Saint Michel, where swarms of tourists move to-and-fro, a cherished residential *quartier* flourishes side by side with the academic stronghold of the city.

V[e] ARRONDISSEMENT

The emblem of this section of town is the eminent Sorbonne college, from where many a philosopher and learned professor has emerged since its origins in the 12th century.

University complexes and libraries fill the area. This is also the place where secondhand bookshops and record shops, and independent movie-houses thrive. The streets are crowded with a lively medley of characters, who animate this youthful *quartier*. Three times a week, the Maubert market adds a burst of color, welcoming the crowds and remaining faithful to the locals, who have been shopping here for many generations.

The Panthéon, seen in the background, holds the remains of many of France's luminaries such as Victor Hugo, Antoine de Saint-Exupéry, Emile Zola, and Voltaire.

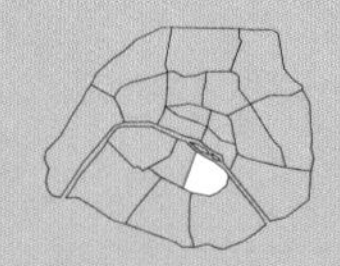

BOUCHERIE
CHARCUTERIE
C LIMOUSIN
LIVRAISON

LITERARY LEGUMES
The Maubert Market

One of Paris' oldest markets stands at the foot of the Panthéon, on a busy square, in the heart of the 5th arrondissement. Just off the bustling Boulevard Saint Germain, Marché Maubert caters to the inhabitants of Ile de la Cité, the academics of La Sorbonne, and the droves of tourists who enjoy strolling through this genuine marketplace that was established so many centuries ago. Set up alongside a row of food shops and café terraces, this convivial area is covered with generous cheese displays, wooden crates of tightly-packed oysters, tempting rows of sausages dangling above trays of steaming *choucroute*, mounds of sweet fruits, crisp vegetables, and bunches of colorful flowers. A veritable treasure island is waiting to be discovered when the market is in full swing on sunny Saturday mornings.

As you meander through the streets of the 5th arrondissement, known as the "Latin Quarter," perhaps finding yourself lost amongst the eager tourists en route to the Notre Dame Cathedral, the hippies loitering on Place Saint Michel, and the window-shoppers on the traffic-infested Boulevard Saint Germain, you might not believe that this was once one of Europe's foremost centers of religious and secular academia. The first "modern" civilization here was established by the Romans, who chose to settle on the Left Bank, building beautiful dwellings, thermal baths, and an amphitheater on the gentle slopes overlooking the all-important river Seine and Ile de la Cité. Various religious orders followed in their footsteps, constructing churches and abbeys during the 6th century, including three of the largest outside of Rome: Sainte Geneviève, Saint Victor, and Saint Germain. The churches soon dominated the Left Bank, establishing vast libraries and covering the fertile land with vineyards and vegetable plots. Over the centuries, for the crowds milling around Place Maubert, the abbots began lecturing on theology and philosophy, exclusively in Latin—hence the name, "Latin Quarter". By the mid-1200s, the first universities and colleges of Paris were established in the *quartier*, transforming it into a place of learning and culture whose character endures to this day.

Left: Marché Maubert may be one of the oldest markets but it is still one of the most popular and draws quite a crowd on the weekends.

Marché Maubert was founded in 1547 to cater to the flourishing Left Bank, which was in desperate need of a marketplace. Having originally been a square where theology and philosophy were taught under the clear blue sky, the location was later converted into the site for gruesome executions spurred on by the cries of rowdy onlookers; so it was a relief when Place Maubert was chosen as the new site for Paris' oldest market, Marché Palu, which had outgrown the confines of Ile de la Cité. In those days, the square was covered with *maraîchers* who would sit surrounded by crates of garden-fresh vegetables, picked at dusk and brought to market when the first rays of sun peeped through the towers of the Notre Dame cathedral. An elderly couple, born and raised a few blocks away from Place Maubert, told us about the days when "La Maube," as the locals call the market, was "a family affair," with three members of the same family setting up three separate stands: one with cheese and milk; one with homemade cakes and tarts; and the other with chickens, rabbits, and eggs. Shoppers would congregate every

other day to visit their favorite vendors and pass the morning exchanging snippets of gossip before heading back to prepare the midday meal. We were struck at how closely their descriptions still fit with today's La Maube, where locals carefully put down their baskets to chat amongst themselves, vendors arrange their displays as would their forefathers, and a camaraderie lost in other places endures here. A small market in comparison, there is a unique atmosphere at La Maube, generated by the mix of tourists eagerly tasting and inquiring about the many specialties, along with elegant women loaded with purchases, lone professors absent-mindedly meandering through the aisles, elderly shoppers carefully counting their change, and children prancing around the lively square.

Left and above: Steaming trays of choucroute garnie can be found at charcuterie stands at every market. Choucroute combines sauerkraut with a variety of pickled and smoked pork cuts and sausages.
Following pages: Often farmers bring their regional specialities to the market. Here stacks of hams and air-dried sausages from Auvergne tempt the shoppers on Rue Mouffetard to buy them.

We always enter this market from the Rue Carmes and are greeted with a treat for the senses: first by a splash of multicolored petals from the corner flower stand, and then by the bright yellow awning of *Le Soleil de Provence* with its olives, honeys, spices, herbs, soaps, and oils that come directly from producers in that sunny southwest region of France. Having lived there for many years, Monsieur Brocker, the owner, appreciates the genuine flavors of these products and prefers not to alter them; so most of the olives are sold *nature,* while a few of them are delicately seasoned with a pinch of *herbes de Provence*, crushed garlic cloves, cracked fennel seeds, or sprigs of thyme. He will gladly give you a taste to help you choose. The fresh *fougasse*, baguettes, olive breads, and quiches are baked using Monsieur Brocker's own herbs, olives, and nuts, at the popular organic bakery Boulangerie Kayser around the corner on Rue Monge. As soon as you bite into one of the many specialties here, you will most certainly feel transported to the fragrant south.

1- SAUCISSE - SECHE
pieces = 60 F
1-SAUCISSON-PUR-PORC
+
1-SAUCISSE-SECHE
LE LOT = 100 F
Les 3
BOITES
DE
PATÉ
DE
L'AVEYRON
PAVÉ
de
L'ARDECHE
55 F
pièce

500F
FOIE GRAS
380

Though the tradition of *maraîchers* has for the most part disappeared at Maubert, you can still find a solid selection of fruits and vegetables. Beginning with the large display on the first aisle, baskets of earthy mushrooms, fine *haricots verts,* knobby heads of cauliflower and broccoli, bright-green brussels sprouts, delicate herbs, mesclun, plump cherry tomatoes, baby eggplant, and radicchio are arranged along one table. Clusters of golden Muscat grapes, fresh yellow dates, baby bananas, pyramids of sugary peaches, figs, plums, and punnets of blueberries, raspberries, and red currants adorn the other. This stand is always busy, with a lively crew that takes advantage of every free moment to replenish the baskets and diminishing pyramids before the next customer stops to diminish them again. Towards the center of the market, the smallest of the stands is run by Jeanine, the lady dowager; clad in a wool hat and gloves, she carefully selects the choicest items from a small array of her homegrown vegetables. Together with her son-in-law, Pierre, who sells their produce at the Port Royal market, she drives into Paris three times a week and charms her customers; they all swear that her homemade *cornichons* are the best in town. At the end of the market,

the brothers Cronauer, who are the third generation to sell at Maubert, drive in from the Seine et Marne region with a selection of vegetables from their own and their neighbors' farms. Having been here for so long, they know their customers well; we heard Jean tell a fragile elderly woman, "you don't have money, it's okay, pay me next time," as he briskly tossed a few extra potatoes into her basket. The newest arrival here is the organic, bio-dynamic stand that occupies the entire farmost corner of the market, with a cascading display of tasty salads, herbs, and local vegetables; though a head of lettuce and a bunch of prickly nettles can cost more than double, their produce vanishes as quickly as it does at the popular organic market Raspail.

When weaving your way through Maubert, you will notice that there is no logical path. Stuck between two métro entrances, the stands fill every inch of pavement—a maze of colors and tempting stops. We enjoy ambling around, discovering the specialties of the season at any time of year. One popular spot is La Boutique Créole, run by a group of friendly, chatty, entrepreneurs who bring a touch of the Caribbean in the form

Accras Morue
22 Frs / 12 pièces
2 Frs / pièce

A FROG'S JOB

Everyone knows that the French love to eat frogs' legs swimming in garlic and butter. This delicacy dates back to the Middle Ages, when the frogs were caught on the banks of the river Seine. A fishing cane and a string with a piece of red cloth attached as bait were used to lure the frog, which was knocked on the head and placed in a burlap sack. The catch would be taken live to Les Halles, where the hind legs were pulled off, and the torsos were left to die.

There were a few whose destiny was decided otherwise. Some amphibians died in the name of science at the university's Faculty of Science, under the unsteady hands of students. The luckiest, however, began careers as fly-catchers at the Maubert market. A minuscule leash was reputedly attached to the frog's hind leg as it sat beside the displays of meat and fish, where the animal would swiftly zap whatever insect that landed on its "employer's" produce. We do not know how long this system lasted, or if the workforce eventually landed in a pan, but in any case we haven't seen any working frogs standing guard at Maubert or at any of the other 61 open-air markets of Paris!

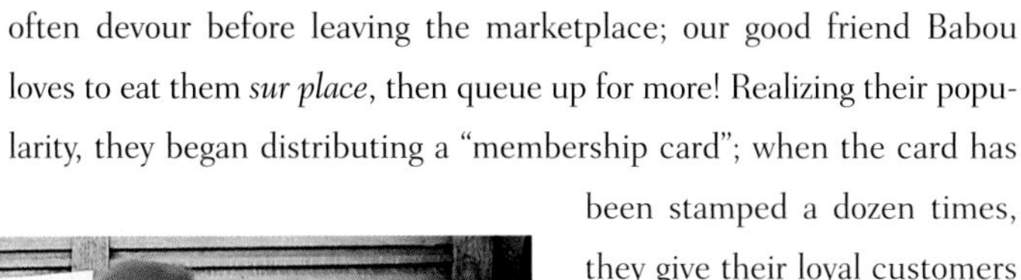

of delicacies from their native French Antilles. There is always a queue in front of their stand, as they casually cook batches of crispy, spicy, garlicky wonders, all the while calling out lyrically to their fellow vendors with the latest gossip or news of the day. Aficionados stop by all morning long to buy piping hot *accras de morue*, or deep-fried fish balls, traditionally made with salt cod as well as their own variations on this delicacy using tomato or chicken. In the Antilles, *accras* are a festive food, eaten to celebrate All Saints Day and Good Friday. Parisians, however, seem to find the little mouthfuls a treat on any day of the year, picking up a dozen of one and a dozen of the other, which they will often devour before leaving the marketplace; our good friend Babou loves to eat them *sur place*, then queue up for more! Realizing their popularity, they began distributing a "membership card"; when the card has been stamped a dozen times, they give their loyal customers a free bottle of specially concocted Planter's Punch. Those bottles are flying!

The shops that line Marché Maubert merge with the market, their displays tumbling out onto the sidewalk. Along with the butcher and fishmonger, there is a bakery that is owned by a woman who spends half her morning visiting all of the vendors at the market, while her efficient staff sells freshly baked baguettes and pastries at breakneck speed. The elegant *charcuterie*, with its beautifully prepared hams, terrines, and quiches, is a pleasure to enter, if only for a peek. If you need wine, you can choose

Left: Carol sells hot and spicy codfish balls at La Boutique Créole.
Above: The Limousins age their cheeses in the stone cellar beneath their small shop La Crémerie des Carmes located in front of the Maubert market.

from the baskets in front of La Cuvier, or step inside to see what the owner has in stock. One of the oldest shops in the area is the Crémerie des Carmes, owned by the Limousin family. A trim man with an impeccable mustache, Monsieur Limousin is a fourth-generation cheese maker, who has been aging his cheeses at the same location for the last 22 years. He specializes in fresh *chèvres* and is very proud of his four-year-old *comté* and *beaufort*. On Saturdays his wife takes over, while he and his son set up a stand at the center of the market to capitalize on the weekend rush.

Left: In France, poultry is cleaned and trussed for you on the spot. Here, Jean-Marie Loren singes the feather off a guinea hen. Above: The traditional attire for butchers is an apron draped over one shoulder. At La Maube, the butchers are gracious and helpful.

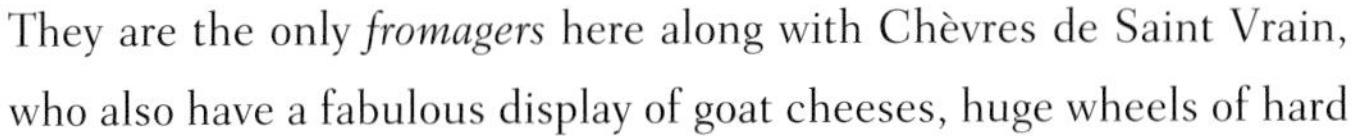

They are the only *fromagers* here along with Chèvres de Saint Vrain, who also have a fabulous display of goat cheeses, huge wheels of hard mountain cheeses, and velvety triple-cream cheeses.

The first chill of Autumn means oysters. Come the second week of September, the owners of L'Huitre du Chouan, clad in blue overalls, set up their display of limpid-green oysters brought directly from their oyster farm on the island of Noirmoutier, just below the Brittany coast. Packed in wooden crates and sold 13-to-a-dozen, with a lemon to go, these *fines de claires* oysters travel 250 miles to be sold at the market. For the inquisitive few, they have a plastic-covered board tacked with photographs of their farm, showing them sloshing around in rubber wading boots, transferring the young oysters from

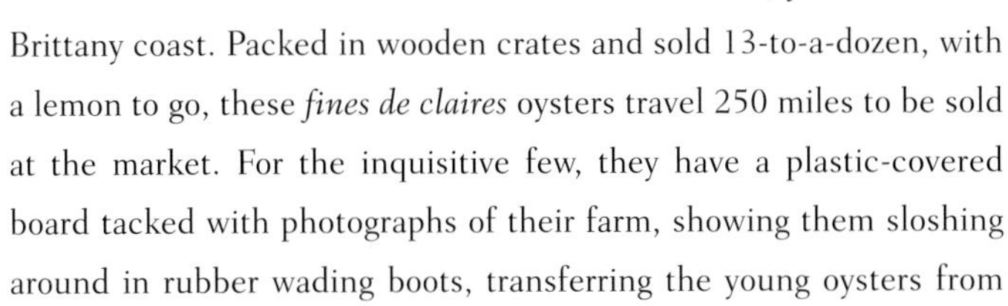

one bed to another where the precious bivalves are left to reach their full maturity for up to three years. Although oysters can be eaten all year-round, it is not very common to find them during the summer months, as this is the oyster's reproduction phase; at that time, their consistency is milky and their flavor slightly acrid—an acquired taste that most people do not appreciate. The saying that one should only eat oysters during the months containing the letter "R" stems from this fact; also, when this expression was born, refrigeration was a rarity, so the oysters sometimes did not weather the long trip from the coast in the middle of summer. This has all changed with modern storage and transport techniques; so if you find a nice terrace or bistro selling oysters at any time of the year, why not try a dozen of these aphrodisiac, cholesterol-reducing mollusks with a glass or two of chilled Muscadet?

There are a handful of butchers, *charcuteries*, and poultry vendors present at the market who are always busy trimming, chopping, and tying prime cuts, sausages, and fowl; or assembling containers of *choucroute garnie*; or pulling a crispy, golden chicken off the spit. Among them is a convivial young poultry farmer from the Perche region who avidly sells his free-range chickens, ducks, guinea hens, and rabbits to loyal customers who stop by for a bird and a chuckle—which he always provokes. Jean Marie's perpetual good mood even attracts the local policeman, Fabrice, who drops by every market day for his midday snack of pâté, made by Jean Marie's mother, with some country bread. Jean Marie gave us a great recipe for rabbit that he rattled off while singeing the remaining feathers off a guinea hen, simultaneously posing gleefully for a picture. Having decided to enter the Parisian markets eight years ago, he has been quite a success; and his many clients could only agree that this is the place to come and buy *"de la très, très bonne volaille."*

Another cheerful character who has become a fixture at the market is Ibu Tall, who stands, six-feet tall, beside his display of African statuettes and masks that are neatly arranged on a colorful tapestry. Maubert is a good place to sell this type of art, because of the diverse public that frequents the market. When you come by the stand, you will always find someone enjoying the soft-spoken manner of this Senegalese merchant, who has an interesting selection of artifacts with some very fine pieces that he will gladly point out to you. He knows all of the other vendors; just after noon, he makes his rounds to see how everyone is doing and to pick up a few snacks for aperitif time "chez Ibu." Some sections of the 5th arrondissement might remind the visitor of a package tour to Athens, with Greek restaurants cramped into narrow side streets and flocks of tourists gawking at ancient ruins. Yet this is the heart of "Gay Paris!" As you walk up the hill towards the impressive Pantheon, the *quartier* regains more of a Parisian flair: cafés, antique shops, and quaint restaurants are edged in between the numerous universities, schools, churches, and libraries that inhabit the ancient buildings. The streets are always crowded with students milling about the many bookshops, secondhand record stores, tiny movie theaters that show only classics, smoky coffee shops, and noisy bars, making this a youthful corner of old Paris.

A great advantage of shopping at Marché Maubert is the nearby street market on Rue Mouffetard, which is open every day (except Monday!) and definitely worth a detour. If you are not too loaded down with purchases, walk to the summit of Mont Saint Geneviève, past the Pantheon, until you

Below: Oyster farmers from the Normandy and Brittany coasts bring their catch to Paris' open-air markets ready to go at 13 to a dozen.

come to Place de la Contrescarpe. This is a perpetually animated square, dotted with café terraces, sandwich and crèpe huts, and bicycles and cars twirling around its central fountain. Winding down the hill from the Place, the narrow Rue Mouffetard has a quality about it that is so "Paris"—despite the fact that this picturesque nook has become "The" tourist destination, lined with wonderful little food shops, street vendors, and bars. Stop at the well-stocked organic shop Rendez-vous de la Nature, at number 96. Then head toward the fish store Quoniam down the way, and check out their great selection of fresh and saltwater fish, shellfish, and crustaceans. Next, step into the *fromagerie*, Quatre Homme, which has an *affinage* chamber where you can see how the aging process is carried out. Although their selection of cheeses is small, their quality is excellent; we picked up an oozing *saint marcellin* and a perfectly ripened camembert. At the bottom of the hill, in a beautiful building decorated with ornate swirls of mosaics depicting boar and deer, the owners of the Italian delicatessen Facchetti have been rolling out pasta and other delicacies since 1929. This is a rather pretty spot in the market, where the street widens near a 12th-century church and a nicely planted roundabout.

Now is the moment for a well-deserved *kir*, before heading out to explore the rest of the arrondissement. Along the river, on Quai de la Tournelle, *bouquinistes* open shop, unloading stacks of paperbacks, antique books, and prints, which they store in green, metal boxes that are perched upon a stone wall that borders the Seine. Browse your way down to the very famous, very expensive, and oldest restaurant of Paris, La Tour d'Argent, which welcomes its privileged clientele to wine and dine as they behold the spires and towers of Notre Dame. The more affordable sister restaurant next door, La Rotisserie du Beaujolais, may not have the pomp; but the great, spit-roasted specialities and the good, traditional French cuisine are certainly worth a try. Farther ahead, the modern and ingenious building, L'Institut du Monde Arabe, offers its visitors not only an excursion through its museum and library, but also a rooftop-terrace restaurant where you can enjoy a tasty Lebanese lunch with an awe-inspiring view of Paris. The beautifully landscaped Jardin des Plantes is a great stop for a picnic, before venturing to the newly refurbished Natural History museum, a taxidermist's dream, with its herds of extinct species, dramatic lighting, and "New Age" music wafting through its exhibition hall. And last but not least, the elegant mosque next door opens its interior courtyard, adorned with fig trees and gurgling fountains, to a faithful crowd who comes here to sip sweet mint tea or lounge in the "A Thousand and One Nights" aura of its café through a haze of cigarette smoke and muffled voices.

Above: Bouquinistes set up along the Seine selling old and new etchings, books, postcards, and magazines.

THE ORIGIN OF THE RESTAURANT

The restaurant as we know it today is a French invention of the 18th century. During the Middle Ages, Parisians dined in auberges and taverns where the main courses were plunked down in the center of a communal table for everyone to help themselves. The fastest eaters feasted for their money's worth, while the more timid customers often had to console themselves with the remains, if any! This rowdy free-for-all was not an enticing dining experience for the more refined folk, who would rather not have to rub shoulders with a crowd of hungry strangers. So it became fashionable for the fortunate few to have a *traiteur* bring succulent roasts and stews to their homes, so as to be able to enjoy their supper in a civilized manner.

Things progressed during 1765 when a certain Monsieur Boulanger started serving piping hot bowls of hearty soup at his establishment and waiting on customers at individual tables. He called his soups "restaurants" from the French word *restaurer,* meaning to bring something back to its original state; which is what he concluded his soups would do for his customers.

At the time, different professions were very well defined. The *traiteurs* had their own union and a monopoly on stews, sauces, and sophisticated dishes. So when Boulanger decided to enhance his menu by adding pieds de mouton au sauce blanche (lamb's feet in white sauce), he caused quite a stir. The *traiteurs* took him to court, but he won the case; the parliament agreed unanimously that lamb trotters in white sauce was not a stew!

The scandal brought quite a bit of attention to Boulanger's little soup shop, drawing Parisians who wanted to try his new dish and be waited on by the renowned patron. The concept of a "restaurant" was well on its way to success.

Le Marchand d'Art

Standing proudly beside his display of African statuettes and masks, the art dealer Ibu Tall is an unusual but welcome addition to the open-air markets. This soft-spoken, gentle-mannered, Senegalese merchant is a magnet for every passer-by, whom he immediately engages in conversation. Everyone seems to know him at the markets, and he regularly makes his rounds to say hello to his fellow vendors.

Having originally come to France in 1981 to study notary law in Lyon, he soon realized that his future could never be in this profession, which he described as extremely closed and elitist. He moved to Paris and found a job managing a supermarket, but he always had an eye open for new opportunities. A friend of his had the idea of selling used car parts from France to various West African countries. Soon Ibu was filling containers with motors, doors, and chassis, and shipping them off to his associate in Senegal. The business thrived, but when the local currency of the region was devalued, his luck turned. With a container en route to Dakar, Ibu rushed there to try to recuperate his costs; eventually he returned to Paris with a dent in his pocketbook but with a few African gifts he had brought back for his friends. Surprisingly, this launched his new career.

Ibu began importing hand-carved chairs and masks and set himself up at the open-air markets. His business slowly developed from simple artifacts, such as one might find on any street in Dakar, to more precious objects and pieces that he had especially made in Togo and Benin, where the craftsmen are famous for their woodwork.

Although most of Paris' roving markets are centered around food, it is not uncommon to also come across clothes, tablecloths, soaps, candles, healing products, lingerie, shoes, crockery, and once in a while, art. These items are generally sold by hawkers, known as marchands volants, who set up haphazardly in vacant spots. Ibu, however, is a permanent fixture at the markets; after five years in this business, he has become well-known for having quality pieces and has quite a following.

Ibu is present at the Maubert and Richard Lenoir markets.

PORT ROYAL

The Port Royal market is a great shopping outing, despite being a bit out of the way, at the back of the 5th arrondissement. On a lazy Saturday, you will be accompanied by bicycles, baby carriages, caddies, walking sticks, and roller blades casually making their way through the market. Over 40 vendors with a selection of wonderful products set up under a row of ancient chestnut trees on one side of Boulevard de Port-Royal.

Pleasant surprises await you down the narrow aisle, beginning with an abundant display of garden-fresh salads and a rôtisserie with succulent pork ribs, shish kebabs, country-style sausages, and chickens; all sitting behind a long table spread with mouth-watering dishes. It is hard to pick and choose here, but you will always walk away with the best catch of the day, tasty olives, a loaf of crunchy bread, a slab of pâté, great fruits and vegetables, oozing cheeses, and a bag full of fresh walnuts.

For those who are not in the mood to cook, you will find: a good Asian *traiteur*, fresh buckwheat crêpes and Bertrand Didier's sweet and savory cakes. We often wander up and down the market several times before buying a bunch of flowers and heading back with brimming baskets to the Jardin de Luxembourg for a late breakfast in the park.

MONGE

Marché Monge sets up on a tree-shaded square bordering Rue Monge, just one block away from the bustling market street Mouffetard. Approximately 40 vendors offer this residential section of the 5th arrondissement a good selection of products, in a tranquil, country-like setting. Walking through the aisles you will find: a great selection of salad greens at the *maraîchers* stands, such as tender *cornes de cerf* and pungent wild *roquette*; an unusual assortment of potatoes at Leo Zamba's, who fills cardboard boxes with such varieties as the Chinese truffle and monalisa briard; prime pork cuts, hams, pâtés, tempting *quiches feuilletés* and savory tarts at the *charcuterie* of Michel Stunault; and miniature twirly *queue de cochon* (pig's tail) sausages at Produits Regionales des Alpes. Along with the freshly baked breads, delicious honeys, wines brought by viticultures, and even homemade chocolate-chip cookies, you will find tempting displays of cheese, meat, fish, and flowers.

If you want some ideas on how to prepare your many purchases, make sure you drop by La Librarie des Gourmets at number 98 rue Monge, where cookbooks and other books about food abound.

Above: The Port Royal market has a great selection of fish.

HUITRES A LA NAGE
Oysters in a Riesling and Cream Broth

Literally, the name of this dish is "Swimming Oysters," which comes from their being cooked in a sauce that is made with wine and the oysters' own water. Shucking the oysters is the only time-consuming part of this recipe—we asked the vendors from L'Huître du Chouan to open them for us and made sure that they retained the oysters' water in a small container. This dish is delicate and delicious for a light supper or an appetizer.

20 minutes 8 minutes

24 oysters
1 bunch chives
1 large shallot
2 tbs sweet butter
1 cup white Riesling wine
2/3 cup crème fraîche
Twist fresh black pepper
A few long chive stalks, for garnish

1. Shuck oysters, draining the water into a separate bowl. Clean oysters gently under slow, running water to remove any shell bits; and set aside in a cool place. **2.** Drain oyster water through a fine sieve or cheesecloth (or paper towel), and put to one side. **3.** Clean and cut chives into 1-inch (3-cm) pieces with scissors, and set aside. **4.** Chop shallot and sauté in the butter, until translucent, in a large sauté pan. Lower heat, add the white wine, and let simmer for 1 minute. Then gently add the oysters and enough oyster water to cover them. **5.** As soon as the mixture begins to simmer again, carefully stir in the cream, and warm another minute. Remove from heat, add the chives, and serve immediately. **Serves 4.**

Aromatic Alsatian whites: Riesling, Pinot Gris, Tokay

Huîtres à la nage

LAPIN AU CALVADOS
Normandy-Style Rabbit Stew

Jean-Marie Loren from the Maubert market rattled off this recipe for us while he was preparing a guinea hen for one of his customers. The rabbit is cooked in sparkling cider and Calvados, which are both produced in Normandy, near the Perche region where Jean-Marie has his poultry farm.

20 minutes 45 minutes

4 shallots, chopped
2 tbs butter
1 rabbit, cut into pieces
Salt and pepper, to taste
1/4 cup Calvados
1 tbs flour
2 cups (approximately 1/2 bottle) sparkling cider
2 carrots, peeled
4 baby turnips, peeled
1/2 lb (250 g) snow peas, stems and strings removed
Chopped parsley, for garnish

1. In a heavy-bottom pan, sauté the shallots in the butter over medium heat until translucent. Add the rabbit, and brown on all sides. Season with salt and pepper. **2.** Raise the heat, add the Calvados, and flambé. **3.** Sprinkle the flour on top, and mix well. Pour in the cider, add the carrots and turnips, mix, and cover. Cook over medium heat for 40 minutes, stirring once in a while. **4.** Meanwhile, boil some water in a small pan, add the snow peas for one minute, remove from boiling water, and run under cold water. Set aside. **5.** As soon as the rabbit is cooked, add the blanched snow peas, and cook an additional 5 minutes. Adjust the seasoning, sprinkle with chopped parsley, and serve immediately with boiled potatoes or wild rice. **Serves 4.**

Rich, full-bodied whites or delicate, round reds: Meursault, Chablis, Moulis

ARTICHAUDS A L'ANCHOIADE
Artichoke Anchoiade

This delicate recipe is made with the small artichokes known as *poivrade* or *violets*, which are slightly purple in color and have a nutty flavor. They are grown in Provence, picked during the summer months, and normally eaten raw as in this recipe, or sautéed with a bit of garlic and parsley, to make a perfect summer appetizer. The sauce that accompanies this salad is as simple as it gets: only anchovies and extra-virgin olive oil blended for a light and delicate result that is neither salty, nor heavy. A dish refined through its simplicity.

15 minutes

1 dozen small artichokes (pick the ones with the leaves tightly closed)
1/2 lemon
10 anchovy fillets (or 1 tbs anchovy paste)
1/2 cup extra-virgin olive oil
12 niçoise olives, for garnish

1. Rinse the artichokes and cut off the stems. Peel down to the yellow, very tender leaves. Place in a bowl of cold water with the juice from half a lemon to keep from discoloring. **2.** If using anchovy fillets, place in a bowl, and make a smooth paste using the bottom of a spoon; then place in a blender. (If using the paste, put it directly in the blender.) Drizzle the olive oil slowly, while blending on a low speed, until the oil is completely integrated into the sauce (you can add it all at once and blend together, but the result will not be as creamy). Place to one side. **3.** Pat the artichoke bottoms dry, and slice as thinly as possible. Place in a bowl with the anchovy sauce, and toss lightly. **4.** When ready to serve, arrange onto four plates by spreading each piece like a flower from the center of the plate to the edges; drizzle with remaining sauce; and decorate with the olives. Serve with a fresh baguette. **Serves 4.**

Delicate, fizzy whites: Côtes de Provence, Vinho Verde

Artichauds à l'anchoiade

The 6th arrondissement has always been the center for literature and art in Paris, dating back to the Middle Ages when the Benedictine monks of the Abbey of Saint-Germain-des-Prés prided themselves in having assembled the largest library in Gaul. In the 1950s and 60s, Saint-Germain-des-Prés was home to many of Paris' famous painters, writers, and musicians. It was also the birthplace of the existential movement, origin of the trend of dressing from head to toe in black, and the location of choice for the hippest art galleries and bookshops.

In today's Saint-Germain-des-Prés, the quest for beauty prevails in the fashion boutiques that have replaced many of the bookstores and galleries. Local residents, known as *la gauche caviar,* are characteristically wealthy,

VIe ARRONDISSEMENT

nonchalant Left-Bankers who enjoy a comfortable existence in ample apartments—while preaching liberal ideas. The ever-appealing renowned cafés and restaurants still rest on their laurels, offering the same menus, décor, and service—but at much more generous prices.

Like the *quartier* in which it is located, the Raspail Organic market has become a very fashionable scene. Actors, celebrities, and wannabes revel in its conviviality and pace. The market attracts the hardcore organic advocates as well as those who just enjoy the idea of healthy eating when convenient. The place makes for a wonderful Sunday morning stroll through mountains of hardy vegetables, towers of fresh bread, and unusual specialties that are hard to come by.

Marie de Medici commissioned the landscaping of the Luxembourg gardens in the 1600s. It is a splendid sanctuary in the heart of Paris.

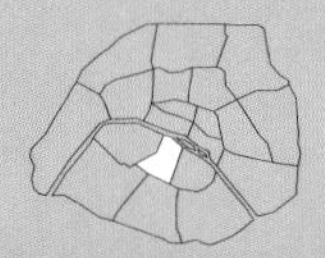

THE GREENS OF SAINT-GERMAIN
The Raspail Organic Market

The Marché Biologique Raspail is the largest organic market in Paris, with a lavish selection of healthful produce, although it appears that many people come here just to check out the crowd, while nibbling on whole-grain *galettes*. Not only is Raspail located in the chic *quartier* of Saint-Germain, Paris' favorite hang-out since the 1920s, but eating *bio* ("organic") has become a growing fad in France over the last few years. Recently, even the major supermarket chains have added an aisle dedicated to fresh and packaged organic produce. So, it is no wonder that you will find celebrities, famous chefs, designers, tourists, and artists among those milling around the market and lining up to buy these excellent though expensive products.

Near the heart of Saint-Germain-des-Prés, the Raspail market runs along the center alley of Boulevard Raspail, between Rue de Rennes and Rue du Cherche-Midi. During the week, this is a bustling section of the 6th arrondissement. Parisians and tourists alike scurry about visiting trendy shoe shops on Cherche-Midi, expensive lamp shops on Raspail, chic fashion boutiques scattered throughout, and the elegant department store Le Bon Marché with its enticing food hall. On Sundays, however, the shops are all closed, the streets abandoned, and Raspail's tree-lined stretch of colorful canopies is the only source of activity—and what a crowd it pulls! Visitors from every corner of Paris come to see and be seen at the *bio* market. Trendy shoppers stroll along admiring vibrant green displays of lettuces and herbs, rows of creamy milk and homemade yogurts, baskets of freshly picked fruits and vegetables with pearly remnants of morning dew, and stacks of healthy-looking organic breads and pastries. Everything here is prepared and grown according to strict organic guidelines.

Left: The Raspail market has evolved from being Paris' first organic market to a fashionable place to be seen on Sunday mornings.

Before heading for the Marché Bio, start your morning with a little contradiction: indulge in a *café crème* and a (non-organic) croissant, at either the local café, Le Raspail, with your head immersed in a cloud of smoke, or at the more elegant and airy Hotel Lutetia. Thus fortified, begin your visit of the market on the Rue du Cherche-Midi side, where time and again we find shoppers gathering at the first corner stand, gawking at the splendor of Claude Conard's enormous display of baskets heaped with cascades of crisp lettuces and aromatic herbs. With up to 15 varieties of salad greens, including mesclun, watercress, dandelion, arugula, *frisée*, oak leaf, endive, *chervil*, *mâche*, and *escarole*, the sight is irresistible. Claude specializes in bio-dynamic fruits and vegetables from all over the world, identified by the denomination "Demeter." This is one of the few stands in Paris where you can actually pick your own greens without sending the vendor into convulsions! Across the way, piping hot potato-onion and carrot-wheat galettes sizzle away on the griddle before being quickly devoured by the conoisseurs. At La Ferme de la Table au Roy, free-range chickens and rabbits are roasted on a spit until golden brown, with fresh eggplants, tomatoes, and onions simmering in the juices below.

Although many farmers have been organically tending their land for generations, it was not until 1980 that an official denomination was

C.A.A.E.
ECOLÓGICA
Nº OG94433
ANDALUCIA

BIO-DYNAMIC

Bio-dynamic is an agricultural process that follows the same basic principles as organic production but also uses a stellar calendar indicating the best days for planting and harvesting. Initiated by the German philosopher, Rudolf Steiner, in the 1920s, organic methods of cultivation respect the natural harmony of the land. Bio-dynamic takes these principles a step farther, by using the many forces that exist in the cosmos, beginning with the rotation of the sun and the seasons. For example, the morning which represents spring is the best time for sowing the fields and for germination, while the evening which represents autumn is the best time for the seedlings to be planted and to take root. The land is also homeopathically treated with minute doses of plant extracts to help it renourish itself and fight against the many pollutants that surround us. This very complex and sophisticated method is closely linked to the constellations of the zodiac and follows the traditional methods of crop rotation, composting, and pollination used in organic farming. Bio-dynamic agricultural practices are internationally recognized.

This page: The organic market offers not only a great selection of regional organic produce but *bio* imports from all over the world as well. You will find a whole array of fresh fruits and vegetables, fish and shellfish, a variety of cheeses and dairy products, and free-range poultry and meat.
Following page: Unusual breads can be found at the organic markets; bakers often use rare types of flour.

CINQ CEREALES
0,6KG
17F
SEIGLE
PUR
0,6KG 19F
SEIG
PUR
1KG

KAMUT
0,6KG
22F
KAMUT
1KG
32F

established for organic goods: *Agriculture Biologique* (*AB*). And not until 1989 was an organic market founded, namely Marché Raspail. Today, the regulations for organic production in France are established and enforced by the Ministry of Agriculture. They require that farmers use no chemicals in the cultivation of their land nor in the raising of their animals. Crop rotation, composting, and pollination are used in cultivating the soil instead of chemical fertilizers and pesticides. These procedures require a more labor-intensive operation, which results in a more expensive product. In order for farmers to receive *AB* certification, they must pay a yearly fee to the ministry, based on a percentage of their earnings. This all came about in order to protect the customers who, prior to this, had no assurance that the product they were buying was actually organic. At the Raspail market you will only find *AB*-certified foods and goods.

For Americans lost in Paris, a tiny stand tended by another American lost in Paris sells delectable homemade brownies, banana muffins, and English muffins which combine perfectly with the milk found at the nearby Fromagerie Saumière. Although these munchies are made with only organic products, they seem like a naughty treat among the wholesome crunchy carrots and tender sweet peas that surround them. A few steps down, on a tiny table covered with a red, Provence-style tablecloth, are neatly arranged jars of more than 25 types of honey gleaming in the morning sun. There are wooden paddles for tasting and a list specifying the attributes of the acacia, lavender, and chestnut honeys, to name a few. Passers-by swarm around the table like bees.

This market is generally packed, so it is best to come early if you want to avoid the rush. By 11 a.m., however, the hurried shopper will not be at ease; although the market is congested, the atmosphere is exceedingly tranquil—everyone seems to have inexhaustible patience, as if intoxicated by the incense wafting in the air! Few lose their temper while they wait for the customers ahead of them to go through their interminably long shopping lists. As Raspail is the only organic market on this side of Paris, and it is convened only once a week, shoppers tend to buy in large quantities and enjoy the time queuing chatting to their neighbors.

At two junctures in the market, you will see roundabouts where small specialty stands sell a variety of curios. We have tasted algae bread, algae soup, algae *tartare,* plain algae, and algae salt—all made from seaweed collected off the coast of Brittany by Monsieur Courtois. We bought his algae *tartare* spiced with capers, onions, and vinegar to spread on toast

Although it is always a joy to spend the morning picking and choosing from the displays, some of the vendors will do the job for you and deliver upon request.

MARCHE
BIO
DOMICILE
PROCHE BANLIEUE
France
Echalotte

SAINT-GERMAIN

A few blocks away from the Raspail market on Boulevard Saint-Germain, is the Eglise Saint-Germain-des-Prés, the oldest church in Paris. It was originally built in the 6th century according to the wishes of the Bishop Germain of Paris who chose this fertile land outside the walls of the city as the site for his parish. During the attack of the Norsemen, the church was destroyed and eventually rebuilt in 1163 with an adjacent abbey where over one hundred Benedictine monks lived and studied, establishing the most important library of the region. Besides being considered the center for artistic and intellectual study, the church and abbey became a strong economic power due to its agricultural infrastructure and real estate which made up most of what we know today as the 6th and 7th arrondissements. During this time, the monks chose to host an annual fair at the site of the present Marché Couvert de Saint-Germain, which was known as La Foire de Saint-Germain. It became the most imporant cultural event in the country where tradesmen and artists from far and wide would come to display and sell their wares. Coffee made its first appearance in France here, as did the rhinoceros. The fair ran for many days and functioned not only as an exhibition center for merchants, but also as a stage for artists and performers who entertained both noblemen and commoners alike. The fair became so popular that although it was stopped a number of times, it resurfaced over and over again until finally disappearing in 1811. The site and facade of the church are the only original remains from this era besides the deeply rooted reputation of Saint-Germain-des-Prés as the seat for the intelligentsia and the arts.

Above: One of the oldest and most famous venues in Saint Germain, Brasserie Lipp, was born in 1922 (photo) and is still going strong today.
Right: The sunny terrace of Café Deux Magots offers its clientele a view of l'Eglise de Saint-Germain-des-Prés in the heart of the *quartier*.

LE PROCOPE
JOURNAL PARLÉ

COFFEE

The legend of coffee speaks of a shepherd from Yemen who was concerned by the lack of sleep of his sheep and summoned the advice of the head monk at the monastery down the path. The monk accompanied the shepherd and noticed the sheep's preference for a bush adorned with little red berries. Wise as he was, he decided to pick a few and threw them into a vessel of boiling water. After drinking this brew, he found that he too could not sleep but neither did he feel fatigued. Quite enthralled by this miraculous drink, he began serving it at the monastery to assure that his monks would not nod off during prayer. Coffee slowly traveled through Arabia during the early 1600s reaching the shores of Istambul where it became a very popular medicinal and pleasurable drink, known as Cahué. Louis XIV was the first Frenchman to taste this brew when it was brought to him by Soliman Aga Mustapha Raca, the emissary of Mohammed IV, known as "Le Grand Turk," in 1669. It did not reach the people until 1671, when two Armenians showed up at the famous Foire de Saint-Germain with the magic brew. Due to the medicinal properties the drink was entrusted with, Parisians were skeptical and not easily won over. It was not until 1686, when a visionary Sicilian nobleman, François Procope, opened the first café in Paris, "Le Procope," that the success of coffee was ensured. Due to the popularity of his establishment which even had its own society magazine (left), coffee became a fashionable drink and finally captured the hearts of the Parisians. Cafés, derived from the name of this novel drink, also became popular meeting places, and by 1716 more than 300 had sprung up around the city while coffee peddlers wandered the streets of Paris serving cups of this popular drink.

for our apéritif. It is an acquired taste, but delicious nonetheless. The plain seaweed makes a nice salad tossed with rice vinegar and sesame oil. During the winter months, Dominique Martino (*) shows up at the market weighed down with truffles which her dogs and pigs unearth in the forests of her native Luberon, in the southeastern part of France. She will tempt you to purchase these aromatic rarities, by offering you truffle-butter spread on thin slices of baguette, as she describes the techniques used to find the knobby black nuggets. If you would like to find out firsthand, she organizes personal tours to "truffle land." If not, a mail order service is available for truffle emergencies.

For centuries, Saint-Germain-des-Prés has been the locus of the intellectual and artistic community of Paris; the tradition dates well before 1686, when the first Parisian café on Rue des Fossés-Saint-Germain, Le Procope, was established. Important writers, philosophers, and painters are known to have spent hours on end conversing here and in the first-floor lounges of Aux Deux Magots and Café de Flore. Up-and-coming jazz musicians such as Duke Ellington and Charlie Parker flocked to cellar jazz bars in the area, where they developed and showcased new rhythms before enthusiastic audiences. Today, chic Parisians and tourists rest on the terraces of these famous cafés, taking a few minutes (or hours) to watch the crowd passing by, as they sip overpriced espressos and flutes of champagne. On occasion, you may find one or two remnants of times past, nursing a *ballon de rouge*, consumed in their writing, hoping to become the Ernest Hemingway, Henry Miller, or Simone de Beauvoir of our time.

The aroma of pitch black vanilla beans mingling with the flowery scent of Chinese teas will lead you to one of the most popular *traiteurs* at the market. Here, protected behind a glass case, a selection of delicately prepared dishes will seduce you. *Taboulé,* barley, and lentil salads, vegetable terrines and duck pâtés, tasty quiches, savory curries and soups, and a variety of homemade desserts always run out before the end of the morning. We like to pick up a few with a fresh loaf of bread and head over to the Luxembourg Gardens just a few blocks away...

Smack in the middle of the market, across the aisle from each other in front of towering stacks of whole wheat breads, stand two vendors reminiscent of old-fashioned rural bakers selling the same loaves at opposite ends of the village square. There are many varieties of whole wheat breads available: some are packed with different grains; others rolled in sesame, poppy or sunflower seeds; and some are also made with natural leavening which leaves a tangy aftertaste. All are delicious and a change from the classic French bread. The shapes vary from baguettes and enormous country rounds, which are sold by weight, to square-shaped loaves and small individual rolls. Some bakers offer traditional French pastries: eclairs, croissants, seasonal fruit tarts and vegetable tarts filled with leeks, spinach, carrots, and onions—all made with whole wheat flour. One of the aspects of organic bread, besides the healthy grains and the stoneground flour, is that no artificial leavening is used and only a small amount of natural leavening, so the result is slightly denser. Often shoppers will pick up a tart or pastry and sit with their baskets on the park benches that sporadically appear along the market in order to re-energize at the halfway point. Alternatively there is a whole wheat crêpe stand a few steps down, where you can savor a crêpe filled with cheese or, for those who prefer it sweet, one with either brown sugar, chestnut purée, or jam.

The emphasis at this market is not meat, nor dairy, nor fish, nor beauty products (though you can certainly find all of these), but rather an abundance of fruits and vegetables. Some of the stands offer local produce that is picked and brought to the market directly by the farmers, known as *maraîchers*, while others carry organic produce imported from all over the world. You will find piles of deep green, leafy spinach beside delicate, white-tipped, tasty turnips and snappy, slim string beans—all bursting with vitamins and a farm-fresh complexion. The outcome is rich in quality, taste, and nutritional value, if not always in appearance. Many of the dedicated organic shoppers who come to buy here are young parents, conscientious of what goes into their children's mouths, willing to pay the extra francs for an *AB*-guaranteed carrot or apple.

As you make your way through the market, you will pass many small cheese stands. Some sell fresh cheeses draining in earthenware pots, while others offer wedges of hearty mountain varieties. In winter, an oyster stand sets up where if you supply the tray, the vendor will shuck a couple dozen oysters for you while you do your shopping. You will pass by a fishmonger who prides himself on his salmon and sole; and a baker who has flaky croissants, *pains au chocolat*, and a very expensive but very delicious fruit-and-nut bread packed with figs, dates, currants, hazelnuts, walnuts, and almonds. You can also pick up a bottle of young fruity Côtes du Rhone at La Cuvée de la Coccinelles, where the owners will

Top: Freshly unearthed truffles and algae from Brittany are but a fraction of the unusual offerings found at Raspail. Bottom: Most of the fruit and vegetable vendors at Raspail grow their own produce.

enthusiastically insist that you try their latest vintage of reasonably priced table wines. If you are planning a party, you can buy a five-liter recyclable container of this wine which will be very much appreciated by your guests.

Once you have seen it all and are ready to concern yourself with more important matters—such as where to go for lunch!—there are several restaurants to choose from only a few blocks away (sorry no organic ones open nearby). You may want to walk over to the Boulevard Saint-Germain for an aperitif at the Café de Flore, and then settle in at the famous Brasserie Lipp across the street for a leisurely lunch, or enjoy a plate of *antipasti* and *prosciutto* with a carafe of wine at the Cherche-Midi, on Rue du Cherche-Midi, just around the corner from the market.

ORGANIC WINE

Don't let yourself be fooled by the term "organic" wine:

Although the grapes are grown following strict organic guidelines without the use of chemical fertilizers or pesticides, the actual wine-making process is done according to traditional wine-making practices, which means that there is no guarantee that sulphates and preservatives (known to cause the occasional headache) will not make their way into the bottle!

You can also wander over to the beautiful Luxembourg Gardens, spread out your goodies on a park bench, and watch the miniature sailboats glide across the pond. After tossing the remaining crumbs to the sparrows and the giant carp inhabiting the waters, finish your picnic with the perfection of an espresso at one of the outdoor cafés. The cafés also serve lunch; the one located near the tennis courts serves good salads with plates of scrumptious sautéed potatoes. Most shops and galleries are closed on Sundays, but it is still nice to stroll around the streets of Saint-Germain-des-Prés window-shopping and relaxing in the many cafés.

Right: Even the least experienced cook can put together a heavenly salad at Jean Conard's bio-dynamic vegetable stand.

Le Fermier Bio

We met the organic farmer Henri-Jean Giboulot at the Batignolles organic market, lost behind a display of vibrant fruits and vegetables, handing out a bouquet of lily of the valley to one of his customers. Besides his garden-fresh produce, he also grows a variety of grains, presses extra virgin-oils, tends to a vineyard and raises a herd of Charolais cows. We thought that this young *bio* farmer would be the ideal person to introduce us to this method of farming and asked if we could come and visit.

One glorious spring morning, we found ourselves in the heart of Burgundy at the Domaine Giboulot in the small village of Combertault. The region is famous for its wines, its wheat, its cooking, and its beautiful snow-white Charolais cows, all of which we were about to discover. Dressed in a *bleu de travail,* this tall, friendly man with a shock of curly hair gave us a hearty handshake, ushered us immediately into his jalopy, and off we went to see his herd and crops.

As we bumped along country lanes, Henri-Jean explained to us why almost thirty years ago his father Paul converted to organic farming. Although he had initially adhered to the new postwar system of high intensity, chemical-ridden cultivation, in due time he realized that his cattle and crops were becoming immune to treatments and plagued by diseases. He searched for alternative methods of farming, and in 1970 decided to change his whole approach and adopt organic guidelines. The results have been satisfactory, with high yields and healthy cattle, and his two sons, Henri-Jean and Emanuel, continue to perpetuate this ideology. From a young age the two brothers were drawn to different areas; Emanuel began studying oenology early on while Henri-Jean's dream was to own a herd of *Charolais* cows and he bought himself a calf with the money he received for his first communion. To this day, Emanuel is solely in charge of the family vineyards and Henri-Jean is the proud owner of a herd of forty. We sloshed through the lush pastures of buttercup, alfalfa, clover, and swaying grass, trying to keep up with Henri-Jean's long strides until we came upon his herd that was grazing peacefully. There was one impressive smug bull in charge, and each cow had a calf at her side that would dash to hide with every whir and click of our cameras. These beautiful specimens spend the spring and summer months outdoors and the winter fattening up, eating only organically grown grains in the barn behind the house.

A short drive away, Henri-Jean has 35 hectares where he grows various types of wheat, including the ancient variety *epautre*, oats, lentils, corn, soya, and sunflowers, and down the way a lush garden plot filled with lettuces, zucchinis, strawberries, herbs, radishes, leeks, melons, sweet peas, and string beans. After our tour, Henri-Jean graciously invited us to lunch, and along with his wife and children, we sat down to what looked like half a side of beef along with delicious *pommes frites*, a garden fresh salad and a bottle of their organic red wine.

As the sun began to set, with soggy shoes and socks and a car load of goodies, we ventured deeper into Burgundy, land of wine and castles, and almost never made it back to Paris.

Henri-Jean Giboulot is present at the Batignolles and Raspail organic markets.

RUE DE SEINE-BUCI

This popular street market, located in the heart of Saint-Germain, is often wrongfully confused with an open-air market. Lined with vendors and food shops that open up to the street, the offerings are mixed; people mostly come here to people-watch and to experience the "real" Paris.

As you walk along Rue de Buci, you will come to a minuscule shop at number 34, Aux Vrais Produits d'Auvergne, which dates back to 1947. It is packed with wonderful delicacies from the region: enormous jars of duck *cassoulet*, fresh and air-cured sausages of every shape and size, earthenware jars of *rillettes*, and delicious cooked and smoked hams. The latest arrival, Oliviers & Co. at number 28, sells vintage olive oils that have been preselected from all over the world. At number 18, there is a *traiteur* selling pre-cooked Italian specialties: cannelone, lasagna, and egg-plant parmesan, as well as fresh paninis that can be heated up, layered with *bresaola*, *provolone*, and marinated bell peppers, or with *prosciutto*, mozzarella, and tomato. Farther along, there is a Chinese take-out, a few bakeries, and an Alsatian specialty store with a pushcart out front that is always stacked with prepared sandwiches.

Along Rue de Seine, you will find that most of the fruit-and-vegetable stalls are affiliated with the supermarket and have decent but commercial produce. The butcher, fishmonger, cheese, and wine shops on the other hand offer a nice selection although a bit on the pricey side.

MARCHE COUVERT SAINT-GERMAIN

The Marché Couvert de Saint-Germain is the original site of the Saint-Germain fair, which was held at the beginning of the Middle Ages. This fair became the most important cultural and economic event of Paris, attracting performers, artists, and merchants from all over the world. Such rarities as coffee were introduced by tradesmen eager to barter their goods while artists showed their works and performers, acrobats, and musicians entertained the public. The fair thrived for over three centuries until it finally petered out after the Revolution, at which time Napoleon I ordered the covered market to be built. It was completed in 1813.

In the early 1990s, the market underwent a complete overhaul, leaving the original facade as the only reminder of days past. The vendors were assigned a quarter of the covered market; the remaining space was turned into a pristine shopping mall with a public swimming pool and parking lot below. A far cry from the days of the fair, the food hall is now devoid of all charm; instead of hearing the hawkers promoting their wares, one quietly goes about one's shopping in a subdued and antiseptic atmosphere. Still, all is not lost: 19 of the 40 original vendors remain, offering good quality and a fair selection. You will find two fishmongers, a handful of vegetable and fruit stands, two excellent butchers, a baker, a florist, a health-food stand, Chinese, Greek, and South American *traiteurs*, a wine merchant, an Italian fresh pasta stand, and even a seamstress and a cobbler.

RASPAIL

Founded in 1920, the Raspail market is one of the oldest open-air markets in Paris. Located on the same spot as the Sunday organic market, it is smaller and caters to a different crowd. Approximately 30 vendors, offering some decent quality products, set up here, among them: Michel Gaigner's popular fish stand; Catherine Faure's tempting display of mushrooms; and the Ardeche speciality stand that has robust, flavorful hams, pâtés, and sausages carefully arranged beside an assortment of wine, cider, and little baskets of onions and garlic.

There are several butchers, *fromagers*, vegetable stands, a *triperie*, and a very nice *volailler* who makes roasted chickens and, on occasion, baby goat *(cabri)* that just melt in your mouth.

This is a fine place to do your shopping when in the neighborhood, but if you are looking for something more sophisticated drop by the impressive food hall La Grande Epicerie de Paris, behind the department store Le Bon Marché; at the Epicerie you will find a nice selection of prepared foods and unusual delicacies from all over the world, plus a well-stocked wine section and informed staff to help you.

Above: Lining up at Michel Gaigner's fish stand at the Raspail weekday market.

MARKET RECIPES

SALADE DE MACHE ET DE BETTERAVE
Parisian Beet and Lambs Lettuce Salad

This is one of the most traditional *brasserie* salads, which you will still find at select establishments throughout Paris. One of our favorites is at the Brasserie Lipp, which makes this salad to perfection. It is a great appetizer, and the combination of flavors is perfect. Beets are normally sold cooked at the markets; but if you cannot find them cooked, there is nothing simpler than cooking a beet!

30 minutes 25 minutes

1 cooked beet
1 lb (500 g) mache (lambs lettuce)
2 hardboiled eggs
1 handful peeled walnuts

For the vinaigrette:
3 tbs olive oil
1 tsp walnut oil (optional)
1 tbs vinegar (optional: raspberry vinegar)
Salt and pepper, to taste
1 tsp Dijon mustard (optional)

1. To cook a beet: Cut off the stalk, and place in boiling water. Reduce heat, and cook approximately 25 minutes until you can put a knife through it easily. Remove from water, let cool, and remove skin. If you make more than the recipe calls for, the best way to store them is in vinegar water (cold water with a tsp of vinegar) in the refrigerator; they will keep a few days. **2.** Cut the beet in half, and slice each half. Set aside. Wash the mache several times, spin dry, and set aside. Boil the eggs, run under cold water, peel, cut into quarters, and set aside. Leave the walnuts whole. **3.** Whisk together the ingredients for the vinaigrette. It can be as simple or as sophisticated as you want. The basic olive oil and vinegar can be pepped up with a spoonful of mustard; and you can experiment with different oils (add a tsp of walnut oil) and vinegars (raspberry, for example). **4.** When ready to serve, place the mache and beet in a large bowl, and toss with the vinaigrette; then decorate with the egg and walnuts. **Serves 4**.

Fruity, chilled reds or crisp, aromatic whites: Brouilly, Côtes de Blaye, Graves

SOUFFLE AUX FLEURS DE COURGETTE
Squash Flower Soufflé

Zucchini flowers are one of the wonderful things about summer. The minute we see a vendor with these delicate yellow-and-orange flowers decorating his stand we quickly search for a new recipe. The following was offered to us by Joseph Jacart, who is one of the pioneers of organic farming in France, having begun in 1959. This recipe is quite easy to make and always a special treat. Make sure your eggs are at room temperature!

30 minutes 30 minutes

For the dish:
1 tbs butter
3 tbs parmesan cheese

For the soufflé:
2 cups zucchini flower petals and bottoms (approximately 16)
1 tbs butter
3 tbs diced shallots
Salt and pepper, to taste
2 tbs butter
3 tbs flour
1 cup milk
3 egg yolks
1/2 cup (45 g) gruyère
1 pinch nutmeg (optional)
4 egg whites
1 pinch salt

Soufflé dishes

1. Prepare a 6-cup soufflé dish or 4 individual ones by rubbing them with butter and sprinkling the sides and bottom with grated parmesan cheese. Preheat the oven to 400 °F (205 °C). **2.** Prepare the flowers by removing the pistil, pulling the petals away from the base, and tearing them into slivers. Slice the base of the flower thinly. Set aside. **3.** Melt 1 tablespoon of butter in a pan over medium heat. Add shallots and cook until translucent. Add the flower bottoms and sauté a couple of minutes. Add the flower petals, season with salt and pepper, and cook a few more minutes until soft. Set aside and let cool. **4.** Scald the milk and set aside. **5.** In a small saucepan, melt 2 tablespoons of butter over low heat, add the flour, and whisk together. Add the milk, and whisk continuously for 5 minutes until the mixture has thickened; do not allow it to boil. Let cool. **6.** Place the milk mixture in a large bowl, and add one egg yolk at a time. Mix in the cheese, the flower mixture, and nutmeg if desired. **7.** In a separate bowl, beat the egg whites with a pinch of salt until stiff. Pour one third of the egg whites into the other bowl, and mix together, then fold in the remaining two thirds. Make sure not to over-mix. **8.** Gently pour into the soufflé dish, and bake for 30 minutes until golden, puffed, and moist inside. Make sure that your guests are seated before taking the soufflé out of the oven. Serve immediately. **Serves 4**.

Delicate reds and whites: Roussette de Savoie, Saumur, Chinon

ONGLET A L'ECHALOTE
Seared Steak in a Shallot and Red Wine Sauce

Generally Henri-Jean Giboulot prefers his *Charolais* steaks plain but, for this particular cut which has a strong flavor, he makes a sauce with wine and shallots. *Onglet* is not always easy to come by, as the butcher usually puts this cut aside for himself. It can be substituted with other cuts; but make sure you use a well-aged piece of sirloin or rump steak. This particular cut is quite thin, about 1 inch (2 1/2 cm) thick, so ask your butcher to slice the steak of your choice accordingly.

10 minutes 10 minutes

4 shallots
4 6-oz (170 g) boneless steaks
3 tbs butter
1 tbs peanut oil
Salt and pepper, to taste
1/2 cup red wine
1/4 cup beef stock

1. Finely chop the shallots, and set aside. **2.** Pat dry the steaks with a paper towel, and heat a large frying pan over a medium-high flame. **3.** Put 1 tablespoon of butter and the oil into the pan. When hot, add the steaks. Sear for 2 to 3 minutes, turn over, add salt and pepper, cook another 2 to 3 minutes, and salt and pepper the other side. Continue cooking and turning until the desired *cuisson*: rare, medium or *bien cuit*. Remove onto a warm plate, cover with aluminium foil, and set aside. **4.** Put 1 tablespoon of butter in the pan, lower heat to medium, add the shallots and a pinch of salt, and stir continuously for 3 minutes. Raise the heat to high, and deglaze the pan with the wine. Allow to evaporate 1 minute, then add the stock. Whisk in the remaining tablespoon of butter, and reduce by a quarter. Adjust the seasoning, and spoon onto steaks. **Serves 4.**

Either a light, fresh red or a coarse, full-bodied red: Saumur Champigny, Côte Rôtie, Saint-Julien

SOUFFLE AUX FRAMBOISES
Raspberry Soufflé

This light, fluffy dessert makes a nice finale for an elegant dinner; and it is a change from the traditional cakes and ice creams. You can prepare the raspberry mixture ahead of time, leaving it at room temperature. Then add the beaten egg whites, and place the soufflé in the oven, half an hour before serving. Make sure to serve immediately, as they fall quickly.

30 minutes 30 minutes

For the molds:
1 tbs butter
4 tbs sugar

For the soufflé:
1 lb (500 g) raspberries
2 tbs sugar
1 tbs butter
4 tbs flour
4 egg yolks
5 egg whites
1 pinch salt
4 tbs sugar

Confectioners' sugar and raspberries, for garnish

1. Butter 4 individual soufflé dishes, and sprinkle the sides and bottoms with sugar. Place in refrigerator. Preheat oven to 475 °F (250 °C). **2.** Place the berries, reserving 8 for garnish, and 2 tbs sugar in a saucepan. Cook over low heat for approximately 15 minutes, until you have a marmalade-type mixture. Remove from heat and let cool. Press through a sieve to remove seeds. **3.** In a separate saucepan, melt butter over low heat, add the flour, and whisk together to form a roux. Mix continuously for a couple of minutes; do not worry if it separates. When cool, add the raspberry mixture, and mix in one egg yolk at a time. **4.** In a separate bowl, beat the egg whites with a pinch of salt until stiff. Add the additional 4 tablespoons of sugar at soft peak to help stiffen. **5.** Pour one third of the egg whites into the other bowl. Mix together, then fold in the remaining two thirds; make sure not to over-mix. **6.** Gently pour the mixture into the 4 soufflé dishes, and bake for 5 minutes. Then lower temperature to 400 °F (205 °C), and bake 15 to 20 more minutes until golden, puffed, and moist inside. Sprinkle with confectioners' sugar, place each soufflé dish on a plate, garnish with raspberries, and serve immediately with a bowl of *crème anglaise* and a plate of butter cookies on the side. **Serves 4.**

Champagne

RESTAURANT
OPTIQUE
ILE DE RE
122 BHA 92

Housing Paris' most symbolic monument, the 7th arrondissement could be the most visited area of the city. Surprisingly enough, this is not the case—after having admired the Eiffel Tower, most visitors turn right around and head elsewhere, leaving the 7th in peace.

Ever since it became a sought-after neighborhood in the 17th century, where the privileged built enormous private mansions,

VII[e] ARRONDISSEMENT

the 7th has discreetly housed some of the most exclusive residents of Paris. One of the less-populated areas of the city, it exudes a reticent quality: quiet streets where the inhabitants live behind massive portals and high walls surrounded by greenery. Oddly enough, for such an upscale, sober neighborhood, its market, Saxe Breteuil, is one of the most convivial and lively in the city, with a charming country-like appeal.

2.5 million people climb the Eiffel Tower every year but few venture into the residential neighborhood that surrounds it.

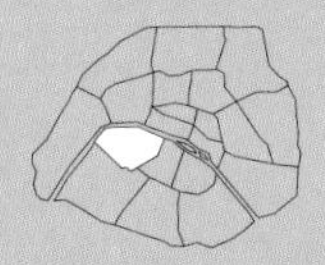

René GAILLARD
FRAMBOISES
FRAMBOISES

IN THE SHADOW OF THE EIFFEL TOWER

The Saxe-Breteuil Market

In a quiet, elegant neighborhood where shops and cafés are few and far between, the Saxe-Breteuil market is an oasis, its colorful awnings rising against the pale sandstone backdrop of the surrounding buildings. This part of the 7th arrondissement houses two of the most important monuments of Paris: the Eiffel Tower and Les Invalides. Once you have ascended to the skies to admire the breathtaking view from the tower, and descended into the crypt to behold the Tomb of Napoleon, venture forward into this prestigious neighborhood to see a very local side of Paris.

The neighborhood is regarded as one of the best sections of town to inhabit, with its luxurious apartments and green esplanades. Through the centuries, the area has maintained a very elitist aura: in 1682, when the King's court left the Louvre and moved to Versailles, the aristocracy was eager to move out of the Marais, which had by then become too crowded. The nobility decided to settle across the river, where land which lay en route to Versailles was available. By 1689, the bridge Pont Royal was built, linking the 7th arrondissement directly to the Tuileries gardens. The 7th, with its beautiful palaces and enormous gardens, was becoming firmly established as a center of aristocratic life. Most of the development in the area was completed in the late 1800s. Elegant, Haussmann-style apartment buildings, considered to be regal and spacious by modern standards, replaced what used to be vast meadows. Nowadays, most of the grand properties have been split up and the original palaces converted to government offices or foreign embassies. One of the few contemporary standouts is the UNESCO building erected in the 1950s, just up the street from the market.

Hidden behind the Ecole Militaire, the Saxe-Breteuil market stretches down the broad, tree-lined Avenue de Saxe, from Place de Fontenoy to Place de Breteuil.

Nestled amidst all this elegance and wealth, stands the Saxe-Breteuil market. Like at a village farmers' market, one feels transported from the city to a place where the mood is friendly and calm. Even on busy Saturdays when there are over 120 stands offering an outstanding selection, you can comfortably stroll along chatting with vendors and customers alike. Yet, with one glimpse upward, you will be reminded that you are in the heart of Paris with the Eiffel Tower hovering overhead.

Residents armed with baskets and shopping carts venture to Saxe-Breteuil not only to shop, but also to socialize and exchange cooking tips. Shoppers and vendors alike address each other by name. We have often overheard people discussing their children's vacations, the latest elections, and how the pork roast was cooked to perfection. The formality of the French is not so apparent here—one day, a local proudly introduced us to "the singing salad-lady", Monique Quillet, who has been selling leafy greens here for over 20 years as she continues to pursue a professional singing career.

Start your visit to the market at Place de Breteuil, where on sunny days you will find a man seated at his piano serenading the shoppers. We always walk down the left-hand aisle first, checking out the homemade jams, jellies, *Paris Brest*, eclairs, and other traditional pastries which are sold at the first stand you encounter. As you wander past displays of colorful fruits and vegetables, tempting Italian specialties, and homemade sweet and savory pound cakes (we love to sample them all!), you may hear the sound of a gong—a ringing you might imagine encountering while climbing the Himalayas.

You will discover that it is Jean Falconnet, at his Savoie specialty stand, chiming a monstrous cow bell that the robust *Savoiard* cows somehow manage to wear around their necks while grazing in the pastures. The cheese that they produce is just as hearty: oversized wheels of *gruyère debacles* and *tomme de savoie* with thick crusts, pungent aromas, and earthy flavors; these stand next to rounds of the more refined *reblochon*, *abondance*, and *beaufort*. Claiming to be the best-looking vendor in the market, Monsieur Falconnet will charm you with his enchanting "Grimm-like" depiction of Savoie, a mountainous region in the southeast of France that shares a border with Italy. Besides cheese and sausages from the region, he also sells pasta and polenta, which are commonly eaten in Savoie as an accompaniment to hearty meat stews. Unlike in Italy, the Savoie people eat large-grain polenta which they cook in chicken stock, mix with sautéed onions, cover with grated cheese and finish off under the broiler. Laughingly, Monsieur Falconnet admits that after such a meal a long walk in the mountains is recommended, if you can manage!

In 1873, Saxe-Breteuil was one of the many open-air markets established to replace the covered markets, which were dwindling in popularity. Back then an administrator was designated for each market, and rules and regulations were enforced: spaces were allocated, awnings were set up, and parking was reserved for each vendor's carriages and carts. The organizing spirit continues to this day, as Saxe-Breteuil was recently the first market to establish an official vendors' association, with an elected committee which represents the concerns of the market community and work together to promote its popularity and well-being. While visiting this market, you have the feeling of it as a strong focal point for the neighborhood, bringing life into the otherwise staid vicinity.

After getting your little taste of Savoie, continue your aperitif with some of the best and most varied olives we have ever come across. René Melet decided to plunge into the olive business after escaping from the weight of the French bureaucracy, which he endured while running a water purification plant of 150 employees. He left to set up his own small business with his son, Michael, where they sell fresh, brine-packed olives, marinated to perfection in a melange of ingredients.

Right: You will be able to taste delicacies every step of the way. Here, Monsieur Falconnet offers a sliver of his hearty *tomme de savoie*.

Tomme de CHARTREUSE
20%
79,90F
10%
69,90F

ARACHIDES GRILLEES
le SACHET
500g 10F

SARDINES SECHÉES
le Kilo 54,80 F

AMUS' GUEULE
123 Bis, Av ANATOLE FRANCE
94600 CHOISY-LE-ROI

AMUS' GUEULE

AMUS' GUEULE

He uses light-tasting oils, such as sunflower, grape seed, and corn (though he refused to tell us which one) so as not to mask the taste of the particular olives, as can happen when using olive oils. One of our first discoveries was a seasonal olive from Provence, the *Salonenque* variety, which is cracked and marinated with wild fennel and has a delicious, nutty, bark flavor. Buy them in small quantities, for after only a few days they become oxidized and lose their green hue and fresh taste. At Monsieur Melet's stand, more than 40 varieties of olives are displayed in bowls, delicately garnished with sprigs of bay leaf and cured lemons. The lemons, which marinate in the olive brine for five to six weeks, are favored by his clients to use as a tenderizer and flavor-enhancer in poultry dishes.

One day we were offered a few of René's anchovy-filled olives to sample with a Muscadet Sur Lie wine from Emmanuel Bodet, the owner of the Chateau de Souché vineyard in the Pays Nantais region. It's a special treat to be on hand when *viticulteurs* come here from different regions of France to test their young wines on the market. We were fortunate to be there to taste a Sauvignon Blanc du Pays du Retz, in a very unconventional manner: Monsieur Bodet opened up an oyster for each of us and in the empty shell poured a bit of wine to drink with the last trace of oyster. He calls this method of wine-tasting "chabrot," an expression used in the countryside when the peasants add wine from their glass to their bowls to finish off the remaining spoonfuls of soup.

As you float along past butchers, cheese displays, and a kitchen bazaar, you will come across an exotic stand. Although this market, like other markets, offers several Italian, Portuguese, and African commodities, as well as regional French specialties from Auvergne, Normandy, and Corsica, it is rare to find delicacies from Armenia. La Table D'Armenie prepares light and flavorful Armenian dishes, such as: *dolma*, eggplants stuffed with a sweet and savory rice mixture; *beurek*, triangles of phyllo pastry filled with tasty meat, ricotta, or spinach; charcoal-grilled eggplants, generously mixed with tomato, garlic, and mint; stuffed grape and cabbage leaves; and as accompaniments, homemade *tarama*, creamy yogurt and freshly baked flat bread. They also offer an array of deeee-licious pastries, including *baklava* and *burma,* which are not as sweet and heavy as one usually finds; we recommend that if you are buying two, buy three; and if your are buying four, buy six...

Left: *Epiciers* offer a wide selection of olives, nuts, dried fruits, and delicacies like these salt-cured sardines from Portugal. Following page: The *viticulteur*, Emmanuel Bodet offers a sample of his wine sipped from an oyster shell.

OLIVES

Green and black olives come from the same trees, but are picked at different stages: green olives are unripe and generally picked in the summer, black olives are ripe and generally picked in the winter, wrinkled black olives are overripe and are picked at the beginning of the following season.

Fresh olives directly off the tree are extremely bitter and virtually inedible. It is necessary, therefore, to treat them in two stages: in order to remove the bitterness, the olives (green and black) are soaked in baths of fresh water, which are changed on a daily basis, for approximately ten days depending on the variety. Generally, the green olives need more time. Sometimes ashes or chemicals are added to the water to accelerate this process but purists prefer only water.

Once the bitterness disappears they are placed in a brine solution, for approximately two weeks, to achieve their full flavor and for storage. At this point, the olive can be eaten and this is the best moment to distinguish between the different varieties. Hereafter, the traditions of each country and the creativity of the merchants come into play.

Réne Melet, our friend at the Saxe -Breteuil and Edgar Quinet markets, has olives from all over the world. He sells the finer varieties such as the *Caillater* and *Picholine*, plain or with very delicate spices added like *Herbs de Provence* for his *Noir Douce de Provence* or fennel seed for the *Salonenque* variety. For the heartier varieties, like the Moroccan and Tunisian olives, stronger condiments are added such as garlic, pimentos, and lemon (often a combination) with names like *Les Delices D'Izmir* and *La Mexicaine* or they are stuffed with either anchovies *Farcie Aux Anchois*, almonds or pimentos. All of the olives are mixed with oil when displayed at the market and are returned to the brine solution with their condiments for preservation.

We enjoy trying the different varieties and preparations that are available and often take home the plain varieties and come up with our own concoctions adding spices like cracked coriander seeds, toasted fennel seeds, cumin, juniper berries, bay leaf, garlic or dried chilies and fresh herbs such as parsley, dill, coriander and mint.

TAPENADE
Olive Caviar

We used this *tapenade* recipe as one usually uses a pesto, mixed with freshly cooked pasta. It is easy and delicious.

For 4 people, combine 1 cup pitted black olives with half a clove garlic, 1 tablespoon capers, 1 anchovy, and 3 tablespoons olive oil and blend in a food processor for a few seconds until a chunky paste is formed. Drain the cooked pasta retaining a cup of the cooking water, and toss with the *tapenade* to form a smooth sauce adding a few tablespoons of the water as needed. Sprinkle with chopped parsley, Parmesan cheese, and freshly ground pepper, to taste. You can experiment with different varieties of either black or green olives always taking the saltiness of each into consideration and compensating with the above recipe.

1995
Sauvignon Rouge de Retz
Vin de Pays
1995

On your way towards the end of this aisle you will pass by Jacky Lorenzo's fish stand and the organic breads on sale at Grain de Vie. Over the last five years there has been an influx of young entrepreneurs selling bread at the open-air markets. This is a new phenomenon. Formerly, market shoppers were forced to stop at the bakery on their way home, unless they picked up a loaf of the famous *Poilane* country bread that some cheese vendors sell. Before that, at the beginning of the 18th century, over 1,500 bakers sold their breads at specific open-air markets, known as *marché aux pains* (bread markets). By the end of the century, however, the tradition faded as bakery shops were established. Now, over two centuries later, there is a trend to return to the original methods, not only of selling bread at markets, but also of using old ways of preparing them. Historic recipes have been revived and adapted to create new varieties. Nowadays one can find whole wheat baguettes, raisin-nut breads, five-grain breads, *fougasse* (a flat bread from Provence baked with olive oil), flavored breads, and a whole array of country-style wheat breads at almost every market. This, of course, does not deter Parisians from sneaking out every morning for their customary hot baguette and buttery croissants at the local bakery. By the way, there is a stunning, old-fashioned bakery, founded in 1906, and definitely worth a visit: Le Moulin de la Vierge, located nearby at 166 Avenue de Suffren.

From this end of the market, in the distance you can see the Ecole Militaire, which was built at the request of Madame de Pompadour, the official mistress of Louis XV. She envisioned an institution where destitute young men would have the opportunity to become officers. Unfortunately, she passed away before its completion in 1773. The future Emperor Napoleon I finished his studies here and graduated as an artillery lieutenant. It is still a military school for higher officer training, and if you are lucky you might see some of the cadets riding their immaculately groomed horses about the grounds. The property is enormous, as you will notice if you skirt around it to get to the Champ de Mars, the park that leads up to the Eiffel Tower. When the Ecole Militaire was built, this section of Paris was marshland where the clergy grew vegetables to sell at the city's markets. In order to accommodate the needs of the school, the Champ de Mars (named after the Roman God of War) was cleared to be used for military exercises of up to 10,000 soldiers. At the end of the 19th century, the Champ de Mars was landscaped and converted into a public park that was chosen as the location for the Universal Fair in 1889 when the Eiffel Tower was built.

Continuing down the second aisle, you will come across two farmers from Normandy who display baskets of farm-fresh eggs, free-range chickens, ducks, and rabbits. They also sell a very unusual delicacy: fresh camembert, which is double the height of an aged camembert. It is eaten either sweetened with sugar or honey, or with chopped herbs and fresh-cracked black pepper. Farther down, Signor Daga from Sardinia sells fresh, appetizing raviolis overstuffed with salmon, spinach, wild mushrooms, or the traditional ricotta. He also makes nests of tagliatelle on the spot, which we cooked one evening with our olive man's recipe for *tapenade*.

There are all manner of fruit and vegetable stands on this aisle: from farmers with their homegrown produce displaying steamed ruby-red beets and garden-picked salads to merchants with a variety of local and exotic goods such as lychees and mangos. Fortunately, many products still remain seasonal, so you have the pleasure of looking forward to fragrant Cavaillon melons and strawberries from the Périgord region in the summer; and enormous plump artichokes from Brittany, quinces from Normandy, and earthy truffles from Dordogne in the autumn and winter.

Top and right: With the tempting array of freshly baked breads available at the market and the local bakery, Au Moulin de la Vierge, one is never at a loss for a crunchy baguette or a divine croissant.

Pain de Mie
15F

THE EIFFEL TOWER

The Eiffel Tower was constructed for the Universal Exhibition in 1889, the 100th anniversary of the French Revolution. It was designed by Gustave Eiffel and two engineers with the idea of it being only temporary and, therefore, easy to assemble and take apart. In total, 12,000 pieces were cast and riveted on site with 2.5 million custom-made bolts. The exhibition jolted a stream of enthusiasm and unity for the city in its excitement for this international event. Once built, the 318 meter (1,000 foot) Tour Eiffel at once shocked and thrilled the Parisians. It was considered by many to disturb the aesthetic homogenity of Paris besides being a useless structure, and petitions were signed for its removal. On the other hand, there were those who found it magnificent, especially being the tallest structure in the world until the Chrysler building in New York City was built over 40 years later.

Even medical teams, searching for a legitimate use for the tower, carried out experiments to monitor human physical reaction to such heights.

Ultimately, its savior was the short-wave radio as La Tour Eiffel proved to be the best location for the city's antennas. The aesthetic Parisians consented, and since then it has become the emblem of the city of Paris, drawing over 125 million visitors, certainly justifying its survival.

Every few years, volunteer painters from all over Europe flock to Paris for the best view in town while dangling from the girders, dunking their paint brushes in over 40 tons of paint needed to freshen up the complexion of this grande dame.

Farther along on the left-hand side, you will come to the perpetually busy Aux Delicieuses Cochonnailles, a stand with an impressive spread of free-range pork and pork products, tended by three charming characters who move in choreographed motion. You will find an array of different pâtés that you can pick up to eat with a fresh baguette and crunchy cornichons, or you might want one of their homemade sausages, bacons, or hams. In France, butchers traditionally specialize—you will never find beef, lamb, or chicken sold at an *artisanal* pork-butcher stand like this one.

The last of our favorite stops at this market is the family-run Trouville fish stand back at Place de Breteuil. Clad in yellow slickers and boots, father and son offer seafood caught fresh off the Normandy coast. Monsieur Auguet, a former fisherman, selects the best catches from the small boats at the quaint port of Trouville every morning, then drives into Paris to sell them at the market. Trouville, neighbor of the renowned Deauville, is a popular weekend destination for Parisians. Only two hours away, it is full of seaside hotels and restaurants stretching down a mile-long beach. The invigorating ocean air and fresh seafood are a double pleasure for the city's inhabitants, which may be part of the reason clients flock to this stand to buy up the delicious soles, scallops, and turbots.

As you finish your visit, you will probably be famished! So why not drop by the restaurant D'Chez Eux, located on Avenue Lowendaal. They specialize in cuisine from the southwestern part of France, including a well-made *cassoulet*—a delicious stew from Toulouse made with white beans, *confit* of duck, and other meats and sausages; this is one of the most savory dishes of France. Or you might choose from one of the numerous restaurants on the Avenue de la Motte-Piquet. Afterwards, if you are not too heavily loaded down with purchases, take a stroll to the nearby Rodin Museum, located on rue de Varenne. This is one of the few original palaces and gardens constructed in the area during the 18th century. The museum is one of the most stunning examples of the buildings of the era, and it holds a significant portion of Rodin's lifetime work, which he donated to the state. The artist lived and worked here from 1904 until his death in 1917. The garden, which you can visit separately from the museum, is absolutely breathtaking. If you are heading in the opposite direction, walk over to the Champs de Mars, where you can spread out your picnic in the gardens or have a twirl on the turn-of-the-century carousel, and take a boat tour along the Seine on the Bateaux Parisiens that dock just below the Eiffel Tower.

The bantering amongst the vendors of Aux Delicieuses Cochonnailles makes for an amusing shopping outing.

AUX DELICIEUSES COCHONNAILLES
FELTEN

tous
la ferme

RUE CLER

Besides the wonderful roving market Saxe-Breteuil and a few scattered supermarkets, the very popular market street Rue Cler is the only shopping area in this tranquil part of town. Lined with flower shops, butchers, bakers, wine shops, *traiteurs*, fruit-and-vegetable stands, and even a health-food store, everything that you may need is spread along this pedestrian way.

There are some very popular shops, including our favorite Italian *traiteur*, Davoli, which is filled to the brim with every delicacy imaginable, and packed with customers lining up along the two counters all the way out the door! If you are missing Italy, go to the right-hand side and buy some *prosciutto di parma*, salamis, *bresaola*, and real *parmigiano reggiano* (a rarity in France). If you would rather try one of their French specialties, line up on the left-hand side to buy their many terrines, fresh salads, and smoked salmon. You can also pick from one of their prepared dishes, or see what they have cooking outside; we have tried their delicious suckling pig and their tender *osso buco*. For oysters or a lobster, go to the fishmonger La Sablaise; for a steak, try the Aux Gourmets butcher shop; and for cheese, go around the corner to the well-reputed cheese shop, Marie Cantin, on Rue Champs-de-Mars—the prices may seem high, but if you consider that these are the cheeses that you will find at some of Paris' most renowned restaurants, it is well worth the splurge.

Left: The countryside brought to Paris: eggs straight from the farm.
This page: Despite the great selection at Saxe, locals never miss going to Davoli on rue Cler.

Le Fromager

Sporting an oversized Basque beret during the winter and a wide-brimmed Savoie felt hat the rest of the year, Philippe Perette is one of the most popular *fromagers* at the open-air markets. His fabulous display is dominated by huge wheels of mountain cheese atop wooden milking stools, plus an eclectic assortment of goat, sheep, and cow's milk cheeses carefully arranged on straw trays and wooden crates. Aided by a handful of young students, Philippe drives in from his farm in the Essone region, where he and his associate Claude prepare all of the goat-milk cheeses.

A native of Perpignan, Philippe moved to Paris as a young man to pursue his studies. Rather than settle down in the big city, he joined the surge of young entrepreneurs in the 1970s who decided to go back to their roots in the country. Instead of heading south, however, he bought himself a small farm, a half-hour drive away from the city, on which to tend his herd of 60 goats. He raises his furry friends with loving care, giving them full reign of the six hectares of tree-studded meadows. His motto is, "Only a happy goat will produce the right milk; and only the tastiest milk will make the perfect *chèvre.*" After a few years as an apprentice, Philippe developed his own unique style; he believes the character of the individual cheesemaker and *affineur* is apparent in the finished product. He compliments his own production with a selection of cheeses from artisanal farmers, from different regions of France, who adhere to the same principles as he.

Although Philippe's pride and joy are his fresh *chèvres*, from which he claims you can taste the goodness inherent in his happy goat's milk, he also offers an exceptional selection of other types of cheeses. We are partial to his fruity *saint félicien*, always ripened to perfection; *tomme crayeuse* from the Haute-Savoie region, with a lush, creamy texture and a mild flavor that differs radically from the more common, heartier *tommes;* and his *roquefort*, which is marbled just right, with blue veins of mold giving this sheep's milk cheese its particular bite. Whatever you choose will be delicious; and Philippe will be happy to introduce you to some new surprises.

Philippe Peret and his crew from Les Chèvres de Saint Vrain are present at the Président Wilson, Maubert, Grenelle, and Saint Charles markets.

MARKET RECIPES

TARTE AU CHEVRE
Zucchini and Fresh Chèvre Tart

This light alternative to the classic quiche given to us by Philippe Perette from Chèvres de Saint-Vrain has a fabulous combination of flavors. Although the recipe calls for zucchinis, we also like to make it with a cup of sautéed spinach (with all the liquid squeezed out), and seasoned with nutmeg. You can make it with asparagus, broccoli, yellow squash, or anything you fancy. You can make your own dough or buy it if in a hurry!

15 minutes 30 minutes

For the dough:
5 oz (100 g) flour
1 pinch salt
4 oz (125 g) chilled butter, cut into cubes (you can substitute 1 oz [30 g] of butter with 1 oz [30 g] fat or lard)
For the filling:
3 eggs
1 lb (500 g) fresh goat cheese
1 tsp *herbes de Provence*
Salt and pepper, to taste
2 tbs olive oil
1 onion, finely chopped
3 zucchini, sliced thick
2 tbs chopped basil
1/2 cup (45 g) gruyère, grated

For the crust: **1.** Put the flour and salt in a bowl. Cut in the butter with two knives or with your fingertips; incorporate well. Add the water and blend quickly into a ball. Add up to 1 tablespoon more of water if absolutely necessary. **2.** Place on a lightly floured surface, and knead the dough with the heel of your hand in small quantities by pushing the dough away from you in one clean sweep. Make sure not to over-knead as the warmth of your hands will heat the butter and result in a chewy dough. **3.** Form the dough into a ball, sprinkle with flour, and cover in plastic wrap. Refrigerate for at least 2 hours or overnight. **4.** Remove from the refrigerator and roll out on a floured flat surface. Place in the buttered pan, press into shape. Prick the bottom with a fork, place a piece of buttered wax paper on top and weigh down with dried beans. **5.** Bake 8 to 10 minutes in an oven preheated to 400°F (205 °C).

For the tart: **1.** Mix together the eggs, goat cheese, *herbes de Provence*, salt, and pepper. **2.** In a sauté pan, cook the onions in the oil until translucent, about 3 minutes. Add the zucchini, basil, salt, and pepper and cook about 8 minutes until soft. Remove from heat, discard any liquid, and set aside. **3.** Lower the heat of the oven to 350 °F (180 °C). Place half the egg mixture on top of the crust, arrange the zucchini on top, and cover with the remaining egg mixture. Sprinkle with the gruyère, place in the oven, and bake for 35 minutes. It will rise while baking and settle once removed from the oven. **Serves 6 to 8.**

Easy drinking, chilled reds: Sancerre, Beaujolais, Anjou, Pinot Noir

PALETTE DE PORC FERMIER AU FOUR
Thyme Roasted Pork Shoulder

Monsieur Michel Felten from Aux Délicieuses Cochonailles at the Saxe Breteuil market gave us his family recipe for roasted pork which is simple and ideal for a leisurely Sunday lunch *à la Francaise!*

15 minutes 2 hours

1 pork shoulder roast (approximately 3.5 to 4.5 lbs./1.6 to 2 kg)
5 garlic cloves
2 large onions, chopped
1/2 cup dry white wine
2 bay leaves
1 bunch of fresh thyme
1/4 cup olive oil
2 lbs roasting potatoes, quartered or sliced
Salt and white pepper, to taste

1. Ask your butcher to debone and tie a pork shoulder. **2.** Cut cloves in half and insert them into the roast. Coat the roast with the olive oil, season with salt and pepper and place in a roasting pan on top of the bay leaves and a couple sprigs of thyme. **3.** Distribute the remaining stems of thyme around the roast along with the chopped onion and pour in the wine. **4.** Place the roast in a cold oven and set temperature to 350° F (180°C). Cook for 1 1/4 hours, basting every once in a while. **5.** Add potatoes and put back in oven for 45 minutes until the roast and potatoes are cooked. Slice the roast, surround with the potatoes on a serving dish and strain over the juices from the roasting pan. **Serves 6 to 8.**

Coarse, full bodied, spicy reds: Hermitage, Corbières, Saint-Estephe

DOLMA

Dolma refers to vegetables that are stuffed with either a vegetarian or a meat filling which can be eaten warm or cold with a drizzle of olive oil and chopped mint on top. Edouard Boghossian from La Table d'Armenie gave us this recipe which can be made with either eggplant, zucchini squash, cabbage, or bell peppers.

40 minutes   1 hour

2 large eggplants, uniform in shape
For vegetarian stuffing:
1/3 cup olive oil
1 small onion, chopped
1 clove garlic, chopped
1 cinammon stick
1 anis star
1/4 cup (40 g) pine nuts, coarsely chopped
1/4 tsp ground coriander
1/4 tsp aniseed
1/4 cup (40 g) corinth raisins
1 cup (250 g) rice
1 cup (250 g) chopped seeded tomato
3 tbs chopped fresh parsley
3 tbs chopped fresh coriander
3 tbs chopped fresh mint
1 tsp salt
1/2 tsp pepper
2 cups light veg or beef broth
For meat stuffing, to above add:
1/2 lb (250 g) ground meat or sausage meat

1. Slice tops and bottoms of eggplant and cut cross-wise leaving two identical pieces. Scoop out the middle leaving 1/4 inch shell forming a hollow tube open at either end. Coarsely chop pulp and set aside.
2. Heat oil, add onions, garlic, cinammon stick and anis star and cook until translucent. Add pine nuts and dried herbs and brown for 5 minutes. Add fresh herbs, raisins, raw rice, tomato, chopped eggplant, salt and pepper (and meat if desired) and cook for 5 additional minutes stirring constantly until slightly brown. **3.** Fill the eggplant tubes with stuffing, pack from both sides, and place standing, tightly fit in a heavy bottom pot. Pour enough stock in the pot to almost cover eggplants (approximately 2 cups). **4.** Cook for about 1 hour, covered at low heat until eggplants are cooked. Spoon some stock on top of each one from time to time and check that the liquid does not evaporate completely and that the eggplants are not sticking to the bottom of the pot. If so, add more water. **5.** When cooked, remove from heat, allow to cool 10 minutes and serve immediately or let cool completely at room temperature. Place each one on a plate, drizzle with plain or spicy olive oil and garnish with chopped fresh mint. If serving cold, you may like to serve them accompanied by a bowl of plain yogurt for everyone to help themselves.
Serves 4.

Fruity rosés or crisp, fragrant whites: Pouilly Fumé, Sancerre

GATEAU AUX AMANDES ET AU CHOCOLAT
Almond and Chocolate Cake

Substituting ground almonds instead of flour, this chocolate cake becomes a light alternative to traditional chocolate cake with a nutty flavor. Served with a dollop of *crème fraîche*, a raspberry coulis, or simply on its own, it is a delicious dessert.

20 minutes   30 minutes

5 oz (150 g) bitter chocolate or 6 tbs cocoa
5 oz (225 g) sugar
7 oz (200 g) butter, room temperature
10 oz (300 g) ground almonds
3 tbs flour
5 eggs, separated
1 tsp baking powder
Pinch of salt

1. Grate chocolate by hand or in a food processor (or measure cocoa). Mix with the sugar, the egg yolks, and the butter until blended and smooth. **2.** Add the almonds and flour and mix well. **3.** Beat the egg whites with a pinch of salt, at soft peak add the baking powder and continue beating until firm. Carefully fold into the other ingredients. Do not over-mix. **4.** Preheat oven to 375°F (190°C). Rub an 8-inch mold with butter and sprinkle with flour. Pour the mixture into the mold, smooth even with a spatula and place in the oven. Bake approximately 30 minutes or until a toothpick placed in the center of the cake comes out clean. **5.** Let cool, remove from mold and sprinkle with confectioner's sugar. Serve with a spoonful of *crème fraîche* and/or raspberry coulis on the side. **Serves 6 to 8.**

Note: to make the coulis, place a container of raspberries (fresh or frozen) in a blender. Add sugar if desired and blend until smooth. Pass through a sieve and serve on the side.

Sweet wine: Beaumes-de Venise, Muscat

Left: Dolma

The Champs Elysées is often deemed representative of the 8th arrondissement. Actually, this often-mispronounced, tourist-flooded promenade, packed with movie theaters, crowded shops, fast-food restaurants, and overpriced cafés, is but a minute facet of the area. The 8th epitomizes the refinement and glamour of Paris. Its glorious, sweeping vistas filled with monuments, and its beautiful squares and avenues in perfect symmetry, make this neighborhood one of the most grandiose in the world.

VIIIe ARRONDISSEMENT

Not exactly the quaint side of the "City of Lights," this is the regal, polished seat of luxury, on view through the elegantly bedecked shop windows and polished revolving doors of the grand hotels and restaurant that line the avenues of this sparkling *quartier*. Here every visitor to Paris comes to be dazzled and indulge in the best of what France has to offer. The Marché Aguesseau may be the smallest open-air market of the city, but, complemented by the gourmet food shops that surround it on Place de la Madeleine, it is quite representative of the significance and tradition of French cuisine.

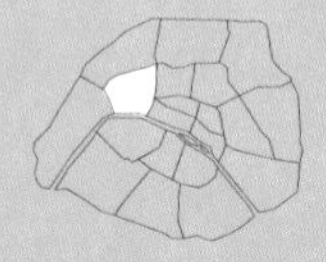

Place de la Concorde is one of the most spectacular squares in the world.

A LA MADELEINE
The Aguesseau Market

Dwarfed by the towering columns of the Madeleine church, the Aguesseau market appears incongruous amidst a swirl of traffic. A survivor from the days when horses and carriages paraded fashionable passengers around the elegant *quartier*, the only open-air market of the 8th arrondissement stands firm. Once a prestigious residential neighborhood, the majestic buildings that define the face of the *quartier* are now mostly occupied by banks, corporations, scintillating jewelry and clothes shops, upscale restaurants, and tempting gourmet food shops. The few tenacious inhabitants who still occupy ample apartments here enjoy the luxury of this thimble-sized market that most visitors fail to notice.

Originally bordering the edge of the city, the 8th arrondissement was once mostly marshland interspersed with vegetable plots and scattered with small villages that the nobles would cross en route to their country homes in Longchamp. In order to beautify these expeditions, Marie de Medicis, the wife of Henry IV, decided in 1616 to have a tree-lined carriageway made, beginning at the edge of the gardens of her current home, the Louvre. The passage was named "Cours-la-Reine." Following suit, the landscape gardener of the monarchy extended the central alley of the Tuileries gardens beyond its gates up the hill of Chaillot, planting trees the whole length of the way, gracing the lower end of the slope with beautiful, English-style gardens. These efforts gave this western section of Paris its primary cachet. During the mid-1700s, Louis XV had a square built at the entrance to the Tuileries gardens, in which to place a glorified statue of himself depicted as a Roman emperor crowned with laurel leaves and draped in a flowing toga. Around the same time, the nobles constructed lavish *hotel particuliers* along the nearby Rue du Faubourg-Saint-Honoré, among them the presidential mansion, Palais de L'Elysée—a grandiose example of the time, replete with rolling gardens and stylish fountains.

These were the foundations of the future arrondissement, which expanded in every direction throughout the coming century. The Cours-la-Reine was to become the main throughway along the river. The extended promenade was to become the Champs Elysées. And the square Louis XV was to become the regal Place de la Concorde. The area underwent its biggest transformation in the mid-19th century with the input of Baron Haussmann, who not only laid out the wide boulevards and avenues that criss-cross the neighborhood but also built the grandiose apartment buildings and esplanades that line them. The location and prestigious layout of the area attracted wealthy residents, followed by upscale restaurants, ritzy hotels, *haute couture* fashion houses, theaters, and food specialty shops. By the turn of the century, the 8th arrondissement had established itself as the *quartier* of lavishness, a reputation that it has kept up ever since.

Named after the magistrate Antoine Aguesseau, the Aguesseau market was founded in 1723, when this area was slowly becoming residential. Nowadays, despite the efforts of the seven vendors who invariably set up their stands every Tuesday and Friday, the Aguesseau market seems

The minuscule Aguesseau market stands proudly along one side of the monumetal church of the Madeleine and is surrounded by numerous specialty shops.

a bit lost in the haven of gourmet food shops and restaurants that define Place de la Madeleine. Like no other section of Paris, this has been the center of gastronomy since such establishments as Hédiard, Fauchon, Caviar Kaspia, Ladurée, and Maxim's opened their doors on the square and surrounding streets at the turn of the century. To this day, one can indulge in the many specialties associated with France for which these houses have become renowned: *foie gras*, truffles, champagne, caviar, smoked salmon, fine spirits, chocolates, and pastries.

En route to the market, if you are coming from Place de la Concorde, it is highly advisable to stop for a creamy *café au lait* and a sweet *madeleine* at Ladurée, an ornate tea parlor and pastry shop that is always packed. You can sit here at little round marble tables and thumb through the newspaper while sipping your coffee. As you leave, take a moment to admire the magnificent view along Rue Royale: Place de la Madeleine and its church on one side and Place de la Concorde, the Seine, and the National Assembly on the other. The Madeleine church, down the road, was rebuilt in 1764 to top off Rue Royale, which is why it faces south instead of the traditional east-west orientation. In truth, this regal structure looks like anything but a church, with its Greco-Roman facade and 52 towering columns that took many years to complete. Originally, the structure was conceived as the future home for the stock market, or a court house, or the Bank of France, or a theater, but Napoleon chose to commemorate his army, dubbing it his "Temple of Glory." It finally became a place of worship in 1817, and despite its lack of tolling bells or a steeple, it is still a favored location for prestigious weddings and funerals.

Marché Aguesseau is tucked away on the western side of the square, where it can be easily overlooked. Under a row of trees, a native of the Picardie region sets up an extensive display with plump free-range ducks and chickens, camembert and Pont l'Evêque cheeses, mounds of sweet and salted butter, trays of fresh and aged *chèvres,* buckets of thick cream, and large mesh baskets filled with dark brown eggs carefully cushioned on beds of straw, all of which he brings straight from his farm. Two vegetable stands, a *charcutier*, a fishmonger, a baker, and a florist make up the rest of this tiny market.

Aguesseau, which caters to the few, mostly elderly residents of the neighborhood, was on the brink of extinction 11 years ago. The vendors

Although the Aguesseau market is one of the smallest in the city, the handful of vendors nevertheless carry a delectable assortment of products.

SAUCISSON
AUX AMANDES
FAB. ARTISANALE
LE KG 146F/100
SAUCISSON
AU BEAUFORT
FAB. ARTISANALE
SAUCISSON
D'ANE
FAB. ARTISANALE
LE KG 137F/100

Beluga

Sevruga

Ossetra

CAVIAR

Caviar is the "fruit" of the ancient sturgeon species that lives in the Caspian Sea, navigating between the coasts of Russia and Iran as well as the rivers of Siberia and as far as the Pacific shores of Asia. The town of Astrakan at the mouth of the Volga River is considered the capital of Russian caviar, as it is here that the female sturgeons come during springtime, swimming upstream in the river swollen by the melting snow to lay their eggs. They are accompanied on their journey by the males, who after fertilizing the eggs travel back to the open sea. In days of yore, the Cossacks would harpoon the first females of the season, as they were prized for their golden eggs so cherished by the tsar.

Caviar is actually the perfect food, as it contains just about all the vitamins, minerals, proteins, and essential oils needed for the organism. If only it were not so pricey! The quality of caviar lies in its preparation, as the fresh eggs once removed from the sturgeon must be immediately cleaned and salted with the finest of sea salts. The preparation is rapid, but it takes an experienced hand to dose the salt just right. This process takes place directly on the fishing vessel where the caviar is tinned and stored in the hold of the ship at an unwavering 32 degrees Fahrenheit (0° C) until it reaches the port.

There are three different types of caviar: Beluga, Ossetra, and Sevruga. Beluga comes from the largest of the sturgeon family. They start laying eggs only at the age of 20, yielding ten to 15 kilograms of roe. The grains are the largest and of the highest quality, ranging in color from light to steel gray. The Ossetra sturgeon reaches maturity after eight to ten years and yields up to ten kilos of black to golden-brown colored roe, which has a slight hazelnut taste. The Sevruga is the smallest of the three and takes only six years before yielding two to five kilos of roe with a very fine taste, a small grain, and a coloring that ranges from black to dark gray. Whatever the type, caviar should be eaten immediately after the tin has been opened, as the delicious little pearls oxidize rapidly; and besides, who could say no to a lightly buttered toast heaped with Beluga, or a warm blini, a touch of *crème fraîche*, and a spoonful of Ossetra. (Not forgetting, of course, a shot of ice cold vodka or a flute of tingling champagne!)

then formed an association to fight for its survival. One of the most persistent has been the florist, Lucie Langiano, whose family has been a presence at the market for over four generations and cannot imagine working anywhere else. After 20 years of charming her clients with fabulous bouquets, sprays of cherry blossoms, rainbows of roses, gigantic birds of paradise, and beaming sunflowers, she is serious competition for the small flower market on the opposite side of the church. Since the 1950s, when the sale of freshly cut flowers was permitted at food markets, the flower markets of Paris have dwindled. The few survivors are at Place de la Madeleine, Place des Ternes, Place de la Republique, and on the Ile de la Cité. Unfortunately, they have lost their charm, and the selection is quite meager in comparison to the fabulous flower shops that fill the city, along with those at the open-air markets. For the Parisians, buying a bouquet of freshly cut flowers is as routine as picking up a head of lettuce or a baguette—you will always see a burst of petals peeping out of shopping caddies and baskets.

Aguesseau is a treat, but your excursion will not be complete without crossing over to the street-side of the square, where at the corner of Boulevard Malesherbes the radiant displays of Baccarat's red signature windows gleaming with its delicate blown glass objects and jewelry will open your senses. Next door, go into the tiny shop of Caviar Kaspia for a delectable scoop of Ossetra; or splurge on a tin of Beluga and a few thin slices of their exquisite smoked salmon with homemade blinis and cream, to go. This establishment was founded in the Roaring Twenties, after the exodus of Russians who had left their homeland during the Bolshevik Revolution, following in the footsteps of the well-known ballet dancers, artists, and writers who had taken France by storm. Naturally, these expatriates needed their vodka, called *champanski*, and caviar to balance their diet, making this a popular destination after the theater.

Above: Flower vendors, known as *bouquetières*, have sold flowers on the streets of Paris for centuries. Here, Madame Langiano prepares a colorful bouquet for one of her customers.

Continue on for a whiff of earthy truffles at Maison de la Truffe, before exploring the fragrant spices, fresh produce, teas, coffees, and condiments at the enticing grocer Hédiard. At the tender age of 22, Ferdinand Hédiard was so taken by the exotic plants, herbs, fruits, and flowers from the colonies that he decided to introduce these wonders to the Parisians. In 1854, he opened his shop. The red lacquered storefront, with its Ali Babaesque displays decorated with palm fronds, garlands of vibrant chili peppers, gourds, baskets, and masks, was the first of its kind—as was the original idea of having charming *Martiniquaise* women serving the illustrious clientele, adding yet another exotic touch to the image. Despite his never having left France, Hédiard was a connoisseur of international quality, and by procuring exceptional products established for himself a brand name of the highest repute. He became quite a celebrity with the high society. Such famous names as Alexander Dumas would flock to meet him and taste his unique delicacies.

Hédiard was one of the first merchants to choose Place de la Madeleine as the location for a shop, realizing the future potential of the 8th arrondissement, as far back as 1880. Since then, Hédiard has expanded, with five shops scattered throughout the city, offering a wide selection of products, from wines to prepared dishes, candied fruits, marzipan, jams, coffees, and teas; and a brand name that is distinguished all over the world by its trademark red-and-black packaging and octagonal jars. This shop is very enticing; mingling fragrances waft throughout; generous displays of exotic fruits and vegetables greet you at the entrance; tables topped with spices and herbs, shelves neatly lined with jars and bottles, barrels brimming with coffee grains, tins of Indian and Chinese teas, wooden crates of wine, and display cases with tempting prepared foods and pastries fill the store. A nice touch are the straw baskets on hand to carry your purchases while you browse.

The Belle Époque, when art and high culture reigned in *fin de siècle* France, was epitomized along the Grand Boulevards, just east of Place de la Madeleine. Here *tout Paris* strolled down these wide thoroughfares to see and be seen. Cafés and restaurants catered to elegant theatergoers who came into the neighborhood to be dazzled by the new opera house, Palais Garnier, or the beautiful leggy damsels at the Folies Bergère. After being entertained, the carousers would stop for a regal supper and bottle of tingling champagne at Café Riche, or for a delicious sorbet at Café Tortoni, which was reputed to sell up to 1,000 scoops on a balmy summer night! It was therefore only natural for talented couturiers, jewelers, and other artisans to establish themselves in this burgeoning *quartier*. With the steady influx of more popular folk, attracted by the scintillating lights and glamour, towards the end of the 1800s the fortunate and fashionable set moved westward, embracing the new 8th arrondissement with its many fine restaurants and stores. They settled around the Madeleine, Rue Royale, and Faubourg-Saint-Honoré.

Next on your journey, cross over to the handsome wine shop Nicolas, an establishment founded in 1822 by Etienne Nicolas. He was the first merchant to sell bottled wine and send delivery boys, clad in burgundy aprons and caps, to haul clinking wooden pushcarts to every corner of the city. The company grew rapidly. Today they have 337 shops in France, of which 114 are in Paris. Recognizable by their bold gold lettering and

Above: Hediard's exotic storefront circa 1854; fancy folk at Café de la Paix in 1910.

THE TINGLE OF MUSTARD

A little jar or crock of mustard is omnipresent in France, on every restaurant table and in every household. This is not a recent fad, but a tradition that dates back to Greek and Roman times, when the virtues of this ochre-colored condiment, then known as "sinapi," were appreciated. A versatile paste made from crushed mustard seed and mixed with either vinegar, water, wine, or grape extract, mustard was used to enhance the flavor of roasted meats. The grains left whole were also added to various dishes.

As well as being a flavor enhancer, mustard was also considered a cure for numerous ailments: poultices were applied to wounds or used to sooth rheumatism, bronchitis, or aches and pains; when taken orally, mustard was considered to liven the senses, help digestion, and ward off scurvy. One can still buy mustard flour at the pharmacy, called *sinapisme,* for the healing of bumps and bruises.

As early as 1390, the city of Dijon in the Burgundy region defined itself as the mustard capital of the world. This was due to the fact that wine and *moût* (grape extract), of which Burgundy always had an abundance, were necessary to coax the essential oils from the mustard flour and give it its fiery taste. During the 17th century, over 600 *marchands de vinaigre et moutarde* hawked their much-coveted commodity, wheeling through the streets of Paris pushcarts with two wooden kegs containing vinegar and mustard. The most renowned *marchand* was Monsieur Maille, whose reputation surpassed the frontiers of France, making him the official supplier for the courts of all of Europe. This was proven when an earthenware crock bearing his name was recuperated from the belly of a ship that sunk in 1785—*en route* to deliver his mustard to the tsar of Russia. Today you will find jars of Maille mustard in every store and supermarket. Today, 69,000 tons are consumed yearly in France. Nowadays, "Moutard de Dijon" refers mainly to the type of mustard and not the origin.

The most classic of all French salad dressings is made with a generous teaspoon of fine Dijon mustard and one tablespoon of red wine vinegar whisked together with three tablespoons of mild-tasting oil, such as peanut or grapeseed; add a twist of pepper and a pinch of salt, *et voilà!* This creamy vinaigrette is delicious with any type of salad and is perfect poured over a plate of steamed leeks. You can multiply the amounts and store the mixture in the refrigerator for a number of days. Remember that once a jar of mustard is opened, it must be kept in a cold place in order to preserve its kick.

Above: The Maille mustard shop on Place de la Madeleine

burgundy storefronts, they stock a wide choice of wines and spirits preselected from the vineyards of France. They offer a bottle for literally every taste and purse. The one on Place de la Madeleine is the largest and most complete, allowing it to compete with the cellars of Fauchon and Hédiard.

As you continue along you will come to Rue Tronchet, which leads up to Gare Saint Lazare and the famous Printemps and Galeries Lafayette department stores. If you are here during the wintertime this is the best vantage point to see the elaborate holiday displays of snow-covered Alps, gingerbread houses, and sleighs gracing the facades of Fauchon, the specialty shop across the way. In 1886, shortly after Hédiard, August Fauchon established his business with the intent of offering the best quality products to the elegant clientele of the neighborhood. Specializing in the *crème de la crème* of French cuisine, he elaborated on traditional dishes. The mouthwatering window displays always draw a crowd of awe-struck tourists. Standing side by side, the three gourmet shops offer a mind-boggling selection: 119 kinds of jams, 44 different sorts of mustards, 56 flavors of vinegar, and 90 types of tea are but a fraction of their offerings. *Foie gras,* rabbit pâté, vegetable terrines, lobster in aspic, *quenelles*, *escargots de Bourgogne*, smoked salmon and sturgeon, as well as delicately assembled hors d'œuvres complement the rich selection of pastries, chocolates, candied fruits, breads, and cakes. This is a must for any food lover coming to Paris. Regardless of your budget, there is always a little something to buy that will be carefully placed in their signature black-and-white-lettered paper bag.

The last of the signature stores worth a visit is the small Maison Maille mustard shop, whose reputation and name date back to 1747, when Monsieur Maille supplied the courts of Europe with vinegar and mustard. The tradition of pumping freshly prepared mustard into earthenware crocks is still alive at this shop. You should take advantage of tasting the uncommon tangy and fruity flavor. There are over 16 varieties from which to choose, stored in the beautifully hand-painted porcelain containers decorating the shelves.

If lunch is in order after your tour of the market and shops, you will have to backtrack to either Hédiard, with its discreet dining room on the mezzanine, serving traditional and exotic dishes; or to Fauchon's tea room, or upmarket restaurant. Caviar Kaspia is also open for those who are ready to spend a long afternoon sampling different caviars and vodkas. Or, if you have already had too many tastings and your appetite is satiated, you can visit the *haute couture* fashion boutiques that line Rue du Faubourg-Saint-Honoré and Avenue Montaigne, or wander through the gardens of the Tuileries. Take a peek at the Jeu de Paume Gallery that hosts interesting contemporary exhibits, or the Orangerie Museum that houses great impressionist paintings, including Monet's water lilies. You may also decide to attack the Champs Elysées; en route, browse at the stamps and telephone cards that collectors display on park benches and trestle tables along Avenue Matignon—this tradition has persevered every Thursday, Saturday, and Sunday, since 1939. When the city lights start to twinkle towards the end of the afternoon, stop for coffee or an apéritif at Fouquet's… and watch the world go by.

EUROPE

The covered market Europe is lost in a drab section of the 8th arrondissement. Although the handful of vendors filling this small food hall offer good quality produce, the neon lights and sterile atmosphere make for an uneventful outing. Constructed in 1972 to replace an original Baltard-style glass-and-iron structure, the actual building is nothing more than practical. It houses a fruit-and-vegetable stand, a florist, a butcher, a fishmonger, and a *charcutier*, who cater to the locals and the office workers.

Les Volaillers de Luxe

The Miolanes are among the younger generation of vendors at the markets—but by no means are they new to the gourmet poultry business. Their long table is lined with an appetizing array of top-notch poultry and game. Laurence has beautifully fanned the tail feathers of a *poulet de Loué* and delicately fluffed a capon's snow-white neck mantle; and Pascal has lent his touch with a row of bobtailed hares, hung above a plump suckling pig, propped up next to *terrines* of their homemade *foie gras*. This feast for the eyes is always animated by Pascal's continuous bantering along with Laurence's embarrassed smile.

Laurence was born into this *métier.* As far back as she can remember, she helped out her parents selling at the market or preparing their savory stews, roasts, and *pâtés*. When we joined her one cold winter morning, on her rounds at the wholesale market Rungis, she reminisced about when she came here as a young girl. Her history here was in evidence from the moment we stepped into the brightly lit poultry pavilion: Laurence was warmly greeted by several vendors with the familiar four-time kiss on the cheek—most of them have known her all her life. She was immediately shown the plumpest pigeons, quails, guinea hens, prized *bresse* chickens, pheasants, and partridges. We followed her, peeking into the various crates as she placed her orders. That day, capons, fresh goose livers, and *magret* of duck looked especially good; and though the prices were steep, she did not hesitate to purchase—this kind of quality produce always sells.

Pascal comes from a different background. As a young boy, he had aspired to be a chef, even though he applied for both the butcher and the cooking school in Paris. Though he chose to go to the former, his passion for cooking never subsided; and the market offers the perfect outlet for his talents. Pascal met Laurence just as she had started her own poultry business, after a bout with becoming a professional hairdresser. The two have been running their successful *volailler* stand together ever since.

After ten years of market presence, they have become well-established vendors; and their large clientele put full trust in their choice and preparation. An expert with a knife, Pascal seems to be perpetually deboning and trimming. We have often watched him carefully slip thin slices of truffle beneath the skin of a capon, or bard a pheasant, for his customers. They have developed a variety of sophisticated dishes: you will always find a casserole of boar or venison stew, chicken and tarragon in aspic, or wild duck *aux deux fruits* ready to be taken home and devoured. The Miolanes form a perfect team: their enthusiasm and commitment harkens to the many generations that have come before them.

The Miolanes are present at the Grenelle, Président Wilson, and Convention markets

SALADE DE COQUILLES ST JACQUES AU MONBAZILLAC
Scallop Salad with Monbazillac Vinaigrette

Combining fresh scallops and slim *haricots verts* from the Aguesseau market, the "Chinese truffles" from Hediard, and a good bottle of Monbazillac wine from Nicolas, we came up with this delicious recipe. Chinese truffles are small potatoes that have a deep purple color and a chestnut flavor; if you cannot find these, you can use any combination of boiling potatoes—for the presentation, the smaller the better. This can be served as an appetizer or main course; just change the quantity of scallops (2 to 3 per person for an appetizer; 4 to 5 for a main course).

30 minutes   5 minutes

For the vinaigrette:
2 cups Monbazillac wine (or other dessert wine)
1 tsp Dijon mustard
1 pinch salt
Freshly ground pepper
3/4 cup sunflower oil
2 tsp lemon juice

For the salad:
2 new potatoes
2 Chinese truffle potatoes (or new potatoes)
1 lb (500 g) *haricots verts* (French string beans)
2 tomatoes
1 small bunch chervil
2 tbs butter
12 large sea scallops (with roe, if possible)
Shaving of black truffle (optional, for garnish)

For the vinaigrette: **1.** Reduce wine, over medium heat, to one half. The liquid will change color and will resemble liquid honey. **2.** Combine the mustard, salt, pepper, and reduced wine in a bowl. Add oil and lemon juice, and mix together with a whisk. Set aside.

For the salad: **1.** Boil new potatoes and Chinese truffle potatoes 10 to 15 minutes, until cooked. Cool, peel, and julienne. **2.** Trim and blanch string beans in boiling water for 2 minutes. Remove, retaining the water, and rinse under cold water. Return to boiling water for an additional 2 minutes until cooked but still crunchy. Strain and rinse again. **3.** Peel the tomatoes by making a cross on the bottom of the tomato with a knife and placing in boiling water for 1 minute. Remove from water and peel. Cut in half, remove the seeds, and julienne. **4.** Wash chervil, and discard stems. Mix together with string beans, tomato, and vinaigrette in a large bowl. Add potatoes and mix gently. Set aside. **5.** Heat the butter in a skillet over a medium-high flame. When it is foaming, sear the scallops for 2 minutes on each side. Season with salt and pepper and remove from heat. **6.** Make a bed of the string bean salad on each plate, distribute the scallops accordingly, and serve.

Dry, full-bodied, aromatic whites: Meursault, Condrieu, Pinot Noir

CHEVREUIL AUX PRUNEAUX
Venison Chops in a Prune and Cognac Sauce

Come Christmas time, venison makes its appearance at the markets. Though the beautiful displays are tempting, one often associates preparing game with overnight marinating and long hours of cooking. This recipe, given to us by the Miolanes from the Président Wilson market, calls for tender chops which cook in a jiffy, quickly seared like a steak. This lean meat should be eaten rosé and served with fresh tagliatelle. You can also prepare boar chops in the same manner.

10 minutes   25 minutes

20 pitted dried prunes
1/4 cup armagnac
1/4 cup water or stock
Salt and pepper to taste
4 venison chops, 1 1/2-inches (4 cm) thick
1 tbs heavy cream

1. Soak the prunes in a bowl of cold water overnight, or if need be, a few hours ahead of time. **2.** Strain the prunes, and simmer uncovered in the armagnac and water for 15 minutes. Remove from heat and set aside. **3.** Preheat a frying pan over a medium-high flame. Salt and pepper the chops, and cook the venison for 3 minutes on each side (depending on thickness and preference). Do not overcook; rather undercook as they will continue cooking while you make the sauce. **4.** Remove the chops to a warm serving dish. Deglaze the pan with the juice from the prunes, add the prunes, stir in the cream, adjust the seasoning, and heat for a minute. **5.** Pour the sauce over the chops, spoon the prunes on top, and serve immediately. **Serves 4.**

Sophisticated, full-bodied reds: St Julien, Pauillac, Gevrey-Chambertin

Left: Salade de coquilles Saint Jacques au Monbazillac

TERRINE DE FOIE GRAS
Foie Gras

Foie gras has such a reputation that many of us believe that it falls from heaven; and few of us imagine that we could cook a terrine of *foie gras* ourselves. Both the Criés and the Miolanes generously shared their secrets with us, thus demystifying the procedure. The following recipe is made with the fresh liver of a fattened duck. Goose liver can also be used, but it is more sensitive to heat and requires an experienced cook.

3 to 4 hours 35 to 55 minutes

1 fresh *foie gras* of duck, 1 1/10 to 1 3/4 lbs (550 to 875 g)
1/2 cup milk
1/2 cup Sauternes wine
2 to 3 tsp salt (depending on size of liver)
1/2 to 3/4 tsp ground white pepper (depending on size of liver)

Thermometer
Terrine
Baking dish

1. Remove the liver from the refrigerator and let stand at room temperature for 1 to 2 hours. **2.** Gently pull the two lobes of the liver slightly apart. With the tip of a small knife, carefully remove any veins or bile that may be visible on the underside. **3.** In a large bowl, macerate in the milk and Sauternes for 2 hours. **4.** Remove from the liquid, and place on a clean kitchen towel to drain for approximately 1 hour. **5.** Rub the liver with the salt and pepper and gently pack the whole liver into the terrine. **6.** Meanwhile, place some water in the baking dish with the thermometer and place in the oven. Heat oven to 176°F (80°C). **7.** When the thermometer shows 176°F (80°C), place the terrine in the bain marie, and cook for 35 to 45 minutes for 1.1 pounds (500 grams) or 55 minutes for 1.75 pounds (800 grams). It is very important that you keep an eye on the terrine while it is cooking—the thermometer should never go above 176 °F (80°C), as the liver risks melting! **8.** When cooked, remove from heat and allow to cool. For best results, it is recommended to let the cooked *foie gras* stand in the refrigerator for a minimum of 2 days before eating. **9.** Remove from refrigerator 15 minutes before serving. If serving individual portions, slice a 1/2-inch (1.25 cm) portion per plate, along with toasted white bread. If serving whole, place the terrine in hot water for a few minutes, turn over onto a serving platter; and serve with toast. It can be accompanied by coarse sea salt and fresh cracked black pepper. Refrigerated, it will keep approximately 10 days after cooking.
Serves 10 to 12.

Champagne, vintage Port, or smooth, full-bodied sweet wines: Sauternes, Beaumes-de-Venise, Vouvray

MADELEINES

Madeleines are the quintessential French tea cake. This traditional recipe calls for a touch of honey; but one can also add a little grated lemon or orange rind to make it even more fragrant. The batter should rest in the refrigerator for at least 2 hours before baking and can even be made the night before.

15 minutes 15 to 18 minutes

5 oz (100 g) flour
1 cup (100 g) finely ground almond
1 3/4 cups (250 g) confectioners' sugar
8 oz (250 g) sweet butter
1 tbs honey
1 1/4 cups egg whites (approximately 7 to 8 eggs)

Madeleine cookie mold

1. Preheat oven to 350 °F (180 ° C). **2.** Mix the flour, almonds, and confectioners' sugar together in a bowl. **3.** Melt the butter with the honey in a small saucepan. Let cool. **4.** Using a fork, mix the butter, honey, and egg whites (not beaten) together; then incorporate the dry ingredients until smooth. The mixture should be thick but still pourable. Place in refrigerator for at least 2 hours for best results. **5.** Butter the mold, put 2 spoonfuls of the mixture into each shape, and bake until golden, approximately 15 to 18 minutes. The cake will rise a bit and form a small dome with a crack in the middle. Remove from oven, remove from mold, and cool on a cake rack while preparing the next batch. **Makes about 16**.

Sparkling wines

NORD
NORD

Some visitors may vaguely remember the 9th and 10th arrondissements of Paris as the section they saw through a taxi window en route to their hotel from the Gare du Nord. Others may associate this urban part of town with tiring shopping sprees at the renowned department stores Galeries Lafayette and Printemps. Few, however, venture to the heart of the *quartiers*. It is true that besides the Grand

IXe-Xe ARRONDISSEMENTS

Boulevards and the Opera Garnier there are not many obvious attractions. Nevertheless, pockets of everyday life survive amongst all of this commotion; here you can catch a glimpse of old Paris: family-run restaurants, curio shops, tempting bakeries, private mews, hidden courtyards, lively playgrounds, and the largest covered market in the city, Saint Quentin.

Twenty-two statues adorn the monumental facade of the Gare du Nord, each representing a northern city that can be reached from this train station.

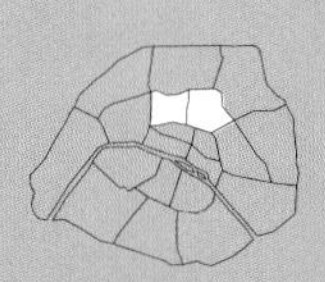

XPO
aits d'humour
rée gratuite
VILLE DE PARIS
MARCHE SAINT-QUENTIN
La
num

SLIM PICKINGS
The Saint Quentin Market

The 9th and 10th arrondissements cannot help being the most urban section of town. Crisscrossed by main arteries linking the eastern and westernmost extremities of Paris; housing three of the main train stations, two of the largest department stores, the Opera Garnier, and many theaters, large brasseries, offices, and shops; these neighborhoods are focal commuter points for the city. It is here that the Saint Quentin, along with the neighboring Saint Martin and newly established Alibert markets, cater to the local residents as well as to the incessant flow of commuters. Having at one time been at the core of this pulsating section of the city, they continue to offer quality produce in an original setting; their importance, however, has diminished significantly over time.

Once a peaceful country setting, this area was incorporated into Paris when Louis XIV decided to remove the protective ramparts surrounding the city and replace them with the tree-lined promenades, Boulevard des Capucines and Boulevard des Italiens. Most of this outlying, northern land was occupied by the clergy up until the end of the 18th century; it was only upon their decision to move to the Left Bank that the nobles were free to take up residence and built elaborate *hotels particuliers*. Slowly the countryside was inhabited; but the most significant urbanization took place in the mid-1800s, when Baron Haussmann barged through the area demolishing many of the private mansions to make room for his new city layout. He built wide boulevards that extended past the existing promenades of Louis XIV, as well as major railroad stations, apartment houses equipped with plumbing and elevators, the Paris métro, and the first electric lamps sparkling on Place de l'Opera. The *quartier* exemplified the new and modern Paris.

The 9th arrondissement became the center of entertainment, with restaurants, bars, and brasseries opening on every corner, and theaters and clubs dazzling the crowds. During the Belle Époque at the turn of the century, champagne flowed; and dandies arm-in-arm with their elegant ladies strolled down the avenues or stopped for after-theater supper at the fashionable Café de Paris.

The arrival of the train stations and the métro transfigured the 10th arrondissement in a different way. Though the energy was similar to its western neighbor's, the pomp here was missing. Throngs of people were continually disembarking from the train stations and many settled in the neighborhood, making this section of Paris both transient and residential. Filled with bars, clubs, and restaurants, this *quartier* catered to a more popular crowd. For the elite, the dominating train station made for a less desirable milieu.

Today, the 9th arrondissement is the more residential and tranquil of the two, with private mews and village-like enclaves scattered throughout.

Left: The lofty Saint Quentin covered market was constructed in 1865 and restored in 1982. Above: A tranquil haven, the Canal Saint Martin in the 10th arrondissement.

The southern end does fall prey to some congested boulevards, bustling department stores, hotels, shops, and cafés, as well as the busy Gare Saint Lazare. But the northern tip of the arrondissement is more low key. It houses a few clubs and restaurants that spill over from the adjacent red light district, Pigalle, but it is mainly inhabited by the elderly, who have been here since the good old days; and by the trendy, who have streamed down from the 18th. As there is no open-air market in this *quartier,* the residents depend on Rue des Martyrs for their food shopping, as well as the neighboring Rue Lepic, where tempting shop windows line the steep street that leads up to the picturesque Montmartre.

Rue des Martyrs winds down from Place Pigalle, into the heart of the 9th, housing some very good shops, such as the *fromagerie* Maison Molard at number 48, a small, old-fashioned store with excellent specialties from Savoie and a tempting selection of *artisanal* goat cheeses arranged on marble counter tops. Jean Molard's family has been in this business for generations. Today he stands guard at the shop, while his wife Josiane and son Arnaud sell their specialties to several open-air markets throughout the city. They gave us a selection from their wide range of *chèvres,* which they identified with neatly handwritten markers. They also suggested an order in which to eat them so as to best appreciate and distinguish the characteristics of each. All were delicious, but our favorite was the bite-sized *bouton d'Oc*, which has a fine, mild flavor and just melts in your mouth.

Another gem in the neighborhood is Charcuterie Lyonnaise at number 58, which is reputed to be one of the best sources for specialties from Lyon. Among them: the delicious *rosette de Lyon*, France's ultimate air-dried sausage; freshly prepared *jambon Persillé*, a ham that is cooked in a flavored stock, left to set in its own juices to form an aspic, and then cut as a pâté; and their own light and fluffy *quenelles de brochet*, a favorite dish made with freshwater pike.

If you continue down the hill in the direction of the opera house, Palais Garnier, you will be swept away by the waves of frantic shoppers who mill about the eternally busy department stores, Printemps and Galeries Lafayette. Let yourself be carried up the escalators to the first floor of Galeries Lafayette; and escape into the gourmet supermarket with its

Left: Maison Molard's delicious sausages, cheeses, and mouthwatering pâtés.
Right: Saint Quentin is the largest covered market in the city encompassing 2,500 sq.m. (27,000 sq. ft.)

b.e quesson
tel 47.70.55.33
Livraisons
à Domicile
B & E QUESSON
Quesson
Bœuf Braisé
39 F Kg 50
Quesson
Côtes
d'Agneau
59 F Kg 50
Quesson
Bœuf Braisé
Sans os
39 F Kg 50
Côtes
d'Agneau
Palette
Caisse

19,80
drôle
quel
goût

PALAIS GARNIER OPERA HOUSE

The Palais Garnier Opera House was *the* place to be during the luscious Belle Epoque. More precisely, *the* place to be was in the foyer, as here theatergoers could flaunt the latest fashion, expose their slender, white necks sparkling with diamond necklaces, and throw coy glances at the handsome dandies. The architect, Charles Garnier, had planned his sumptuous theater just so. Although it was designed to meet the needs of the most demanding stage sets, and comfortably sit 2,156 guests in the most modern auditorium of its time, it was above all planned to be a stage for socialites. Inaugurated in 1875, it is a classic example of ornamental neo-baroque style. In later years, Chagall's pastel-colored ceiling painting added a final touch, inspiring guests before the lights dimmed and the curtain rose.

The Palais Garnier also had its dark side: in 1896, during a famously anticipated performance of Faust, the gargantuan crystal chandelier hanging from the ceiling crashed down upon the spectators, injuring many and killing one woman. This incident inspired the renowned novel, Phantom of the Opera.

bountiful displays of fresh produce and specialty upmarket products from all over the world. We were pleasantly surprised by the quality and selection of the merchandise, as well as by the ever-present counters where tired shoppers can rest, sip a glass of wine, and savor half a dozen oysters, a salad, or a steaming bowl of *bouillabaisse*.

Although the 10th arrondissement accommodates two covered markets within a few blocks of each other, it is not a very residential part of town. Dominated by two important train stations, it is hard to make this a nice market outing. But if you do find yourself in the vicinity of Gare du Nord and Gare de l'Est, take the time to visit Marché Saint Quentin, a huge edifice emerging along one side of the congested Boulevard Magenta. One of the last original structures of its kind, this lofty market hall of glass and iron has a great deal of potential, which was sadly overlooked when it was restored in 1982. Instead of being flooded with light, one feels claustrophobic in the cramped maze of aisles that do no justice to this beautiful structure. Despite the lovingly displayed selection of excellent quality meat, cheese, fish, fruits, and vegetables, there is a lack of warmth and atmosphere. Most of the people who shop here during the week are commuters on their lunch break or heading home, leaving the vendors to fend for themselves for the rest of the day. Things liven up on the weekends, when the locals are about.

Left: A succulent choice of fruits including fresh lychees is available at the covered market Saint Quentin.

We stopped at the lovely display of game, rabbits, and free-range chickens of Monsieur Picciotto, who was busy plucking and cleaning a grouse but took the time to chat. He recommends cooking the grouse in two stages: the breast is best when it is quickly seared in a heavy-bottom pan, as you would a steak; the other parts are tastier if marinated and cooked in a stew, as they tend to dry up otherwise. We also admired the fabulous variety of vegetables that Yolande Vallais had arranged in baskets spread out along her stand including: Chinese truffles, *cèpes*, fresh hazelnuts, passion fruit, kumquats, lychees, asparagus, *girolles*, and figs, for which this generous, soft-spoken woman's customers line up and patiently wait to be served. In the center of the hall, there is a small café/restaurant where you can stop for a little apéritif or coffee at the bar; or swing around to the other side and sit down to a *plat du jour*. They say the food is decent, and the most amusing thing is to watch the barman/chef/waiter negotiate around this tiny space.

After Marché Saint Quentin, you can continue your tour along Rue du Faubourg-Saint-Denis. Passing some nice, traditional food shops, you will reach the arcade Passage Brady, also known as "Little India." A bit on the dilapidated side, it is packed with tiny restaurants and grocers where one can stop to eat a spicy curry or buy a bag of henna, basmati rice, or hot dried chili peppers; or, if you are game, have your head shaved by one of the many barbers that set up shop here. The arcade is always filled with people, especially at lunch and dinner time, and one feels trans-

Lingots
le kg
12,00

ported to another land as soon as you set foot under the high glass ceiling. As you exit on the other side, cross the street to the Passage du Marché. This will lead you directly to one of the more disappointing covered markets of the city, Marché Saint Martin. Back in 1850, this was one of the main covered markets of the time; as many as 100 merchants occupied the space. When it was rebuilt in 1989, the original structure was destroyed and robbed of all of its charm. Replaced by a large apartment building with a food hall inhabiting the main floor, this shopping experience has a supermarket-like aura, dominated as it is by neon lighting and Muzak. Only ten vendors inhabit this enormous space. Though they have very good quality produce, it seems wasted on so few customers, and they were thrilled by a little bit of conversation.

The neighborhood surrounding the Canal Saint Martin is the only really quaint section of the 10th, which might be why the youngest of the open-air markets, Marché Alibert, was established here two years ago. This miniature market sports a handful of courageous vendors offering a small but complete selection of flowers, cheese, prime cuts, fruits, and vegetables. They set up once a week on a quiet street beside the large Saint Louis hospital. One can only hope that their efforts will be richly rewarded.

If you find yourself in the neighborhood, take the time to enjoy the canal—a part of Paris that is still quite a secret. Here the locals enjoy fishing for carp in the murky waters. Once in a while a barge chugs past, with children and barking dogs chasing it along the banks. You might decide to pick up a few slices of ham and some cheese at the market, and wander over here to spend a quiet Sunday afternoon enjoying the scenery. Alternatively, you could venture back to Rue du Faubourg Saint-Denis for lunch at the authentic Art Nouveau brasserie Julien, or enjoy a *choucroute garnie* at the Alsatian brasserie Flo located a few blocks further down the road.

Left: Lingot white beans and other legumes are staples used in many of France's most popular dishes such as *agneau aux haricots blancs* and *petit salée aux lentils*.

Le Tripier

Tripe butchers are an uncommon profession in most of the Western world; and most people are hesitant when they come to a stand decorated with veal heads, ears, hooves, brains, livers, kidneys, and other indecipherable organs. But Raymond Neveux is quite at home here. After more than half a century dissecting and preparing these items, it is second nature to him.

In France, this *métier* dates back to the Middle Ages, when *tripiers* did all of the rudimentary work of cleaning and skinning the animals for the butchers; they were given the tripe and hooves as compensation. It was not until 1643 that this became a profession in its own right. *Tripiers* were officially recognized by Louis XIV, who specified that they were solely authorized to sell what was commonly known as the *cinquième quartier* ("fifth quarter"), meaning whatever remained after the carcass was divided into four equal parts; that is, head, skin, blood, hooves, innards, and offal. Although the "fifth quarter" was originally considered to be the least appealing section of the animals, reserved for the poor and underprivileged, over the years these items have become an integral part of sophisticated French cuisine.

In 1945, Raymond Neveux began the two-year course at the famous butcher school in Paris, choosing to follow in his grandfather's footsteps. After completing his apprenticeship at the abattoir La Villette, he joined his parents at the open-air markets. Other than a short break for his military service, he has been there ever since. A real artisan, Raymond can identify every muscle and organ imaginable and knows how to prepare it to perfection. Although innards and offal are not as popular with the younger generation, Raymond is confident that there will be a resurgence. After 20 years as president of the Tripe Butchers Union, he has handed down his know-how to both his children, assuring the continuation of this profession. Like their father, both Murielle and Christian have their own stands at several of Paris' open-air markets. Though Raymond is now officially retired, he likes to help out his son at the Président Wilson market where you will find him expertly preparing his clients' favorite items behind his huge wooden chopping block.

The Neveux family is present at the Président Wilson, Bobillot, Raspail, and Edgar Quinet markets.

ROGNONS DE VEAU A LA CREME
Veal Kidneys in a Cognac Cream Sauce

Kidneys are very lean fare, believe it or not, so one should not feel too guilty about being generous with the butter and cream. As they should be eaten rosé, the preparation time is short, and you will savor in a matter of minutes a special and original dish given to us by the tripe butcher Raymond Neveux.

10 minutes   12 minutes

18 oz (500 g) cleaned kidneys, (4 to 5 oz [120 to 150 g] per person)
2 tbs peanut oil
3 medium shallots, chopped
2 tbs butter
1 pinch sugar
Salt and pepper, to taste
1/4 cup cognac (optional)
1 tbs whole grain mustard (or smooth Dijon mustard)
4 tbs heavy cream
1/4 cup (75 g) chopped parsley
Finely chopped parsley, for garnish

1. Slice kidney lobes into 1/4-inch (1/2-cm) thick pieces. Put 1 tablespoon of oil in a large pan, and sauté sliced kidneys for 1 minute—do not brown. Remove from heat, and place in a sieve to drain; this procedure will yield a more delicate taste. **2.** Sauté the shallots over medium heat with 1 tablespoon of butter and 1 tablespoon of oil; add a pinch of sugar (which stops the shallots from burning); and cook for 5 minutes or until translucent. **3.** Briefly rinse the kidneys, and pat dry with a paper towel. Add the remaining tablespoon of butter to the shallots; add the kidneys; and turn up the heat to medium-high. Salt and pepper, and cook for about 4 to 5 minutes, turning often. Optionally, if you want to flambé them with the cognac, do so now. **4.** Stir in the mustard and cream, adjust the seasoning, and heat for a short minute. The kidneys should be pink in the center. Remove from heat, sprinkle with finely chopped parsley, and serve immediately accompanied by boiled potatoes or white rice. **Serves 4**.

Full-bodied, coarse, spicy reds: Côtes de Nuits, St. Emilion, Pomerol

COQ AU VIN
Burgundy Style Chicken Stew

Traditionally this dish is made with a rooster, but a plump roasting chicken is easier to come by and does not need to simmer for hours before becoming tender! Choose a good, hearty Burgundy wine for the sauce to make the taste noticeably more delicious. If you have the green tip of a leek hanging around in the refrigerator, use it instead of cheesecloth to assemble your bouquet garni.

30 minutes   1 1/2 hours

1 roasting chicken (3 to 4 lbs [1.5 to 2 kg])
2 thick slices of bacon
Salt and pepper, to taste
2 cups red Burgundy wine
1/4 cup cognac
2 tbs flour
1/2 cup chicken stock
1 bouquet garni (2 sprigs thyme, 1 bay leaf, 2 cloves, 5 peppercorns, and 1 sprig parsley)
2 garlic cloves, peeled and crushed
3/4 lb (375 g) small, white, button mushrooms, stemmed and cleaned
2 tbs butter
1 lb (500 g) boiled potatoes
Chopped parsley, for garnish

1. Cut the chicken into pieces (keep the back for making stock); and dice the bacon. In a large skillet, sauté the bacon until brown, remove with a slotted spoon, and set aside. Sauté the chicken parts until golden in the bacon fat, about 10 to 15 minutes, in batches if necessary. Season with salt and pepper. **2.** At the same time, reduce the red wine in a saucepan until 1 1/2 cups remain. **3.** Put all the chicken back in the skillet, pour the cognac over it, stand back, and flambé by lowering a lit match to the pan. Shake the skillet until the flame extinguishes. Remove the chicken to a plate. Sprinkle the flour into the skillet over medium-high heat, stirring continuously. Scrape up all the brown bits and juices. Bit by bit, add 1/2 cup of wine, whisking continuously until the mixture is smooth. **4.** Place the chicken into a Dutch oven, and strain the sauce on top; some of the flour will remain in the sieve—do not force it through. Add the remaining wine and the stock. **5.** Bring to a full boil, add the bouquet garni and garlic, and partially cover. Reduce heat to low, and let simmer for 1 1/2 hours or until the chicken is tender. If the sauce reduces too much, add a bit more reduced wine and a bit of stock. **6.** Fifteen minutes before the coq au vin is ready, add the bacon bits, sauté the mushrooms in a bit of butter for 10 minutes, drain, and add to the chicken. Adjust the seasoning, discard the bouquet garni, garnish with chopped parsley, and serve with plain, boiled potatoes. **Serves 6**.

Coarse and robust reds: Nuits-Saint-Georges, Chambolle-Musigny

SARDINES FRAICHES PRINTANIERES
Marinated Sardines with Spring Vegetables

This delicious dish looks like a very elaborate and sophisticated appetizer, perfectly suited for an elegant dinner party; but in fact it is very easy to prepare. To make it look extra special, debone the sardines carefully, julienne the vegetables very finely, and use a good olive oil. You can prepare them ahead of time and keep them in the refrigerator; this allows all of the flavors to develop.

30 minutes

8 medium sardines
1 zucchini
1 yellow squash
1 carrot
1 green bell pepper
1 red, orange, or purple bell pepper
3 tbs olive oil
1/2 lemon
2 tbs pink peppercorns (baies roses)
Salt and pepper, to taste

1. Wash sardines carefully to remove the scales, gut them, and place on a plate. Remove the heads, and carefully debone the sardines, leaving the two fillets joined at the tail. Put to one side. **2.** Julienne the zucchini, yellow squash, and carrot into 1-inch (2.5 cm), extra-fine strips. Blanch in boiling water for 1 minute. Rinse in cold water and set aside. **3.** Julienne the bell peppers the same way, and mix with the other vegetables. Add the olive oil, lemon, pink peppercorns, salt, and pepper; and toss gently. **4.** On a plate, put a thin layer of olive oil seasoned with salt, and dip the sardines to cover the skin and interior. Place a tablespoon of vegetables in between the two fillets, and arrange on a serving dish. These can be served immediately or covered with plastic wrap and placed in the refrigerator for a few hours. **5.** To serve, place two sardines on each plate and garnish with a couple of scallions, a wedge of lemon, and a little mound of sea salt on the side. **Serves 4.**

Lively, light whites with a citrus aroma: Muscadet de Sèvres-et-Maine sur Lie, Poully Fuissé, Vinho Verde

SORBET DE KIWI
Kiwi Sorbet

Sorbet is a refreshing and light finale for any lunch or dinner. The jade-green scoops garnished with fresh mint leaves and berries make a pretty sight. This fruit-filled sorbet is simple to make and does not require being stirred continuously in an ice cream maker, but only occasionally, by hand. With a stainless-steel bowl (which conducts the cold faster) and a few stirs with a fork, you will have a fine result in just a few hours. Try this recipe when you are planning to spend a day at home. Once the sorbet is ready, it will keep for several weeks in the freezer.

 15 minutes   4 to 5 hours

I cup water
I 1/2 cup (325 g) sugar
2 cups (500 g) puréed kiwis (about 8 whole) Note: one can use any firm fruit, such as strawberries, peeled peaches, bananas, or apricots
I lemon
Chiffonnade of mint leaves and fresh berries, for garnish

I. In a saucepan, bring the water and sugar to a boil. Stir until the sugar is completely dissolved. Remove from heat. **2.** Peel the kiwis and purée in a food processor or pass through a food mill. Add the juice of one lemon. Pass through a sieve to remove the small black seeds. **3.** Stir the kiwi purée into the sugar-and-water syrup. Mix until homogeneous. Pour into a stainless-steel bowl. Cool to room temperature, and place in the freezer. Leave a metal fork in the bowl. **4.** Stir after I hour to break down the first frozen crystals. Repeat every I to 2 hours, until the sorbet is firm. Depending on your freezer, this can take between 4 and 5 hours. Do not forget to give it a vigorous stir at regular intervals—otherwise it will freeze up into a solid block. To serve, form oblong scoops by using two spoons; dip them into hot water between scoops. Put 2 or 3 on each plate, sprinkle with mint chiffonade, and surround with fresh berries. As this type of sherbet melts quilckly, it is best to use chilled glass dessert plates or bowls. **Serves 6 to 8.**

PAINS
SPECIAUX
au cumin
au pavot
razowy
biologique
beigels
&
letze
SPÉCIALITÉS
YIDDISH
SPECIALITES
SALEES
tarama
gehakte herring
gehakte leber
caviar d'aubergine
blinis
pirojkis

All those in vogue are sure to head straight to the Bastille, the burgeoning new *quartier* of Paris. Far from the often-overlooked arrondissement that it once was, the 11th has emerged as a fashionable part of the city.

This area has always been a stronghold of the working class, where artisans set up their workshops and dwellings. It remained unchanged until the 1980s, when President Francois Mitterand chose its Place de la Bastille as the site for Paris' new opera house. Overnight, money started pouring into the neighborhood, transforming ateliers into chic lofts and art galleries, replacing old wine bars with hip cafés, and flooding the area with

XIe ARRONDISSEMENT

trendy international restaurants. This has become *the* place to be, especially on the week-ends, when it is chockablock with a colorful mixture of people dallying on café terraces, wandering the streets, peeking in trendy boutiques, or grabbing take-out sushi.

Along with its neighborhood, the lively Richard Lenoir market has taken off—it has become one of Paris' most popular markets. Extending from under the golden wing of the Genie de la Bastille, the market is packed every Sunday with a bustling crowd of young and old, buying from the numerous stands, while musicians and entertainers animate the passers-by.

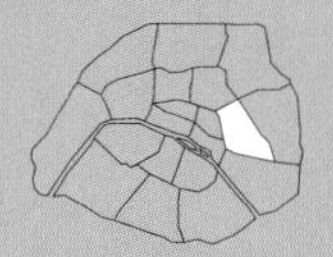

Stocking up on challah bread at one of the Jewish bakeries along Rue des Rosiers in the Marais.

L ORIENTAL

STORMING THE BASTILLE
The Richard Lenoir Market

As a rule, weekend markets are by far the liveliest. In terms of atmosphere, the Richard Lenoir Sunday market is the *crème de la crème*. The tree-lined central promenade of the Boulevard Richard Lenoir, where the market sets up, represents the seam between two historically distinct areas: the once noble and bourgeois Marais and the proletarian Bastille. Both areas have become more homogeneous, so the demographic divides no longer exist, but still each has a very distinct feeling. The Marais' architecture, with its magnificent Place des Vosges and its elegant palaces, represents a traditional, aristocratic epoch in French history. The Bastille's less elaborate buildings, on the other hand, portray the soul of the working class and the symbols of the Revolution of 1789. Today, both neighborhoods serve as residential, leisure, and professional districts, as well as popular attractions for visitors.

The Marais continues to be a place to discover or rediscover old Paris—through its numerous libraries, museums, and promenades with pretty shops and galleries; the Bastille is where one goes to see what is new and changing—including international restaurants, funky shops, and the latest clubs. The overload from these two popular neighborhoods naturally spills into the market, which stretches down the boulevard from the Place de la Bastille. Whether people come to shop, meet friends, or pass the time, you will notice enclaves of people chatting and laughing among themselves or exchanging witty comments with the vendors. All here enjoy the luxury of a Sunday morning.

Dating as far back as the end of the 19th century, Boulevard Richard Lenoir has been host to an open-air market.

As you approach Boulevard Richard Lenoir from Place de la Bastille, a carousel at the edge of the market gives you the feeling of entering a fair. Above the reverberating tunes piped from the loudspeakers, you can hear the calls of the vendors, reminiscent of the early 1900s when this boulevard was the site of the "Ham and Scrap-Iron" fair. This unusual fair originated in the Middle Ages, when ham was sold at the Cathedral of Notre Dame during Holy Week. Over the centuries, the fair moved to different locations around the city, until 1869 when it settled at Boulevard Richard Lenoir. It remained there until the 1970s, when it was moved to the periphery of the city and a flea market was added; hence the name, "Ham and Scrap-Iron."

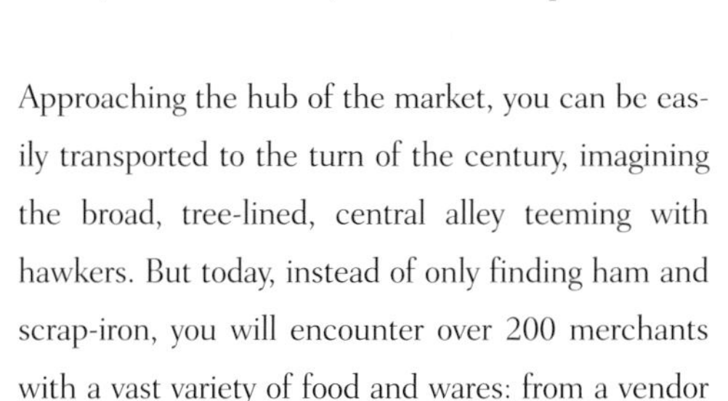

Approaching the hub of the market, you can be easily transported to the turn of the century, imagining the broad, tree-lined, central alley teeming with hawkers. But today, instead of only finding ham and scrap-iron, you will encounter over 200 merchants with a vast variety of food and wares: from a vendor of *artisanal* brie to an African woman selling her prepared traditional foods; from the organic vegetable producers with their carrots caked in dirt to the Portuguese and Italian specialty stands with layers of *bacalhau* and rows of salami and *prosciutto*; from the *viticulteurs* selling their wines to the butchers with choice cuts waiting to be transformed into delicious *steak frites*; from the bountiful fish stands with pyramids of pink *langoustines* to a small kitchen bazaar cluttered with baskets and cooking gadgets; from bakers with various rustic breads, crunchy baguettes, and Provence-style *fougasse* to fruit vendors with local and exotic displays; the choice seems endless. Indeed, for the newcomer, it is hard to decide what and from whom to buy—so just let yourself be carried forward by the tide...

AVOCAT
S
Pour
5

In the first section of the Richard Lenoir market, the stalls sell the herbs, vegetables, and fruits used in most North African dishes. As you work your way down the market, you will have to pick one of three aisles to follow first. If you begin on the right-hand side, an enormous cheese stand will most likely catch your eye. The atmosphere here is always convivial and relaxed, as the owners hire students and aspiring artists to help them on the weekends. A friend of ours gets so carried away with the array and affordable prices here that he often takes home a carload to Germany as gifts for his friends. If you are looking for a more sophisticated selection, with the higher priced *artisanal* aged cheeses, you can visit Michel Lucien. He makes his own brie and *chèvre*, as well as fresh farmer's cheese, and the delicious *Fontainebleau* (a light, airy cream dessert usually served with fresh berries and a touch of sugar). You might also ask Arnaud Molard, from La Ferme de Megeve in the center aisle, to help you select from his neat display of goat cheese and specialties from the region of Savoie.

Continue down through the aisle packed with butchers, vegetable displays, and flower stands, until you reach Jacky Lorenzo's hard-to-miss fish stand. You will come upon heaps of shellfish, crabs, sea urchins, and all the bright-eyed catches of the day. On the weekend, Jacky has an army of enthusiastic, blue-clad workers tending to the customers who cram against the counter. In the center of the enormous stand, several fish-cleaners scale and gut the purchases, while a cashier sits amassing the francs. If you are lucky enough to see Jacky himself, you will certainly recognize him: energetic and boisterous, flaunting his latest catch, and encouraging the customers to buy and buy and buy. He is present at three different Paris markets throughout the week and prides himself in having the largest stands with fish of exceptional size and the choicest quality at the best price. Whenever he sees us approaching, he briskly picks up the largest species within his reach, such as an enormous sea bass, or two gigantic crabs, or he embraces a pile of mussels, posing for a picture and enthusiastically bellowing about the freshness and affordability of his fish.

When you come to the end of the market, by the métro station Bréguet Sabin, you can twist your way around one of the two remaining aisles; the Genie de la Bastille in the distance will guide you back. Right next to the Art Deco métro exit you will find a small stand tended by an apiculturist selling his many varieties of honey, fresh honeycomb, soaps,

PLACE DE LA BASTILLE

Place de la Bastille, as we know it today, was completed in the 1830s. Previously it had been the site of a fortress built in 1356 to protect the city's expansion towards the east. During the 18th century, it served as a prison for naughty aristocrats punished by the reigning kings. There, elite prisoners' lifestyles apparently were not disturbed being behind bars; they continued their lives of luxury with endless bottles of wine, delectable food, and even sultry lovers. Characters such as the Marquis de Sade and Voltaire were among those incarcerated. Nothing remains of this former bastion; it was torn down after the Revolution; but you can find its markings in the pinkish slabs of stones embedded in the pavement at No. 3 Place de la Bastille. The golden-winged Genie de la Bastille sculpture graced the Place in 1840 as a tribute to the fight for freedom and liberty that this area represents.

Left: Cavaillon melons make their appearance at the beginning of summer.
Right: Provence-style fougasse; Michel Lucien and his fluffy Fontainebleau.

Céteaux

candles, and sweets. You might also bump into Monsieur Lory, who, even in the dead of winter, is perpetually soaking his feet in a tub of green water! He will inform you about the miraculous attributes of his *Sel Au Pin des Landes* (bath salts), for the softest feet in town. For your other ailments, there is a wise old man wearing a beret selling little pots of tiger balm, curious roots, and various powders; if you give him the chance, he will rattle on about each potion for hours—until you are healed.

Down the center aisle there are many vegetable and fruit stands. Among them are one of the few organic (referred to as *biologique*) producers present at this market; Vergers du Bois Veneaux, who sell pears and apples straight from their orchard; and an exotic fruit stand with produce from all over the world, including dwarf bananas from the Ivory Coast, star fruits from Malaysia, baby pineapples from Thailand, avocados from Mexico, and papayas from Brazil—all of which the French enthusiastically purchase at any price.

Another interesting stall along this central aisle sports a young farmer lost behind outsized baskets packed with eggs. If you stop to buy a carton, do not be disconcerted by his apparent nosiness when he asks what you are going to do with these eggs and when you are going to use them—this is normal in France: the freshest eggs are reserved for *oeuf à la coque* (soft boiled eggs); week-old ones for omelettes; two-week-old

Filling the orders and measuring out mussels by the liter at Jacky Lorenzo's stand.

ERIE MARIA
CRUSTAC

SEL AU PIN DES LANDES
ACTIVE
ELIMINE
REGULARISE
CALME
PREVIENT
SEL AU PIN DES LANDES
ACTIVE
ELIMINE
REGULARISE
CALME
PREVIENT
50F LE PAQ

ones for baking; after three, throw them out! Along with chicken eggs and quail eggs, goose eggs are sold in the winter; the latter are triple the size of a chicken egg, with a more gelatinous texture and a paler yoke—they are considered to be very healthy. We tried them and were not impressed! Farther ahead, we hope that you will be serenaded by the splendid voices of the Zalkalyne sisters, in their turn-of-the-century black dresses and red feather boas, singing old French classics accompanied by their *Barbarie* organ. As you watch the audience flocking towards them, you will notice everyone mouthing the songs along with them. The sisters are two of the many performers, who normally appear in cabarets and small clubs around town, yet choose to also use the open-air markets as their stage. They are perpetuating a French tradition that dates back to the 14th century, when popular *chanteurs des rues* sang about their woes, hopes, and loved ones at their favorite venue, the Pont Neuf bridge.

A few steps away, Madame Henia displays her prepared escargots, which are precooked, filled with garlic and parsley butter, and ready to pop into the oven. This is a real treat, as she receives the snails live from farms in Provence and Burgundy and prepares them for sale herself. The escargots are left to drain in burlap sacks for two or three days in order to get rid of all their impurities. The snail is then removed from its shell, trimmed, and cooked briefly in a *court bouillon*. The empty shell is cleaned and bleached, and then refilled with the snail and the prepared butter. We learned that 95% of escargots come from origins other than France and do not receive the same care, being usually mass produced. So if you have access to an oven and can buy these farm fresh snails (even if you have never tasted them), buy a dozen, a bottle of wine, and a fresh baguette to sop up the melted parsley butter.

Left: Street performers and vendors alike will go out of their way to animate the crowd. Here the Zalkalyne sisters play their Barbarie organ and Monsieur Lory soaks his feet in bath salts.

There is a little breathing space in the momentum of the market at two points along the boulevard. Entertainers use these areas to perform; and activists invade them to distribute their pamphlets promoting a specific political party, candidate, or concerns of the neighborhood. You can take a rest beside the fountains and munch on one of your purchases while reading the various pamphlets, and enjoy the scene. Boulevard Richard Lenoir was originally the Canal Saint Martin, which was covered over in 1859; and the fountains and small planted sections actually hide the light ducts

HUNTING FOR ESCARGOTS

At the end of the 19th century, there existed a profession that consisted solely of reselling escargot shells. The "escargot shell merchant" would rummage through the garbage of the upscale restaurants along the Champs Elysées, picking up the used snail shells. These he would carefully dust off, but not wash, as the remaining traces of butter were the key to his profession. Popular bistros that could not afford butter would buy these old shells to flavor the meager margarine with which they filled them when adding new snails. The clients were tricked but happy dunking their bread after savoring a "buttery" escargot.

Top: Escargots are sold already filled with a parsley and garlic butter. Bottom: The vendors at the African *traiteur* Taranga are always keen to explain their prepared ethnic dishes. Right: From quail, to chicken, to goose eggs, Monsieur Brocker has them all.

En Promotion
plateaux

OEU

AMANITE
de César

Le Journal du Dimanche
LE COUP DE GUEULE DE VOYNET
Pasqua
Ce qu'il prépare

PUR CHEVRE
CENDRE

for the canal below, which is still in use. One can take a boat tour up the canal from the nearby harbor, Bassin de l' Arsenal, on the opposite side of Place de la Bastille.

Continuing down the center aisle, take a look at the bountiful mushroom display of Meyer Champi. Mounds of *girolles, cèpes, chanterelles,* and rare varieties such as the cultivated, orange-capped *amanite des Césars* (not to be confused with its deadly cousin, the *amanite Phalloïde*). This variety can be savored raw—sliced paper thin, with a drizzle of olive oil, a pinch of parsley, salt, and pepper. Across the way, rows of golden-brown chickens are roasting at Michel Chamillard's poultry and rabbit stand. He also tempts the palate with roasted stuffed capons, guinea hens, quails, and ducks ready to be taken home. Next door, stop at Taranga, the mouth-watering, prepared, African food stall, where you will find such exotic dishes as: *yassa,* a popular Senegalese chicken dish, and *moyo*, a grilled fish dish from Benin served with *ablo*, the African version of polenta. They also sell bottles of an invigorating fresh ginger root drink as well as hibiscus tea.

As one o'clock draws near and the stalls begin to be dismantled, you can either venture with your purchases to the promenade of the Bassin de L'Arsenal and picnic in the gardens by the canal; or wander off in the direction of the Marais for an apéritif at one of the cafés under the arches of the Place des Vosges, where you can people-watch. You might also continue on to Rue des Rosiers, to top off your purchases at one of the many Jewish pastry shops, and stay for lunch. On the other hand, you could choose to visit one of the restaurants near the Place de la Bastille, such as the brasserie Bofinger on Rue Bastille, for a great tray of oysters. After lunch, you may want to check out the afternoon Sunday dancing at the Balajo on Rue de Lappe from 3 to 7 p.m., a tradition still alive and well at this epic dance hall. So come have a spin and go back to the times when Robert Mitchum, Rita Hayworth, and Edith Piaf used to party here.

Previous pages: Richard Lenoir is one of the largest and most animated markets in Paris with over 200 stands. Below: Place des Vosges, formerly known as Place Royale, circa 1740 and today. Right: A cheerful *charcutière* at the "Ham and Scrap Iron Fair" in the 1930s.

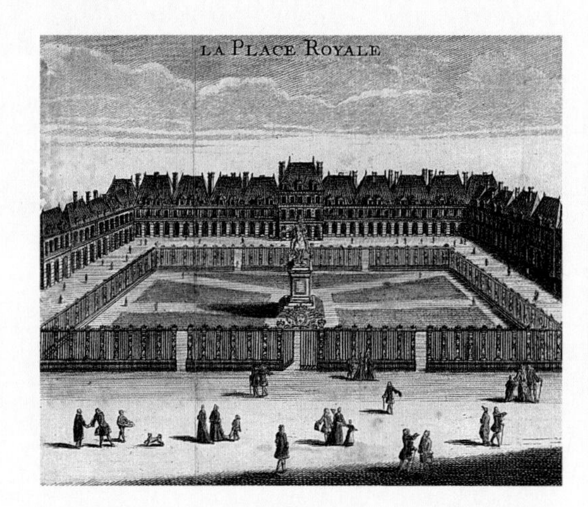

PLACE DES VOSGES

Originally planned as the first public square for festivities and leisure for the aristocracy by King Henry IV, the Place des Vosges became the emblem of what this neighborhood represented when it was built in 1612. It was named "Place Royale" in honor of the inauguration party held to celebrate the regal double-wedding of King Louis XIII to Anne of Austria and Princess Elizabeth of France to Philippe IV of Spain. After the Revolution of 1789, this square and the entire neighborhood were neglected for many years. Then in 1965, it was declared a protected zone by the government, and gradually many of the palaces and squares were restored to their original splendor. Perhaps Place des Vosges, with its many visitors, is at last used in the way that Henry IV originally intended—the only difference is that now it is open to all; you can even sit on the grass, which until recently was a big "no-no" in all Parisian parks.

PRODUITS
SCHMID
3F 75
PRODUITS
SCHMID
3F 00
PRODUITS
SCHMID
3F 00
SCHMID
1F 50
SCHMID

CHARONNE

As you exit the Alexander Dumas métro station, you will find the expansive Charonne market on either side of the tree-lined Boulevard de Charonne. This market is characteristic of the working-class community that still persists in this section of the 11th. The atmosphere is friendly and serene, with a mixed clientele, and vendors who personify *la vielle France.*

The selection is not sophisticated, but it is customarily French—with the main focus being meat and vegetables. In these categories, the choice is vast: a number of *charcuteries*, some well-stocked poultry stands, classical butchers, and a couple of horsemeat and tripe butchers.

There are some wonderful *maraîchers* dispersed throughout the market, with lovely garden-fresh vegetables and cut flowers. You will not find fancy greens here; the salads are classic bib lettuce, batavia, escarole, rougette, and frisée, presented in wooden crates along with cooked beets, carrots, leeks, turnips, and whatever the season brings.

Once you have had a look at the cheese, fish, olives, flowers, and the rest of the stands, have an aperitif and buy a lottery ticket (Loto) at the sunny corner café-tabac.

POPINCOURT

The Popincourt market is located a few blocks to the north of the Richard Lenoir market, stretching along the same tree-lined central promenade. A weekday market, the atmosphere at Popincourt is more serene than the lively shopping Sundays at Richard Lenoir. With approximately 65 vendors here, you will find an extensive selection of fruits and vegetables, fish, meat, chicken, cheese, regional specialties, flowers, bread, and even wine.

The quality can vary considerably from stand to stand, as can the prices, but on the whole this makes for a very nice shopping outing. Look for: a small stand run by an Italian farmer who sells cultivated and wild mushrooms, which he picks near his home in the region of Saint-Germain-en-Laye, northwest of Paris; the hard-to-miss Savoie speciality stand Alpage, with strings of salamis hanging in front of a deep red backdrop; and the extensive vegetable stand Les Delices du Jardin, which sets up across the way, tended by a quiet, friendly woman who sells choice produce that she buys from the *maraîchers* in various regions of France.

Above: The Alpage stand is always a treat at the Popincourt market.
Right: Mountains of produce at the Belleville market.

BELLEVILLE

On the edge of two distinct quartiers, the Belleville market is like a gateway from the traditional, French, working-class section of the 11th to the multicultural and multiracial neighborhood of the 20th. The disparity between the tranquillity at the Père Lachaise market just one block south and the havoc at this market is mind-boggling; from one moment to the next, you will feel transported from Paris to a city somewhere in North Africa. It is an experience; so gather your energy to fight the crowds, venture forth, and let yourself be swept through this kilometer-long whirlwind.

Keep you eyes open! An experienced shopper can get a good selection at dirt cheap prices; while the less experienced one may walk home with a bag of bruised tomatoes. Watch what goes into the plastic bags; and if you can, select the items yourself.

Starting at the Menilmontant metro stop, the Belleville market is a constant flow of fresh produce, winding the full length of Boulevard de Belleville. Out of the over 150 stands that line the boulevard, there are only three that sell dried fruits, nuts, spices, and olives; two that carry Portuguese specialties; one selling honey; a handful of fishmongers; and one butcher; the rest display rows and rows of fruits and vegetables. You will find yourself surrounded by mountains of green beans, carrots, eggplants, zucchinis, onions, chilis, tomatoes, herbs, apples, oranges, grapefruits, melons, bananas, figs, avocados, lemons, and fresh dates.

PERE LACHAISE

The Père Lachaise market is the epitome of the small neighborhood market, although it appears a bit forlorn on this wide boulevard. With only 15 stands on a good day, it is often so quiet that it resembles a school fair, with the vendors visiting each other as they casually keep tabs on their stands. You will still find a nice selection, with most everything that an everyday shopper would need: flowers, bread, fish, cheese, nice veggies, a butcher, and a *charcutier.*

Truite
68 00
Rouget Barbet
1 kg
88 F 00

Le Poissonier

The man orchestrating the enormous displays of fish at Lorenzo's stands is stocky and vigorous, with an easy smile and mischievous eyes. Jacky Lorenzo is constantly moving about, rearranging pyramids of langoustines and heaping piles of crab, calling to the passers-by, instructing his employees, and giving his favorite customers a peck on the cheek. Since beginning his career in 1977, he has gained a reputation for having vast displays, competitive prices, and a booming voice that carries over the buzz of the market.

Of Italian origin, Jacky came to Paris to pursue a career as a professional soccer player. In order to support himself, he started working at a fish shop owned by the president of the Fishmongers Association. He was very impressed by his boss, "an elegant man who smoked cigars and drove a luxury car"; and he aspired to be like him. Eventually, he quit soccer and took the plunge into the fish business.

Since the overheads of opening a shop at that time was too high, Jacky opted for a spot at the open-air markets. From the beginning, he decided to specialize in unusually large fish that until then had been available only at a few fish shops. He bought himself a secondhand truck, and on the first day that he ventured to Rungis, Paris' enormous wholesale market, he filled it to the brim with all of the sea bass that he could get his hands on. En route back to the market, he was "blessed" by a storm that covered the whole Atlantic coast and created a sea bass shortage. A literal overnight success, Jacky was immediately the most popular fish vendor in town. Not only did customers line up at the newcomer's stand, but also other fishmongers and restaurateurs turned to him for supply.

Over 20 years later, aided by his wife Christelle, his daughter Aurelie, his two sons Fabrice and Giovanni, and a staff of 15 that swells to 25 on the weekends, he is present at three of the best open-air markets in Paris, turning over an impressive quantity of up to three tons of fish and shellfish per week. Although Jacky is by far not the only fishmonger at the markets, he certainly keeps all the others on their toes!

Jacky Lorenzo is present at the Richard Lenoir, Saxe Breteuil, and Popincourt markets

MARKET RECIPES

SALADE DE POULPE ET DE POMMES DE TERRE
Mediterranean Octopus and Potato Salad

Many people avoid cooking octopus as the outcome can be rubbery and tasteless. Our experience has been otherwise, with a special secret that several fishmongers have shared with us. For best results, buy a whole fresh octopus at the market, clean it, and freeze it overnight; this helps to tenderize the meat. The day of cooking, defrost it, and gently lower it into a boiling *court bouillon*; the result will be tender and flavorful. If you are cooking it ahead of time, leave the octopus in the *court bouillon* and refrigerate until needed.

30 minutes   45 to 60 minutes

For *court bouillon*:
1 bay leaf
4 peppercorns
A few parsley stems
1 small onion
1 carrot
1 tbs sea salt
8 cups water

For the salad:
1 octopus (2 to 3 lbs [1 to 1.5 kg])
The *court bouillon*
6 new potatoes
1/4 cup olive oil
1 tbs lemon juice
1 tbs *court bouillon*
1/2 cup (125 g) packed flat parsley leaves
Salt and pepper, to taste
A few red peppercorns

1. Put the ingredients for the *court bouillon* in a large pot, and simmer for half an hour. **2.** Clean the octopus, removing the eyes, beak, and innards (or ask your fish monger to clean it for you); and rinse. **3.** Bring *court bouillon* to a boil. Gently lift the octopus by its head and place into the pot, tentacles first. The tentacles will curl up as you slowly lower them in. Repeat, dipping in and out of the *court bouillon*, 3 times. Cook uncovered at a slow boil over medium heat until you can pierce the meat with a knife, approximately 45 minutes to 1 hour. Allow to cool in the *court bouillon*. **4.** Cook the potatoes whole about 10 to 15 minutes until cooked but firm. Let cool. **5.** Remove octopus from liquid and slice at an angle into 1-inch (2.5 cm) pieces. Place in a bowl, add the olive oil, lemon juice, a tablespoon of the *court bouillon*, parsley, and salt and pepper to taste. **6.** Peel the potatoes and slice into thin rounds (or use an egg slicer). Place the potato slices overlapping each other to form a small circle, on individual plates. Spoon the octopus salad into the middle, sprinkle with a few red peppercorns, and serve. **Serves 6.**

Fine and delicate whites: Côtes de Provence, Bandol

YASSA DE POULET
Spicy Lime Yassa Chicken

Madame Ndongo, the owner of Taranga, gave us this simple recipe made with chicken and lime. The trick, she says, lies in the quality of the chicken; she prefers to use free-range chickens, and she selects only the legs and thighs for a juicier result. This recipe calls for only 1 hour of marinating, but you can marinate the chicken overnight if you prefer a more tangy flavor. This dish is traditionally served with white rice.

1 1/4 hours   1/2 hour

4 chicken thighs and legs (or breast)
2 tsp salt
1 tsp black pepper
6 medium onions, sliced
4 cloves garlic, crushed
2 tbs Dijon mustard
2 carrots, sliced
6 Bird chili peppers (tiny, hot, red, dry peppers)
3 tbs peanut oil
Juice of 6 limes or 4 lemons
1 tbs fresh ginger (optional)

1. Season chicken parts with salt and pepper, place in a bowl with the rest of the ingredients, including the lime (or lemon) juice. Leave to marinate for 1 hour, longer if you prefer. **2.** Heat broiler or barbecue. Remove chicken parts from marinade, and place under the broiler. Cook each side approximately 5 minutes, turning once, or until brown. **3.** Drain liquid from marinade, and set aside. **4.** Sauté the marinade ingredients (not the chicken) with the oil in a heavy-bottom pan, at medium-low heat, until the onions are translucent. **5.** Add the chicken parts to the rest of the ingredients, as well as the liquid from the marinade, and 1 cup water. Cover and cook at medium heat for 20 minutes. Adjust the seasoning, and serve. **Serves 4.**

Chilled, fruity reds and aromatic rosés: Saumur Champigny, Tavel

Left: Salade de poulpe et de pommes de terre

DORADE AU FENOUIL
Fennel Baked Sea Bream

This delicate fish with a hint of fennel is wonderfully complemented by the braised fennel hearts and the delicate green sauce that is added at the table. Once removed from the oven, Jacky Lorenzo suggests that you flambé the fish with a shot of Pastis to intensify the aniseed flavor.

15 minutes — 35 to 45 minutes

For the fish:
6 fennel bulbs (top two layers and the stalks)
1 lemon
1 large whole sea bream or sea bass (3 to 4.5 lbs [1.5 to 2.25 kg]), cleaned and scaled
Salt and pepper, to rub onto the fish
1/4 cup olive oil
1/4 cup white wine
1 shot Pastis (optional)

For the fennel hearts:
2 tbs butter
The fennel hearts
1 tsp sugar
Salt and ground pepper, to taste

For the sauce:
The fennel leaves (feathery tops)
1/2 cup olive oil
1/2 lemon
Salt and pepper, to taste

1. Preheat oven to 400 °F (205 °C). **2.** Remove the feathery tops from the fennel, and set aside. Cut off the stalks, clean the bulbs, and slice in half. Remove the two top layers, slice, and arrange half of them along with the stalks on the bottom of a baking dish. Place the hearts in a bowl filled with cold water and the juice of a lemon; and set aside. **3.** Wash the fish, pat dry, and rub with salt and pepper, inside and out. Place on top of the sliced fennel; stuff the cavity; and cover with the remaining slices. Pour the olive oil on top of the fish; and pour the white wine into the baking dish. **4.** Place in preheated oven; and bake, basting occasionally. After 20 minutes, turn the fish over, and cook an additional 15 to 25 minutes, until the meat slides off the bone. **5.** For the fennel hearts: Meanwhile, in a large sauté pan, melt the butter, and place the fennel hearts face down. Sprinkle with sugar, salt, and pepper; and cook covered over medium heat. After 10 minutes, turn, cover, and continue cooking an additional 10 minutes, until tender. Keep warm, to serve when the fish is ready. **6.** For the sauce: In a small bowl, prepare the sauce by cutting the tiny leaves off the fennel stalks, chopping them finely, and adding them to the olive oil, lemon juice, salt, and pepper. Serve in a side dish. Optionally, when the fish is cooked, remove from the oven, remove the vegetables, place back on a baking dish or serving dish, and pour a shot of Pastis on top and flambé before bringing to the table. **Serves 4 to 6.**

Dry, fruity, aromatic whites: Sancerre, Meursault, Côtes de Provence

GATEAU AU FROMAGE BLANC
Fresh Farmer's Cheese Cake

This light and delicate cheesecake recipe, made with Michel Lucien's *fromage blanc*—the equivalent of farmer's cheese—and a touch of orange, is a perfect mid-afternoon treat.

30 minutes — 1 1/4 hours

Butter for pan
Puff pastry (store-bought)
2 cups (500 g) *fromage blanc* (farmer's cheese), 40% fat content
1/2 cup (100 g) sugar
3 tbs potato starch
3 eggs
2 egg yolks
Grated rind from 1 orange
1 tsp vanilla extract (or one vanilla bean)
1 pinch salt

8-inch (20 cm) round cake pan

1. Butter the pan, roll out the pastry, place in the pan, and poke with a fork. Place a sheet of waxed paper or aluminum foil on top, and weigh down with beans or rice. Precook 15 minutes at 350 ° F (180 °C). **2.** In a large bowl, mix the *fromage blanc*, the sugar, and the potato starch; add the eggs and egg yolks one at a time, mixing well. Finally, add the orange rind, vanilla (if you use a vanilla bean, cut it lengthwise and scrape out the grains), and a pinch of salt. **3.** Pour the mixture into the precooked pie crust, and cook at 350°F (180°C) for 11/4 hours or until a knife inserted in the center comes out clean. A golden-brown crust will have formed on the top. The cake puffs up considerably when baking, but it will settle once removed from the oven. **4.** Let cool and serve. **Serves 6 to 8.**

Gateau au fromage blanc

LIGNES
Nos 6&8
LIGNES
Nos 6&8
29

For many, the 12th arrondissement is the section of town that one drives through *en route* to the park Bois de Vincennes or the Gare de Lyon train station. Most Parisians consider it to be just a tranquil, residential neighborhood, far from the goings-on of the rest of the city—they are unaware that this *quartier* has evolved considerably. Since the construction of the Opera Bastille, the government has chosen to modernize sections of the 12th. Besides erecting large apartment complexes and the new finance ministry, they chose to relandscape an abandoned aqueduct and wine depot, bringing a burst of greenery to the area. The streets bordering the 11th have caught on to

XIIe ARRONDISSEMENT

the buzz of the Bastille: a slew of trendy bars, restaurants, and boutiques have opened up, replacing old storefronts where local butcher shops, cobblers, and grocers once stood. For the most part though, it is true, this middle-class neighborhood peacefully goes about its daily routine, with children running off to school and locals walking their dogs on the way to pick up a baguette for lunch. Popular markets are scattered throughout this expansive arrondissement, among them the oldest and most renowned, the lively Marché d'Aligre.

Only a handful of the original Art Nouveau métro stations can still be found in Paris, this one on Place Daumesnil.

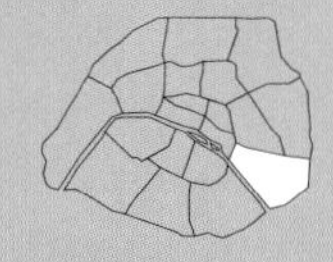

LEADER PRICE

THE NOTRE DAME OF MARKETS
The Aligre Market

As you reach Marché d'Aligre, you will be swept away by the continuous movement at the market's hub. Characteristic of the 12th arrondissement, there is a mingling of people here of all ages, nationalities, and backgrounds. The young and trendy, clad in their latest flea-market finds, buy bouquets of sweet-pea blossoms and a garden-fresh lettuce. They line up alongside French grandmothers who have been shopping here forever. Beggars in search of a few centimes make their way through the crowd, past groups of Arab men in *fezzes* basking in the sun. Meanwhile, night owls nurse their hangovers at the corner café. Located off the busy artery Faubourg Saint Antoine, which connects Place de la Bastille to Place de la Nation, Marché d'Aligre extends along two streets, spreading from the central Place d'Aligre. It is the only market in Paris that combines a covered market, an open-air market, and a flea market. It is also the only market open every day of the week (except the sacred Monday).

The 12th arrondissement was originally located on the outskirts of the eastern side of Paris and made up of garden plots and hunting grounds. The dominating institution in this rural land was once the prosperous Abbey of Saint-Antoine-des-Champs. Founded in 1198, the abbey housed repentant women, souls who had strayed from the path of morality but now chose to dedicate their lives to charity. The abbey owned extensive properties pervading not only the 12th, but also sections of the 11th and 20th arrondissements. Because of its strong ties to the reigning kings and aristocracy, the abbey oversaw most of the affairs in its domain.

The popular Aligre market is a must for anyone in search of genuine Parisian atmosphere untouched by tourism.

The wide Faubourg Saint Antoine, where the church and abbey were located, was the main road out of the city to the vast woods and castle of Vincennes. Along the Faubourg, in the vicinity of Place de la Bastille, France's most renowned carpenters chiseled away in their ateliers, creating the elaborate furniture that decorated the palaces of Europe. The section hugging the shores of the Seine, known as "Bercy," became famous at the beginning of the 19th century for housing the world's largest wine depot. Bercy was suited to the task because at the time it was just outside of the city boundaries—and, therefore, exempt from taxes. This port evolved into a small village with tree-lined lanes that carried the names of different wines, such as Sauternes, Chablis, and Pommard. Along these lanes, stone houses with red tiled roofs stored an enormous quantity of alcohol. They also housed lively wine bars, known as *guinguettes*, to which Parisians flocked to dance and make merry at the large outdoor tables overlooking the river, while downing the untaxed wine.

The 12th has undergone numerous changes over the years, particularly since the 1960s. Then the government began a strong initiative that resulted in the construction of good, bad, and controversial landmarks. Today, instead of the boisterous and colorful wine depot of Bercy, one finds a maze of modern buildings and squares that hold little of the sparkle of former times. At Place de la Bastille, the boxy opera house is juxtaposed with the wonderfully landscaped and restored viaduct, known as "La Coulée Verte," and the picturesque port, Bassin de l'Arsenal. Doddery apartment buildings have been replaced by utilitarian complexes, complete with underground parking, playgrounds, and

supermarkets. Nevertheless, some aspects of this neighborhood remain the same. One still comes across a few carpenters' ateliers tucked away in quiet courtyards; charming, tree-lined squares and boulevards; and the enduringly authentic Marché d'Aligre.

As you exit the métro station Ledru-Rollin, walk up the Faubourg Saint Antoine until you come to Rue d'Aligre, where throngs of people converge into the market. Along this crowded stretch there are approximately 40 stands selling fruits and vegetables. Shoppers make their way past vendors who call at the top of their lungs, offering tastings to all who pass by. When buying vegetables amidst this whirlwind of activity, keep your eyes open, as the pyramids of tomatoes, cherries, figs, and oranges may have a few surprises on the back side. Also, the pace can be so fast that you might not notice a few blemished peaches slipped in with the nice ones. There are vendors who specialize in particular items, such as garlic and lemons, or potatoes and onions, but most sell the same selection of seasonal fruits and vegetables, at competitive prices. Before filling your baskets, make a tour of the whole market to find the best buy.

We enjoy weaving in and out of the aisles to see what the shops that are lined up behind the stands have to offer. Our first stop is usually Café Aouba, the small coffee roaster, for a little espresso and a chat with the owner. Next we cross over to Priet, the cheese shop that has been around for years. It recently changed hands, but the new owners continue the tradition of Monsieur Priet, selling cheeses that still carry his name, aged in their cellar. Next door, a Greek couple, Sofia and Petrit, offer tasty hors d'oeuvres. Sofia cooks them in the kitchen at the back of the shop. Petrit helps you select from the great variety of olives,

stuffed phyllo pastries, savory dips, octopus salad, stuffed grape leaves, and marinated anchovies. A new addition to the street is a Thai *rôtisserie* that sells spicy chickens, quails, and rabbits roasted to perfection with side orders of stir-fried rice, noodles, and Asian vegetables.

There are a few spice shops that are bursting with exotic ingredients for preparing dishes from all over the world. It is fun to browse through them and discover hidden treasures on the shelves: ground and whole spices, dry and fresh herbs, rice, lentils, couscous grains, beans, aromatic waters, soaps, oils, honeys, dried rose buds and fruits—every inch filled, prices exotically low. Along this half of Rue d'Aligre, you will also find several Muslim butcher shops as well as a traditional French butcher, a baker, and a few fishmongers—all complementing the sea of fruits and vegetables.

As you reach the center of the market, you will be heartened by a wall of flowers propped up on a wooden cart at the corner of the covered food hall, Beauvau. Opposite the flowers, a charming mother-and-daughter team stand in the middle of a U-shaped display covered with bunches of lettuce, artichokes, radishes, and onions. They bring the produce from the region of Fontainebleau. They are always cheerful, full of pep, and so popular that they barely have time to wrap up the purchases before attending to the next customer. Thanks to them and a few other old-timers, the tradition of *maraîchers* is kept alive at Marché d'Aligre.

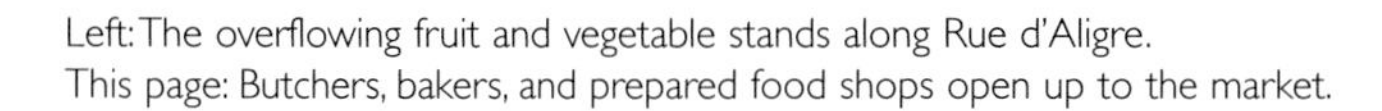
Left: The overflowing fruit and vegetable stands along Rue d'Aligre.
This page: Butchers, bakers, and prepared food shops open up to the market.

Marché d'Aligre had its boom during its first 150 years. At its peak, it was as important a market for the city as the famous wholesale market, Les Halles. With up to 1,000 vendors setting up pell-mell at Marché d'Aligre, outside the food hall, on the square, and along the connecting streets, the area was always crawling with people from every walk of life. Noticing the number of those in dire straits, the nuns decided to bring old clothes to distribute among the poor; and the square was nicknamed "Square des Vieux Habits." It is also rumored that here, on Place d'Aligre, the kings "generously" donated the remains from their feasts to distribute to the needy.

The tradition of recycling old clothing, begun by the nuns, developed over the years. Though no longer given away, heaps of inexpensive garb

The stretch between the flea market and food hall is the hub of the market, where the best quality fruits and vegetables are sold. Here shoppers mill about the picturesque guardhouse, with its small turret and clock, referred to as the "Notre Dame d'Aligre." In the midst of the commotion, a flower lady sets up a small table covered with buckets of water in which she has been displaying her garden-cut flowers for the last 50 years. From behind the colorful petals of hearty daisies and delicate violets, she peacefully observes the crowd, gives a toothless smile to clients, and reminisces about days of yore.

The first historical mention of the Marché d'Aligre was in 1643, when eight butchers installed themselves in a small covered structure in front of the Abbey Saint-Antoine-des-Champs, a few blocks east along Faubourg Saint Antoine. *Maraîchers* and hay merchants added to the ever-growing popularity of the market, which eventually overflowed onto the streets, obstructing the entrance to the abbey. In 1777, with the consent of King Louis XVI, the abbess, Madame Craon-Beauvau, had the market transferred to one of the abbey's plots of land: the Place d'Aligre, where a food hall was erected. Nuns from the abbey who tended large vegetable patches would accompany the *maraîchers* from the surrounding area to the front of the newly built Marché Beauvau to sell their freshly picked produce. Here meat, fish, and cheese were sold, making Place d'Aligre a popular and lively center of activity.

Top: A sea of produce and vendors on Place d'Aligre, 1905; the *maraîcher* stand of the mother-and-daughter team. Right: A flower vendor who has been selling pretty petals in front of the covered market Beauvau since 1950 and a customer.

PLACE
D'ALIGRE
ROLSER
ROLSER

RAG PEOPLE – CHIFFONNIERS

Armed with lanterns, laden with large wicker baskets strapped to their backs, and brandishing long poles with hooks on the end, the rag people of Paris, known as *chiffonniers,* once scurried down the dark streets and alleys in search of treasures that could be salvaged from the city's piles of garbage. Wearing badges indicating their name and profession so as to be distinguished easily from dubious night prowlers, these humble people, who numbered 30,000 in the second half of the 19th century, roamed the streets recycling the waste of the more fortunate.

Many were proud of their *métier,* enjoying the vagabond life, free souls who managed to make a meager living reselling their finds. Whole families dedicated their lives to this existence, and a very defined hierarchy reigned among them. The *pokers* were the poorest of the lot; with hooks in hand, they would recuperate odds and ends such as a discarded crust of bread, a gnarled bone, an old shoe, rags, metal, coal, or anything that could be mended and reused. One step above them, the more established denizens of the street owned a pushcart and staked their claim on a particular neighborhood, profiting from the favors of restaurants and apartment-building concierges. At the top of the heap, the *chef chiffonniers* owned storage rooms, where they would stock the finds they bought from the lower ranks before, bringing the refurbished treasures to sell at the flea markets.

This marginal profession slowly disappeared after a law was imposed in 1884 by the prefect of Paris, "Monsieur Poubelle" ("Mr. Garbage Can"), who introduced the poubelles and forbade the chiffonniers from facilitating their salvaging by emptying them out onto the streets.

Although the vocation no longer exists, the chiffonniers are the forefathers of the antique and bric-a-brac dealers known as *brocanteurs,* who sell their rarities at the well-established and much-cherished flea markets of Paris.

Above: A *chef chiffonnier* at the end of the 1900s. Chalked on his board reads: "I have a large supply of hats and furs - CHEAP!" Right: For centuries, a flea market has been held on the square at the center of the Aligre market.

ROPA

are sold alongside trunks of attic treasures. From time to time one can make a real find. Approximately 30 *brocanteurs* and secondhand clothes vendors set up on the square surrounding the "Notre Dame." Some come equipped with trestle tables, while others spread out blankets directly on the ground with such varied items as framed watercolors, old pots and pans, mismatched dishes, and the odd pair of shoes. There are new and old garments as well as swaths of elaborately embroidered cloth prized by the Arab women for making veils and dresses. You can buy a blue Mao suit for a song, costume jewelry, old vinyls of Claude Brassens, African statues and beads—delve into the piles and see what you come up with!

In the early 1900s, many small bistros lined the Square des Vieux Habits. Here, in this working-class neighborhood, such prominent figures as Ali Khan, Cary Grant, Rita Hayworth, and Dwight Eisenhower would crowd into the popular restaurant, La Boule d'Or, famous for its simple atmosphere and delicious cuisine. Those fortunate enough to have been here during the 1930s and 40s recount the lavish gowns that crossed the threshold, and the beautiful people who sat together at long wooden tables passing the night away. Sadly, these buildings were deemed insalubrious and replaced with a modern structure in the 1960s. La Boule d'Or and its neighboring watering holes were forced out and replaced by a supermarket. One can still picture the black Citröens and Peugeots lining the street, and their chauffeurs loitering about, having a smoke while steamed-up windows hid the illustrious diners from sight. Standing at the edge of the square with your back turned to the modern buildings, you can enjoy a view of Marché Beauvau and the guardhouse, reminiscent of those days with its lively bustle of shoppers.

After having finished your tour of the open-air market, step into the food hall. Here the din from outside abruptly vanishes. Under the lofty framework of crisscrossing wooden beams, the vendors each have an individual hut complete with kitchen and storage room, where they tranquilly go about preparing their fare. Marie, of Marie D'Antan, has a great variety of pâtés, hams, *rillettes*, *foie gras*, and fresh, smoked, and air-dried sausages that she buys from *artisanal* producers in the region of Aveyron. One of her specialties is *rillons*—thick chunks of bacon that have been cooked to a crispy golden brown, eaten thinly sliced at room temperature with tart *cornichons* and cocktail onions. A few steps away, you might find Patrick Hayée busy preparing *chipolatas*—fresh pork sausages made with herbs, ideal for grilling and savoring with a nice spicy mustard and a cool beer. One morning, we watched Patrick stuff paper-thin intestines with his special sausage mixture of meat and spices, then twist the long coil into identical links, as he shared a few market anecdotes with us.

It is rumored that the wooden structure of Beauvau was once a stable, and the fountain in the center was the drinking trough. Though we never had this historically confirmed, it sounds quite picturesque! A wide range of vendors here—including the enormous poultry stand in front of the fountain, a delectable Italian specialty stall, an organic food shop, a well-stocked Portuguese stand, a few fishmongers, and cheese stalls—will satisfy any of your heart's desires. Though the prices might be higher than those outside, for the quality you will find that it is well worth the investment.

After you have finished your rounds at Marché Beauvau, exit on Rue Théophile-Roussel and cross over to the recently opened bakery, Moisan, which bakes delicious organic breads on the premises. Then head over to the famous wine bar, Le Baron Rouge, for an aperitif and a *tartine* generously spread with pâté. Behind the deep red storefront, huge wooden barrels line one side of the room, with small blackboards attached indicating the provenance. Simple table wines such as Gamay, Rosé de Provence, and Côtes du Rhone are poured into one-liter bottles, corked, and sold at very reasonable prices. If you want something a bit more sophisticated, the wrought-iron wine rack across the room always holds a few wonders. As noontime approaches, this former hat shop fills up. Shoppers stack their purchases wherever they can while having a drink and chatting with the regulars. In winter, an oyster vendor sets up outside. Trays of freshly shucked *belons* and *fines de claires* are swallowed down with glasses of chilled Vouvray. The crowd spills out onto the street, balancing their glasses on cars, wine barrels, garbage cans, and window sills; and the jamming of the bartender's jazz band adds to the decibels.

Right: A tranquil atmosphere reigns inside the covered market Beauvau where you will find a whole array of specialties freshly prepared on the premises.

A number of small restaurants are scattered about the *quartier*, including L'Ebauchoir, a fun and affordable place for lunch, located a few blocks up the Faubourg at 45 Rue des Citeaux. Nearby, the vintage Square Trousseau restaurant looks out onto the nearby planted square of the same name. Its turn-of-the-century decor is as authentic as it gets. Though the food is not very consistent, the owner has a flair for discovering delicious wines from small *viticulteurs*. If you would rather sit outside, take a stroll over to Avenue Daumesnil and have a bite at the Viaduc Café. Afterwards, investigate the spacious shops recently installed under the arches. Known as "La Coulée Verte," this restored viaduct is the showcase for young artisans from all over France, displaying crafts, original furniture, blown glass, pottery, and hammered copper objects—all make wonderful gifts. Take a stroll along the planted promenade that runs on top of the viaduct, above the shops, from Place de la Bastille to the reaches of the forest of Vincennes. Endless trails, a lake, the city zoo, and swans await you.

Above: Several butchers offering excellent quality meat have shops inside the food hall. Right: Shucking oysters for the crowds in front of the wine bar Le Baron Rouge.

APERITIF

The word "apéritif" comes from the Latin word *apérire*, which means "to open." In former times, one would drink a cup of chicory or special mineral waters before a meal in order to induce the appetite to open.

Though the aperitif is still an important part of lunch and dinner in France, the waters have been replaced by the flute of champagne, or kir made with white wine and crème de cassis; these not only open up the appetite but the other senses too.

Le BARON
rouge
cfp
cfp

M4

SAINT ELOI

The small Saint-Eloi market sets up in the courtyard of a modern building. Although the atmosphere is certainly not charming, over a dozen vendors offer a good selection to the locals. A few vegetable stands run by Asian families are always overflowing with great-quality produce, and several *maraîchers* bring garden-fresh seasonal greens from their farms.
A vendor sets up a small table where she sells oozing *bries* and camemberts that are hard to resist, as well as a basket of speckled-brown eggs and a bucket of *crème fraîche*. A flower stand adds a touch of color, and the butchers, fishmongers, and *charcutiers* top off the list. Although this section of the 12th is not necessarily a place you would come for a stroll, if you are in the area, do your shopping here; you will not be disappointed.

COURS DE VINCENNES

The enormous Cours de Vincennes market begins at Place de la Nation and runs along one side of this wide boulevard for approximately five blocks. It is fun to take advantage of the ample space to walk along the length of the market, admiring the displays, before starting your shopping spree on the way back. Numerous *maraîchers* offer wonderful fresh produce at very affordable prices, inducing you to fill your basket with bunches of herbs, boxes of berries, tangy watercress, plump steamed beets, curly endive, seasonal fruits, and baby zucchinis with their flowers still attached. You will always find an extensive array of poultry and game, as well as prepared *ragouts* and roasts at Nathalie Crié's, and excellent-quality fish and shellfish from Michelle Doyen. The prices here are low; there is a wonderful selection; and the quality is consistently good. If you like big markets, this is a great place to shop. Its only drawback is its location—a bit off the beaten track, on the periphery of the city.

DAUMESNIL

Bronze lions spewing forth jets of water welcome you to one of our favorite weekday markets, the Daumesnil, which stretches down both sides of the tree-lined Boulevard Reuilly. There are always plenty of

shoppers making their way through the aisles, picking and choosing from the generous displays of the over 80 vendors that cater to this upmarket section of the 12th arrondissement. The selection is endless and of very good quality: extensive fish displays, butcher stands, seasonal fruits and vegetables, French specialities, exotic foods and spices, and plump, free-range poultry will lure you through the market. With the abundance of offerings, it might be hard to decide what to buy, but the prices are right, and the atmosphere is very becoming.

LEDRU ROLLIN

A few blocks away from the bustling Marché d'Aligre along Avenue Ledru-Rollin, the small neighborhood market Ledru-Rollin has a wonderful selection of offerings. There are approximately 15 stands, including *maraîchers*, *rotisseries*, fishmongers, butchers, and bakers. Among them, Josianne Molard brings a selection of tasty *chèvres*, hard cheeses, and delicious air-dried sausages. And Monsieur Labarthe comes up from the Landes region twice a month to supply his faithful customers with plump, free-range poultry and farm-fresh eggs. In wintertime, he also brings *foie gras* and capons; and he gladly takes Christmas orders, when his products are most in demand.

PONIATOWSKI

Adjacent to the expansive Bois de Vincennes, the Poniatowski market sets up on one side of the boulevard with vendors displaying their produce under colorful canopies. A bit meager during the week, on Sundays this market fills up with vendors offering bouquets of country flowers, tempting *charcuterie*, fruit, vegetables, fish, cheese, bread, olives, grains, meat, and poultry. You might consider picking up some succulent peaches, a roast chicken, a slab of pâté, a baguette, and a creamy *camembert* for a picnic in the Bois de Vincennes park.

Above: A wife-and-husband team at Marché Saint Eloi.

Le Boucher

The butchers Jean and Lucette Allain stand behind their long glass countertop, cheerfully chatting with the clients, as they slice and trim their prime cuts. An immaculate display of perfectly marbled *faux filets* and *côtes de bœuf*, leg of lamb and tender chops, meticulously tied veal roasts and pink transparent *escalopes* await their customers. After 45 years, Jean is an expert in his trade and is still as enthusiastic and friendly as when he started his apprenticeship.

Originally, Jean was destined to take over his family's farm in Provence—growing wheat, cabbage, and beets—but instead he listened to the wise words of his grandmother, which seemed far more appealing. "Become a butcher," she said. "It is a good profession, and you will always have something to eat!" A day after his 14th birthday, he enrolled in the butcher school in Lemans; and when he was 17, he left the sunny region of Provence and came to try his luck in the big city.

He worked as head butcher at a shop, honing his skills; and at 26, he decided to start his own business. Alongside his new bride, Lucette, he set up shop at the open-air markets in the suburbs of Paris; and he taught her all there is to know about his *métier*. They eventually shifted to the city markets, and since then they have acquired a long list of customers who would not think of purchasing their steaks or roasts anywhere else. The Allains sell only meat from France's renowned Limousin region, delivered weekly, directly from the *abattoir*. Tending their stand together as on their very first day, they continue to manage happily on their own. Their three children have all pursued other careers.

The Allains are present at the Président Wilson and Jeanne d'Arc markets.

MARKET RECIPES

AGNEAU AUX HARICOTS BLANCS
Lamb and White Bean Ragout

This savory dish given to us by Jean Allain will brighten any gray winter day. It is best to use dried Lingot white beans, soaking them overnight in a bowl of cold water. In the morning, strain them and use in the recipe as indicated. If you choose to use tinned beans instead (though the taste will not be the same), add them 45 minutes before the stew is ready so that they do not overcook.

20 minutes 2 hours

1 carrot
1 small onion
2 garlic cloves
2 lbs lamb shoulder, cut in chunks
3 tbs peanut oil
2 tbs tomato paste
2 tbs flour
1/4 cup white wine
2 cups peeled and crushed tomatoes (tinned ones can also be used)
1 *bouquet garni*
12 oz (350 g) white beans (or 4 cups cooked)
3 cups chicken or beef stock
Salt, to taste
Chopped parsley, for garnish

1. Finely chop the carrot, onion, and garlic; and set aside. **2.** Brown the lamb chunks in a large, heavy-bottomed pan until golden, adding oil as needed. Remove from pan; add a bit of oil; and sauté the carrots, onion, and garlic. After 5 minutes, add the meat and tomato paste, mix well, sprinkle with the flour, stir, and cook an additional 5 minutes over medium heat. **3.** Add the white wine, tomatoes, *bouquet garni*, strained white beans, stock, and salt to taste. **4.** Reduce heat to low, cover, and cook for approximately 2 hours or until the lamb and beans are tender. Adjust seasoning if needed. **Serves 4 to 6.**

Delicate, full-bodied reds: Graves, Haut Medoc, Côtes de Beaune

MAGRET DE CANARD AU PORTO
Seared Magret of Duck in a Sweet Port Sauce

What we had imagined to be a complicated process of grilling, basting, and pampering, was reversed by Dominique Loi, who told us that cooking a *magret de canard* was as simple as grilling a steak. Since it is one of the top sellers at his shop, Comptoir de la Gastronomie, he should know. Using his suggestions, we cooked the duck breast to perfection in less than 10 minutes; here is the recipe.

20 minutes 10 minutes

1/4 cups (40 g) Sultana golden raisins
1 cup port wine
2 duck breasts (magret)
Salt and pepper, to taste
1 golden apple, cut into 8 thin circles

1. Simmer the raisins in 1/4 cup of port wine for 10 minutes. Hold. **2.** Heat heavy-bottomed frying pan over high heat. **3.** Pat dry the duck breast and score the fat side with a sharp knife. **4.** Place the breasts fat-side down in the frying pan for 8 minutes. Baste with a spoonful of rendered fat from time to time to help cook the top. Continuously spoon off the excess fat and save it in a bowl. **5.** Flip the breast, and cook for 1 minute. Remove from heat, and season with salt and pepper. Place on a plate, and cover with aluminum foil to keep warm. **6.** In the same pan, carefully sauté the apple slices in a spoonful of duck fat for 30 seconds on each side. Remove the apples, add another tablespoon of duck fat and deglaze the pan with the remaining 3/4 cup of port wine. Bring to a boil at high heat, then add the raisin and port mixture. Lower the heat and let simmer a couple of minutes. Remove from heat. **7.** Slice the duck breasts into 1/4-inch (1/2 cm) slices, place on top of the apple slices, and cover with the sauce and raisins. Serve immediately with mashed potatoes or polenta. **Serves 4.**

Robust reds: Mercurey, St. Estephe, Côtes de Languedoc

RAIE A LA VINAIGRETTE TIEDE
Skate with Warm Capers and Olive Vinaigrette

Skate is a delicious fish, which is traditionally drowned in butter and capers in French cuisine. Madame Diget at the Raspail organic market gave us this lighter alternative which still has a bite and complements the delicate flavor of the fish.

30 minutes   20 minutes

For *court bouillon*:
3 cups water
1/2 cup white wine
1 whole clove garlic
1 celery stalk
1 peeled carrot
1/2 onion
1 bay leaf
1 tsp peppercorns
A few parsley stalks

For the fish:
4 portions skate (*raie*)
The *court bouillon*
1 lb (500 g) potatoes, boiled
Chopped parsley, to garnish
2 medium tomatoes
1/4 cup olive oil
1/4 cup (75 g) pitted black olives, sliced
1 tbs capers
1 tbs vinegar
Salt and pepper, to taste

1. Combine ingredients for *court bouillon* in a large pot with enough water (approximately 3 cups) to just cover the 4 portions of skate. Simmer for half an hour, and remove from heat to cool. **2.** Gently place the skate pieces in the *court bouillon*. Turn heat to medium, and cook 15 minutes from simmering point (it should never boil). **3.** When cooked (fish should separate from bone), remove immediately from water, and remove skin. Put on platter, and cover with aluminum foil to keep warm. Keep 1/4 cup of *court bouillon*, and discard the rest. **4.** Have ready: warm plates, boiled potatoes, and a handful of chopped parsley. **5.** Peel the tomatoes as follows: in a small saucepan, bring some water to a boil; crisscross the top of the tomatoes; dip into the water for 30 seconds; run under cold water; and peel off the skin. Remove the seeds; and cut the meat into small cubes. Set aside. **6.** In a large pan, over a medium flame, heat a tablespoon of olive oil, add the olives and capers, sauté a couple of minutes, remove from heat, and place in a bowl. In the same pan, without washing it, pour in the rest of the olive oil, the vinegar, a tablespoon of *court bouillon*, and salt and pepper to taste. Bring to a simmer over low heat; add the tomatoes, olives, and capers; remove from heat, and serve. **7.** You may leave the bone, or carefully fillet the fish; and place the portions onto warm plates. Spoon the warm vinaigrette on top, sprinkle with chopped parsley, and serve with boiled potatoes. **Serves 4.**

Refreshing, crisp whites: Pouilly Fumé, Sancerre

TARTE AUX MIRABELLES
Yellow Plum Tart

For this recipe, we use the French mirabelle, which is a small, yellow-and-green plum; but you can use any type of plum, cherry, apricot, or peach. This basic tart pastry is spiced up with cinnamon, nutmeg, and vanilla bean, which marry perfectly with sweet, late, summer fruits.

45 minutes   1 hour

For the pastry:
2 cups (360 g) flour
1 1/2 tsp cinnamon
6 tbs sugar
1/8 tsp salt
1 pinch nutmeg
1/2 vanilla bean
8 oz (250 g) butter
2 egg yolks, beaten
3 lbs (1.5 kg) mirabelle plums, pitted
2 tbs sugar
2 tbs apricot jam
1/2 tbs water

1. Sift the flour, cinnamon, sugar, salt, and nutmeg together in a bowl. Add the vanilla by cutting the bean in half lengthwise and grating the grains from the center. **2.** Cut the butter into the flour mixture with two knives until well incorporated, then add the egg to quickly form a dough with your hands; add a few tablespoons of water if necessary. Wrap in plastic wrap and leave sit at least half an hour in the refrigerator. **3.** Preheat oven to 400 °F (205 °C). **4.** Do not roll the dough; instead, press the dough into the mold, making sure that every part is evenly covered.
5. Arrange the fruit on top of the dough and sprinkle with sugar. Bake for one hour. Remove from oven, and let cool on a cake rack.
6. In a small pan, melt the jam over medium heat together with the water for 3 minutes; and gently baste the fruit so as to glaze the top of the tart. Serve either warm or at room temperature, plain or with a spoonful of whipped cream.

Demi-sec whites: Muscat, Maury

Tarte aux mirabelles

司
67
限公司
KIM 金

Home to the largest Chinatown in the city, one tends to associate the 13th arrondissement with Peking duck, wonton soup, and fried rice. For many, the thought of a succulent eight-course meal at one of the numerous restaurants, or a stop at the popular Asian grocers, is the sole reason for coming clear across town to this out-of-the-way neighborhood on the periphery of the city. Now home to the state-of the-art library and a high-tech cinema complex, on Place d'Italie, the area draws a few more visitors, but most still do not take the time to

XIIIe ARRONDISSEMENT

explore the rest of the *quartier*. This is a residential neighborhood dominated by modern, nondescript architecture and divided by broad avenues. So it is a surprise when one tumbles onto back streets lined with doll-sized houses and flowering gardens; the cobblestone lanes of La Butte aux Cailles, dotted with convivial bars and restaurants; and most especially, the delightful, rambling Auguste Blanqui market. Generous displays, good-humored vendors, and a never-ending selection make this one of the most enjoyable markets of Paris.

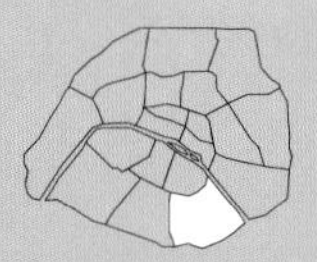

Paris' Chinatown lies a few blocks away from the August Blanqui market.

Au Canon d'Italie
Café
Café
Brasserie
AU CANON D'ITALIE
CAFE
BRASSERIE

A DAY IN THE COUNTRY
The Auguste Blanqui Market

Marché Auguste Blanqui is one of the city's most charming and ample markets. It is filled with tempting displays and friendly faces. Although it is located in one of the least glamorous and most overlooked arrondissements, a shady crown of soaring chestnut trees transforms this stretch of pavement into a country lane. Shoppers turn their backs to the surrounding modern apartment buildings, leave the hurly-burly of the city behind, and dally the morning away. They push prams and caddies, leading children and dogs down the rambling aisle. For them, the trek across town is well worth the effort—when the market is in full swing, it is the perfect place to spend a lazy Sunday morning.

The atmosphere at the Auguste Blanqui market is reminiscent of the days when the 13th arrondissement was a peaceful hamlet thriving on the outskirts of the city. Windmills dotted its lush valleys and vast meadows, and the meandering Bièvre river ran through it. This important source of water determined the future of the area, beginning in the mid-15th century when the Flemish dyer, Jehan de Gobelin, came to live by the river and discovered that the water's composition was ideal for his dyes. He set up a tapestry workshop that over the centuries gained worldwide renown; it is still in existence today. In the mid-16th century, Charles IX declared that industries were forbidden to open within the congested city center, and the banks of the Bièvre became the ideal alternative.

Left: Shoppers stream into the Auguste Blanqui market from the busy Place d'Italie. Marchands volants choose this spot to sell a variety of items.

By the time the 13th was annexed to the city in 1860, over 100 tanneries, draperies, laundries, textile mills, and breweries lined the two-kilometer stretch of the Bièvre that linked up with the Seine. They spewed filth and waste into the waters until it became insalubrious; neither a frog nor a bulrush managed to stay alive on its shores. The neighborhood fared no better. The area bordering the river had become dark and dingy, as squalid as Victor Hugo's portrayal of it in his masterpiece, *Les Miserables*. The northern section was chosen as the site of La Pitié Salpêtrière, an enormous hospital, hospice, and prison. La Pitié Salpêtrière housed the ever-growing number of destitute, mentally deranged, and disreputable women who roamed the streets of Paris. By the end of the 1800s, there were over 8,000 people incarcerated and interned within its walls.

The area had become an undesirable zone shunned by most of the Parisians. In fact, it was not recognized by the municipality until the beginning of the 20th century, when massive restructuring began. You will still come across remnants from the last century, but in 1910 the river was covered up, new roads were paved, and dilapidated buildings were demolished. These efforts were stalled by the two World Wars, but by the 1950s the area finally began to be transformed into a modern *quartier*. The building frenzy reached its peak in the 1970s and 80s, culminating in massive apartment complexes monopolizing the periphery of the arrondissement, alongside the characteristic sandstone facades and townhouses. While the older sections remained primarily occupied by the French middle class, the new buildings were attractive to the influx of immigrants. The most prevalent in the 1970s were people from

Southeast Asia who quickly settled in, establishing the southern tip of the 13th as the largest Chinatown in Paris. This residential neighborhood with its conglomeration of nationalities and a slightly off-beat modern flavor, may be far from the typical Paris setting, void as it is of monuments, museums, parks, beautiful vistas, and famous restaurants, but it has an endearing charm and some interesting places to visit.

The 100-year-old Marché Auguste Blanqui sets up along one side of the wide Boulevard Auguste Blanqui, under a yellow hue cast from the trees overhead. More than 80 vendors line the sidewalk, catering to the diverse community that inhabits this large arrondissement. Start your visit with a little *café au lait* and a *pain au chocolat* at the tranquil Café de France, overlooking the sunny Place d'Italie. If you prefer, stand elbow-to-elbow with the locals at the bar Le Celtique on the corner of Rue du Moulin des Prés, where many of the vendors come to warm up with a glass of rosé.

At the entrance to the market, *marchands volants* sell clothes, blankets, jewelry and other odds and ends, next to fruit and vegetable stands heaped with inexpensive produce. As you descend the hill, the market gains in momentum with shoppers piling up in front of their favorite stands. The first long line will lead you to a red awning sprawled with the name "Cabanes." Here bright-eyed *dorades royales*, salmons, *rougets*, mackerels, and soles are neatly fanned out on top of mounds of crushed ice, surrounded by crates of *tourteau* crabs, sea urchins, oysters, and mussels. In September and October, you may come across a box of *eperlan* fish. These are eaten deep-fried, head and all, with just a squeeze of lemon and a pinch of salt and known as *friture*. The finger-length fish are caught with square nets, known as *carrelets,* in the mild mixture of fresh and saltwater estuaries found in the Baie de la Somme along the English Channel.

The fabulous seafood display competes with the color-coordinated mushrooms at the stand down the way. Big brown *cèpes* are arranged next to purple *mousserons*, blue-black *trompettes-des-morts*, orange *girolles*, yellow *chanterelles*, hazy pink *rosés,* pearl gray shitakes, and white *champignons de Paris*. Monsieur Bouclet lovingly scoops them into paper bags while giving cleaning and cooking instructions and suggesting fresh herbs, watercress, and asparagus accompaniments. Across from him, Jacqueline André, wearing her navy blue apron, sets up over a dozen crates of oysters which she brings from her oyster farm in the Vendée just off the Atlantic coast. She specializes in *claires,* the leaner variety of oysters, with an iodine taste and a green tinge; and *speciales,* which are more plump and richer tasting. There is always a plate of shucked oysters nestled on a bed of seaweed, to demonstrate the quality of the mollusks—the clearer the better, and if you ask, she will certainly offer you one to taste.

Further into the market, Jean Claude Vincainnes brings bushels of apples and pears from his 60-acre orchard in the Picardie region. Here also, the Loiseau family neatly aligns jar after jar of honey on top of a bright yellow tablecloth, next to blocks of honeycomb, pots of invigorating royal jelly, and freshly-baked spice and honey cake, called *pain d'epice.* The Loiseaus are representatives of a cooperative that groups apiculturists from every corner of France. Among their selections, you will find mountain pine flavored honey from the Vosges region, lavender from Provence, sunflower and grape seed from Ile de France, lime tree blossom from Loiret, and rosemary from Languedoc. They also sell the wonderworking *propolis*, whose healing properties are said to be as strong as any antibiotic. This substance can be bought either in its natural state or diluted in alcohol. Evidently, a very small amount is needed to boost your immune system or to ward off any cold or heal any cut.

At the end of the first section of the market, on the corner of Rue du Moulin des Prés, the *fromager*, Maurice Carpentier, sets up a glass display case packed with cheeses that he buys from *artisanal* cheesemakers at Rungis. His selection varies in price and quality, and he always has several special offers of the day, indicated with bright orange and yellow signs: *deux pour dix francs*! (ten francs for two!) for a couple *crotins de chèvre* or creamy *Saint Marcelins*; these always seem to vanish by the end of the morning.

Above: The oyster farmer, Jacqueline André, shows off her fines de claires oysters.
Right: The *fromager* Maurice Carpentier promotes his special offers of the day.

2 CROTTINS
DUBERRY
Lait CRU
10
PROMO

On the weekends, a band sets up at the crossing to entertain the shoppers and add to the festive bustle. We put down our baskets to snap our fingers to "La Planche a Dixie," whose leader wears thimbles on his fingertips to tap out the rhythm on a washboard while his colleagues strum away on guitars and toot on horns. If you leave the market for a moment, and follow Rue des Cinq Diamants up the hill, you will come to a picturesque *quartier* with winding narrow streets, known as "La Buttes-aux-Cailles." In former times, it was reputed to have had one of the best views overlooking the city, the river, and the surrounding meadows. In 1783, the inhabitants of this area were among the first to marvel at the maiden voyage of a *montgolfière* (hot-air balloon). The vessel floated by their vantage point and landed yonder in the meadows between two windmills. In their excitement they ecstatically ran down the hill and nearly tore it to bits.

At the tip of La Buttes, you will find a pool that derives its water from a 500-meter well which was dug in the mid-9th century in order to flush-clean the water of the Bièvre river. The well bubbled over with warm sulfuric water, which was prized for its curative properties, but which had little effect on the river that eventually was covered up and turned into a sewer. Although the beautiful vista and artesian well have long since disappeared, this remains a lovely, secluded corner of the 13th, far removed from the towering concrete palaces below. Recently, the area has been adopted by many young artists.

Above: Under a row of trees and canopies, one is sheltered from the hectic pace of the city.

This second part of the market is always bustling, with shoppers forming long lines at their favorite stands. The charcuterie Teodoro attracts a crowd, who come for steaming trays of succulent *choucroute garnie* and *cassoulet*. Across the way, Nacer Kendel offers a consistently wonderful supply of fruits and vegetables. During the winter months, she has exotic mangoes, baby eggplants, and crunchy brussels sprouts; in the spring, fresh herbs, snow peas, and plump cherries; and come summer, succulent peaches, faultless melons, and juicy apricots. When we visited her during the month of October, she had sweet clementines, enormous artichokes, and a wooden crate of very alluring fresh chestnuts. She addresses her female customers in the familiar "*Ma cherie*," tends to one customer at a time, and always throws in a little something *en plus*. Her neighbor, Jean Louis Grimaldi, who runs La Graine de Vie,

HOW TO PEEL A CHESTNUT

Chestnuts have a very hard skin. The easiest way to peel them is to score them with a sharp knife on the flat side then place them in boiling water with a tablespoon of oil for 15 minutes. Remove them from the heat, and peel one at a time, leaving the others in the hot water. It is imperative that you remove all the inner skin, as it can be very bitter. Once peeled, you can either: add them to the roasting pan 30 minutes before a pheasant or guinea hen is cooked; sauté them with a bit of butter as a tasty side dish; simply mash and purée them like a potato with a little butter and cream; or make a creamy soup (see recipe).

MARRONS GLACES

Marrons glacés are a favorite treat that make their appearance all over France during Christmas and New Year. The Rhône and Provence regions are the renowned headquarters for producing *marrons glacés*, candied delicacies made using plump *marron* chestnuts.

The chestnuts are carefully peeled, and the whole plump kernel is poached in a water-and-flour solution, to which a vanilla bean is often added. They are then drained and plopped into a sugar syrup that progressively gets hotter and sweeter until the chestnut is saturated through and through. Set to cool, they are finally given a protective sugar-coating, called *glaçage*; hence the name, *marron glacé*.

The *marron* chestnut's sister, the *châtaigne* chestnut, is used for simpler dishes; its dividing segment, separating the two kernels, makes it unsuitable for the glacé's delicate preservation procedure.

Nowadays, to meet the demand, *marrons glacés* are commonly manufactured on a large scale. One should keep an eye out for the artisanely produced ones, which might cost a bit more but are well worth it. Have no regrets, as once you have removed them from their gold paper wrappings, their delicious creamy texture and sweet nutty flavor will send you to heaven and back.

charms his clients with his wit and humor while selling homemade tarts, pastries, and over 30 types of organic breads that are filled with every grain, dried fruit, seed, and nut imaginable.

As we were walking along one day, we were approached by an inquisitive gentleman wearing a beret with a pompom that bobbed up and down with every enthusiastic *oui*! and decisive *non*! He told us about his great uncle: a blacksmith who was beckoned by the authorities in 1860 to design a structure that would give more order to the open-air markets. They had become an utter disarray, with vendors setting up pell-mell, surrounded by their baskets, crates, and pushcarts. The man's old relative designed the first wrought-iron stands to snap into a mechanism buried in the pavement. Vendors could place boards on top of them to display their products, and canvases overhead protected their wares from the pelting rain and blistering sun. The system became so popular, that he had to employ an army of helpers and decided to patent this ingenious design, which is still in use over a century and a half later at every open-air market in the city. Jean Claude Cordonnier's family eventually became the market administrators, known as *gestionnaires*, and though he has recently retired, after 50 years of managing 27 markets, he still comes here to visit his colleagues and do his shopping. The Auguste Blanqui market is an endless treat, especially on sunny Sundays when the vendors are in a great mood (anticipating their late lunch and day off!). You will come across stand after stand of delightful delicacies, tended most often by couples, some of whom have been working at the markets six days a week for up to 40 years—such as the fishmongers Lacroix and the *fromagers* Bouvet. Despite the upside-down hours and the heavy manual work that the market entails, they all insist that there is a great satisfaction derived from the human exchange and freedom that this lifestyle offers, and they are proud to continue a tradition that is so ingrained in their culture. Other old-timers are the Criés, who have been working together for over 30 years, but now split up to cover two markets on the same day. Even without the expert eye of his wife Claudine, who is busy at Marché Jeanne D'Arc, Jean Claude Crié manages to set up an impressive display of fowl and game. During the hunting season, you will stop in your tracks in front of the magnificent row of pheasant, hare, boar, and wild duck adorning the stand, as well as the delicious *foie gras*, *magret de canard*, venison, and whole fattened goose and duck livers lining the counter.

As you continue down the hill, take a peek at the Portuguese and Italian specialty stands. These carry exceptional products from these sun-drenched lands: *bacalhau*, fresh gnocchi, olives, custard-filled *natas*, *prosciutto*, *chorizo*, pesto, lasagne, and homemade cornbread are among the mouthwatering choices. La Corbeille de Normandie is another tantalizing stand, overflowing with all the specialties from the lush northeastern region of France. The husband and wife team, Danny and Blondine Jacqueline, select the best from over 35 producers, offering stacks of buckwheat crèpes, jars of marmalade, oozing Camemberts, fresh *chèvres*, stoneware bowls brimming with farmer's cheese, mounds of sweet and salted butter, baskets of free-range eggs, and an array of chickens, ducks, and rabbits. They also have the old-fashioned Normandy dessert, *teurgoul*, a rice pudding that is cooked very, very slowly in a wood-burning oven for five hours, preferably after the bread has been baked so as to take advantage of the warm hearth. A delicious brown crust forms on the top of this slightly caramelized pudding, whose name in the dialect of the region means "to burn ones palette." Apparently, few could resist this bubbling hot custard the minute it was pulled from the oven. Instead of letting it cool, everyone would quickly grab a spoon and dig in—"Ouch! *Teurgoul!*".

The last stretch of the market, believe it or not, still offers a wonderful selection of products: The Benkritlys have an abundant display of tray after tray of grains, legumes, spices, dried fruits, nuts, olives, North African pastries, and candied fruits. *Fromagerie* Lovenian offers a tempting selection of perfectly ripened cheeses, farm-fresh dairy products, and delicious organic breads from the popular Moisan bakery. Produits des Alpes has an array of hearty mountain cheeses and tasty *saucisson*

Freshly prepared delicacies tempt you every step of the way.

Pétri lentement

Halva pistache
70,00
Halva nature
80,00
K'SRA
galette de semoule
12 fr pièce

L'ETOILE D

JAMBON DE BAYONNE
FR LE KILO

sec. The Brouard family contributes vitamin-rich fruits, vegetables, and bouquets of country flowers from their farm in the Maine region. And two *charcuteries*, owned by the elegant and friendly Michel Flao and the chipper and amusing Alexi Nougaro, both offer tempting displays of hams, sausages, *choucroute*, prime pork cuts, pâtés, and pickled meats. The buckets of cut dahlias, roses, lilies, anemones, chrysanthemums, fleur-de-lis, gladiolas, tulips, and sunflowers end the market on a fragrant and colorful note.

If you want to remain in this country atmosphere, bear left up the hill to have a little apéritif at Les Oiseaux de Passage on the corner of Rue Berrault and Passage Berrault. Here you can rest in the casual ambiance and enjoy a slice of toasted country bread spread with *rillettes* at the bar. When you are restored, venture up the hill to the heart of La Butte aux Cailles. You will probably find yourself daydreaming as you walk up the charming lane lined with beautiful gardens and ivy-covered houses. At the top, you will discover a minuscule neighborhood that is home to a young artist community. There are some interesting little shops, galleries, and restaurants here. Our favorite among them is Chez Gladines, where you can enjoy a heavenly meal in a quaint, cramped, festive place that specializes in food from the Basque region. The fresh salads topped with sizzling bacon, the hearty stews served in casseroles, and the homemade tarts will make a lazy afternoon walk essential. You can meander back down the hill, where you might find an antique book or *brocante* (bric-a-brac) fair under the métro overpass, along Boulevard Auguste Blanqui. You can also wander up to Place d'Italie to catch a film in the new cinema complex or check out Paris' Chinatown. The galleries along Rue Louise Weiss are the most recent on the contemporary art scene. The most recent and controversial architectural addition to Paris' landscape, the new national library, Bibliothèque National de France, is the latest haunt in academic circles; wander up and down the long corridors, browse through the books, visit the exhibits, or stop at one of their state-of-the-art computers to pass the afternoon watching the film *Le Jour Se Lève* starring the very French Jean Gabin

Parisians have a predilection for ham and sausages so *charcutiers*, like Mr Flao (left), offer a range of regional and imported smoked, air-dried, and cooked hams and other delicacies.

JEANNE D'ARC

The picturesque Jeanne d'Arc market winds around a church on a tranquil square in the middle of one of the most modern settings in Paris. The quality of the products here is very good, and there is an easy-going atmosphere. The choice of fruit and vegetables is great, with *maraîchers* displaying crates of freshly picked produce at reasonable prices; orchard owners with their many varieties of crispy apples and juicy pears; and vendors like the Balmisse's and the Kendel's showing off a top quality selection consisting of baby vegetables, crisp salads, aromatic herbs, tasty fruits, and other delicacies. You will find an excellent selection of poultry, cooked specialties, and homemade *foie gras* at Claudine Crié's stand; and roasted specialties at Les Trois Coqs. There are *charcutiers* with tempting displays, butchers, fishmongers, and on occasion an oyster farmer who comes in on the weekend from the coast. One of our favorite stops is the fabulous cheese stand run by the charming Philippe Radenac; he ages his enormous selection of cheese himself and will gladly pick his favorites for you. Finally, flowers, bread, olives, cakes, oils, and sweets will lure you around to the front of the church, completing your tour of this bountiful market.

The Balmisses' immaculate fruit and vegetable stand at Marché Jeanne d'Arc.

SALPETRIERE

The Salpêtrière market is a bit lost under the métro overpass that swoops into the adjacent Gare d'Austerlitz train station. Sheltered from the traffic on the busy Boulevard de l'Hopital, only a handful of vendors set up to cater to the residents of this northeastern section of the 13th arrondissement. Although the atmosphere here is a bit glum, you will find a decent selection and some good quality regional French specialities.

BOBILLOT

This market is located in a quiet residential section of the 15th that is very difficult to get to unless you walk or take the bus. There are only about a dozen vendors that set up along this busy avenue hugging the southernmost tip of the city, offering a selection of good produce. As this is a small market, each vendor tries to be as diverse as possible. Monsieur Lecleu has a wide array of cheeses; the Vacca family brings seasonal produce from their farm; the butcher, tripe butcher, and *chevaline* butcher offer their best cuts; and the fruit-and-vegetable vendors set up generous displays. With a bakery, butcher, barber shop, and Chinese *traiteurs* across the street, Bobillot portrays a pleasant local color.

VINCENT AURIOL

Marché Vincent Auriol sets up under the soaring steel underbelly of the métro overpass that runs above the central divider of Boulevard Vincent Auriol. Protected from the elements, approximately 30 vendors build their trestle tables and stands. Along one generous aisle, displays of fruit and vegetables, cheese, fish, honey, flowers, and meat await the shoppers, who arrive with their caddies and baskets from the towering apartment buildings that line the boulevard.

Pierre Vasseur, an *artisan* butcher, trims delicious *faux filets* and *entrecotes*; while further along at Poissonerie Evelyne et Gerard, piles of *Bouchot* mussels and little round coques clams are bought for lunch. The cheese display of Philippe Radenac is one of the best we have seen. He neatly arranges them behind a refrigerated glass counter, giving the impression that almost all of France's 350 cheeses are on view. In addition, there are quite a number of *maraîchers*, including an organic produce stand, a *chevaline* butcher, a bread stand, and a handful of *marchands volants*.

MAISON BLANCHE

Avenue d'Italie is a congested throughway leading to the suburbs of Paris, but the side streets that branch off from this main artery are very residential. To one side lies Chinatown and to the other the quaint *quartier* of La Butte aux Cailles—the two neighborhoods for which the Maison Blanche market caters. Setting up along one side of the avenue, in front of shops and boutiques, approximately 40 vendors display their produce. Although the area is not very inviting, the market has a bit of everything, with decent quality.

The Chassels bring wicker baskets heaped with apples and pears from their orchard in the Ardeche region. Daniel Brockers arrives at the market with hundreds of free-range eggs. Pierre Vasseur has excellent quality beef from the Limousin region and veal from Corrèze. The *charcuterie* Felz sets up an abundant display of sausages, hams, prepared dishes, and *terrines*. And you can pick up a good *coulommiers* or an oozing wedge of *saint félicien* at the cheese stand La Ferme d'Antan.

Below: Philippe Radenac's extensive selection of cheeses at the Vincent Auriol market; buying coques clams to sauté with shallots, butter, and a dash of white wine.

La Charcutière

Impeccably dressed in a pristine, white, lace apron, the pork butcher Ginette Leconte briskly moves behind her tempting display of home-cured hams, sausages, and bacons, as well as countless trays of mouth-watering dishes. She expertly selects, cuts, slices, and weighs out the orders, all the while chatting cheerfully with her customers. The Lecontes' reputation is irreproachable, always meeting the expectations of their demanding clientele and catering to Parisians' every predilection.

At the carefree age of 13, Ginette began working as an apprentice at the Charcuterie Leconte, learning all the secrets and recipes handed down from generation to generation. She fell in love with the Lecontes' son, Daniel, whom she married; and 43 years later, they represent the fifth generation of charcutiers. Present at four of Paris' best roving markets, together with their son Patrick, they offer some of the tastiest hams, pâtés, and other specialties.

Following the family's traditional recipes, their hams are all homemade. First, they are salted for 48 hours, desalted for 48, and then simmered in a bouillon until the cuisson is just right. Left to cool in their juices, they are brought to market two days later; and as these delicious hams disappear within a couple of days, there is no need for preservatives. All of their pâtés are also fait maison, concocted by Daniel and Patrick, who often invent new recipes, inspired by numerous gastronomic trips that they have made together.
We have tasted their forestier, made with mushrooms and green peppercorns; le courlay, spiked with cognac; and délice maison, made with classified ingredients. They are all perfect accompanied by tart, crunchy cornichons and a fresh baguette.

The Lecontes are present at the Pont du Jour, Grenelle, Saxe Breteuil, and Président Wilson markets.

MARKET RECIPES

TERRINE DE LAPIN ET CONFITURE D'OIGNONS
Rabbit Pâté with Onion Jam

This is a light pâté that is leaner than the more traditional, country-style pâtés. Ginette Leconte gave us her secret recipe that her family has been making for generations. Instead of the traditional mustard and *cornichons*, we recommend a sweet-and-sour onion jam for a perfect match. You can double the amounts for the *confiture*, if you want, as it will keep in the refrigerator for at least a week.

30 minutes 2 1/2 hours

For the pâté:
1 lb (500 g) rabbit, deboned, saving the liver
1 lb (500 g) pork neck or rib meat, cut into chunks
4 tbs white wine
2 tbs cognac
2 sprigs thyme
1 bay leaf
1 onion, sliced
1 carrot, sliced
4 tsp fine salt
1 tbs ground pepper
Grated nutmeg
4 eggs
1 tbs flour
1/4 cup (60 g) hazelnuts
Bard or fatty bacon to line the terrine
6 gelatin sheets

For the onion jam:
6 onions
1 tbs butter
6 tbs olive oil
1 tbs peppercorns
1 bay leaf
1 tsp fresh ground pepper
1/2 generous tsp salt
2 tsp sugar
2 tbs red wine vinegar
1 tbs sherry

To make the pâté:
1. Leave the rabbit in pieces and mix together with the pork, white wine, cognac, thyme, bay leaf, onion, carrot, salt, pepper, and nutmeg. Marinate it for at least 12 hours. **2.** Remove the rabbit, pork, and vegetables and herbs from the marinade; and place in separate bowls. Do not discard the marinade. Cut the rabbit into small cubes. Coarsely grind the pork and rabbit liver. Mix the ground meat together with the rabbit, eggs, flour, hazelnuts, and the strained marinade. Set aside the marinated vegetables and herbs. **3.** Preheat the oven to 400 °F (205 °C). Line the sides and bottom of the terrine with the bard or fatty bacon, and fill with the pâté mixture. Knock the terrine a few times on the kitchen counter to settle the contents, and crisscross the top with strips of bard or bacon. Place uncovered in a *bain marie*, and bake until the top starts to pearl, about 15 minutes. Lower the heat to 300 °F (150 °C), cover with a sheet of aluminium foil, and put the terrine lid on. Bake for 2 1/2 hours. Check the water level of the *bain marie* once in a while and add water if necessary. **4.** Boil the marinade vegetables and herbs in 1 cup of water for 10 minutes. Strain, discard the vegetables, and place liquid back in the pan. Dissolve the gelatin in a bit of the liquid, then mix it back with the remainder, and boil for 3 minutes. Once the pâté is cooked, remove from the oven and pour out any juices it may have, then replace it with the gelatin *bouillon*. Weigh down the pâté with a cutting board or other heavy object. When cool, refrigerate for 48 hours before eating.

To make the onion jam:
1. Quarter and slice the onions thinly. Heat the butter and oil in a skillet; add the onions, peppercorns, and bay leaf; season with pepper and sugar; and sweat for 45 minutes over medium-low heat, stirring from time to time until soft. Add the vinegar and sherry, and cook for an additional 15 minutes. Remove from heat, cool, and refrigerate. **Serves 8 to 10.**

Smooth, elegant, full-bodied whites and reds: Meursault, Lalande de Pomerol, Givry.

SOUPE AUX MARRONS
Creamy Chestnut Soup

Shiny, dark-brown chestnuts make their appearance at the markets during the winter months; and this creamy soup makes a great starter before a main course of game. Nacer Kendel's wooden crates, brimming with plump *marrons* at the August Blanqui market, inspired us to make this recipe.

15 minutes 40 minutes

2 tbs butter
1/2 onion, sliced
1 leek, washed and sliced
1 stalk celery, washed and sliced
1 garlic clove, crushed
2 cups (500 g) (about 2 dozen) chestnuts, peeled and chopped
4 cups chicken or beef stock
Salt and pepper, to taste
3 tbs (50 g) *crème fraîche*

For croutons:
2 slices white bread
1 tbs butter
1 shallot, finely chopped
1 pinch sugar

Note: You may use precooked chestnuts from a can, jar, or vacuum-packed; or use fresh chestnuts. The fresh ones must first be blanched for 15 minutes in boiling water with a tablespoon of oil. Remove from heat, and peel one at a time, leaving the others in the water. Make sure you remove the inner skin, as it can be very bitter.

1. In a large casserole, melt the butter; and add the onion, leek, celery, and garlic clove. Sauté for about 5 minutes, until soft. **2.** Roughly chop the chestnuts and add to the pot. Cook together with the other ingredients for 10 minutes over low heat. **3.** Add the stock, salt, and pepper; stir; and cover the pot. Cook over low heat for half an hour. **4.** Remove from heat and blend until smooth using a hand-blender. (If using an electric blender, let cool before blending.) **5.** Return to pan and heat. Add the cream, adjust seasoning, and serve. **6.** For the croutons: Remove the crust and cut the bread into small cubes. Toast until golden in a hot oven and set aside. In a small frying pan, heat the butter and sauté the shallots until golden over medium-high heat. Add the pinch of sugar so that they do not burn, then add the bread cubes, toss gently, season with salt and pepper, and remove from heat. Sprinkle croutons over individual servings of soup. **Serves 6**.

Full-bodied, flowery whites: Chassagne-Montrachet, Chablis, Macon

PINTADE AU CHOU
Guinea Hen and Crinkly Cabbage

Guinea hen, or pintade, is one of the least gamey-tasting birds available at the market. This traditional recipe, prepared with braised cabbage and beer, was given to us by Madame Crié from the Jeanne d'Arc market. It is easy to make as the perfect, hearty, winter meal.

20 minutes 45 minutes

1 guinea hen
Salt and pepper, to taste
3 oz (90 g) thick-cut bacon, cut into strips
1 medium onion, chopped
1 cup beer
1 crinkly-leaved green cabbage, finely sliced

1. Remove the innards, rinse the guinea hen, pat dry, and rub—inside and out—with salt and pepper. **2.** In a large, heavy-bottomed pot, brown bacon and onion for approximately 5 minutes. Place guinea hen in the pot and brown on all sides, about 10 minutes. **3.** Pour in beer, stir, and cover. Cook for 1 hour, turning the bird every once in a while to cook in the juices. **4.** Bring a large pot of water to boil, add a teaspoon of sea salt, and parboil the cabbage 10 minutes. Strain and hold. **5.** Add the cabbage to the pot 15 minutes before the guinea hen is cooked. **6.** Adjust seasoning and serve. **Serves 4**.

Easy drinking reds or coarse rustic reds: Chinon, Côte-de-Bourg

POMMES DE TERRE AU CANTAL
Pan Gratinéed Potatoes

Marinette from Fromagerie Bouvet, at the Auguste Blanqui market, gave us this simple recipe that works as a supper dish accompanied by a green salad, or as a side dish to a juicy roast, rack of lamb, or grilled steak (the cantal cheese adds a spicy kick to the meat).

10 minutes 40 minutes

8 medium potatoes
2 onions
6 tbs butter
Salt and pepper, to taste
4 oz (110 g) cantal cheese, thinly sliced

1. Thinly slice the potatoes and onions into rounds. **2.** In a non-stick pan, melt the butter, add the onions, and cook for approximately 5 minutes until translucent. **3.** Add the potatoes, and sauté, turning constantly for 10 to 15 minutes. Season with salt and pepper, to taste. **4.** Sprinkle the cheese on top, and cover until potatoes are completely cooked (approximately 10 minutes). Serve immediately. **Serves 4.**

Fresh, fruity reds: Gamay, Chiroubles

Above: Compote de fruits secs

COMPOTE DE FRUITS SECS
Stewed fruits in white wine

This tasty fruit stew makes a pleasant wintertime dessert and keeps for up to 8 days in the refrigerator. Laurence Benkritly from the Auguste Blanqui market likes to prepare it with white wine, but you can use red wine as well, or substitute it with grape or orange juice.

10 minutes 2 hours

1/2 cup (124 g) sugar
3 cups white wine
3 cups water
1 cinnamon stick
1 1/2 cups (200 g) dried prunes
1 1/2 cups (200 g) dried apricots
2 cups (250 g) dried peaches, pears and apples combined
1 cup (150 g) dried figs
Peel of 1 orange
1/2 cup (100 g) peeled almonds

1. Combine the sugar, wine, water, and cinnamon stick in a large pot. Bring to a boil, and cook, stirring until sugar is dissolved. Add all the other ingredients, cover, turn heat to low, and stew for 1 1/2 to 2 hours. **2.** Remove from heat and let cool. Serve at room temperature with a spoonful of heavy cream or farmer's cheese. **Serves 4 to 6.**

Fruity whites: Condrieu

31

Your first encounter with the 14th arrondissement will most probably be Boulevard Montparnasse, crowded with throngs of people filing into movie theaters, waiting in lines at packed Tex-Mex restaurants, or edging by the café terraces that occupy most of the sidewalk. Once the haunt of famous artists who would dally the night away at the renowned brasseries that filled the street, Boulevard Montparnasse stands as an icon of the postwar years. Most of the nightspots have been replaced by huge movie complexes, fast-food restaurants, and noisy cafés; and though the few survivors may still be flooded with diners in search of that genuine "something," they have

XIVe ARRONDISSEMENT

lost much of their charisma and "old Paris" flair. Once you pass the hectic junction that is overshadowed by the unsightly Tour Montparnasse, if you walk a block in any direction, you will come to the calm residential neighborhood of the 14th. Besides the addition of the state-of-the-art Fondation Cartier museum, this *quartier* has not changed a great deal. Small streets lead you to secluded courtyards, church squares, and cobblestone alleys, where the locals go about their everyday lives. This tranquility is revealed in the pocket-sized Montrouge market, where the vendors seem so familiar and the surroundings so inviting.

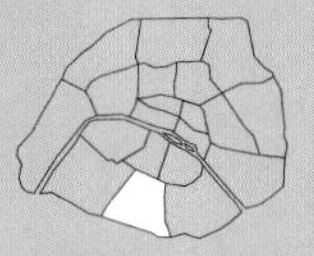

In its heyday, the 14th arrondissement was home to many famous artists. Their ateliers can still be found scattered throughout the *quartier*.

A HIDDEN GEM
The Montrouge Market

Nestled behind busy streets in the heart of the 14th arrondissement, the Montrouge market sets up on a shaded square beside a school and playground. Over 30 stands are squeezed between the trees, offering quality products to neighborhood regulars, who faithfully come here to do their weekly shopping and to catch up on the local gossip. This charming market is what you least expect to come across, after having visited the eerie catacombs at Place Denfert-Rochereau or the famous Montparnasse cemetery just a few blocks away. The atmosphere here is lively, reminiscent of a small village, with three tiny aisles filled with enticing displays, vendors chatting across to one another, and shoppers happily making their way through the market with their overflowing baskets.

Although Montparnasse is known for the bulky brown architectural mishap, La Tour Montparnasse, which dominates the *quartier*, and for its movie theaters and nightlife, the 14th arrondissement is actually one of the nicer residential areas of Paris. Wandering down the side streets, you will find a thriving neighborhood: shops filled with unusual objects, tiny restaurants with fogged-up windows, and hidden courtyards where artist ateliers look out onto small secluded gardens. Originally this area was made up of fields and meadows, with over 60 windmills twirling their sails on the horizon; and below, the foundation was a maze of underground quarries, which had been exploited since the Middles Ages for sandstone and gypsum to build the characteristic facades and monuments of the city. Bit by bit, the quarries were abandoned and used to cultivate mushrooms or to store beer and wine, in the cellars of the neighborhood brasseries. Nowadays, the former quarries have mostly been blocked to the public; although occasionally they have become popular hotspots, for "underground" parties, hosted by the cognizant who somehow manage to open up the otherwise abandoned world.

Like most of the outlying areas, the 14th was integrated into the city in the 1860s. It then remained a rural haven that developed slowly, without the building frenzy that took place on the northern side of the city. The neighborhood was always an attractive destination for artists; since the early-19th century, writers, painters, and sculptors such as Chateaubriand, Balzac and Bourdelle, settled here; they were soon followed by the likes of Picasso, Modigliani, Man Ray, and Fugita in the 1920s and 30s, when the area was in full swing. Montparnasse became the center of the art world and home to artistic innovation and freedom. Cafés, bars, and *brasseries* sprouted up along Boulevard Montparnasse, drawing the international avant-garde scene to their smoky interiors.

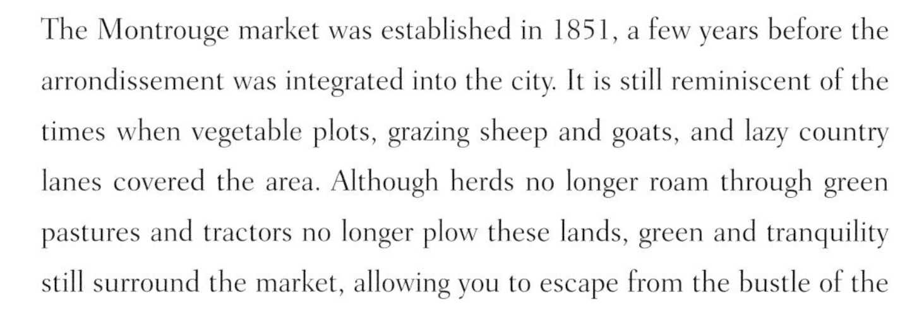

The Montrouge market was established in 1851, a few years before the arrondissement was integrated into the city. It is still reminiscent of the times when vegetable plots, grazing sheep and goats, and lazy country lanes covered the area. Although herds no longer roam through green pastures and tractors no longer plow these lands, green and tranquility still surround the market, allowing you to escape from the bustle of the

Since this is a weekday market, there is never the rushing of people that you will find at weekend markets; vendors as well as visitors here seem very content in maintaining the calm.

grand boulevards and the enormous train station, Gare Montparnasse. Rebuilt in 1969, with the aim of creating a communal space and modernizing the landscape, Gare Montparnasse has proved quite a failure: the pedestrian feels stranded in an expanse of concrete and billboards; and crossing from one side of the *place* to the other is a real obstacle course.

As soon as you cross Rue Mouton-Duvernet and step into the market, with trees overhead and colorful canopies engulfing you, you will sink into a relaxed pace, where shoppers quietly go about making their purchases. Having a chat with Michel Meret is a nice way to start your visit: he comes from his farm and sets up a long table draped in a tablecloth covered with cow motifs, sparsely decked with his farm produce. Three plump chickens and a duck or two lie next to a couple of baskets of speckled brown eggs and small containers of fresh farmer's cheese mixed with fruit compote. The neighboring farms in the Loire Valley supply him with a crate of apple juice, several jars of homemade jellies and jams, and a box of pears or cherries to sell along with his delicious raw milk that his faithful customers all request. He often throws in a small, round cheese that his wife makes at the farm: the very hard ones, aged for up to six months, are to nibble on with your apéritif; the fresher ones are to add to your cheese tray.

Tuesday is generally a quiet day at most markets; some vendors choose not to show up, preferring to use this time to prepare their specialties for the following days. On Friday, each spot is occupied. Along the first aisle next to Monsieur Meret, a stand decorated with baskets of coffee, tall, red-and-green tins filled with tea, and trays of moist brownies and chocolate-chip cookies tempt you with their fragrant aromas as you walk by. Further down, past the fishmonger, a very popular *triperie* sells perfectly prepared offal and meat; and the *maraîcher* Monsieur Chevalange has boxes of sweet, homegrown potatoes, crispy lettuces, and pungent onions, which he continuously replenishes from wooden crates stacked in the back of his truck. The neighboring stand specializes in Italian vegetables that are not very often found at the markets: broad beans, baby zucchini, broccoli rabe, and if you are lucky, a box of green figs. There is also a selection of Portuguese delicacies, such as spicy *chorizo*, slabs of salt-caked *bacalhau*, and an assortment of wines and ports.

Across the aisle, the mother hen of the market, Claudine Crié, stands proudly behind her elaborate display of free-range poultry and steaming trays of *lapin forestier* and *coq au vin*. Jean-Claude and Claudine Crié have been selling their delicacies here and at other markets for over 30 years; and their daughters, Laurence and Nathalie, have followed in their footsteps, perpetuating all the family secrets. In front of a green-and-white backdrop, wearing matching uniforms, they offer high quality poultry and game. Taking pride in simplifying sophisticated dinners, the Criés do the more time-consuming preparations for you: small *paupiettes* of deboned rabbit decorated with a sprig of rosemary; turkey roasts rolled with onions and basil; and guinea hen barded with bacon and filled with a morel mushroom and cognac stuffing—ready and waiting to be picked up and simmered with a dash of wine. They facilitate

Despite being one of the smaller markets of the city, Montrouge offers top-notch quality. Here, the selection of apples, marmalades and juices at the Nochet's stand.

EUR
POMM
S ET POIRES
DE
CONFITURES
AVEC ET......
SANS SUCRE!
COMPOTE DE POIRES
GELÉES
POIRES
CROQUANTES
FORELLE

things even more with their delicious prepared dishes: *paella; ragoût de marcassin;* and, roasted on a spit, a selection of ducks, rabbits, chickens, and pigeons, as well as the occasional leg of lamb, suckling pig, or baby goat. Circumventing French formalities, Madame Crié *tutors* everyone, and often addresses her elderly customers as *"ma petite biche"* ("my little deer") or *"mon petit coeur"* ("my little heart") while she prepares their tiny quails or weighs 100 grams of chicken livers for them. This type of market jargon was common practice at the time of Les Halles; and although it always more has been used affectionately and in jest, one hears it less and less, despite it always inducing a smile and chuckle from the clients.

Next door, the shiny apples and pears carefully arranged at the *Pommes de Touraine* stand are each more unusual than the next. Twelve years ago, Jean-Claude and Evelyne Nochet bought their apple orchard near Touraine, with 40,000 Granny Smith apple trees. What started as a hobby developed into a passion. Nowadays, you will no longer find any bright green Granny Smith apples at their stand; now they specialize in rare and ancient varieties. They also experiment with various hybrids, grafted from samples that Jean-Claude has brought back from all over the globe. Through trial and error, they have selected and cultivated the most succulent, tasty, and interesting apples. They open up a whole new world for those in search of this sweet, tart, delicate, and pungent fruit. Every new graft takes two years before yielding fruit, and only three out of every 20 buds are left on the tree, to develop into plump, healthy apples that are harvested from mid-August to mid-October. Each specimen is carefully laid in a Styrofoam tray with individual compartments to keep them from becoming blemished. Evelyne handles them with loving care, while explaining the different flavors and uses of the more than 35 varieties christened with unusual names such as *calville blanc, court-pendu,* and *sainte-germaine*. You have to dig deep into your pocket to purchase a few, but once you sink your teeth into them you will not regret it. The Nochets are present at the markets until the end of June, at which time they dedicate the summer months to the orchard in order to prepare the trees for the following season.

When the 14th arrondissement was integrated into the city, it was one of the few areas of Paris where people from every group intermingled. Artists originally ventured to this slowly emerging *quartier* because of the inexpensive rents and the empty stables and warehouses that could be

CATACOMBS

Underneath the cobblestone streets of Paris, a maze of over 190 miles winds its way deep into the city's foundation. Dating as far back as the Gallo-Roman times, these subterranean quarries were exploited for their gypsum and sandstone, used until the 20th century to construct many of the buildings and monuments of the city. During the 18th century, the defunct quarries under Place Denfert Rochereau in the 14th arrondissement were chosen to house the largest ossuary in the world. Over six million skeletons were transported from all of Paris' cemeteries, and piled tibia-to-tibia, hip bone-to-hip bone, in what was to be known as "Les Catacombes."

Les Catacombs came into existence because the small churchyard cemeteries could no longer hold the growing number of deceased. Horrific sanitary problems had arisen. So the city undertook its biggest sanitation effort ever. During a two-year period, Parisian bones were exhumed and transferred by nightfall, among them the likes of Robespierre and Danton, to the newly refurbished quarries, which were dug in a 5,000-foot-long labyrinth. Since the day of its completion, Les Catacombs has attracted a steady flow of visitors.

Right: Madame Crié sells superior quality poultry and game as well as seasonal products like *cèpes* mushrooms and prepared dishes like *paella* (this page).

FERMIERES
Préparées par la Maison
Lièvre FRAIS FRANÇAIS
FOIE GRAS DE CANARD
ESCALOPES DE FOIE GRAS DE CANARD CRU
FOIE GRAS CRU
FAISAN A ROTIR FRAIS PIECE
CAILLES FARCIES AUX RAISINS COGNAC
PINTADE FERMIERE
Poulette de BRESSE à Rotir 49,95
PIGEON TENDRE A ROTIR PIECE 50F
GROSSES CAILLES TENDRE A ROTIR PIECE 18F

converted into ateliers. During the 1920s, the area attracted a flow of international artists from Eastern Europe, South America, and the United States. Talent abounded, with the likes of Chagall, Zadkine, Archipenko, Mata, and Soutine, to name but a few. It is said that the Surrealist movement began here also, headed by the Dadaist, André Breton. Political activists such as Lenin and Trotsky hid out in this *quartier* and once in a while could be seen socializing at the newly opened bars and brasseries that had become popular meeting spots. As in other parts of Paris, the mixture of cultures and social classes converging at these establishments proved to be inspirational. Bricklayers would stop for their morning coffee and Calvados before stepping out to lay the new streets and boulevards; artists would come for a warm meal, a few drinks, and conversation; and the upper-class residents from other parts of the city would venture here for a little action, mixing with the artists and also mingling with the new arrivals.

Obviously not everyone came to Montparnasse solely for intellectual inspiration, as it had become the center of nightlife, with restaurants, clubs, theaters and the famous Rue de la Gaîté generating a constant source of entertainment. Montparnasse had its roaring years between the two world wars—with the opening of great brasseries such as La Coupole and La Rotonde; and theaters such as Théâtre de la Gaîté and Bobino, where *tout Paris* came to enjoy the free-wheeling spirit of the 14th. Celebrities such as Edith Piaf, Yves Montand, and Charles Trenet graced the stages of these grand theaters, while an intriguing mix of people occupied the tables and partied until dawn. With all of the bright lights and goings-on, it is of no surprise that the oldest profession in the world thrived here! At the Gare Montparnasse, a steady flow of young women from Brittany could be spotted disembarking from the trains, lured to the big city with exciting job prospects. Unfortunately, upon arrival, most found themselves duped, caught in the clutches of pimps and the world of prostitution. It was a time of wild parties, creativity, and growth which lasted until after the second World War, when the area was cleaned up, never returning to its former glory.

Left: Butchers in France are obliged to attend a two-year course and five-year apprenticeship before opening shop. Right: Jean Louis Grimaldi with his selection of organic breads.

Back at the market, at the end of the first aisle, the Crédaro family sets up a long display with colorful bouquets of field-cut flowers at one end of the table, and at the other, baskets of berries and a selection of farm-fresh produce that varies, depending on what is ripe on their garden plot. They cultivate their land following old-fashioned methods, not using chemical fertilizers or insecticides; they could easily qualify for the *AB* (organic) denomination, but choose not to, due to the levies and membership fees that would increase their costs. So if you want to find untreated beets, carrots, sweet peas, Jerusalem artichokes, and baskets of sun-ripened strawberries—at affordable prices—this is the stand to visit. The mother-father-and-son team also brings fresh eggs, herbs, preserves, and potted plants from the neighboring farms; and they are always ready to explain the best way to cook this or that vegetable. Along the same wholesome line, across the way, Jean Louis Grimaldi, from Graine de Vie, sells over 30 varieties of whole-grain breads that are each more interesting and delicious than the next. An actor by passion and baker by profession, Jean Louis is quite a character, always chatty and charming when convincing you of the quality and originality of his breads.

Surrounded by fruit-and-vegetable stands, the expansive display of the *charcuterie* Chez Joël et Eliette seems to take up most of the central aisle. This lively pair sells all of the traditional pâtés, sausages, hams, and prime pork cuts, as well as scrumptious pizza *Provençale*, *taboulé* salad, and *jambon persillé*—all hard to resist. Walking down this rather short stretch, you will encounter another *maraîchère*, Madame Tregouet, whose vegetables, fresh cheeses, yogurts, and free-range chickens look quite delicious but are spoiled by her perpetual bad mood. She is always moaning and groaning about something or other; one day we saw her shooing away a woman from the front of her stand as the woman was juggling many purchases, trying to rearrange them in her basket. Not the best way to hold onto your customers! We always make a huge detour around her stand in order to avoid her unpleasant manner. At the end of the aisle, the horse butcher stand run by Marie-France Lafforgue is, on the other hand, welcoming—if you are into eating this very lean and healthy meat. The horse's finicky eating habits and their allergies to hormones assure a clean meat,

6

MONT D'OR RACLETTE

Vacherin can also be eaten warm! Jean Jacque Lainé, a cheese vendor at the Montrouge market, gave us this simple recipe that resembles Swiss Raclette. Just place the cheese in its wooden box on a shallow, ovenproof dish, make small "chimneys" (holes) in the cheese with a knife, pour a cup of white wine on top and let sit one hour. Optionally, garlic slivers can be inserted to give it an extra kick. Place it in a preheated oven (350°F/180°C), box and all, for 15 to 20 minutes, peel off the top crust, and voila! A fresh baguette, a fruity white or red wine, perhaps a salad, some boiled potatoes, *cornichons*, and you have a delicious meal! (see photo above)

CHEESE

Although there are farmers who age their own, most cheeses achieve their full character in the cellars of cheese merchants, known as *affineurs*. *Affineurs* receive the cheeses directly from the farms at a young stage, often already having formed their moldy crust which is vital for aging. They bring the cheese to full maturity through a variety of techniques. In cellars (see photo left page) usually located below their shops, the cheeses are placed on shelves which are covered with either straw, wood, paper, or plastic, in either a humid or dry room, depending on the variety. Each cheese is individually tended to: rubbed with either brine, beer, or alcohol, rolled in ashes, or left to develop its own personal character. This procedure can take anything from two weeks to several months and requires daily attention. Unfortunately, most *affineurs* are very secretive about their special techniques. They may explain the basic procedures, but few are willing to reveal specifics. Fewer still will show you their cellars. The personal taste of each *affineur* is reflected in the final product, Of course, the best way to distinguish the differences is by tasting several of the over 350 varieties produced in France. When comparing two *affineurs*, you may like the *chèvre* from one because of its bite but the *camembert* from another because of its almost overripe creamy texture. It is for you to investigate and for you to decide!

Mont d'Or is, like most foods in France, seasonal. Towards the end of autumn, aficionados stick out their noses in search of this creamy cheese with its peach-colored, undulated crust, individually packed in round, spruce-wood boxes. *Mont d'Or*, commonly known as "*vacherin*," makes its official appearance at the markets in the beginning of November, after having been carefully matured over a period of four months. We were told that the secret to this sinfully creamy cheese is that the Franche-Comté region's cows, known as *Montbéliard* and *Pie Rouge de l'Est*, produce a very rich and fragrant milk after having spent the summer months grazing on the over 50 varieties of grass and herbs found on the mountain pastures of the region, along the Swiss border. The maturing process begins in August, when the milk is used to make the raw cheese; it is then molded, wrapped with spruce-wood bark, and placed on spruce-wood boards, where it is carefully treated with brine, and routinely flipped until a thin outer layer forms; at this time, it is placed in an individual box and left until properly aged.

Traditionally, one leaves this wonder out at room temperature for at least an afternoon, and serves the cheese in its encasing, with the top crust carefully removed and a large soup spoon to serve. This cheese should never be cut, and the real glutton can scrape the last bits from the shell once everyone else at the table has finished eating. You find *vacherin* all through the winter; it is very popular at Christmas time, when it is at its peak. The season sadly peters out after the holidays and finally comes to an end in February.

Savourez l'onctuosité du
Fromage Frais
La Ferme de L'Isle
40% MG.
PONT-L'

which is sweeter in taste, and has less cholesterol than beef, and is often recommended by doctors. Although it seems to be a dwindling trade, *chevaline* butchers in France still have a faithful following; after her 30 years selling at the markets, Madame Lafforgue believes that the demand will persist.

The Montrouge market has fantastic fruit-and-vegetable stands, many of which are run by Southeast Asian families, reputed to have excellent quality produce and a great selection. Many of these families supply traditional fruits and vegetables, such as asparagus, baby spinach, mesclun, green beans, bananas, melons, and strawberries; as well as more exotic items, for which many clients especially come, such as Chinese cabbage, black turnip, ginger, soy beans, lemongrass, mangoes, rambutan, and passion fruit. These vendors have, for the most part, entered this business by chance. For example, our friend Jean Luc Lor, at the far end of the last aisle, worked as a taxi driver, store manager, and cook before establishing himself at the markets. Usually the rhythm at these stands is fast, very courteous, and meticulous. The displays are impeccable. Generally, you have to pay a hefty amount for your purchases, but you can be certain of the quality, and you will never walk away with tasteless fruit or tired lettuce that has to be thrown out the next day.

One of the only cheese stands at Montrouge is run by a couple that has been selling here since 1977. The Lainés buy directly from small *artisanal* cheese makers. They specialize in *chèvre*, but they have a complete array from every cheese-producing region of France. Monsieur Lainé is very active in market politics—he is concerned about the new rules and regulations in production and sale of food that will be imposed by the European Union, and he is intent on protecting the methods and traditions of French gastronomy. A native of the Limousin region, he is a true food lover. He is also a coordinator for an English gourmet travel group, "Market Discoveries"(*), organizing visits to cooking schools, food shops, and of course Parisian markets. An enthusiastic salesman, he will have you pinching, smelling, and sampling each variety from his display. We enjoyed the creamy goat milk, *monthais à la feuille,* and the rich and aromatic *epoisses de bourgogne* that is rubbed with *marc*, a strong brandy from Burgundy. We also walked away with his favorite recipe for *mont d'or* (see p. 209).

Left: When buying cheese in France, *fromagers* like Monsieur Lainé will ask you when you plan to eat it and press the center to check its ripeness.

From time to time, the market is subject to a fair amount of animation, generated by the 14th arrondissement's town hall; but generally, serenity prevails. If you are looking for a sunny terrace, with a few passers-by to observe, wander over to Rue Daguerre, a daily street market that hosts a number of very nice food shops, bookstores, and boutiques. Along this pedestrian lane, you will find the newly opened Androuët and Fromagerie Vacroux for excellent cheeses, Nicolas and Caves Péret for a good bottle of wine, and a few butchers, pastry shops, fruit-and-vegetable stands, and the bountiful fish shop Daguerre Marée for every fish and shellfish imaginable. A few blocks down from this hub is the delicious bakery Le Moulin de la Vierge, where you can indulge in a perfect *fougasse* or a sourdough roll, and watch flour-dusted breads being popped into wood-burning ovens.

After all this shopping, if you are in the mood for lunch, either scout out one of the many small restaurants serving French, Indian, or Asian fare; or try the small wine bar Le Vin des Rues, at 21 rue Boulard, known for its frogs' legs and list of wines by the glass. Instead, if you have purchased the ingredients for a picnic, walk over to the rambling Parc Montsouris and install yourself by the lake or under an ancient tree, and enjoy the tranquility. When you have had enough of blue skies and chirping birds, you may venture into the catacombs, where three centuries of Parisians are neatly stacked; or walk a bit further, to the Fondation Cartier on Boulevard Raspail, to see a more recent side of the city and enjoy the current exhibition.

ALESIA

Located on a small square a few blocks away from the beautiful Montsouris park, the Alesia market caters to the inhabitants of this residential neighborhood. The two large flower displays make a warm welcome, as does Fromagerie Lovenian's abundant cheese stand (above), with its wide selection of goat's milk cheeses and baskets of freshly baked organic breads. Monsieur Lacroix and his wife offer a small but good selection of fresh fish from the Normandy and Brittany coasts; and Monsieur Jouastelle sets up a select display of plump free-range chickens, ducks, and guinea hens, which he brings from his farm in the Saône region. Past a number of *maraîcher* stands, stacked with crates of salads and garden-fresh vegetables, you will find one of the old-timers at the market: the *charcutier* Monsieur Nougaro, who sets up a large display brimming with delicate quiches and tarts, tasty hams and sausages, and quality pork roasts, chops, and ribs. The atmosphere is calm and friendly, and you will find everything you need, but make sure you get an early start as the locals seem to buy up all the produce before noon.

EDGAR QUINET

If you turn your back to the ugly tower of Gare Montparnasse, and walk along the tree-lined central alley of Boulevard Edgar Quinet, the attractive Edgar Quinet market will distract you from the hustle-and-bustle of the busy Boulevard Montparnasse. Although it is a relatively large market, Edgar Quinet has a calm and traditional pace, reminiscent of times past; it is a pleasant place to pass the morning.

Besides the occasional tourist, the clientele at this market is very local. The most popular vendors all know their clients by name, and they do not mind the customers' demanding style and meticulous scrutinizing of every item. Although the selection and quality can vary at many of the stands, you will always find a fantastic array of wild and cultivated mushrooms at Meyer Champi; a wonderful variety of exotic fruits and vegetables at J & M Boulay and Gasche-Lecroc; and delicious hams, salamis, and prepared pasta dishes at Daniel Capocci's Italian specialty stand. In addition, there are a handful of fishmongers, butchers, and *charcutiers*, some tempting *fromagers* and bakers, an apiculturist, an African *traiteur*, and a plant stand, all of which are well worth a peak. Pick and choose in the tranquil atmosphere of this charming market before going to one of the sunny café terraces that line the boulevard.

VILLEMAIN

Situated on a square, the Villemain market seems sadly abandoned on Wednesdays, when only a fraction of the vendors show up to cater to just as thin a turnout of customers. Holding the fort is Monsieur Heron, who seems to be the only source of animation as he enthusiastically calls to the passers-by to sample his plump *burlat* cherries or smooth-skinned apricots. There are a handful of other vendors offering a small but complete variety of items. If you happen to be in the area on Sunday morning, a visit here can be combined with a visit to the Convention market located on Rue de la Convention, just one métro stop away.

BRUNE

Marché Brune is one of our favorite markets, where you will find quality goods at very reasonable prices. Its only drawback is the location, on a large, busy boulevard at the edge of the city. But as you wander through the aisle, you will find yourself engulfed by the pleasant and convivial atmosphere and vast selection.

Among the over 70 stands, *maraîchers* abound; as do *fromagers*, butchers, and *charcutiers*. They are intermingled with colorful flower stands, expansive fish displays, and poultry vendors. The market draws quite a crowd, and there is something tempting every step of the way.
A special treat is a roaster who bastes her chickens, rabbits, and ducks with a Thai marinade spiced with ginger, lemon grass, cumin, and coriander before roasting them to a crunchy golden brown.

If you are planning to visit the nearby flea market at Porte de Vanves, you should take the time to come here as well, and also to the newly opened fish hall nearby on Rue Castagnary, a wholesale market where the prices are low and the offerings are as fresh as can be.

BRANCUSI ORGANIC

Having opened as recently as October 1999, Marché Brancusi is an emblem of how important organic produce has become. Located on a quiet square, this miniature market has about a dozen stands offering organic produce, dried goods, cheeses, meats, breads, prepared foods, and fish. Complemented by the excellent Max Poilâne bakery, this may be one of those out of the way havens that is yearning to be discovered.

Le Traiteur Italien

George Capitano is a portly man who always has a smile draped across his face, even when he is discussing serious issues such as how to cook his raviolis. With a blue woolen cap perched on top of his head, he beams behind his tempting display of homemade Italian delicacies. His large hands are continuously covered in flour from scooping into his trays of raviolis. He quickly wipes them off on his white work frock to slice paper-thin layers of Parma ham, before plunging them right back in for the next customer. Everyone comes to him for his delicious raviolis, George's pride and joy. From the quality of his pastas, salamis, hams, antipasti, and crumbling blocks of parmegiano and pecorino cheese, one would think that George is following a long line of family tradition. The fact is, seven years ago his sister had the idea of owning a pizza van. As George had just left his computer-programming job, he found this to be an appealing prospect. He headed for Italy to learn how to make the perfect pizza, which he describes as having a thin crust topped with just the right amount of tomato sauce, cheese, and basil; this was the key to his success. One thing led to another; he was soon twirling out nests of fettuccine in the back of the van, and customers were lining up for a jar of his tomato sauce. Things were going well, and the little pizza business was thriving, but of course nothing inspires a Frenchman—let alone an Italian—more than love. When he met the charming Françoise, a chemist at one of Paris' main flour mills, he had visions of them setting up shop together, surrounded by trays of delicate pasta.

With Françoise's more scientific approach, and George's love for food, they make a great team. The raviolis are gloriously light and delicious. George bases most of his ravioli recipes on his mother's; but he likes to experiment as well. He has come up with such tasty and inspired combinations as walnut and eggplant, balsamic vinegar and spinach, and ricotta and pesto. Once the various mixtures are cooked, he often adds a dash of white wine, a pinch of nutmeg, or a drizzle of fragrant olive oil before stuffing the raviolis—so that each plump mouthful is bursting with flavor. Decked with all the different *salumeria*, wine, and oils that they bring directly from Italy, as well as trays of marinated artichoke hearts, bell peppers, grilled eggplant, and zucchini, their stand is irresistible. There is always a line of shoppers waiting to purchase a little something from the Capitanos.

The Capitanos are present at the Convention, Président Wilson, and Saxe Breteuil markets

MARKET RECIPES

CHAPON AU CHAMPAGNE
Capon with Champagne and Truffles

Capon is a festive dish best reserved for a special occasion. As the birds are always large, one will easily suffice for 6 to 8 guests, and even a bit more depending on the choice of appetizer. Capons are no ordinary fare, so it is best to order them well ahead of time. In this recipe, the truffles may be exchanged for morel mushrooms (fresh or dried). If you choose to use dry morels, remember to soak them beforehand; and if you use tinned truffles, add the juice as well for extra flavor.

20 to 30 minutes 2 hours

1 capon (6 to 9 lbs [3 to 4.5 kg])
2 shallots
1 large truffle or 2 oz (60 g) dry *morilles* (morel mushrooms)
2 tbs peanut oil or goose fat
Salt and pepper to taste
1 bottle of champagne
2 heaped tbs heavy cream

1. Cut the capon into pieces, chop the shallots, and julienne the truffle (or soak the morels). **2.** In a large Dutch oven, lightly brown the capon pieces in the oil or goose fat over medium-high heat for about 10 minutes. Remove and set aside. Do them in batches to make sure each piece gets a chance to brown. Spoon off excess fat before continuing. Add the shallots to the pan, and sauté until translucent. **3.** Place the capon pieces back in with the shallots, season with salt and pepper, pour in the champagne, and boil for 2 minutes to let the alcohol evaporate; then add the truffle juliennes or the morels. **4.** Cover, and cook over low heat for 2 hours, stirring from time to time. **5.** Before serving, stir in the cream and adjust the seasoning. Heat, but do not let the cream sauce come to a boil. Place in a serving dish and serve immediately with plain or wild rice. **Serves 6 to 8.**

Vintage Champagne or sparkling wine, Burgundy white wine

GATEAU AUX POMMES
Warm Butter Apple Ring

Evelyne Nochet's apple cake is a winner! When we made it, we were surprised at how little batter was needed—just enough to barely coat the apple slices. The ratio of cake to apple is heavenly, and the butter-and-sugar topping added at the end is a delicious touch.

15 minutes 30 minutes

8 tsp flour
3 tsp sugar
1 tsp baking powder
1 egg
1 tsp vanilla extract
2 tbs sunflower oil
7 tbs milk
4 Jubilé apples (or other baking apples), peeled, quartered, and sliced
Butter, to grease mold

For the topping:
4 tbs salted butter
6 tbs sugar

1 ring mold

1. Sift flour, sugar, and baking powder into a bowl. **2.** Mix egg, vanilla extract, oil, and milk. **3.** Add liquid ingredients to dry ingredients, mix together, and add apples. **4.** Grease mold. Pour mixture into mold, and bake for 25 minutes at 350 °F (180 °C). **5.** Melt the butter in a saucepan over medium heat. **6.** Remove cake from oven, pour the melted butter on top, and sprinkle with the sugar. Put back into the oven, and bake for an additional 5 minutes. **7.** Let cool for a few minutes, then remove from mold, and serve with fresh cream or vanilla ice cream. **Serves 4 to 6.**

Demi-sec white or rosé: Anjou, Vouvray

A buttery apple tart from the Max Poilâne bakery.

Max

The 15th arrondissement has neither the panache of Paris' more stylish *quartiers* nor the typical staggering number of monuments and historical nooks and crannies. It is one of the city's younger areas that boomed during the Industrial Revolution, when most of Paris' factories were concentrated here along the banks of the Seine. In the early 1960s, the area underwent massive restructuring: noisy and unsightly industrial facilities were transplanted to the suburbs. This modern *quartier*, with its proximity to the posh 7th and 16th arrondissements, appealed to young executives and families; it quickly established

XVe ARRONDISSEMENT

itself as a residential neighborhood. Over the years, it has not changed much, except for the addition of a new commercial center on the riverfront. A number of hotels, movie theaters, and businesses settled there, in ultra-modern high-rises, which seem out of sync with the rest of Paris' architecture. Not many guide books will recommend a tour through the 15th, and you will rarely see a tourist navigating the streets; but this low-key neighborhood has a pleasant atmosphere and houses a handful of lively markets, including the delightful weekday market, Saint Charles.

Thirty-seven ancient and modern bridges cross over the river Seine linking the right and left banks of Paris.

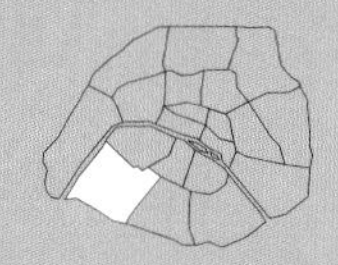

TO MARKET! TO MARKET!
The Saint Charles Market

Marché Saint Charles is the quintessential Parisian neighborhood market: tempting aromas and sights accompany you at every turn. Makeshift stands, in front of beckoning shop fronts, line the sidewalks on either side of Rue Saint Charles in the highly populated southwest corner of the city. This weekday market is always full of baby carriages, shopping carts, and shoppers scurrying through narrow aisles filled with specialties representing every Parisian predilection. The butchers offer hearty *côtes de bœuf* and veal roasts; the *maraîchers*, bushels of new potatoes, onions, and garden-fresh greens; the fishmongers, whole salmons, deep ruby-red slices of tuna, and perfectly trimmed fillets; and the cheese vendors, wedges of gruyère, *cantal*, and wooden boxes of creamy camembert.

Bordering the river Seine on the outskirts of the city, the 15th arrondissement was originally made up of two hamlets: Vaugirard and Grenelle. Both were owned by the powerful Abbey of Saint-Germain-des-Prés. While Vaugirard evolved into a village of over 6,000 inhabitants by 1825, there was little change on the plains of Grenelle until the 1830s when, due to its vast expanses of unused land and proximity to the river, it became the industrial center of Paris. During the Middle Ages, it was on Vaugirard's lush pastures that the cattle who provided Paris with most of its meat were grazing. Also here Benedictine monks planted rows of vines from which they derived a much-cherished red wine. The land of neighboring Grenelle was less fertile and subject to continuous flooding, but the pure drinking water of the area was treasured. As both towns lay on the outskirts of the city, past the toll walls and therefore exempt from taxes, they were popular spots for small indulgences. Carousers would come to drink dry the cellars of the many taverns in Vaugirard. Then they would stumble past the windmill in Grenelle to the small fishing port on the bank of the river, where they swam and feasted on crayfish.

Shoppers stream along the narrow sidewalk of Rue Saint Charles caught between tempting shop windows and the stands.

The Saint Charles market was established under the name "Javel" in 1879, to cater to the workmen and their families who settled in the area. They toiled in the numerous local tanneries, foundries, and other factories. The most famous enterprise was the French car manufacturing plant Citroën, acclaimed for designing the presidential limousines and sleek aerodynamic vehicles that sped gangsters away in every French *film noir*. The oldest factory was a chemical plant, built on the site of the windmill of Grenelle in 1777; here bleach was invented, baptized *eau de javel* after the islets known as *javeaux* that appeared along the riverbank following excessive flooding. The speed with which this area developed, up through the 1950s, was overwhelming. The resulting industrial landscape, with smokestacks spewing forth billowing clouds of black smoke, excessive noise, and clawing air, was far from a pretty sight, sound, or smell. It was a relief when the factories were moved, and the area became the tranquil, residential neighborhood that it is today.

As you exit the métro station, Charles Michel, a jumble of shops and cafés will welcome you into the spirit of the open-air market that sets up every Tuesday and Friday along the tree-lined stretch between Rue de Javel and Rue des Cévennes. Stop at the inviting Moule a Gâteau, which has buttery pastries to dunk in your coffee. Then head over to admire the first stand on the left. Run by a mother-and-daughter team, its tables are overflowing with homegrown produce displayed in baskets and crates on a bright-blue plastic covering. In the summer months, you may encounter the friendly, talkative tablecloth salesman who sits next door to them; he watches in awe as people line up to buy fruit and vegetables, no doubt wishing that they would be just as motivated to buy one of his Provence-style tablecloths.

At mid-morning, you will be pulled along as the aisle fills up with locals, their baskets, their dogs, and their babies. Though it can get a bit tight, there is no push-and-shove here; everyone is very courteous and friendly. This is not a market where vendors shout to hawk their produce—there is no need to draw the shopper any closer than he already is! The first store you'll come across is a butcher with a succulent display including individual servings of *carpaccio* that are made for you to take home, serve to your guests, and return the clean plates the following day. Next door is Buongiorno, an Italian haven that is not more than six-feet wide and twelve-feet long, crammed from floor to ceiling with fresh pasta, cheese, wine, ham, salami, coffee, *antipasti*, and homemade desserts. Here you can pick up a bottle of extra-virgin olive oil and thinly shaved parmesan to sprinkle on top of your *carpaccio*. At the Flûte de Gana bakery a few steps away, stop and watch the famous *flûtes* being shaped, left to rise in linen forms, and then slid into wood-burning ovens. These yeasty baguettes are some of the best you can buy in the city, with a crunchy crust and a slightly chewy center.

As you continue past displays of fish, flowers, and vegetables, you will come to the hard-to-miss *charcuterie* stand of Madame Boulanger and her daughter Nathalie. We often bump into Nathalie having a coffee at the delicatessen Rebuzzi, another Italian haven, directly in front of the Boulangers' display. Madame Boulanger is one of the only *traiteurs* at the market who actually cooks some of her dishes on the spot. Besides the multitude of quiches, tarts, pizzas, grilled sardines, tomatoes *Provençal*, roast suckling pig, hams, pâtés, *terrines*, rice pudding, *clafoutis*, and baked apples, you can buy roasting potatoes with *Auvergnat*-style sausage, steaming *petit salé aux lentilles*, blood sausage with braised onions, or hearty *cassoulet*.

If you do not find enough here to fill your every desire, walk a bit farther to the corner shop. Au Cochon Rose has been around since 1936, and it prides itself on its award-winning blood sausages and *fromage de tête* as well as its mind-boggling display: feast your eyes on stuffed poached salmon, quail in aspic, *bouché à la reine*, monk and sole fish *terrines*, lobster halves with avocado; 20 varieties of salads, including the ever-present grated carrot, as well as potato, shrimp and grapefruit, cabbage and raisin, endive and walnut, tomato and onion, *salade Russe*, Baltic herring, and *céleri remoulade*; and don't forget the warm, steaming trays of *veau Printanier,* roast loin of pork stuffed with prunes, *morue a la Provençale*, herb-roasted hams, *bœuf en daube*, and mashed potatoes, creamed spinach, and braised endives to accompany all of the above. If that is not enough, there are plenty of sumptuous desserts to choose from as well. Best of all, they offer special menus for every purse: from 29 francs to 54 francs for a lunch box. Naturally, the place is always packed!

In the 1960s, after most of the industrial plants had migrated to the suburbs, new apartment complexes were built, attracting the up-and-coming, people who aspired to live in the nearby posh 7th and 16th arrondissements but could not afford to do so. As a result of some haphazard city planning, the neighborhood is a mishmash of modern and old architecture. The northern edge of the arrondissement still has an elitist flair, but on the whole, this is a family oriented neighborhood. There is a community of older residents who have been here since well before the war, and a growing number of young families attracted by the functional, modern buildings and the proximity to the *peripherique*. The 15th is not really a place to come and enjoy the sights; this is a thriving middle-class neighborhood with a mainstream tradition of daily food shopping. The many markets and specialty shops attract Parisians who prefer to buy their cheeses from a favorite *fromager,* chat with the *maraîchers,* and ask the *marchand de vin* to select a good bottle for a family lunch—rather than visit an antiseptic supermarket where they can finish their shopping list in an uneventful 20 minutes. You will rarely encounter a tourist wandering the streets of this vast arrondissement; if you come here you will find that though the sites may be less than spectacular, they do reflect the everyday life of a typical Parisian.

Italian specialty shops, *traiteurs*, butcher shops, and bakeries line the street complementing the selection at the market.

The market continues past the intersection of Rue de la Convention, which is often filled with clothes stands. You will then encounter Monsieur Mallet, fussing over his tiny table decked with chickens, quails, pigeons, and rabbits, fresh goat cheeses, sausages that he spices with basil and black trumpet mushrooms, and a basket with one or two varieties of mushrooms that he brings from his native Loire Valley. One of our favorite stops is the Les Chèvres de Saint Vrain stand, with its mouthwatering spread of fresh goat cheeses attractively displayed next to rounds of *comté de fort saint antoine*, *mimolette*, *brebis fermier*, *morbier,* and creamy *pont l'eveque*. The young vendors here enthusiastically explain the eclectic assortment and offer good advice on what to buy. We always follow their suggestion and have never been disappointed.

The sparkling butcher shop owned by Monsieur Mahier, with a handful of experienced helpers clad in red work coats, always has perfectly tied roasts and a delicious selection of lamb, pork, veal, and beef. In the autumn, the still life of hares, pheasants, deer, grouse, and wild boar hanging from the storefront, decorated with brass hunting horns and autum leaves, makes you dream of venison stew and the feast to come!

The remarkable number of butcher shops found along Rue Saint Charles may be due to the tradition dating all the way back to the Middle Ages, when the plains of Vaugirard were the grazing pastures of Parisian cattle and the area housed an important slaughterhouse which closed only in 1970. The great following that butchers have here is not unusual—the French will never give up their grilled *entrecôtes* and *steak tartares*.

At the small roundabout, the wine store Cellier Saint Charles is filled with enormous wicker baskets holding simple table wines, and wooden shelves where more sophisticated *cuvées* are displayed. Its location is ideal, as based on your preceding purchases, you probably will have decided upon a menu, for which you will need a good wine recommendation which the charming owner will certainly offer.

The last stand before crossing over to the other side of the market is a rose farmer who sets up stacks of freshly cut roses: tiny vibrant pink, pale yellow, tangerine orange buds, long-stem cardinal red, and luscious pale-pink country roses—he often sells out before 10 a.m.

BUTCHERS

The butchers' union is the oldest and strongest in Paris, dating as far back as 1146, when it was established during the reign of Louis VII. For centuries, an outsider could enter the trade only with an official letter from the king; otherwise, the know-how and title legally had to be handed down exclusively through family members. The union had a monopoly on raw meat. They were not rivaled until the 1500s, when the *charcutiers* were allocated the sale of cooked and fresh pork. Meat was not an expensive commodity in Paris during the first centuries of the city's existence; humble workers as well as nobility dined on lavish stews and roasts. Livestock were bought either from cattle markets held in the neighboring villages, from which they were herded to the city; or from the well-stocked pastures of the clergy, who often made a little pocket-money selling off their extra cattle. Then, in the mid-16th century, a growing population and economic crises pushed the price of beef way out of reach for most commoners; and a juicy *côte de bœuf* became a rarity. In response, the *charcutiers* ingeniously began transforming the less-expensive pork into countless varieties of sausages, hams, *andouilles*, and pickled meats, using everything but the oink of the affordable pig.

Paris was not equipped with a slaughterhouse until the 19th century, so it was customary for butchers and *charcutiers* to kill and prepare the animals in the courtyards behind their shops. Often the terrified beast would escape—wreaking havoc in the streets; and the stench and filth from the slaughter was nauseating. This prompted the creation of five *abattoirs* between 1808 and 1818, and another five in 1860. The humongous La Villette *abattoir* was still in use up until the 1970s, and was one of the last to close in the city. As a reminder of days past, an original metal pavilion graces the site of the Vaugirard *abattoir* in the 15th arrondissement, where a weekly antiquarian book fair has replaced the heads of bellowing cattle.

There is a special section at the beginning of the other side of the market made up of the four organic producers who come here every Friday. The bastions of organic food in Paris are Marché Raspail and Marché Batignolles, but the vendors here attract quite a number of customers. Monsieur Savier sells his homegrown vegetables along with some imported fruits; his is a bountiful display of products, including peaches, mangoes, baby eggplants, and slim *haricots verts*. The family-run La Ferme de la Bourgere has wooden crates filled with whatever vegetable is ripe at their farm. These, along with the organic cheese and butcher stands, make this a small but complete alternative for the conscientious shopper.

Although most of the stores along the last part of the market sell clothing and shoes and are not very interesting, there is still quite an array of stands left to investigate. The vegetable vendors include Monsieur Occaer, who sells fresh *cornichons* that you can pickle yourself or purchase already prepared with vinegar, sprigs of tarragon, bay leaves, and garlic, in large preserve jars. Fishmongers also seem to like this stretch, with crowded displays of octopus, sardines, mackerel, swordfish, cod, sole, tuna, and shrimp.

Occupying an old dairy, and discretely opening its door to the flow of shoppers, is a bric-a-brac shop called Au Facteur Cheval, worth peeking into. Beautiful antique porcelain and glassware, furniture, paintings, and odds and ends can be bought at reasonable prices. It is a perfect place to escape from the hurly-burly of Saint Charles and swiftly browse through the centuries.

As you continue down the street, a dry-goods vendor arranges burlap sacks full of grains, beans, and rice next to a low table with heaping buckets of olives, spices, and dried fruits. The Meyer Champi stand has a display of mushrooms that changes depending on the week. *Girolles,* chanterelles, *mousseron,* shitakes, *cèpes*, black trumpets, morels, and *champignon de Paris* are neatly arranged on a yellow tablecloth. Each variety is separated by bouquets of fresh herbs and parsley, selected to enhance the flavor of each type of mushroom. A Savoie cheese and sausage vendor complements the fishmonger and bakery shops that signal the end of the market.

If you follow Rue Saint Charles back toward the métro, you will encounter an old-fashioned cheese shop trimmed with wooden paneling.

Right: Besides selling top-quality meat, the butchers that line rue Saint Charles offer excellent game. The season for boar starts at the beginning of November.

The owner ages his own cheeses in the cellars and two enthusiastic saleswomen tend to the customers. There is a large organic supermarket at 20 Rue de l'Eglise. On the corner, at the end of Rue Saint Charles, there is a minuscule Auvergnat specialty shop, where you have to duck under hams and sausages to approach a display case filled with earthenware crocks of *rillettes, confit de canard,* and homemade pâtés.

Unfortunately, once you come to this intersection there is not much in terms of beautiful sights or things to do. You may want to walk over to Quai André Citroën by the river, named after the first Citroën car that drove down this stretch when peace was restored in 1919. From here you can see the replica of the Statue of Liberty and the Eiffel Tower in the distance. Follow the promenade down to the new André Citroën Park that replaced the old auto plant, and admire the artistic landscaping. Its slightly complicated scheme includes a playground in the "White Garden," trimmed lawns in the "Black Garden," greenhouses in the "Central Park," seasonal displays in the "Changing Garden," swaying rushes in the "Garden of Movement," and the "Theme Garden" with items for each of the five senses. If this seems too multifaceted for what you have in mind, go instead to the smaller and more tranquil Georges Brassens Park. This site once accommodated the slaughterhouse of Vaugirard, but it has been transformed into a modern park, with vineyards, an apiary, a herb garden, and an antiquarian book fair that is held in the iron-and-glass hall on the weekends. Directly across from the book market, you can stop for coffee at Le Café du Coin; and treat yourself to an irresistible buttery *tarte aux pommes* at the lovely Max Poilâne bakery. Otherwise, if you just wander around the neighborhood, you will come across some quaint restaurants serving not only French fare but Vietnamese, Moroccan, Korean, Indian, and Lebanese cuisine.

Above: The bric-a-brac store, Au Facteur Cheval, near the end of the market is a must for all treasure hunters.

Riz
Semoule
Pois Chiches
1kg 3F50
Riz
1kg 7F50
Haricots
Rouges
1kg 13F50
6F75
Pois Cassés
1kg 6F00
1/2 kg
3F00
Lentilles
9F90

Le Traiteur

Annie Boulanger's *traiteur* stand, which sells prepared dishes, rarely goes unnoticed. Her abundant displays are a feast for the eyes: a myriad of quiches, onion tarts, *pissaladières,* grilled sardines, marinated bell peppers, *terrines*, pâtés, mounds of *rillettes*, cooked and smoked hams, fresh and air-dried sausages, baked apples, *clafoutis*, fruit tarts, and rice puddings. It seems a remarkable feat to set up this enormous spread; and as if this were not enough, Annie cooks many of the dishes on the spot. Claiming to be one of the first to offer this service at the markets, she stands proudly behind her sturdy, cast-iron gas burners, stirring away at piping hot skillets of *fricassé Auvergnat*, and gently poking at coils of blood sausage with translucent, golden onions simmering in goose fat.

Every evening Annie delves into her repertoire of traditional French recipes, planning for the following market day. In her *laboratoire* on the outskirts of the city, she is aided by a handful of homeless and handicapped. She employs them to peel, trim, and chop the mountains of ingredients; while she prepares and cooks her numerous dishes throughout the night. At daybreak, her daughter Nathalie loads tray after tray, platter after platter into the truck and sets up the display at the market; while Annie has a few hours' rest, arriving just in time for the *casse-croute* and the rush of customers.

Annie speaks with pride of her 25-year attendance at Paris' roving markets. She has become quite a celebrity and has stashed away piles of magazine and newspaper clippings praising her generous cooking. Having come from a family of fishermen off the Normandy coast, upon her arrival in Paris as a teenager, she immediately found work as an apprentice at a fish store. A few years later, she met her husband-to-be, a *charcutier*, and she switched *métiers*. Together they started the *traiteur* business which she now runs on her own, with the help of Nathalie.

Annie and Nathalie are present at the Président Wilson, Richard Lenoir, and Saint Charles markets.

CONVENTION

Sunday is the day to come to this enormous market, which stretches along Rue de la Convention, filling every inch of free space on the narrow sidewalk with rich displays. Similar to Marché Saint Charles, here over 100 stands line up side by side, directly in front of food and clothing shops that open their doors only a few feet across from them. The aisles can get crowded, so it is best to come early; but the atmosphere is relaxed and good-spirited.

When you exit the métro, along the left-hand side of Rue de la Convention, there is a carousel that twirls children around, while their parents watch live bands performing on the sidelines. The market has a wide selection of excellent-quality fruits and vegetables, and it is a pleasure to walk along unable to decide which beets to buy, whose watercress looks greener, or who has the crunchiest apples. There is also fresh fish selling at a rapid speed from several large stands, as well as oysters, which seem to be just as popular, from oyster farmers who come during the winter months. Other favorites include: Bernard Duval's tempting display of olives; George Capitano's great selection of Italian specialties; and Meyer Champi's heaping mounds of mushrooms. In addition, you will find numerous *charcuteries*, *fromageries*, *volaillers*, and *boulangers* that have great displays and are tended by helpful merchants—all making this market one of the more agreeable ones to visit.

LECOURBE

Even though the Lecourbe market has to fight against an ugly backdrop of modern apartment complexes, it manages to maintain a little charm. Setting up along Rue Lecourbe, vendors such as the Lainé's with their eclectic cheese stand, several fishmongers, butchers, fruit-and-vegetable merchants, and a dozen others offer a decent selection to the inhabitants from the immediate surroundings. Like other markets, Lecourbe suffers from the mid-week blues, when only a portion of the vendors show up, and the vacant spots are occupied by *marchands volants* selling mattresses, blankets, tablecloths, and other odds and ends.

CERVANTES

Located on the edge of the 15th arrondissement, Marché Cervantes is held in a very uninviting setting, overshadowed by a modern apartment complex. In the center of a cement courtyard that prevents the sun from shining in, this market caters to the neighborhood residents. You will find a bit of everything, including fruits and vegetables, cheese, bread, meat, fish, and flowers; but the quality is, for the most part, average—this is not a market to go out of your way for.

LEFEBVRE

The Lefebvre market lines the traffic-ridden Boulevard Lefebvre, which is dominated by the Porte de Versailles convention center and sports stadium across the way. Hugging the city, it is not the ideal destination for a market outing and functions more as a neighborhood market catering to the locals. But if you find yourself in the area, perhaps on your way to the Georges Brassens park, you will find some decent options to put a good picnic together at very reasonable prices.

GRENELLE

The bustling Marché Grenelle sets up under the Motte Piquet métro overpass in a long stretch of colorful stands. Spanning the length of two métro stops, the selection is never ending; and even on a miserable rainy Sunday, Marché Grenelle makes a great outing. Over 60 vendors display their produce, sheltered from the busy Boulevard de Grenelle that runs on either side of the market. Among the numerous stands, you will come across farmers with their homemade dairy products, *maraîchers* with mounds of salads, a handful of butchers and poultry vendors including one who sells organic meats and the exclusive poultry vendors, Miolane, expansive flower stands, an apiculturist, an escargot vendor, and a Provence specialty stand with satchels of lavendar, fresh *fougasse* breads, and olives for sale. If you are looking for good quality in a low-key setting, come to Marché Grenelle.

MARKET RECIPES

PISSALADIERE
Onion Tart

Although Annie Boulanger is writing a cookbook of her own, she was generous enough to share her recipe for *pissaladière* with us. There are many different versions of this recipe: in Provence it is made without egg; in other regions a bit of custard is added; and often a lot of custard is added and it resembles a quiche. We like Annie's version the most and if you love onions this is a dish for you!

30 minutes   1 hour

For the pastry:
1 1/3 cups (240 g) flour
1/2 tsp salt
1/4 cup olive oil
8 tbs ice water

11-inch (26 cm) tart mold

For the filling:
2 lbs (1 kg) onions
3 tbs olive oil
2 eggs
1/2 cup liquid cream
Salt and pepper, to taste
1 pinch nutmeg
1 pinch cinnamon

1. Place flour and salt in a bowl. Add the oil in a slow stream, incorporating it into the flour. Do not over-mix; add the water one tablespoon at a time. As soon as the dough is manageable, cover and let stand for half an hour. **2.** Slice the onions finely. Heat the olive oil in a large pan. Add the onions, and sauté for 20 minutes over medium heat, stirring frequently. **3.** Roll the dough out on a floured board, and place in a buttered mold. Trim the edges, and prick the bottom with a fork. Place a sheet of waxed paper on top, and cover with beans to weigh it down. Bake for 12 minutes in a hot oven, 400 °F (205 °C). Remove from oven, discard the beans and paper, and put back in the oven for 5 minutes more. **4.** Lower oven heat to 375 °F (180 °C). **5.** In a large bowl, mix together the eggs and cream; and season generously with salt, pepper, nutmeg, and cinnamon. Add the onions, mix well, and pour the mixture into the tart shell. **6.** Place in the oven, and bake for 30 minutes. Raise the heat to 400 °F (205 °C), and bake for another10 minutes to brown the top. When slightly cool, remove from mold, slice, and serve. This quiche can be eaten either hot or cold. **Serves 6 to 8.**

Easy drinking, chilled reds: Saumur Champigny, Beaujolais

BRUSCHETTA AUX PETONCLES
Bay Scallop Bruschetta

This delicious appetizer also makes a perfect light supper accompanied by a green salad. The recipe is quick and easy, and makes a nice alternative to the classic tomato-and-basil bruschetta. In France, bay scallops (*petoncles*) are sold in their shells. When removing from the shell, keep the roe (the orange part); it is not only delicious but adds a nice touch of color.

15 minutes   8 minutes

1 lb (500 g) bay scallops
4 2-inch (5 cm) slices of country-style bread
3 garlic cloves
4 tbs olive oil
1 tbs butter
6 tbs flat parsley, coarsely chopped
1 cup white wine
Salt and pepper, to taste
Chopped parsley and fresh ground pepper, for garnish

1. Rinse the bay scallops under cold running water, leaving on the roe. Pat dry with a paper towel. **2.** Toast the bread and rub one side with one of the garlic cloves. Place one slice each on heated plates, and set aside. **3.** In a skillet, heat oil and butter over a medium-high flame with the garlic cloves (these can either be left in or discarded depending on taste), and add the scallops and parsley. Cook for a minute or two until partially cooked, then turn up the heat and add the wine. Cook for a few minutes more until the sauce thickens slightly. Season with salt and pepper. Generously heap the bay scallops on top of each slice of toast, distribute the remaining sauce, and sprinkle with some chopped parsley and a twist of pepper. **Serves 4.**

Spicy, light whites: Bourgogne Aligote, Sancerre, Muscadet

Bruschetta aux petoncles

CAILLES AUX FIGUES FRAICHES
Roasted Quails with Fresh Figs

Quails are a delicious alternative to the traditional roast chicken. Monsieur Mallet at Saint Charles recommended we make them with a fig-and-wine sauce which marries wonderfully with the quails as their taste is slightly gamey. Served with creamy, mashed potatoes and a full-bodied red wine, this one is hard to beat!

30 minutes 45 minutes

Salt and pepper, to taste
4 quails
4 slices thin bacon
Kitchen string
8 black figs
1 cup red wine
2 tbs peanut oil
2 garlic cloves
1 sprig rosemary
2 sage leaves
1/4 cup water
4 sprigs rosemary, for garnish

1. Salt the cavity of the quails, wrap each one with a piece of bacon over the breast, and truss with the kitchen string. Pepper the outside. Preheat oven to 375 °F (180 °C). **2.** Quarter the figs, and place in the wine to macerate. **3.** In a skillet at medium-high heat, brown the quails on 4 sides in the peanut oil for approximately 10 minutes. **4.** Place garlic cloves, rosemary, and sage in an oven dish; add the quails and water; and place in oven. Bake for 30 minutes. **5.** When cooked, remove quails from the dish, discard string, and keep quails warm in turned-off oven. **6.** Strain the baking juices from the quails into a saucepan; and at high heat, add the fig-and-wine mixture. Cook for 8 minutes or until sauce has thickened slightly and figs start to fall apart. Adjust seasoning and remove from heat. **7.** Place quails in serving dish, cover with sauce, and garnish with rosemary sprigs. Serve immediately with mashed potatoes on the side.

Full-bodied, aromatic reds: St. Emilion, Pauillac, Côte-de-Nuits

CREME CARAMEL

Crème caramel is one of those timeless, traditional French desserts that is so easy to prepare yet always induces an "ooh!" and an "ah!" when brought to the table. This recipe calls for a single mold, but the mixture can be baked in individual ramekins. Just test the cooking from time to time—when an inserted knife comes out clean, they are done. Crème caramel tastes just as scrumptious after a few days in the refrigerator, so it can be made ahead of time.

20 minutes 40 to 60 minutes

For the caramel:
4 tbs (60 g) granulated sugar

For the custard:
2 cups milk
1 vanilla bean (or 1 tsp vanilla extract)
3 eggs
3 egg yolks
6 tbs granulated sugar

1 ovenproof dish
2 cups water, for *bain marie*

1. Preheat the oven to 350 °F (180 °C). **2.** In a saucepan, heat the 4 tablespoons sugar over a medium flame, turning the pan occasionally, until it caramelizes. Quickly pour the syrup into the ovenproof dish, coating the bottom. Set aside. **3.** Pour the milk into a saucepan. Slice the vanilla bean lengthwise, and scrape out the grains. Add both bean and grains (or the vanilla extract) to the milk. Scald the milk, remove from heat, cover, and let steep. **4.** Bring 2 cups of water to a boil for a *bain-marie*. **5.** In a large bowl, whisk together the eggs, yolks, and sugar until you have a light and frothy mixture. **6.** Remove the vanilla bean from the milk, and pour slowly through a sieve into the egg mixture, whisking continuously. **7.** Pour the mixture into the caramelized mold. Place the mold into a larger baking dish, and add the boiling water until it reaches the halfway point of the custard mold. Place in the oven. **8.** Bake for approximately 60 minutes. The water of the *bain marie* should never boil; otherwise your custard might become grainy. As oven temperatures tend to vary, test the custard with a knife before removing it from the oven—when done, it should come out clean. Let cool before chilling. Refrigerate at least 2 hours before serving. To serve: run a knife around the sides of the custard, and flip it onto a serving dish. **Serves 4 to 6.**

Madeira wine or sweet Sherry

Cailles aux figues fraîches

17

When you say you live in the 16th, most people "ooh!" because they can imagine you sitting in your luxurious apartment, possibly on your spacious terrace, holding a glass of champagne, overlooking the Seine, with the Eiffel Tower illuminated in the background; or they "eek!" because they are terribly embarrassed to know you and see you as the most boring, bourgeois individual that they have ever met! Both and neither are true. Yes, there are some fabulous apartments throughout the arrondissement, housing the rich and sometimes famous; and, in comparison to other neighborhoods, there is really not much happening. Nevertheless, for such a bourgeois, boring place there are numerous stylish restaurants, tons of greenery and great museums ... and hey, admit it, no one would mind having a little *pied a terre* at this address!

XVIe ARRONDISSEMENT

The 16th arrondissement has always been a retreat for the wealthy. Originally it was on the outskirts of the city, and Parisians would travel to enjoy its woods, natural springs, and vineyards. Since it was integrated into the city, each section of this vast arrondissement has developed its own character: the southern edge is a quiet neighborhood with winding streets; the central part is the heart of activity for the arrondissement, with shops, movie theaters, restaurants, and cafés lining the sidewalks; and the northern section embodies the arrondissement's image of grandeur, with its formal boulevards lined with private mansions and stately apartment buildings, which to some seem isolated from the reality of Paris. It is here that the opulent Président Wilson market sets up twice a week, offering an exclusive selection to a select clientele.

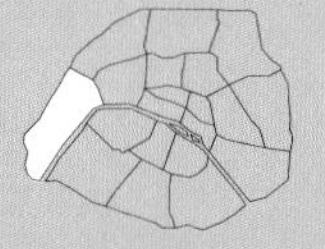

The posh 16th arrondissement hosts the poshest of markets.

FARMERS FOR THE HAUTE COUTURE
The Président Wilson Market

Under the vigilant eyes of George Washington astride his bronze horse, Paris' most upscale and elegant market unwinds along the tree-lined central divider of Avenue du Président Wilson. Between the handsome Museum of Modern Art and the turn-of-the-century Museum of Fashion, the Président Wilson market stands at the gateway to the enormous 16th arrondissement. The market boasts over 60 stands offering top-notch products and catering to a very demanding clientele. Its colorful awnings lead the visitor through lovingly composed displays of fine string beans, polished potatoes, baskets of raspberries, and bursts of arugula. Lavish stands of game, meat, cheese, fish, and flowers transform this strip of pavement into a food worshiper's sanctuary.

Wealthy executives, celebrities, and expatriates have always enjoyed living in this exclusive residential neighborhood. Originally, the 16th arrondissement was located on the outskirts of the city, part of the prehistoric forest of Rouvray that stretched all the way to Rouen. The place was a favorite hunting ground for kings, and its small villages and vineyards made it a popular stopover for travelers en route to Chaillot and Saint-Germain-En-Laye. Luxurious lodges were built in the woods to house the royal guests and to host lavish dinners in celebration of the hunt. Over the centuries, much of the oak forest has been cut down, and the villages of Passy and Auteuil have been integrated into the 16th, thus stretching this *quartier* from the southern edge of the city along the Seine all the way up to Place de l'Etoile. What forest remains is in the large Bois de Boulogne park that runs along the entire length of the quartier. Here Parisians spend their weekends appreciating the lakes, paths, and gardens. Come nightfall, this former haunt of kings transforms into a forest of debauchery—with prostitutes and transvestites appearing behind every tree.

Left: Early risers get the best pick of the day when the market is at its calmest.

The Président Wilson market stretches down the wide avenue from Place d'Iena to the *haute couture* district in the neighboring 8th arrondissement. The pomp and sophistication of the elegant clothes shops on Avenue Montaigne seep into the market in the form of dapper shoppers pulling their *de rigueur* plaid shopping carts and stylish baskets past displays that are often as colorful and elaborately planned as Montaigne's designer windows. This is a bustling market, where customers enjoy taking their time to select the tempting delicacies available at each and every stand: the *volaillers'* wide assortment of specialty fowl and game; numerous *maraîchers* with tasty, delicate vegetables and sweet, unblemished fruits; butchers' quality cuts and perfectly tied roasts; *charcutiers'* refined hams and *gelées*; *fromagers'* artisanal cheeses, wines, and breads; and the dazzling flower stands that adorn the aisle. The offerings are of superior quality—and priced accordingly, so one can easily go broke during the course of the morning shopping!

We always start our tour at the top of the hill, having had our *petit déjeuner* elsewhere, as the avenue is devoid of cafés and shops. It is worth a stop to admire Madame Quennejean's towering display of technicolor blossoms. Unusual flowers, such as delphiniums, bell flowers, orchids, lilies, and long-stemmed irises are placed in buckets of cool water next

Aïl Rose
Nouveau
le Kg 18F 00
CAT 1
Petits Pois
le Kg 28F 00
PRIMEUR DE NOIRMOUTIER
La petite rondeur du palais
ORANGES A JUS
Ile de France
Navets Bio
la botte 12F 00
Provence CAT 1
Carottes
Saumur
POMMES DE TERRE
VARIETE : SIRTEMA
POIDS : 5 KGS
CALIBRE : -35

to stacks of the more common roses, peonies, and daisies of every color and size. Many come here to do their weekly flower shopping, as the prices are reasonable and the selection extensive. There are three and sometimes four florists present at this market. You can pick bunches from the wonderful displays, and have them carefully arrange a magnificent bouquet with beautifully coordinated colors for you while you finish your shopping. At this end of the market, quite a few *marchands volants* set up, hawking various items such as towels, socks, clothes, hand-embroidered tablecloths, earthenware dishes, and other odds and ends.

Once you enter the hub of the market, the real feast begins. You will find a marvelous selection, from local fruits and vegetables to exotic produce. Everything looks as if it was picked that morning. It is so preciously handled and arranged that you would think the vendors were selling diamonds and rubies. Fragile bunches of yellow zucchini flowers and bundles of tender wild asparagus are lined up next to enormous, armored artichokes, baskets of delicate spinach and fragrant herbs, golden-orange mangoes and clusters of vine-ripened grapes. The Balmisses have one of the prettiest stands, where husband, wife, and helper serve their crowd of faithful customers with care. The displays are immaculate; and it is impossible to squeeze a peach or smell a melon, as the vendors are meticulous and prefer not to have their beautiful arrangements disrupted. You will be expected to wait your turn, or risk getting snapped at; but eventually you will enjoy the special attention that they give you and the way that they carefully choose each item so that it is perfectly ripe on whatever day you choose to savor it.

Vendors begin setting up at the crack of dawn. Here the meticulous display of the Balmisses and the mountains of farm-fresh lettuces at Jean Thiebault's.

In comparison to the very formal and pristine Balmisses, Joël Thiébault sets up an enormous *maraîcher* stand with overflowing mountains of rich, tasty vegetables, from which he invites his customers to pick and choose. Aided by a hard-working crew who also man the farm, he fills his stand with salad greens, herbs, leeks, cooked beets, carrots, broccoli, radishes, sweet peas, cauliflower, and turnips. They will inform you how soon the new crop of tomatoes will be picked and when to buy the last of the rhubarb before the season ends. The prices are reasonable, and we always walk away with bulging bags, which then relieve us of the guilt of having splurged on a teeny carton of *fraises des bois*.

At the heart of this exclusive neighborhood is the posh Avenue Foch, with its majestic apartment buildings and private mansions, as well as numerous museums, embassies, and the very popular Place du Trocadéro.

Le kilo 1080

fête
anniversaire

Colin
Saumon

CHAPon EXTRA
1kg
98 00

MORVAN
FRANCE
Cèpes
France
14F
100g
Morvan
140F Kg

Fleurs de
Courgettes
la Pièce 3F00

At Trocadero, the chic and cosmopolitan stop for coffee at Carette; and the young and rowdy linger about the esplanade of the Palais de Chaillot, roller-blading amid the throngs who hike down the hill to the Eiffel Tower. The 16th is so large and self-sufficient that it often seems to be an autonomous entity with pockets of activity dispersed throughout. Children rush off to school, nannies leisurely push strollers through the streets, office workers dash out for a quick lunch, and mothers shop for the evening meal at the local *traiteur* after buying a pair of the latest shoes on Rue de la Pompe.

As you wander through the market, you will come to Laurence and Pascal Miolane's elaborate display of prized *poulet de Bresse*, *poulet de Gers*, *canard croiser*, and *lapin fermier* labeled with their exact provenance; as well as plump *cailles*, pigeons, and suckling pig. The selection here is always fit for a king; one can easily conjure up the multiple-course dinners of the court of Louis XIV. The only difference is that, unlike the deer and boar chased after by the kings in the forest of Rouvray, the wide range of game here will be trimmed and ready to cook. Come September, the season for pheasant, partridge, and wild duck arrives. The Miolanes always have mouthwatering, prepared dishes that Pascal makes himself. During November and December, when wild boar and venison are available, he will tempt you with a pot of *civet de marcassin* or *chevreuil au poivre vert*. If you prefer to cook it on your own, he will marinate the game for you the day before, so that you can have

The most exclusive of products can be found at the Président Wilson market. Clockwise from left: Sea scorpions; porcini mushrooms, pheasants, sea urchins, and zucchini flowers.

THE ROYAL METHOD OF PICNICKING

The kings of France knew how to travel! On their excursions out of the castle, not a moment passed without the reassurance that food was close at hand. In fact, there was a valet whose sole responsibility was to tend to the king's rumbling tummy. If at any moment along the way, the king felt the urge for a bite, a feast consisting of six loaves of bread, six bottles of wine, 20 biscuits, six dozen puff pastries, candied fruit, six oranges, two pâtés, two Bries, 20 cakes, 24 cheese tartelettes, and 24 brioches was promptly laid out. The food and drink was regally presented on silver platters and in silver pitchers, upon red tablecloths that bore the coat of arms. The taster, another indispensable valet, would make sure that no poison would spoil the fun; and within minutes, the king and his entourage would sit down for a little picnic in the woods.

FOIE GRAS

Poor old ducks and poor old geese, but lucky us, who can indulge in a *tartine* or a seared slice of *foie gras*, accompanied by a glass of sweet Sauternes. The ducks and geese from Perigord and Gascony in the southwest part of France, as well as those from Alsace in the north-east, are the chosen fowl to supply the tables of France, with their treasured pale-pink-hued livers. What once used to be a seasonal delicacy, during the festive months of November to February, is now available all year round thanks to modern breeding and imports from Hungary and Israel. *Foie gras*, which means "fat liver," is achieved by force-feeding the fowl for a month just before slaughter, a technique known as *gavage*, to produce an enlarged, rich, firm liver. Though this method sounds quite barbaric, the geese do enjoy a pleasant outdoor life on the meadows the rest of the year before induring their plight. Formerly only the geese's burden, over the last 20 years ducks have gained the upperhand of the market, as they are far easier to breed, produce a liver that is just as good (some will say better), and their delicious breasts, *magret de canard*, are also very much in demand.

Foie gras has a multitude of denominations depending on how it is prepared. The purest form is raw, sliced, and sprinkled with a pinch of the finest quality sea salt (*fleur de sel*), which, due to its stronger flavor and softer consistency, might be best left to the true connoisseurs. *Foie gras mi-cuit* (half-cooked) is one of the most delicious and popular ways to savor it. Only the best livers are kept for this method of preparation, where the whole liver is marinated, deveined, seasoned with salt and pepper, and only partially cooked so as to retain its full flavor. *Foie gras entier* (whole) is cooked further, resulting in a milder taste and firmer consistency.

Foie gras vary in quality and can be purchased either fresh or vacuum-packed. *Foie gras* entier is said to improve with age when canned. There is a large array of lesser-quality *foie gras* available on the market, going by the names *block*, *mousse*, or *truffé*. The liver in these is mixed with a variety of other ingredients, including truffles, pork fat, and chunks of liver—they are tasty but have little to do with the real thing.

FOIE GRAS POELEE

If you happen to find fresh *foie gras*, salt and pepper 1/2-inch thick filets, and pan fry for 30 seconds on each side. Then deglaze the pan with a bit of raspberry vinegar, quickly add a few fresh raspberries and the cooked *foie gras* and *serve*.

it simmering away immediately, and add your own finishing touch. For Christmas, they prepared a capon with *foie gras* and thin slices of fresh truffles carefully placed under the skin—delicious when cooked in the oven as per their instructions. We served the dish with seasonal Perigord chestnuts they supplied and enjoyed quite a feast. It went superbly with a few bottles of Clos de Mouche from the Côtes de Beaune region. We also indulged in a block of the Miolanes' refined and buttery-smooth *foie gras mi-cuit*, to serve on toast at our New Year's Eve party with bubbly champagne.

With such a selection of exquisite products at this market, you will be able to prepare the most sophisticated menu for any occasion. If you are planning an elegant dinner with an air of Nouvelle Cuisine, the very sparse and delicate spread of Thiezaurd's poultry stand, with its minuscule quail legs methodically lined up next to strips of *magret de canard*, glistening chicken livers, and plump frogs legs, is the place to shop. Each little breast is so carefully trimmed that even if you are cooking for 20, the servings will be identical. There is also a handful of very popular fish stands; our favorites are Poissonèrie Diget and Poissonèrie JPB, where they always carry a supply of oysters for *huitres a la nage*; as well as lobsters, crayfish, and crabs to boil and dip into a fresh tarragon mayonnaise; sea urchins to add to a *plateau de fruit de mer*; and an abundant selection of all the freshest fish. Adding to this the perfect vegetables and wonderful cheeses, your diners will never be at a loss.

As the market is located a short stroll from the Champs Elysées and next door to the busy Pont d'Alma (now famous after the death of Lady Di), tourists always come to admire the displays. Although some of the vendors are a bit on the grumpy side, most of them have become accustomed to these visitors. In fact, a few merchants have started warming up to them, trying out the few English phrases they have mastered, and posing for pictures. Monsieur Gremillet (*) is especially fond of tourists. To lure them into buying his tinned Lafitte *foie gras*, he enthusiastically uses the bits and pieces of whatever language he finds necessary. He has even joined the Internet craze; and, in a very un-French manner, he markets his products from the Landes region. So when you are far from Paris, *foie gras* and *cassoulet* are just a "dot com" away!

The atmosphere at the market is generally relaxed, so you often have the chance to speak to the vendors as they prepare a rack of lamb or weigh some potatoes for you. One sunny day, with the picturesque garden of the Musée Galliera in the background, we stopped to talk to a

young man standing by his jars of honeys. He told us the tale of the honey-wine he sells called "Hydromel." It appears that this blend of honey and spring water dates back to the Greek times and has a curious effect on the drinker. Resembling a sweet Muscat wine, Hydromel is generally drunk in small quantities as an aperitif, except for in the region of Brittany, where it is very popular. There, frequently, people get carried away; and instead of falling forward into a drunken stupor, Hydromel apparently triggers a nerve that makes them fall backwards! To avoid this fate, at the neighborhood cafés the well-known drinkers are roped to the side of the bar so as not to crash into the tables behind them. We never gave it a try, opting instead for a soothing jar of aromatic rosemary honey.

Not all of the products sold here provoke such a drastic effect. As you make your way through the rest of the market, alongside elegant women, with their equally patrician dogs peering over the rims of their shopping carts, and well-heeled couples buying provisions for the weekend, you will come to Les Chèvres de Saint-Vrain. Here Philippe Perette in his insignia beret and his young, sporty crew specialize in their own *artisanal* goat and hard mountain cheeses. They also offer pyramids of ash-covered *valençay*, earthy *banon* dipped in *eau de vie* and wrapped in chestnut leaves, and fig-shaped *gaperon* (a dense fresh-farmer's cheese seasoned with pepper and garlic)—all neatly placed on straw trays. Nearby, another *fromager* has a more traditional display with yogurts, eggs, cream, raw butter, wine, bread and a great array of cheeses including delicate *petit quercy* decorated with wild mulberry leaves, creamy *saint marcelins*, soft *pavé d'auge*, *pont-l'evêque*, and flavorful *tête de moine*.

A handful of *charcutiers*, including the mother-and-son team Leconte, offer hearty comestibles on their long tables: *terrines* filled with tasty

pâtés flavored with pistachios and spiked with Cognac, mousses speckled with mushrooms and green peppercorns, blood sausages, *Auvergnat* sausages, knobby *andouillettes*, and whole cooked hams. You will also be tempted by the celeriac salad, grated carrots, *museau de porc en vinaigre*, *choux farci*, and *jambon persillé*, all so typically French. One of our favorites is their delicate *œufs en gelée* (poached eggs in aspic, wrapped in ham, with fresh tarragon and red peppercorns). When you cut into the savory aspic, the yolk runs out creamy orange, making this a heavenly mouthful. To choose them, the Lecontes gently poke the top of each egg with a thumb to make sure that they are *mollet*, as the yolk should never be over-cooked.

Left: The cheese display at Les Chèvres de Saint Vrain is always outstanding.
Above: Shopping with caddies and dogs is customary in France.

Over the years, French cuisine has lightened up considerably but butter, red meat, cream, *foie gras*, and rich cheeses still make their way into the diet of most of France's population. Foreigners regularly gawk in amazement at the mostly slim and trim Parisians, while they, in turn, add inches to their waistlines as quickly as the francs leave their pockets! The secret of this scheme is moderation. The French love their delicacies but, unlike in former times, they will indulge only once in a while. Paris has been the best-stocked city for food since the Middle Ages, when merchants from the surrounding areas would bring fresh fish and oysters, barrels of wine, butter, cream, cheese, chickens, and eggs to sell on Ile de la Cité. In 1868, Paris received 10,000 tons of grapes (most probably in liquid form!), 150 tons of truffles, 1,300 tons of chicken and game, 62 tons of fresh and saltwater fish, 190 tons of oysters, 2,000 tons of eggs, and 12,000 tons of salt(!) when the population of Paris was approximately only 1.8 million, of whom maybe one quarter indulged in these specialties. With these ingredients, one can only begin to imagine the many delicacies that were prepared according to traditional methods that are still followed today. Parisians love to find their shops and markets overflowing with mouth-watering treats—whether they indulge in them or not.

So many tempting sights can be overwhelming. We often give in to the marvels, lugging home much more than we had ever planned to buy or can realistically expect to eat. Still we go right back every Saturday and buy up another storm! For those who, as the French, master the art of moderation and are not weighed down with purchases, you can travel to other wonders in the area. A coffee at the Musée d'Art Moderne bookshop can be a good stop before heading off to visit the numerous musums that fill the 16th. Besides the Modern Art and Fashion Museums

next door; and the Museum of Man and Marine Museum at Place du Trocadéro; there are also the Wine Museum, the Musée Dapper of African art, Le Corbusier Foundation, and the newly restored Musée Guimet of Asian Art, dispersed throughout the arrondissement. You may decide instead to lunch at one of the many terraces around the Pont d'Alma: Marius et Janette is a (pricey) must for fish lovers, the casual Chez André offers a leisurely bistro lunch, and Noura is an informal Lebanese restaurant where you can stand at the counter for a shwarma or enjoy a plate of mezzes on the terrace. This can be followed by envious window-shopping—or serious money-dropping—at the *haute-couture* fashion palaces that line the avenues. Alternatively, you might stroll around Place du Trocadéro and stop at Carette for a sinful chocolate macaroon.

Above: The chic Carette café on Place du Trocadéro, known for its chocolate macaroons. Right: The selection of flowers at the Président Wilson market is unbeatable.

Pivoine
La Botte
25 F.

AMIRAL BRUIX

The small Amiral Bruix market, which runs along a wide sidewalk shaded by trees, is located just off the busy roundabout Porte Maillot. Despite bordering this traffic mayhem, the atmosphere is tranquil and remote, catering mainly to the residents of the immediate area, who live in luxurious apartment buildings overlooking the Bois de Boulogne. The offerings are good and prices reasonable, but with only a dozen stands this is really just a neighborhood market where you can pop over for a bunch of flowers and a bag of cherries if you are staying nearby.

SAINT DIDIER

The small Saint Didier market, built in 1863, is housed in the only Baltard building still standing in the city today. Sadly, the metal roof is the last bit of the original structure still visible, having been covered up by bricks and mortar and stripped of its former glory. Although the vendors do their utmost to offer good quality, the atmosphere inside is pretty dismal; and the handful of vendors that set up outside along Rue Mesnil selling fruits, vegetables, flowers, and fish seem to fare far better.

Above: One of the smaller covered markets, Saint Didier. Right: Auteuil offers a pleasant, country-like atmosphere and excellent produce.

AUTEUIL

When you enter the Auteuil market, after crossing the busy Rue d'Auteuil, it seems as if you are in a village square. This is the countryside brought to Paris—if you block out the occasional honking from the cars, you might feel transported to a sunny town in Provence. You will find the same quality here as at the Président Wilson market, but with far less pomp; and as they are held on the same days of the week, we often hesitate between the two.

Colorful canopies shelter approximately 30 stands that are so tightly squeezed into the triangular market place that some of them, such as Bernard Richaudeau's apple display, tumble out into the street.

This market is absolutely bursting with fruits and vegetables. Dapper customers line up with their baskets and caddies at their favorite vendors. We are especially fond of Madame Gervais, a small, plump woman who wears a straw hat and peers over her spectacular display that is abundant and creative, with garlands of flowers twisted around the poles and little baskets holding the many different lettuces, herbs, and fruits.

Whichever direction you turn, you will find fishmongers quickly running through their stacks of salmon, tuna, and sea bass; butchers hurriedly preparing legs of lamb and trimming *côtes de bœuf*; and *fromagers* skillfully wrapping up piles of camembert, gruyère, *comté*, and yogurts to keep up with the requests of their happy customers. This is definitely a great shopping outing, worth going out of your way for.

POINT DU JOUR

This large market stretches from the Paul Reynaud square, along Avenue de Versailles, all the way to the busy roundabout Porte de Saint Cloud. Over 40 stalls line up in front of a row of shops whose displays spill out onto the sidewalk. You will find a good selection, and some nice food shops, but this is more a market to do your everyday shopping than a place to linger about. If you do come, make sure to drop by the wonderful cheese shop Ferme Sainte Suzanne, located on the square; the appetizing *charcuterie* next door; and the huge wine shop Cave Martino on Avenue de Versailles.

MARCHE COUVERT PASSY

The covered market of Passy is located in an enormous cage-like structure built in the 1950s, with high metal beams soaring above. Over 20 stands offer a variety of good quality products: fine fruit-and-vegetable stands; an Italian *traiteur* with homemade pastas, fresh mozzarella, grilled vegetables in olive oil, and other *antipasti*; a large butcher stand with excellent quality meats and poultry; several fishmongers with good selections of fresh, fresh fish; a Portuguese stand with a delectable display of *chorizos*, olives, and bottles of *Vinho Verde*; and a flower stand that opens up onto the neighboring street, Rue de l'Annonciation. If you need some bread, a tart, or a bottle of wine, continue down this pedestrian street.

GROS-LA-FONTAINE

In a very isolated part of the 16th that is difficult to get to other than on foot, the Gros-La-Fontaine market caters to a faithful and demanding clientele from the immediate area. Here you will find a number of fruit-and-vegetable vendors, cheese stands, butchers, a florist, and a fishmonger, as well as a kitchen bazaar, and a few clothes stands. This low-key weekday market offers you a peek at Parisian everyday life.

PORTE MOLITOR

The Porte Molitor market is hard to get to, as it is located on the edge of the city next to Bois de Boulogne. This is a weekday market that is not very busy, with a pleasant atmosphere and a nice selection of products. If you are planning a picnic in the park, come here and pick up some slices of ham, pâté, and *saucission* at Aux Delicieuses Cochonailles; a freshly baked *fougasse* or raisin-nut bread next door, some garden-fresh tomatoes and peaches at one of the *maraîchers*; and a *crotin de chèvre* at one of the fromagers.

Le Maraîcher

The garden farmer, Joël Thiébault, is as comfortable behind his generous display of fresh, seasonal vegetables as he is tilling the land on his family's farm. His ancestors were among the first merchants to set up at the Président Wilson market when it was founded, in 1873. In fact, he occupies the identical spot where his great-grandmother would set up her crates of garden vegetables. As a child, Joël would accompany his father, who would ride to the market on a horse-and-buggy; and Joël would fill the baskets of many of the customers who continue to be his faithful clients today.

Joël took over the reins from his mother only a few years ago. He now manages a team of 15 that is divided between the market and the farm. His stand specializes in seasonal vegetables, and differentiates itself from the others in that all of the items are heaped into towering mounds from which the customers can pick and choose. He always has a steady supply of salads, fresh herbs, and root vegetables; but he also likes to experiment with new varieties. Large, knobby, garden tomatoes were among the favorites this summer. Despite their irregular shapes and colors, his customers snatched them up to slice thinly and serve with chopped chives and olive oil. Besides large-scale production on his 23 hectares of land, Joël also develops designer strains of vegetables for chefs, such as yellow tomatoes, baby cauliflower, romanesco, broccoli rabe, white eggplant, and chili peppers.

Although his wife is not involved in the goings on at the farm, Joël claims that she is in charge of the cooking; but we have a hunch that he puts in his two cents where the destiny of his peas, beets, and broccoli is concerned !

Joël Thiébault is present only at the Président Wilson market

FLEURS DE COURGETTE A L'ITALIENNE
Crispy Fried Zucchini Flowers

We often enjoy this recipe during the summer months, when zucchini flowers make their appearance at the markets. Although they are still considered a delicacy in France, some *maraîchers*, such as Joël Thiébault, have whole fields covered with them. He cuts them one by one and arranges them in a separate crate that he carries in the front of the truck with him so that they don't get too jostled. Below, you will find his simple recipe for deep-frying them, with an Italian touch added by a friend of ours. Their delicate flavor is enhanced by the luxurious texture of melted mozzarella, the discrete bite of anchovies, and the sweetness of basil. Fried with a light, Japanese, tempura-style batter, these crunchy flowers compose a delicious hors d'oeuvres to accompany a glass of chilled white wine.

15 minutes 5 minutes

12 zucchini flowers
1/2 a mozzarella
3 anchovy fillets (or anchovy paste)
6 fresh basil leaves
Peanut oil, for deep-frying
1 cup (180 g) flour
1/2 cup ice cold water
Salt and pepper, to taste

1. It is best to use the flowers on the day you purchase them, as they are very delicate. Snip the stems of the zucchini flowers, leaving about 1-inch (2.5 cm) of stem; and remove the pistil from the center of the flower. No washing is necessary. Set aside. **2.** Cut mozzarella into 1/2-inch (1.5 cm) strips; quarter the anchovy fillets; and tear the basil leaves in half. **3.** Wrap strips of mozzarella and pieces of anchovy in the basil leaves. Gently open the zucchini flowers, carefully place the cheese-and-basil roll inside the flower, and twist the tip of the flower to hold the stuffing. Set aside. (If you wish, you can prepare these beforehand, and keep in the refrigerator.) **4.** Put the peanut oil in a high-sided pot, and heat over a medium-high flame until very hot. **5.** Gradually whisk together the sifted flour with ice cold water until you have a homogeneous batter that is quite liquid. Add a pinch of salt and a twist of pepper. **6.** Dip the stuffed flowers in the batter so as to coat them completely. Deep-fry them in the oil until golden brown, approximately 5 minutes. Place on a paper towel to absorb the excess oil; and serve. **Serves 4 (3 per person).**

Note: If you are preparing this recipe for many people, you can precook these ahead of time, deep-frying them for 3 minutes; and before serving, refrying them for less than a minute—be vigilant, because they brown very quickly at this stage.

Dry, crisp, citrusy whites: Sauvignon Blanc, Pouilly Fumé, Sancerre

ROTI DE VEAU AUX CAROTTES DOUCES
Veal Roast with Sweet Carrots

Jean Allain suggests that you bard and tie the veal roast to prevent it from drying out while cooking. Another pointer is to place a sheet of wax paper larger than the size of the lid underneath the cover of the pot, so as to keep the moisture within and to assure a juicy and tender roast.

15 minutes — 1 1/4 hours

1 tbs olive oil
3 lbs (1.5 kg) veal roast
1 tbs butter
6 carrots, halved and quartered
10 shallots
Salt and pepper, to taste
1 rosemary sprig
1 thyme sprig
1 bay leaf
1/2 cup water
Chopped parsley, for garnish

1. In a Dutch oven or heavy-bottomed pot with a matching lid, heat the oil over medium-high heat, and brown the roast on all sides. Remove to a plate, and pour off the fat from the pan, discarding any burned bits. Scrape the bottom if necessary, and wipe clean with a paper towel. Return the pan to the burner, and reduce the heat. Add the butter, and sauté the carrots and shallots for 4 minutes, making sure not to brown them. **2.** Salt and pepper the roast and place on top of the vegetables. Add the rosemary and thyme sprigs, the bay leaf, and the water. Reduce heat to low, and cook covered with a sheet of wax paper sealed beneath the lid. Cook for 1 1/4 hours, turning the roast and gently stirring the vegetables once. **3.** Discard the herbs, remove the roast to a cutting board, and carve into 1/2-inch (1 1/2 cm) slices. Arrange on a serving dish, and surround with the shallots and carrots. Strain the juices over the roast, sprinkle with parsley, and serve with boiled new potatoes or wild rice. **Serves 6.**

Delicate, full-bodied reds: Pauillac, Volnay, Brouilly

TIMBALE DE CRABE ET RATATOUILLE
Ratatouille and Crab Timbale

This fresh salad is a perfect and elegant appetizer. The ratatouille is cooked in several steps so as to keep the vegetables firm. Each ingredient is prepared and cooked separately, then combined to make a delicate ratatouille. This dish is best eaten ice-cold; it should be prepared ahead of time so that you can chill it in the refrigerator for a couple of hours.

30 minutes — 15 minutes

1 cup (250 g) lump crabmeat (or 2 whole crabs)
1/4 cup olive oil
1/4 cup sunflower oil
1 garlic clove, whole
1/4 cup (60 g) diced zucchini
1/4 cup (60 g) diced yellow squash
1 small onion, finely chopped
1/4 cup (60 g) diced eggplant
1/4 cup (60 g) diced red pepper
1/4 cup (60 g) diced orange pepper
1/4 cup (60 g) diced green pepper
2 tomatoes, peeled, seeded, and chopped
2 tbs lemon juice
Salt and pepper, to taste
2 tbs slivered fresh basil leaves
Toasted slices of baguette
Basil flowers, for garnish

1. If you are cooking the crab, prepare a *court bouillon* and simmer the whole crab in it for approximately 20 minutes. Let cool, and shell the crab. Put the crabmeat in a bowl and refrigerate. If you buy it, make sure that it is good quality white meat. **2.** Combine the olive and sunflower oils in a cup, and set aside. **3.** Put two tablespoons of oil and the garlic clove in a small sauté pan. Heat the oil over a medium flame, add the zucchini and yellow squash, and sauté for approximately 5 minutes, turning gently, until the squash is cooked but firm. Place in a bowl, keeping the garlic clove in the pan. **4.** Repeat the above procedure for the onions, the eggplant, and the three peppers; add each cooked ingredient to the bowl containing the cooked squash. **5.** Lower heat, add a tablespoon of olive oil and the chopped, peeled tomatoes. Cook 3 minutes to make a sauce. Add the other vegetables, stir, and cook for an additional 5 minutes. Cool to room temperature and place in refrigerator. **6.** When cold, combine the crabmeat with 1 1/2 cups ratatouille. The mixture should have a nice pink color but should not be too runny. Season with lemon juice, salt, and pepper to taste. Before serving, mix in the slivered basil leaves. To serve, pack a small cup or timbale mold with the crab salad, and turn over onto the plate. Decorate with 3 or 4 slices of toast and the basil flowers, and serve. **Serves 4.**

Dry, fruity whites: Sancerre, Pouilly Fumé, Sauvignon Blanc

Timbale de crabe et ratatouille

BŒUF BOURGUIGNON
Beef Stew Simmered in Burgundy Wine

This classic of all classics is still one of our favorites. Whenever we make it for a party, even in these non-meat-eating times, our guests still enthusiastically serve themselves—even if only to soak up the sauce and sugary onions with the boiled potatoes. There are many variations on the basic recipe: some people like to marinate the meat, others dust each piece with flour; some like to use Burgundy wine, and others Bordeaux. We found the recipe of Christian Gardy, from the Président Wilson market, much to our liking.

30 minutes 3 hours

For bœuf bourguignon:
4 oz (125 g) thick bacon, cut in strips
3 lbs (1.5 kg) stewing beef, cut in 2-inch (5 cm) cubes (chuck, rump, or round are best)
2 onions, sliced
2 carrots, sliced
2 tbs flour
1 bottle red wine, Bordeaux or Burgundy
2 cups beef stock
1 lb mushrooms
2 tbs olive oil
1 clove garlic, crushed
1 lb (500 g) baby onions
2 tbs butter
2 tbs sugar
3 lbs (1.5 kg) boiled, peeled potatoes
Chopped parsley, for garnish

1. In a large casserole, brown the bacon. Remove pieces from pan and set aside. In the same oil, brown the meat on all sides. Do this in batches—do not cook the meat, just brown the sides. Set aside in a separate bowl. **2.** Once you have finished browning the meat, in the same casserole sauté the onions and carrots. When they are glistening, add the bacon and meat, and mix together. Sprinkle the flour on top, and mix well to coat the meat. Add the bottle of wine, and cover. **3.** Strain the beef stock, and add to the meat. Cover, bring to a simmer, lower the heat, and allow to cook at least two hours, stirring every once in a while, assuring that the bottom is not sticking and skimming off any fat that rises to the top. **4.** Meanwhile, wash and quarter the mushrooms. Sauté them in a small pan, with some olive oil and garlic if you wish. Remove from heat and set aside. **5.** In a saucepan, parboil the baby onions with their skin on, in a drop of water, for a minute or two. This will facilitate the peeling. Once peeled, melt the butter in a saucepan, coat the onions, mix in the sugar, cover, and cook for 20 minutes over a low flame. Remove from heat and set aside. **6.** When the *bourguignon* is almost ready—the meat should be tender and the sauce should coat the back of a spoon—stir in the mushrooms and baby onions, and adjust the seasoning. Garnish with chopped parsley and serve with plain boiled potatoes. **Serves 6 to 8**.

Rustic, coarse, full-bodied reds: Gevrey-Chambertin, Pomerol

TARTE AU CITRON
Lemon Curd Tart

Lemon tarts are exquisite—the mixture of tangy lemon custard in a fine crumbly crust is a perfect combination. The dough is very buttery, so if you find that it is sticking too much to your rolling pin or table, try rolling it out between two pieces of plastic wrap. Once you have achieved the proper size, peel off the top sheet, and flip the dough into the tart mold. Pat into shape, and remove the remaining piece of plastic wrap. This is a good trick to use with doughs that are hard to work.

1 1/2 hours 35 minutes

For the tart crust:
3.5 oz (100 g) butter
3 tbs confectioners' sugar
1/2 a beaten egg
1/2 a vanilla bean (or 1 tsp vanilla extract)
1 pinch salt
1 cup (180 g) flour
1 tbs ground almonds

For the lemon custard:
2 eggs
3 egg yolks
7 oz (200 g) sugar
1 cup lemon juice (approximately 5 lemons) including the juice of half an orange added to soften the bite
4 oz (125 g) sweet butter

1 tbs grated lemon rind, for garnish

10-inch (25 cm) tart mold

1. Combine the butter, sugar, 1/2 beaten egg, and vanilla; mix well with a wooden spoon until you obtain a smooth paste. Add the salt, flour, and almonds; and knead together, making sure not to overwork the dough. Roll into a ball, and place on a sheet of plastic wrap. Flatten out with a rolling pin to the size of a pancake. Cover with another sheet of plastic wrap, and refrigerate for at least 1 hour. **2.** Meanwhile, in a large bowl, whisk together the eggs, egg yolks, and 4 tablespoons of the sugar until the mixture is creamy and light in color. Set aside. **3.** In a thick-bottomed saucepan, heat the lemon and orange juice, butter, and remaining sugar over a low flame, until the butter starts to bubble. Remove from heat, and slowly incorporate it into the egg mixture, whisking all the while. **4.** Pour the custard mixture back into the saucepan, stirring continuously; and heat until it just begins to boil. Cook for 3 minutes, stirring continuously. Remove from heat, and pour into a bowl. Allow to cool before refrigerating. **5.** In the meantime, roll out the dough with a bit of flour (or if necessary between two sheets of plastic wrap). Place in a buttered tart mold, prick the bottom with a fork, and refrigerate again for 1/2 hour. **6.** Heat the oven to 400 °F (205 °C). Weigh down the tart mold with a sheet of wax paper filled with beans, so that the dough does not rise while you prebake it. Bake for 10 to 12 minutes, then remove the paper and beans and bake for a further 8 minutes.
7. Lower the oven temperature to 350 °F (180 °C). Fill the precooked tart shell with the custard. Bake for 15 minutes. Remove from oven, sprinkle with grated lemon rind, and allow to cool before refrigerating. Refrigerate for approximately 3 hours until the custard sets. Leave at room temperature 15 minutes before serving. **Serves 8 to 10**.

The 17th arrondissement is an enormous *quartier* with very little happening. It is primarily a residential area that takes up most of the northwestern section of Paris, from the Arc de Triomphe to beyond the railroad tracks of Gare Saint Lazare. On one side, you will find a sedate, bourgeois neighborhood with regal buildings and ample boulevards; on the other, bordering the red-light district of Clichy, a more urban region with narrower streets and less-imposing architecture. In the late 1800s, at the time of its founding, this area was a

XVII[e] ARRONDISSEMENT

center of change, creativity, and growth. Baron Haussmann was busy excavating and constructing a modern arrondissement; the brothers Pereire were laying down the first railroad tracks of Paris; and painters, inspired by the novel landscape, gave birth to a new movement called "Impressionism." Today, by comparison, the 17th is a sleepy, residential part of town. Oddly enough, it is also the site of the forward-looking Batignolles organic market, which is anything but stagnant, attracting people from all over the city.

The railroad tracks of Gare Saint Lazare lie at the center of the 17th arrondissement, just a block away from the colorful Batignolles organic market.

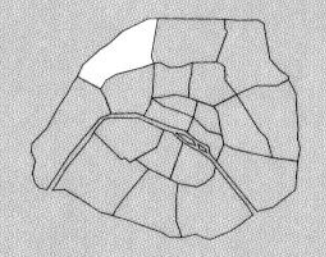

MARCH BIOLOGIQUE DES BATIGNOLLES
TOUS LES SAMEDIS MATIN

encourageons l'agriculture BIOLOGIQUE
respecte l'ENVIRONNEMENT et la SANTE
ne force pas la NATURE
n'emploie pas les PESTICIDES
répond à une DEMANDE
une VRAIE ALIMENTATION riche en FIBRES et VITAMINES
rotations annuelles de LEGUMES VERTS sélectionnés
principes de la BIODYNAMIE
la VIE du sol
semis... ENTRETIEN
PROTECTION
en saison, les DONS de la NATURE
TOUT FRAIS DU JARDIN
J.P. BOURVEN
VENTE A LA FERME
31 rue de neuville
HAMeau des étangs
95 CERGY

A RAILROAD TO GREENER PASTURES

The Batignolles Organic Market

The picturesque Marché Biologique Batignolles, with its leafy trees hovering above, will remind you of a country square. Although it is the offspring of the very popular Marché Raspail, that trendy scene is not in evidence here. Located in a quiet, low-key neighborhood, this market invites you to spend the entire morning wandering about discovering its secrets. You may find out how best to prepare purple-tipped *poivrade* artichokes, or the combination of herbal teas that will ensure the soundest sleep, or what type of lentils you should use for a refreshing salad. The smaller of the two organic markets of Paris, Batignolles is favored by the dedicated organic-food shoppers who want to avoid the crowd on the Left Bank yet require an equivalent selection and quality. Despite being founded as recently as 1994, its popularity is firmly established.

The Batignolles market is generously spread out along the central promenade of Boulevard des Batignolles, in the eastern part of the 17th arrondissement. In the 1800s, Baron Haussmann transformed this agricultural and hunting ground into a modern residential area, with wide boulevards lined with trees and majestic sandstone apartment buildings paving the way to the city center. The bourgeoisie adopted this new development surrounding Parc Monceau and Place de l'Etoile. The already-established eastern section, demarcated by wide railroad tracks, remained home to the working class. The face and character of this quarter has not really changed; it is still quiet and residential.

The sparse central divider of Boulevard des Batignolles is transformed every Saturday by the bustling organic Batignolles market.

As you approach the market, from a distance you will notice a wide banner attached to the trees announcing "Marché Biologique Batignolles." Two squares lined with approximately 40 stands selling organically grown products make up the body of this market, which has an unhurried and spacious feel. The entrance is colorful, with a row of stands displaying homegrown and imported fruits and vegetables. Colombian bananas, Corsican citrus fruits, Spanish strawberries, and Italian kumquats complement the local plump beets, red and green rhubarb, clouds of cauliflower, and rounds of white celery root.

Walking through the aisles, you will be surrounded by tantalizing sights that make it hard to know where to go first. You may want to start on the right, where a farmer sets up her stand of different farm-fresh products every week. Some days she brings apple tarts or pound cakes or cookies, which she bakes the night before; other days, a few trays of very fresh eggs, or blocks of butter wrapped in cheesecloth, or pots of thick *crème fraiche*, or, on occasion, a veal roast, a chicken or two, or a basket of apples. Across from her, the *traiteur* from Raspail, "Madame Annie," has an elaborate display of her prepared salads, quiches, soups, and pastries on a long table topped with teas and honey. In this section, there is also a stand that sells only organic fish, which means not bred in captivity, not treated with artificial coloring nor preservatives, and never frozen. Even the cracked ice used to chill these silvery gems is said to be untreated. This might seem a bit extreme, but at least you will be assured of enjoying fresh local fish, such as wild salmon or river trout, caught at the break of dawn, uncontaminated —and priced accordingly!

Père & Fils

In the center of the square, you will be drawn to one of the largest displays at the market, run by four young entrepreneurs who buy their goods directly from over 30 suppliers at the wholesale market, Rungis. Theirs is a favored *métier* for the new generation; those unable to find work in traditional circles find the flexibility and independence of working at roving markets very attractive. Low tables form a U-shape, behind which Mario, Tarik, Vanessa, and Mickey dash about serving their faithful customers from baskets of white asparagus that spill out next to piles of slim *haricots verts* and vine-ripened tomatoes. Tarik sold us a selection of delicate *chervil* mixed with baby spinach, red Belgian endive, arugula, and the reddish-brown rougette, which we tossed with a few tablespoons of good olive oil, a dash of walnut oil, a spoonful of vinegar, and salt and pepper, to make the perfect green salad!

Farther along, there is a stand selling 100% cotton clothing in various earthy shades, dyed naturally of course—nice and comfortable but also nice and pricey. Next you'll see a bucket of long stalks of fresh aloe which when cut open produce a rich clear gel used to heal burns and cuts, and to nurture hair and skin.

As you browse, you may hear a lost poet reciting his newest compositions. Then you may discover that he is the husband of the charming woman from whom you bought a crêpe at the Raspail market. Thérèse and Michel Beucher come to this market every week to sell traditional Normandy style crêpes, as well as home-pressed organic cider and Calvados, made from the fruits of the orchard that they have been tending in Normandy for over 20 years. If you are a fan of sparkling cider, you should have a chat with Michel, and try a few bottles from his selection. You will quickly appreciate the world of cider by having a taste of the different harvests. The 1997 might be fruitier and more alcoholic, with a golden honey color, while the 1996 may have a stronger citrus flavor and be a lighter shade of blond. Like it or not, Michel will have a poem for every sip, and you may find that you will have to abandon him in mid-verse!

This market is a pleasant surprise for those who like to sleep in. Unlike other weekend markets, you will not have to elbow your way through crowds to get the last liter of milk or tray of eggs for your brunch.

STATUE OF LIBERTY

The 17th arrondissement was the birthplace of the magnificent sculpture that graces Bedloe's Island, the Statue of Liberty—one of New York City's most famous landmarks. Frédérique-Auguste Bartholdi sculpted and cast the massive hand and torch in his atelier and foundry near Parc Monceau, with the help of Gustave Eiffel (best known for the eponymous tower). The statue took shape to the awe of the neighborhood, who applauded its appearance (head and hand only) at Paris' Universal Exhibition in 1878. The 200-ton lady was finally completed in 1884.

Originally, the statue was to tower above the entrance of the Suez Canal but the funds for the endeavor were insufficient and its destiny was decided otherwise. The Statue of Liberty sailed across the Atlantic Ocean and was assembled in New York as the tardy but splendid gift from the French to commemorate the United States' first centenary. Its torch is a symbol meant to light the way for new arrivals who come to America in search of greener pastures.

Organic farmers are cultivating a wider range of fruits and vegetables as the demand increases.

You will come across elderly ladies pulling shopping carts with their Sunday dinner carefully packed away, young parents carrying overloaded baskets while pushing prams and collecting wandering toddlers, and connoisseurs who travel from other parts of Paris to take advantage of this market's specialties. The displays are always abundant and never seem to run out, which is probably because the vendors are well stocked in preparation for the Raspail market the following day.

When you cross the small street to the other square, you will encounter a colorful fruit stand where the vendors wear red-and-white-striped aprons and straw hats. Their display is different from the others as they do not set up tables but instead build walls with crates of either strawberries, mangoes, avocados, or melons, depending on the season. There is also a wall display of over 30 varieties of marmalades, jams, and jellies, of which a selection is available for you to taste on slices of delicious whole wheat bread from the adjacent bakery. Madame Corvaisier at La Ferme de la Metairie makes her preserves with over 60% fruit, concocting interesting combinations such as banana-rhubarb, carrot-orange, and kiwi-pineapple; as well as traditional flavors such as raspberry, orange, and apricot; and unusual ones such as quince, red tomato, and fig. We vouch for the lime and wild blueberry, which we enjoyed on our morning toast.

The clarity of light filtering through the trees of the market here has been celebrated since the days when this part of Paris was home to many Impressionist painters, among them the famous Edouard Manet. This eastern part of the 17th arrondissement, known as "Le Village des Batignolles," was appreciated for its juxtaposition of modern and traditional. The newly laid railroad tracks and accompanying station offered the painters new subject matter, while also being a means of escape from the city center to the nearby fields and forests of Saint-Germain-En-Laye. The neighborhood was filled with inexpensive spaces for ateliers and bars, such as the Café Guerbois, whose gardens and terraces provided a place to gather and engage in heated discussions. The Impressionist movement is actually credited as having originated at this popular café. Only a few blocks away from here, Manet painted his masterpiece *Le Chemin de Fer*, depicting romantic figures in a modern setting.

An array of vintage sparkling ciders is available to taste at Thérese and Michel Beucher's Normandy specialty stand.

ORGANIC ≠ VEGETARIAN

Agriculture biologique, the term referring to organic production in France, is not synonymous with vegetarian but instead only refers to the way that food is produced, that is to say in the most natural and chemical-free way possible.
The classical eating habits of the French remain the same, and the organic market will have the same assortment of foods that are available at ordinary markets.
You will find butchers with pork, beef, and lamb; *volaillers* with chickens, ducks, and rabbits; *charcutiers* with *pâtés*, hams, sausages, and bacon; cheese vendors with *camemberts*, *roqueforts*, and *chèvres*; bakers with chocolate eclairs, croissants, and baguettes; winemakers with red, white, and rosé wines; *epiciers* with oils, coffees, dried fruits, and grains; and a wide selection of fruits and vegetables.
The only differences you might see on the surface are the elevated prices, as all of the ingredients used to make these natural specialties have to be organically produced and cultivated.

Above: *Comté* is one of the more popular cheeses in France, it can be bought at different stages of maturity from 3 to 12 months. Right: Preparing crêpes at the market using a traditional paddle to spread them out and make them as thin as possible. Bottom: Potato and carrot pancakes are a favorite snack to nibble on at the organic markets in Paris.

Since the outbreak of "mad-cow" disease, the lines at organic butchers have multiplied; Parisians now wait up to 20 minutes to buy their much-cherished steaks and veal chops. Monsieur Lessieu, a pioneer in the organic butcher trade, generally sets up his stand on the far left-hand corner of the second square. Since 1975, long before the *AB* denomination was established, he has been raising livestock in a chemical- and hormone-free environment on his ranch in the green valleys of the Perche region, due west of Paris. At all of the organic markets in and around Paris, Monsieur Lessieu sells beef and veal of his own production; as well as lamb and pork from neighboring organic farmers; and a selection of homemade pâtés, sausages, hams, and salamis. Meat sold at organic butchers is generally of superior quality, with a full flavor and prices that are comparable to other high-quality meats sold at local butchers.

Nearby, look for Henri Martin, a hefty man wrapped in a big white apron, who sells the best eggs in the market. He prides himself for vending a rare variety distinguishable by its speckled, deep-brown shell and its rich dark-orange yolk. These eggs are laid by the *poules de maranes*, an ancient breed of hens from Charente. They are scrumptious and best eaten *à la coque*. You will also find a few chickens, goat cheeses, and mounds of creamy, raw butter that Monsieur Martin sells by the pound. He is always jovial, and he loves to converse about his very special eggs. As you are strolling past the various stands, you might catch a whiff of incense from Claire's Les Encens Divins. If you are suffering from anxiety attacks, tell her your woes and she will gladly explain how to create a tranquil atmosphere in your home using an ancient method of burning incense by smoldering traditional mixtures of spices on miniature charcoal burning lamps. Or have a chat with Madame Jacquinet, who will help you select some herbal teas to assuage whatever the incense cannot heal. If these do not suffice, and you want to be cured from the inside out, there is an *epicerie* that has an enormous display of every type of dried and processed organic food imaginable: lentils, rice, peas, linseed, azuki beans, kasha, bulgar wheat, chickpeas, dried herbs,

Above: Legumes and fresh goat cheeses are among the selection at Batignolles.
Right: Henri Martin is most definitely a fan of his farm fresh Poules de Maranes eggs.

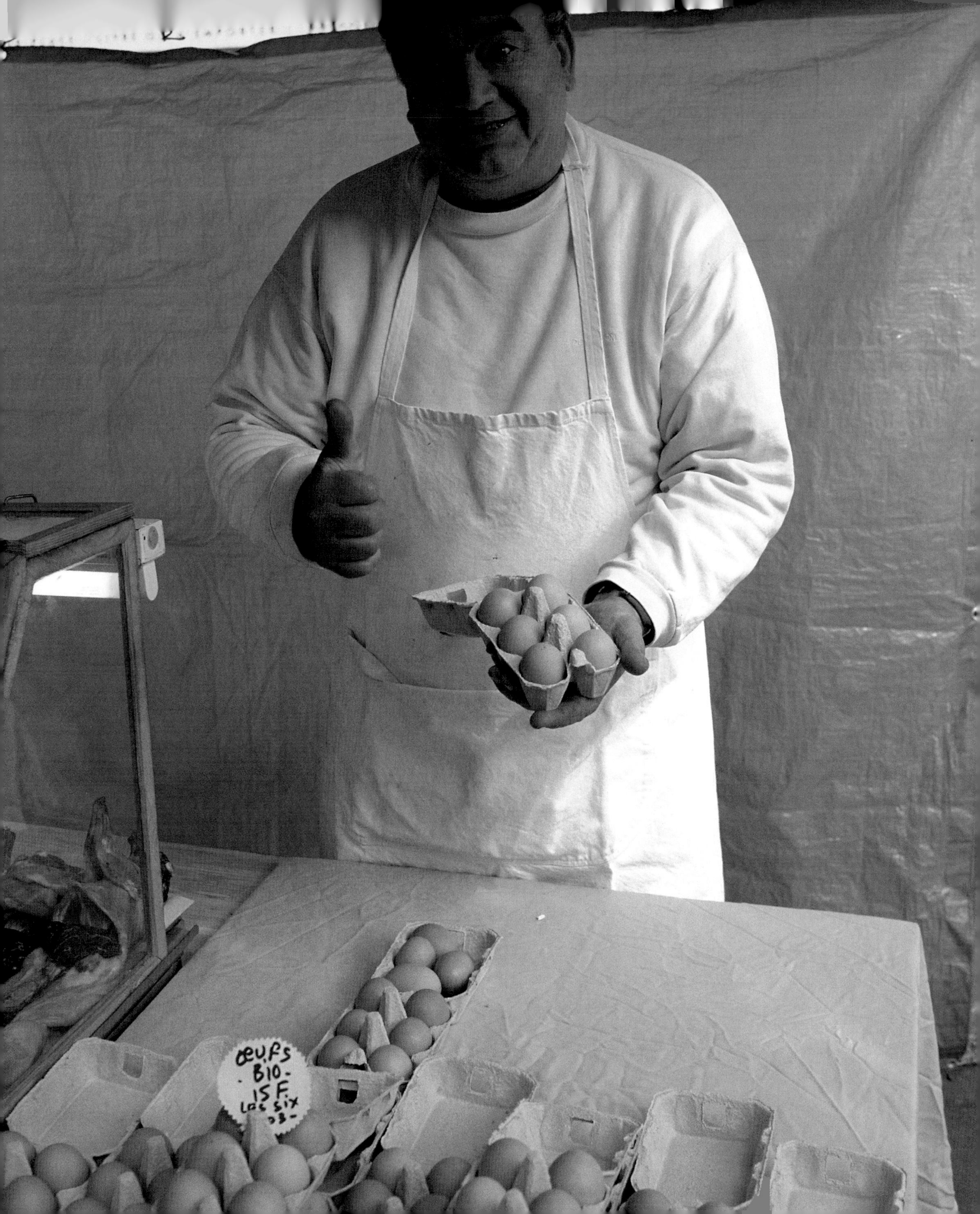
œufs
- BIO -
15 F.
Les six

spices, seaweed, soy milk, soy cheeses, soy patties, coffees, teas, oils, and an array of untreated dried fruits and nuts. There are products from all over the world, and it is a good place to discover new ingredients. Olivier and his team will readily explain how to cook and prepare pitch-black Thai rice, orange lentils, or quinoa, and advise you what to eat them with, and why! We have come across devotees who make pilgrimages here to track down the latest bean, share recipes and book recommendations, and discuss the attributes of eating the different grains.

As you cross back to the first square, visit La Ferme de la Table au Roy on the corner, piled with yogurts, milk, and the best selection of cheeses in the market. Although the organic markets offer the basic types of cheeses—such as goat, brie, camembert, roquefort and some hard cheeses such as *comté*, emmentaler and *cantal*—there is not an extensive variety here. As cheese production in France is very regimented, and the laws surrounding cheese making are as strict as the laws surrounding organic production, we believe that many cheeses in France could easily be approved for the *AB* denomination. But most cheese makers are not interested in joining the *AB* association; hence the limited selection at the organic markets.

Back at the starting point, take a moment to taste some of the organic wine that Monique and Paul Giboulot have been making since 1970 at their vineyard near Beaune in the Burgundy region. Next door, Paul's son, Henri-Jean, sells vegetables that he grows in plots adjacent to his father's vineyard. The tasty Charolais beef that this dedicated family raises is also available at this market, from the Boucherie Bessier.

If you would like to linger in this village atmosphere—if you are not too laden down with purchases—walk to the church of Sainte Marie a few blocks away. Wander down the shop-lined Rue des Batignolles, once the address of the Impressionist painter Edouard Manet, until you reach the church. There you can stop for a drink or lunch at the restaurant, Le Jardin d'Isa, on the left-hand side of this charming square. Browse the antique shops scattered about, before relaxing in the beautiful gardens of Square des Batignolles tucked away behind the church, a haven of greenery and multicolored flowers. If you still have the urge to do a little more food shopping, the market street Rue Levis is only a few blocks due west; there you will find some nice *traiteur* and *charcuterie* shops.

Above: Les Encens Divins offers an ancient way of burning incense that seems to attract even the youngest shoppers. Pebble-like pieces of incense are placed on a burning lamp to release their healing and aromatic properties. Right: All-natural soaps made from a base of olive or almond oil come in many fragrances.

UN DON DU CIEL
LES COPEAUX
SAVON DE MARSEILLE
SAINTE FAMILLE

Haricot Verts
le kilo 60
Cerises Van
le kilo 28
Champignons
le kilo 60
Très Sucrés

RUE LEVIS

Rue Levis is a bustling street market that runs along a pedestrian way, only a few blocks away from the organic market Batignolles, in the residential 17th arrondissement. Though the fruits and vegetables are by far not as farm-fresh as one will find at the *Bio* market, Rue Levis is graced with some excellent shops. The *charcuterie* Schmid Levis specializes in delicacies from Alsace; the *traiteur* Ballereau sets up a table with steaming trays of prepared dishes such as *bœuf bourguignon*, *paella* and *coquelet au fenouil*; and the cheese shop J. Carmes et Fils has an abundant display set up on wine kegs that spill out onto the cobblestone lane. Several bakeries, butchers, florists, and a lovely old shop selling fresh-roasted coffees make this market street complete.

BERTHIER

In this out-of-the-way neighborhood that borders the periphery of the city, this market sets up in the middle of a playground and offers basic, everyday products for the inhabitants of the adjacent buildings. The atmosphere is convivial, and despite feeling a bit isolated from the rest of Paris, you can casually go about your shopping. There is not much variety; but the displays are attractive, the quality is good, and the prices are right. However, unless you happen to be right next door, it is not a must.

MARCHE COUVERT BATIGNOLLES

Having originally been a beautiful structure of glass and iron built by the architect Baltard in 1867, the covered market of Batignolles is a great disappointment. The fabulous *verrière* was torn down and replaced in 1979 by an ugly brick building of several stories. The market is crammed into the ground floor, with artificial lighting and Muzak attempting to bring some life to this otherwise dreary place. Approximately 20 stalls struggle to survive, offering an average selection of meat, cheese, fruits, and vegetables, with the fish and Portuguese stands being the best of the lot. It is certainly not worth a detour!

NAVIER

If you are committed to see every corner of Paris and find yourself in this part of town, come visit this tiny market. You will find about a dozen stands selling very nice produce. You might be pleasantly surprised by this friendly and very French market, as the surrounding neighborhood is anything but appealing. One senses that the clientele rush out to the market every Tuesday and Friday to stock up for the next three days on fresh eggs and chickens, beautifully prepared *magrets de canard*, a couple of *chevaline tournedos*, a filet of sole, along with a sweet-smelling melon, some white asparagus, and a ripe camembert.

Left: A luscious display of summer fruits and vegetables at Batignolles.
Right: Scallops, *coquilles Saint Jacques*, are sold in their shell with the roe attached.

RUE PONCELET

Off the very busy Avenue des Ternes, a fruit-and-vegetable stand juts out to attract the hurried pedestrians. A display of oranges, grapefruits, and strawberries lures the clients into this busy market street that is concentrated on Rue Bayon and Rue Poncelet. An enormous fish shop, Daguerre Marée, complete with tanks and bountiful displays of fish and shellfish, takes up one whole side of Rue Bayon.

Down Rue Poncelet, you will be swarmed by fruit and vegetable shops that offer average produce at rather high prices. A small *chevaline* butcher, recognizable by the sculpted horse head mounted above the entrance, stands next to the enormous Boucherie Roger.

The main attractions are the bakery Paul, which has a trolley set up in front with tempting baguettes, tarts, and *brioches*; Brulerie de Ternes, which roasts its coffee on the premises; the cheese shop, Alléosse, which offers an excellent selection of cheeses that are aged to perfection in the cellars; and the delicatessen, Stubli, which has Nordic specialties ranging from *weisswurst* to *strudel* which can be eaten there or taken away.

MARCHE COUVERT DE TERNES

Despite being one of Paris' oldest covered markets, built in 1852, the *marché couvert* de Ternes is trapped beneath a 1970s architectural disaster. Stands vending an array of meat, poultry, cheese, and dairy products; a Portuguese specialty shop; a few fruit-and-vegetable stalls; and an unimpressive fish stand make up the offerings at this market. Sadly, neither the bit of sunlight that makes its way in, nor the vendors' efforts, nor the row of food shops on the adjacent pedestrian street, Rue Lebon, manage to get this market off the ground. The nearby Rue Poncelet is a much more charming place to do your everyday shopping.

La Patissière

With a carload of buckwheat specialties, the Chauvels travel over 280 miles (450 kilometers) every weekend, from their farm on the border of Brittany, to attend two of Paris' markets to sell their homemade pastries. On a small table draped with a red-and-white checkered cloth, they carefully arrange stacks of buckwheat crêpes, as well as *blinis*, loaves of bread, buttery apple tarts, thick custards, jars of apple jelly and pumpkin jam, and satchels of flour. Well into their 70s, this couple is very determined: even in the dead of winter, bundled in hand-knitted cardigans and heavy wool coats, they stand patiently warming their hands over their crêpe griddle, waiting for the next customer to come along for a hot *galette au sarrasin* smeared with butter.

Once a week, Basil climbs up the wooden ladder to the barn's attic and fills two big buckets with buckwheat. He grinds it in a flint-stone mill and sifts the flour, separating the different grinds. Madeleine then puts the sorted grinds into little, hand-sewn bags which she later uses for baking her cakes, breads, and *blinis*. Come Friday after lunch, the two of them load the car and head for Paris, arriving by nightfall at their second appartment in the center of town. Madeleine immediately sets about making *sarrasin galettes*, 120 in all. She is joined by Basil, who plops down next to the stove to keep her company and dine on piping hot crêpes.

Madeleine met Basil, the son of a miller, while she was working on her parents' farm over half a century ago. Four children down the road, they still occupy the same house in which Madeleine was born. Fifteen years ago, the Chauvels retired, and their son Edouard followed in their footsteps to become the 11th generation of agriculturists. It was his initiative to plant buckwheat that triggered Madeleine and Basil's enterprise of selling the ancient grain in the city. *Sarrasin* (buckwheat) was first introduced to Europe in the 1600s; over the centuries, it was used to make sustaining porridges or breads when mixed with white flour. Nowadays, most of the buckwheat in France is imported; the Chauvels are among the few to keep this dwindling tradition alive.

After all these years, this energetic couple never seems to tire. Once the throngs of shoppers have subsided, at the end of a busy weekend, they pack up—taking with them all the remaining cakes, breads, and *galettes* which they have conscientiously saved to feed to their very lucky pig—and embark on the long trip back home.

The Chauvels are present at the Port Royal and Place Monge markets.

MARKET RECIPES

CREPES AU SARRASIN
Sweet or Salty Buckwheat Crêpes

Madeleine Chauvel shared her crêpe recipe with us so that you can make them at home although she swears they will not have the same flavor if you do not use her stone-ground flour. Crêpes au sarrasin are considered to be healthier (and heavier!) than the more common white-flour crêpes but they are eaten the same way. They can be generously spread with jam or honey, or warmed with grated cheese, ham, or an egg. They will keep a couple of days in the refrigerator and can be re-heated in a pan with a bit of butter and then garnished with your ingredient of choice.

1 1/4 hours   30 minutes

2 cups (250 g) *sarrasin* (buckwheat) flour
1 egg yolk
2 1/2 cups water
1 egg white
Pinch of salt and pepper
2 tsp white flour
2 tsp peanut oil

Butter for the pan

1. In a large bowl, mix the *sarrasin* flour together with the egg yolk and the water, until smooth. **2.** In a separate bowl, whisk the egg white to a peak with a pinch of salt and pepper. Slowly add in the 2 tablespoons of white flour and the oil. **3.** Fold the egg whites into the buckwheat mixture, and add a little bit more water if necessary. The crêpe batter should be fluid. Cover the bowl with a dish towel and let stand for at least 1 hour. **4.** Heat a crêpe pan or non-stick skillet over medium-high heat. If the batter has thickened too much, add a bit more water; it should pour easily. Add a bit of butter to the pan (make sure it does not burn), and pour a ladle full of batter into the pan, tilting to and fro so as to spread the batter evenly. A flat-tipped wooden spatula comes in handy to help even out the crêpe. Cook for 3 to 4 minutes, flip, and cook for another 3 to 4 minutes. Remove onto plate, and keep warm. Continue making them until the batter is finished. To serve, reheat the crêpes in a pan, spread with butter and jam; roll; and eat! Or while still in the pan, sprinkle with ham, cheese, or whatever you fancy; fold in half; heat for 3 minutes; and serve. **Makes about 12 crêpes.**

Dry sparkling cider

PAVE DE SAUMON AVEC SALADE DE LENTILLES
Poached Salmon with "Puy" Lentils

This light summer dish is usually served tepid, but can easily be made ahead of time and served cold. This recipe calls for the small, green, Puy lentils but you can substitute whatever lentil you choose.

10 minutes   45 minutes

1 cup (250 g) Puy lentils
Water to more than cover
1 tsp salt
1 carrot, peeled and chopped
1 small onion, chopped
1 large garlic clove, chopped
1 *bouquet garni*
Slivers of bacon (optional)
1 tbs Dijon mustard
1 tbs vinegar
3 tbs olive oil
Salt and pepper, to taste
Chopped dill, for garnish

4 1-inch (2.5 cm) slices of fresh salmon
Water for poaching
1 tbs white wine vinegar
Bay leaf
1/2 tsp black peppercorns
1/2 onion
1 celery stalk

1. Place lentils in a large saucepan with enough water to more than cover. Bring to a boil, and strain immediately. **2.** Clean saucepan and cover blanched lentils with cold water. Add salt, carrot, onion, garlic clove, and *bouquet garni*. Bring to a boil, then reduce heat. Cook for approximately 40 minutes until soft. **3.** When the lentils are tender, remove from heat and allow to cool. Whisk the mustard, vinegar, oil, salt, and pepper together. Strain the lentils, reserving some of the cooking water, and toss them together with the vinaigrette and dill. Optionally, add a few slivers of cooked bacon. Add a few tablespoons of the water if the mixture is too dry. **4.** If you have a fish poacher, place enough water to cover the four steaks, add the vinegar and seasoning, and bring to simmer. If you do not have a poacher, you can use any large pan or saucepan; just make sure that the salmon pieces fit easily. **5.** Gently place the salmon pieces into the simmering water. Allow 5 to 7 minutes for them to cook. They should be quite rare in the center. Remove from the water, peel off the skin, de-bone, and serve. To serve, place 2 to 3 tablespoons of lentil salad in the center of each plate, flatten out into a circle with the back of a spoon, gently place the salmon pieces on top, and garnish with a few sprigs of dill. **Serves 4.**

Dry, coarse whites or fruity reds: Côtes de Bourg, Mercurey, Saint-Amour

SALADE AUX HERBES
Summer Herb Salad

The celebration of summer begins with all of the green, green bunches of fresh herbs at the market. In order to take advantage of the variety available, we chose to put them together with an assortment of delicate salad greens; this allows the flavor of the herbs to remain distinct but also to combine for an eclectic mouthful. This salad is a wonderful addition to any meal or perfect as a main course accompanied by cheese, bread, and a chilled bottle of white wine. We recommend the following lettuces and herbs, but feel free to mix and match.

15 minutes

1 head Boston lettuce
1 head red oak leaf lettuce
1 head green oak leaf lettuce
1 radicchio
1 bunch fresh basil
1 bunch chervil
4 stalks fresh tarragon
12 chives

For the vinaigrette:
1/4 cup extra-virgin olive oil
2 tbs walnut oil
1/8 cup red wine vinegar
Salt and pepper, to taste

1. Wash all of the lettuces and spin dry. **2.** Wash the herbs, delicately removing the stems from the basil, chervil, and tarragon. Cut the chives with scissors into 2-inch (5 cm) long pieces. **3.** Place the lettuces and herbs in a large salad bowl and gently toss with the vinaigrette. **Serves 4.**

Dry, delicate whites and rosés: Pouilly Fumé, Rosé de Provence, Touraine

Salade aux herbes

GATEAU A L'ORANGE
Glazed Orange and Cointreau Pound Cake

Madame Annie from the Batignolles market gaves us this original cake that is perfect to accompany an afternoon cup of tea or a tingling glass of champagne. The cake mold used in this recipe is important: the best-suited is a spring-form mold with a cone-shaped center.

15 minutes   1 hour

2 cups (500 g) sugar
8 oz (250 g) soft butter
1 vanilla bean (or 1/2 tsp vanilla extract)
2 tbs grated orange rind
5 eggs
3 cups (540 g) flour
1 tbs baking powder
1 pinch salt
3/4 cup milk

For the glaze:
1/4 cup (60 g) butter
2/3 cup (160 g) sugar
1/4 cup orange juice
1/2 cup Cointreau

Spring form with conical center

1. Preheat the oven to 350 °F (180 °C). **2.** In a large bowl, cream the sugar and butter together until very light and fluffy. Cut the vanilla bean lengthwise, and scrape out the grains. Add them to the sugar-and-butter mixture along with the orange rind. **3.** Add the eggs one at a time, beating the mixture very well after each addition. **4.** In another bowl sift together the flour, baking powder, and salt. Alternate adding the flour mixture and the milk to the sugar, butter, and egg mixture. The batter should be very light in texture. **5.** Butter and flour the spring form, shaking off the excess flour, and spoon in the batter. Place in the oven, and bake for 1 hour. **6.** When cooked, a knife inserted in the center should come out clean. Remove from the oven, and prepare the glaze. **7.** For the glaze: In a small saucepan, combine the butter, sugar, orange juice, and Cointreau. Heat over a medium flame until the butter is melted and the sugar dissolved. Do not boil. **8.** Pour the glaze over the warm cake—it should literally be swimming in glaze. Gently move the sides of the cake away from the mold with a knife, so that the glaze can seep down to the bottom. Let stand for at least an hour, or until all the glaze is absorbed, before removing from the mold. **Serves 8 to 10.**

Champagne

Every visitor to the "City of Lights" is sure to climb the endless steps to the top of Montmartre, for a whiff of what most consider to be the quintessential Parisian quartier. Actually, the picturesque hill, topped by the snow-white domes of the Sacre Coeur church, a vineyard, and a maze of cobblestone lanes, is but a single aspect of the 18th arrondissement. Surrounding this quaint village lies one of the most populated and diverse neighborhoods of Paris. The 18th has many facets that flourish

XVIIIe ARRONDISSEMENT

on the different sides of the hill: you might be swept away by an urban flurry, or led down quiet back streets, or find yourself wandering through a bustling, multicultural *quartier*. It may be disorienting if you are expecting just bicycles, baguettes, and berets from Paris; but this is a genuine side of this cosmopolitan city. Twice a week, one of the most advantageously priced markets sets up in the neighborhood. Catering to a sea of shoppers, who come from every corner of the city, the exhilarating Barbès market is a bargain hunter's dream.

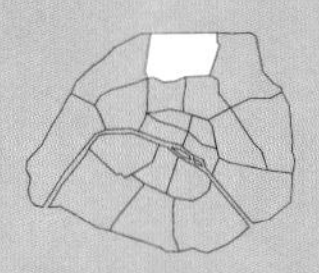

One of the best views of the city can be had from the top of the hill of Montmartre.

205 BEY 77

PARIS PAS CHER
The Barbès Market

The enormous and crowded Barbès market, contained beneath the steel girders of one of the oldest métro overpasses in Paris, bursts with movement and energy. Unlike any other market, Barbès is as teeming and exotic as a Moroccan *souk*. People of all ages slowly filter through the crowded aisles in search of best buys. Located at the crossroads of the congested Boulevard Barbès and Boulevard de la Chapelle, in the very popular 18th arrondissement, it is not your run-of-the-mill Parisian market. Yet it embodies a significant side of this city's culture. Towering piles of fruits and vegetables paint a never-ending banner of color along the central aisle. The stalls reverberate with the bellows of vendors amid the sea of shoppers, who move in unison from one end of the market to the other. Cheap is the norm here, and if it is not cheap enough, the regulars will haggle until the price is right!

This eastern part of the 18th arrondissement is known as "La Goute d'Or." Despite being situated at the foot of Montmartre—a stone's throw from the funicular that conveys visitors up to the church of Sacre Coeur and Place du Tertre—La Goute d'Or is far removed from the folklore of the famous hill. Hence, it is often overlooked by visitors and locals alike. Tourist buses line the neighboring streets, but the camera-clicking hordes rarely cross over to this part of the *quartier*. Here, over 30 nationalities cohabit. There is an established North African community and, more recently, a growing presence from West Africa.

The sea of shoppers seems miniaturized, under the majestic nave created by the massive columns that support the Barbès métro overpass.

At one time a hamlet on the outskirts of the city, La Goute d'Or derived its name (literally, "Drop of Gold") from the famous vineyards that covered its sunny slopes. Like with other outlying areas of the city, during the Industrial Revolution this bucolic village changed dramatically. It became home to the poor and lower echelons of the working class who had come from the provinces to toil in the many factories marring the northeastern face of Paris. Through the last century, La Goute d'Or has been adopted by the immigrant and transient population and slowly become integrated into the life of the city.

As you exit the Barbès Rochechouart métro station, follow the crowd to the outskirts of the market. Here stragglers set up makeshift stands with cartons on dollies, from which to hurriedly sell the items of the day, such as avocados or khobes bread, before the market administrator finds them. If you stand here a moment you will be amazed at the whirlwind of activity where everyone goes about their business seemingly oblivious to one other. It is best not to bring a shopping caddie—it is so crowded that you will spend half your time making sure you don't run over anyone's toes! Instead, buy a ten-franc, plaid, nylon tote bag at the first kitchen bazaar.

Before entering the market, you may find yourself hesitating when you see the swarm of people joining the flow. Between overloaded shoppers squeezing their way in and out of the mob, blind beggars with outstretched hands tapping their way into the hub, and children holding onto their mother's skirts, it may seem as if there would not be a square inch for one more person! Take hold of your shopping bag and venture forth.

As you work your way through the aisle, quite possibly stuck between a man carrying a 20-pound bag of carrots and a baby strapped to her mother's back in a wide band of colorful African cloth, you will notice that most of the market is dedicated to fruits and vegetables. Stands that are four or five times longer than those at other markets line up, side by side, selling most of the ingredients that are used in *Maghrébine* cuisine. Mounds of tomatoes, eggplants, chili peppers, limes, garlic, oranges, watermelons, fresh and dried dates, broad beans, onions, zucchinis, okra, scallions, bell peppers, and turnips fill displays next to huge stacks of fragrant mint, coriander, and parsley. Hordes of shoppers pick at every pile. Vendors miraculously refill displays as quickly as they are depleted, simultaneously handing out plastic bags, bargaining with shoppers, and weighing the purchases. Though the quality is not always top-notch (in fact, it can be disappointing), if you are buying in large quantities and you know how to pick and choose, this market is ideal. Shoppers come here from all over Paris for the notoriously low prices, and everyone exits with two or three overflowing nylon bags.

Besides the herbs for enhancing North African dishes, a few stands sell the grains and spices needed to prepare them. You can find olives for *tajine aux olives*; semolina for a fluffy couscous; the ingredients for *beghirs* (lacy pancakes spread with dates and honey); ground or whole spices such as cumin, saffron, aniseed, and cinnamon to add to savory broths and stews; dried fruits for roasts, soups, and desserts; chickpeas, white beans, and fava beans for salads; and ground chilis, garlic, cumin and coriander seeds mixed with oil—the components of fiery *harissa*, a paste that one finds at every table giving an extra kick to the broth of a couscous or to spread like mustard on *mechoui* (roasted lamb). In France, the people and traditions of Tunisia, Morocco, and Algeria are all referred to as *Maghrébin* (North African), though they each have their own culture and cuisine. They may use the same basic ingredients and often have similar names for dishes, such as couscous or *tajines,* but each country has its distinct style and method of preparation.

Sweeping past the many stands, you might feel drowned out by the din from the rumbling of the métro above, the enormous crowd of shoppers, and the bellowing of the vendors. Though it can be overwhelming, this is part of Barbès market's exotic appeal. The vendors are masters of selling, competing against one another, hawking their wares in guttural Arabic or French, creating a stir to attract shoppers' attention. As most of the produce comes directly from Rungis, with very few *maraîchers* present, the displays are virtually identical; it is up to the vendors to market their goods alluringly, for example, offering you a tempting

The Barbès market is where you will find North African specialties such as fiery *harissa*, salt-cured lemons, khobs bread, and dates.

THE A LA MENTHE

Fresh mint tea is the choice drink of North Africa. Not only is it a delicious and appeasing follow-up to a hearty feast, but it is a symbol of hospitality in Maghrebi culture.

Generally the brew is enjoyed either after meals or as a gesture of welcome, and it is considered an offense not to accept a piping-hot glass of sweet mint tea. Traditionally the tea is prepared by the father or the eldest son of a household; sometimes the guest of honor is asked to perform the ritual; but never a woman.

In a metal teapot, preferably silver, a pinch of Chinese green tea is doused with a small amount of boiling water to remove the bitterness. A generous handful of fresh mint leaves is added, with an equally generous amount of sugar, and then boiling water to cover. The tea is stirred, the teapot is wrapped in a cloth, and the tea is left to steep a few minutes. Then it is stirred once more and poured into small ornate glasses at arm's length, both to aerate it and so that the sound of the cascading fragrant brew might reach the ears of the Almighty.

PICOLINO
Poniente
Poniente

FRESH AVOCADOS
FRESH AVOCADOS

ORANGES
Kilos

YAMATO
Limes
23 Fr 90 /kg

CAPITAINE congelé
25
THIOF congelé
1kg
DISK congelé
Frs 29,95
1kg
SOMPATTE
Frs
1kg
59,95
FRAIS
19 Fr 95
1kg

wedge of juicy melon as they drop their prices. These tactics actually work wonders. One day we found this out first-hand: traffic came to a complete standstill at the center of the market, as customers mobbed the stands of two vendors across from each other, when they cut the price of their tomatoes in half.

While pyramids of fruit and vegetables abound here, butchers are few. Most people go to the neighboring Rue de la Goute d'Or, just a block away, where there is one at every corner. As this area is primarily Muslim, most of the butchers do not sell pork and carry only meat from animals that have been slaughtered and bled according to Muslim tradition. Stacks of singed veal hooves and lamb heads make for an unsettling entrance for the novice, as does the extensive selection of innards and offal on display—beef hearts, lamb tongue, tripe, brain, liver… you name it, they've got it! Packaged sausages, wrapped in bright red and yellow plastic casings, hang like luminous Christmas decorations. Chickens, spicy *merguez* sausages, and cuts of lamb and beef round out the displays. Although observant Muslims abstain from drinking alcohol, many of the shops carry Moroccan and Algerian wine. Vineyards planted in North Africa during the 19th century by the French have become an important industry, and these fruity red and rosé wines make a perfect accompaniment for the savory *Maghrebi* cuisine.

Fish is also a rarity at the market. To find it, you have to venture a bit farther than Rue de la Goutte d'Or, to the pedestrian market street Dejean. Here you will find two large fish shops that specialize in exotic varieties, such as the odd-looking *thiof* and *disk*, species that are frozen and flown in from the Ivory Coast. Local catches include live catfish that thrash about, spraying the passers-by. As you leave Rue de la Goutte d'Or, en route to Rue Dejean, the neighborhood slowly develops a West African flavor — shops are filled with yards of colorful, patterned material used by women for their national dress and matching turbans, known as *"boubous."* In many of the ethnic groups in France, men and children generally wear Western-style clothes, while women continue to wear their traditional attire.

Once in the neighborhood, stay and discover the many specialties available in stores lining the adjacent streets. Along Rue des Poissonniers and Rue Myrha, you can find all of the ingredients used to prepare typical dishes from countries such as Benin, Ivory Coast, Togo, Cameroon, Senegal, and Congo. Parisians from every corner of the city come here to buy rare and exotic vegetables, not available at the Barbès market. Along the outside of the shops, huge, rugged *manioc* (cassava) and

Left: Buying exotic produce on Rue Myrha; a selection of unusual fish on Rue Dejean.
Above: Lining up at the Muslim butcher.

PIGALLE AND THE MOULIN ROUGE

People all around the world have heard of the famous Moulin Rouge, the steadfast symbol of Paris' red-light district, where the frenetic can-can dancers continue to shake their thighs for an ecstatic crowd of night owls. Dating back to the late-1900s, the area of Pigalle became home to the city's nightlife, as cabarets, clubs, and bars sprouted up along the boulevards at the foot of Montmartre, offering more than just entertainment. A poor area located near the railroads and at the periphery of the city, this was prime terrain for squalid goings-on. The mixture of lowlifes and thrill-seeking bourgeoises often ended in brawls, knifings, and theft. It was not uncommon for elegant gentlemen to be framed by pretty *dames de la nuit* and daring mademoiselles to lose their way in the strong arms of virile commoners. Despite this, the area's success was undeniable, quickly becoming the rave of *tout Paris.*

Over the last century, Pigalle has evolved and become a very mixed and lively part of town. The Moulin Rouge has been at the center of it all, attracting famous entertainers from all over the world. Among them: Edith Piaf, Bing Crosby, Yves Montand, Ray Charles, Liza Minelli, Charles Aznavour, Ella Fitzgerald, Ginger Rogers, and Frank Sinatra. Along with the 60 can-can dancers of the nightclub, these luminaries have preformed for just as prestigious an audience. Today, the Moulin Rouge hosts three shows a day and the bustling red-light district filled with sex shops and strip joints has tourist buses lining its boulevards while theaters, concert halls, fashionable bars, and fine restaurants have joined the action.

ligname roots, usually peeled and boiled to make white purée, are lined up next to ginger root, yams, plantains and baskets of *miloukhia* leaves that resemble okra in taste and viscosity. Inside, bottles of spiced palm oil, cans of coconut milk, bags of tapioca, sachets of exotic spices, and baskets of sun-dried fish and shrimp clutter the shelves. Rarities such as live gigantic land snails from the Ivory Coast wriggle in cardboard boxes. These are usually boiled, cleaned with lemon, and fried. We were told that the rolls of cooked manioc wrapped in banana leaves are generally steamed and eaten as an accompaniment to hearty stews and roasted chickens. We bought a neatly tied roll, which we heated up—but we were not very impressed by its bland taste and gelatinous texture. Perhaps this is a delicacy best sampled with an authentic dish prepared by a real connoisseur.

On the way back down the hill to the market, stop at one of the bakeries to pick up a crescent-shaped *corne de gazelle* or a sweet and sticky Moroccan *chabakia* made from fried semolina and honey. You can savor these later in the day with a hot glass of fresh mint tea. You might also want to get a *khobs,* a round flat loaf of bread sprinkled with either sesame seeds or aniseed, to accompany a scrumptious grilled *merguez* sausage and a fresh tomato salad. If you haven't yet finished shopping, hurry to buy up the remaining produce before the boisterous *souk* vanishes back into piles of crates and cartons as one o'clock approaches, leaving only the pigeons to scavenge in the debris of bruised fruits and wilted greens. Vendors often drop their prices even further at this time to sell off the remaining produce to the thinning crowd.

At the end of your tour of the Barbès market and La Goutte d'Or, you may find your tote bag filled to the brim with bunches of mint, spicy olives, gold painted tea glasses, a few yards of African cloth, and maybe even a pot-bellied *couscoussière*. If this is not the case, consider joining the throngs of bargain hunters at TATI, where you will be sure to find the deal of the century! Or walk a few blocks to the scenic park at the foot of Sacre Coeur to rest your weary bones and take in a staggering view of the city. Once you have recuperated, continue your visit of Montmartre. Wander through the maze of picturesque streets until you reach Place des Abesses, where you can catch a bite to eat in one of the many small restaurants and bars. Then walk down the market street of Rue Lepic to the famous Moulin Rouge and adjacent red-light district of Pigalle, with its newly opened Museé de l'Erotisme, to complete your visit of the multifaceted 18th arrondissement.

Right: Colorful fabrics adorn the exit of the market.

TATI

At the crossroads of the congested Boulevards Rochechouart and Barbès, the pink-and-white colors of the TATI shops rule. Throngs of shoppers in search of the ultimate bargain flock to these innumerable discount stores. Pink-and-white-checkered trademark bags are stuffed with clothes, jewelry, beauty products, shoes, and even wedding dresses, sold at rock-bottom prices.

The TATI empire originated in the 1950s, through the vision of the industrious, Tunisian-born Jules Ouaki. He introduced the concept of permanent "*soldes*" (sales) to a postwar clientele. The idea was more than successful, and 40 years later this enormous enterprise is still flourishing and expanding under the supervision of Mr. Ouaki's son, Fabian, who perpetuates the ideology that has made a success of this family affair: that fortunes can be made not at the expense and detriment of others.

RUE LEPIC

As you climb the steep Rue Lepic street market from Boulevard Clichy, displays from shops, overflowing onto the sidewalks, lure you to the top. Rue Lepic borders the 9th and 18th arrondissements, and has the only concentration of food shops in the area, so the inhabitants of Montmartre come here to do their daily shopping. The block has the highest density of butchers that we have ever come across—over a dozen. We are not sure whether this might have anything to do with the extra protein needed to climb the hill of Montmartre, but you will find all types of butchers here: *artisanal*, commercial, *chevaline*, and *triperies*. Of course, you will also find a selection of cheese, fish, vegetables, wine, and flowers; as well as several bakeries, *traiteurs*, and cafés where you can rest your calves. As you get to the top, and wind around onto Rue des Abbesses, the food shops continue: a well-stocked Italian specialty store, more butchers(!), some nice wine shops, and tempting cheese shops. Then gradually the Montmartre atmosphere crystallizes: the food shops turn into clothing boutiques, the cafés spread out onto the streets, and the crowd blossoms. There are many sunny terraces where you can people-watch, before venturing to Sacre Coeur to have your portrait done.

ORDENER

As you exit the métro station Jules Joffrin, in front of the Church Notre Dame de Clignancourt, you will immediately start tripping over shopping carts. Before reaching Marché Ordener, you will come to a market street on Rue Poteau and Rue Duhesme that is always bustling. There are some nice shops here, but before buying anything, you may want to walk down a few streets along Rue Ordener to see what the market has to offer. The roving market runs along one side of the street, creating a narrow aisle squeezed between wine shops, bakeries, and cafés. The selection is vast, with some fabulous *maraîchers*, impressive cheese displays, and some very good butchers. One popular stand sells a selection of olives, dried fruit and nuts, and other specialties such as *tapenade*, *harissa*, and oils to spice up your life. In the winter, you will find an oyster farmer whose selection complements the fishmonger's elaborate displays. Flowers, clothes, and other odds and ends round out the offerings.

CRIMEE

FORGET IT!!! We walked along the interior *périphérique*, with fatigue shaving on our faces, to find the two stalls that make up the Crimée market: bad, bad veggies and awful flowers. Forget it.

ORNANO

Ornano is a very long market, stretching along both sides of the boulevard, selling a range of fruits and vegetables on one side and a bit more variety on the other, with *charcuteries*, cheese stands, fishmongers, and bakeries. The street is busy, with people walking alongside the market and frequenting the many cafés. The quality of products varies a great deal at the market, but if you also visit the different shops along the boulevard, you can fill your basket with an eclectic selection at very reasonable prices. Our favorite stop on this street, at number 7, is La Rose de Tunis, which specializes in oriental pastry from North Africa and the Middle East. There are quite a number of Muslim butchers, a few wonderful spice-and-grain merchants that engulf you with the different smells and tastes, and a handful of French specialty shops. Consider passing by here on your way home from the Clignancourt flea market that is located a few blocks away.

LA CHAPELLE

La Chapelle market is one of our favorite covered markets in Paris. This food hall, built in 1858 by the architect Magne, has been restored to perfection. Although it is located in a very urban part of the 18th arrondissement, the area immediately surrounding the market is still very quaint. On the pedestrian Rue de l'Olive, across from a small square and a church, this brown metal-and-glass structure invites you into a very old Parisian atmosphere. Approximately 30 stands, dispersed under the lofty skylight, offer a variety of good-quality products. Many of the vendors have been here for years, some for over three generations, so you will witness quite a familiar exchange with the older clientele who frequent the market. If you are a fanatic about markets or a fan of Baltard-style buildings, this charming *marché* is worth the detour.

NEY

The large Ney market runs along the traffic-ridden interior *périphérique* on the northern edge of the city. The area is filled with modern apartment complexes, and it houses Paris' biggest flea markets—Puces de Clignancourt, making it not the most quaint place to shop. Despite this, there are some reasonably good butchers, *charcuteries*, and fish stands—even if the fruit and vegetables are of average quality. If you are coming to the flea market on Sunday, consider instead the Marché Ornano which we much prefer, held around the corner along Boulevard Ornano.

L' Epicier

Like a *souk*, the Benkritlys' abundant display of grains, legumes, spices, dried fruits, nuts, olives, pastries, and candied fruits bursts with colors, aromas, and exotic temptations. Having originally been a small stand with a limited selection, Laurence and Abdelrani Benkritly have expanded their offerings significantly over the years. Their stand is now one of the best *épiciers* that you will come across at the open-air markets.

Laurence has been the driving force behind the expansion. An avid cook with a curiosity for cuisines from all over the world, she began experimenting with different ingredients and adopted many of the traditional Algerian dishes from her husband's native land. Gradually they incorporated the new ingredients and dishes into their offerings. Every week, Laurence spends two days cooking up a storm in the family kitchen, preparing crescent-shaped shortbread cookies dusted in confectioner's sugar, called *cornes de gazelle*; as well as stuffed dates; candied citrus rind; layered phyllo pastry with pistachios and honey; stuffed grape leaves; and whatever new ideas pop into her head. One of our favorites is the flatbread *k'sra*, made with semolina, cooked on an earthenware surface, and eaten either warm with butter and honey or spread with her freshly made hummus, *tarama*, or *tapenade*. Laurence has a collection of over 400 cookbooks which she uses for inspiration. She also often jots down recipes to share with her customers.

Abdelrani prefers to stay out of the kitchen, although he does enjoy concocting spice mixtures to add to their many varieties of olives. His main job is to keep the stock of their over 300 products replenished. He goes out of his way to find vanilla beans from Tahiti, apricots from Turkey, giant capers from Andalusia, basmati rice from the Himalayas, dates from Israel, raisins from Chile, and the famous *pruneaux d'Agen* from the south of France.

Abdelrani and Laurence Benkritely are present at the Auguste Blanqui and Lefebvre markets.

MARKET RECIPES

CAVIAR D'AUBERGINE
Eggplant Caviar

Eggplant caviar is a delicious *amuse-gueule* that goes well with a chilled glass of white or rosé wine. Serve a basket of toasted pita bread or thin slices of baguette for your guests to dip into the creamy mixture.

5 minutes 40 minutes

2 medium eggplants
Half a garlic clove, chopped
2 tbs olive oil
1 tbs walnut oil
1/2 lemon
Salt and pepper

1. Preheat the oven to 350°F (180°C). Wash the eggplants, dry, and prick them with a fork. Place in the oven on a sheet of aluminium foil and bake for 40 minutes or until soft to the touch. Remove from the oven and let cool. **2.** Slice open lengthwise and scoop out the meat into a bowl, discard the skins. Add both oils, the garlic, and blend with a mixer or food processor for 2 minutes. The mixture should not be too smooth. Add the salt and pepper to taste and a few squeezes of lemon juice, taste again and rectify if necessary. Serve in a bowl, drizzle a bit of olive oil on top, sprinkle with freshly chopped parsley and a twist of black pepper. **Serves 4**.

Full bodied, fruity whites: Côtes du Rhône, Chardonnay

VICHYSSOISE D'AVOCAT
Avocado Vichyssoise

This is a nice twist to the classic *vichyssoise* substituting the leeks for avocadoes and adding a pinch of cumin to round off the flavors. A light summer soup which has a surprisingly rich and luxurious texture without adding any cream.

15 minutes 2 hours

2 Haas avocados
3 medium boiling potatoes
4 cups chicken stock
1/4 tsp ground cumin
Salt and pepper to taste

1. If making the chicken stock from scratch, prepare ahead of time and let cool. Remove the congealed layer of fat before adding to the soup. **2.** Peel and boil potatoes until well cooked. Let cool. **3.** Combine avocado pulp, potatoes, cumin and 1 cup of cold stock in a blender. Blend to form a smooth purée, adding the remaining stock gradually. The consistency of the soup should be thick and creamy. **4.** Taste, adjust seasoning, and cool for a couple of hours before serving. Stir the soup and serve in four chilled bowls, garnish with a few pink peppercorns and cilantro leaves and serve. **Serves 4**.

Crisp, earthy whites: Vouvray, Saint-Véran

Vichyssoise d'avocat

TAGINE D'AGNEAU AUX CITRONS CONFITS
Tagine of Lamb, Olives, and Salt-Cured Lemons

Traditionally, this savory stew is cooked on top of the stove in a conical, earthenware tagine pot. Laurence Benkritely assured us that a heavy-bottom pot would do just fine—and the result was excellent! The salt-cured lemons give the lamb a very distinct flavor and help to tenderize the meat while cooking. Remember to pick up a North African flat bread when you purchase the spices and lemons.

10 minutes   1 1/2 hours

4 tbs peanut oil
2 lbs (1 kg) lamb shoulder, cut into large chunks, saving the bones
1 tsp ginger powder
1 tsp cumin powder
1 tsp turmeric
1 pinch saffron
4 onions, chopped
Water to cover
1/2 chicken bouillon cube
3 small cured lemons
1 tbs vinegar
8 oz (250 g) cracked green olives, pitted
1/2 bunch parsley, chopped
1/2 bunch coriander, chopped

1. In a heavy-bottomed pot, heat the oil over medium heat, and brown the lamb pieces on all sides. **2.** Add the bones, ginger, cumin, turmeric, saffron, and onions; and cook until translucent. Add enough water to cover, along with half a chicken bouillon cube. **3.** Cut the lemons in half, remove the pulp, and julienne the skin. Add them to the meat. When it comes to a boil, lower heat, cover, and allow to simmer for 1 1/2 hours. **4.** Meanwhile, bring a small saucepan of water to a boil with a tablespoon of vinegar. Add the pitted olives to the water. Boil for 10 minutes. Strain, and add to the meat halfway through cooking. **5.** Once the meat is cooked, add the chopped parsley and coriander, and serve with boiled potatoes and North African flat bread. **Serves 6.**

Rustic or fruity reds and rosés: Morgon, Bandol, Tavel

PASTILLA MAROCCAINE AU PIGEON
Moroccan pigeon pastilla

Moroccan pastillas are delectable flaky phyllo triangles stuffed with a fragrant mixture of herbs, spices, nuts, and savory pigeon that are fried to a finger-licking golden brown. Naturally, the pigeon can be substituted for another meat. The sugar and cinnamon topping adds an unusual touch and heightens the burst of flavors even more.

1 hour   10 minutes

2 cups (500g) minced cooked pigeon meat (about 4 pigeons)
3 tbs oil
1 onion, chopped finely
1/4 cup (75 g) chopped parsley
1/4 cup (75 g) chopped coriander
1/4 cup (40 g) chopped pine nuts
1/4 cup (40 g) chopped almonds
1/4 cup (40 g) chopped raisins
1/4 cup (40 g) chopped dried apricots
1 tbs ginger powder
1 tbs cinammon
2 pinches of saffron
1 tsp salt
Pepper to taste
Phyllo dough sheets
Vegetable oil for frying
Optional: 2 beaten eggs

1. To cook the pigeon: place a bit of oil in a large casserole and sear the pigeon on all sides. Add a cup of water or white wine, cover and cook approximately 45 minutes until cooked. To check doneness, pierce meat, when the juices run clear they are done. Remove from heat. When cool enough to handle, pick meat from bones and chop into small pieces. **2.** Heat the oil in a pan, add the onion and sauté until translucent, then add the parsley, coriander, pine nuts, almonds, raisins, apricots, ginger, cinammon and saffron, cook for about 5 minutes. Add the pigeon, mix well and season generously with salt and pepper to taste, remove from heat. **3.** Remove the phyllo pastry from the package and cover with a damp towel. Cut the sheets in half, place one heaped tablespoon of the mixture on the edge of the pastry dough and fold together to form a 3 to 4-inch-long triangle with the stuffing securely packed inside. Bind the ends together with the beaten egg, hold under a damp towel so they do not dry out. **Optional:** Scramble a couple of eggs in a small skillet, remove from heat and add a spoonful on top of the pigeon meat before folding. **4.** In a large saucepan, pour two inches of vegetable oil and heat over medium-high heat. Place the pastillas into the oil, turning over after 30 seconds and cook for about 2 minutes, or until golden, making sure they do not burn. Remove from oil, drain and place on a paper towel. Sprinkle with sugar and cinammon and serve immediately. The hot pastillas can either be served on individual plates as an appetizer or on a serving dish and passed around as hors d'oeuvres. **Serves 4.**

Coarse Rosés or Fruity reds: Bergerac, Gigondas, Moroccan wine

Far from the monument-studded esplanades and scintillating glamour that one associates with Paris, the 19th arrondissement houses a mishmash of old and new architecture that has mushroomed since the 1970s on the northeastern edge of the city. This is a multicultural neighborhood—with over 67 ethnic groups, a mélange unlike any other. The small shops and restaurants of Chinatown, the flowering mews surrounding the Buttes

XIXe ARRONDISSEMENT

Chaumont park, the promenades along the Bassin de la Villette, and the numerous open-air markets scattered about, bring you to a side of Paris often overlooked. The lively Joinville market—tucked alongside the peaceful Canal de l'Ourcq, with its riot of colors, diverse offerings, and mixed crowd—jumbles all of the many facets of the 19th together in a one-of-a-kind atmosphere.

A picturesque canal runs from the tip of the 19th arrondissement all the way through the right bank of Paris to link up with the river Seine.

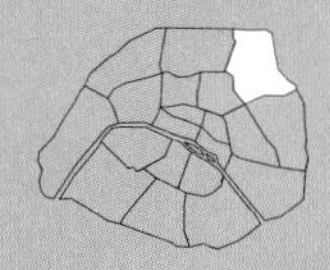

THE MELTING POT
The Joinville Market

The Joinville market comes to life along the peaceful Canal de L'Ourcq, transforming a shaded square with its picturesque church and belfry into a colorful flurry of activity, every Thursday and Sunday. Row after row of fruits and vegetables, stacks of fragrant herbs, dangling clusters of grapes, fresh dates, and corn husks fill the over 100 stands. Interspersed are a handful of fishmongers, butchers, *charcutiers*, and *fromagers*. Just off the busy Rue de Flandre, shoppers dragging shopping carts arrive from every direction to spend the morning in this lively atmosphere, picking and choosing from the abundant displays. With a mixture of nationalities and foreign languages, this market has an exotic appeal. Be prepared for the noise, though, which can be deafening on the weekend. As crowds stream into the four closely packed aisles, the vendors hawk their produce with exuberant bursts of *"dix balles, dix balles!"* and *"Ah, mes belles oranges!"*

Dating back to 1198, the 19th arrondissement was once a village surrounded by vineyards, wheat fields, and meadows. A rich community outside the city walls, this hamlet prospered independently until the beginning of the 19th century, when the area was transformed forever with the building of a canal, slicing through the village. Known as Canal de l'Ourcq, this over 100-kilometer-long canal fed into the river Seine, bringing water to the city center and offering a navigable route from the north all the way to the foot of the Bastille. Docks, warehouses, factories, and small industries sprouted along the waterway. By the time the 19th was annexed to Paris in 1860, its population had swelled almost twenty-fold, to 30,000. The panorama had changed completely. Although the southern end had maintained its village-like quality, with pocket-sized houses and miniature gardens lining quaint mews, the northern and outermost sections had become an unsightly industrial wasteland, with bellowing smokestacks and malodorous garbage dumps.

The bustling Joinville market has been the focal point of the quartier since its inception in 1873.

The placement here of the city's main slaughterhouse in 1876 did not help matters. Not until its closing almost 100 years later was the area finally cleaned up: the factories, sugar refineries, tanneries, and warehouses were relocated outside the city. The abattoir was torn down and replaced by a futuristic museum, Cité des Sciences et de l'Industrie, and a modern park, Parc de la Villette. The streets and gutters were cleaned and paved, and the banks of the canal were relandscaped with tree-lined promenades and park benches. The only section of the 19th that was, for the most part, left in peace were the winding streets running down the hill from the lovely Buttes Chaumont park; the rest was scraped clean and replaced by sweeping towers and apartment blocks. This surge of new housing has attracted a great number of people seeking more affordable apartments; it is one of the most populated and diverse *quartiers* in the city.

Along Rue Joinville, few cars manage to squeeze through the throngs of pedestrians and past the many vendors' parked trucks. This street leads up to the marketplace and is monopolized by shoppers zigzagging from the café to the Asian grocer to the newspaper kiosk to the Muslim

butcher shop, and to the cheese shop before finally reaching the square. The first part of the market sets up on the righthand side of the street. By 11 a.m., this narrow aisle is virtually impossible to negotiate. Flashy gold-embroidered velvets and satins, long North African dresses with matching ornate slippers, and an extensive row of flowers and plants greet you at Joinville. Covering the pavement, buckets filled with dahlias, gladiolas, silvery eucalyptuses, daisies, roses, and sweet-smelling freesias stand next to pots of miniature cacti, ferns, pansy seedlings, baby ivy, and braided ficus trees. The aroma wafting from mounds of turmeric, cumin, curry, red peppercorns, fiery paprika, and anise seed draws an eager crowd. At a festively decorated stand, traditional *espadrille* shoes dangle next to massive hams, garlands of dried red chili peppers, tempting pâtés, *jambon de Bayonne*, and sausages from the Basque region.

Up ahead, the Bourgeois family arranges an array of plump poultry as well as a tempting assortment of ready-seasoned-and-tied chicken tournedos, *paupiettes*, shish kebabs, and saddles of rabbit. They drive in from their farm in the Seine et Marne region, where they raise free-range chickens and rabbits. Propped up in neat little rows, with their red-crested heads folded under (which the vendors will obligingly remove upon request), these succulent chickens need no fancy preparation; just rub with a little salt and fresh ground pepper, add a sprig of thyme, and pop in the oven. If you are in a hurry, buy their pre-roasted chickens, rabbits, and turkey legs, along with some crispy, brown potatoes and a bit of gravy that you can pep up with a dash of Calvados and a dollop of cream. A *triperie* and finally a popular fish stand, with a crew of vendors clad in bright-yellow slickers, bring you to the hub of the market.

The atmosphere on this square is much more hurried. Here you will see shoppers darting from aisle to aisle heading for whatever immediately catches their eye. Even in the early morning hours, the market is a whirlwind, with the wise getting the best pick of the lot. The front section of the market offers a more diverse selection: you will find everything except a classical beef and lamb butcher, whose absences probably date back to the time when the *abattoir* was still in existence and the area was overflowing with butcher shops. Although *chevaline* butchers are less and less prevalent, you will still come across one at practically every market in Paris. The corner stand is tended by a representative of

MARCHANDS DE DATTES

When sugary dates first arrived in France from North Africa, vendors found that few Parisians were interested in buying the dark-brown, sticky fruits. They had to conjure up a scheme to entice the passers-by: not only did they dress up like Turks, with turbans, baggy pants, and pointed slippers, but they invented a nonsense language, hoping to lure a few customers with their exotic-sounding gibberish.

Their plan must have worked! Today you will find moist, plump dates at every market, usually at the dried fruit and olive stands. During the summer months, fabulous treats that take you straight to the *souks* of Morocco are the sprigs of fresh, yellow dates, which are crunchy with a juicy, sugary taste and a much milder flavor.

Right: This is one of the few markets where you can pick and choose your own produce. Normally, the vendors insist on doing it for you.

this trade: Monsieur Denvilly is a gentle character who goes about his work quietly, meticulously trimming and slicing tenderloins and filets as if he hadn't a worry in the world.

If you haven't come prepared, you should buy a ten-franc tote bag to carry your purchases; they are very light and handy. There is a man who navigates the aisles selling them. As you wander around, you will come to a huge wall of eggs over which you can barely see the head of the vendor. The first time we saw this surprising mountain, we thought it to be absurd; but Bernard from the Fromagerie à la Ferme Normande certainly knows his business—by the end of the morning, they were all gone! Nearby is a *charcuterie* with tasty *terrines*, sausages, homemade *chipolatas*, and country-style pâté. The Poissonerie Claude Cabrit displays glistening mounds of Bouchot mussels from the bay of Mont Saint Michel, as well as a good selection of fresh sole, mackerel, sardines, *dorade grise*, sea bass, and from time to time, a crate of finger-length *eperlan* fish with which to make a delicious *friture*.

We always make a beeline for Nicole Denoit's stand, to make sure we have our stash of *cèpes* before they run out. During their short season, which usually lasts from September to November, she brings two precious crates of the small-capped variety, known as *Bolet*, which are reputed to have a fuller flavor and a denser flesh. Wearing her signature glasses and pearl earrings, Nicole has been charming her clients for over 32 years with a wonderful selection of mushrooms—and only mushrooms. She has a great display of cascading heaps of *champignons de Paris*, tumbling next to mounds of *rosés, girolles*, *trompettes-des-morts*; and neatly arranged in wooden baskets, extra-large and extra-special *pied de mouton* and grey and yellow *chanterelles*. She explains that all mushrooms should be cooked for at least half an hour, except for *cèpes* which should be seared in a lightly buttered pan for only five minutes on each side, sprinkled with sea salt, a little ground pepper, *et voila*! She insists that when you cook a *cèpe* you do nothing else, no telephone calls, no last minute fussing—nothing—just stand guard over the pan and serve immediately.

Nicole is one of the old-timers at the market who has witnessed the *en masse* arrival of fruit and vegetable vendors that dominate two-thirds of the square. This surge arose from the need of the community for less expensive produce, which the diminishing number of *maraîchers* could

Left: Ten-franc, nylon, plaid, tote bags have replaced shopping baskets at many of Paris' markets.

CHEVALINE

not always offer. Over 60 stands, each tended by three to four helpers, offer produce that is for the most part imported and ferried directly from the wholesale market Rungis. Pyramids of melons, prickly pears, pomegranates, chili peppers, limes, oranges, mangoes, bananas, grapes, corn, eggplants, tomatoes, and tresses of garlic are sold at bulk prices. Note that they can vary dramatically in quality; the experienced shopper can do very well here, but should always keep an eye on what goes into his basket. The vendors here contribute to the animation of the market, promoting their specialties at the top of their lungs, while offering tastings and joking with the clients. They attract a large crowd of every age, size, shape, and nationality. The mixture milling about the square makes this market a fun and unique place.

The few remaining *maraîchers* at the market still do a thriving business. Among them, Monsieur Gueddour, a native of Morocco, is hidden behind stacks of mint, parsley, coriander; and heaped crates of radishes, turnips, and carrots. Unlike the many other herb vendors who import the fragrant bouquets used in most North African dishes, he is one of the few who grows his own. From his small garden plot near Fontainbleau, he sells up to 7,000 bunches per week. Nearby, the lumbering Didier Cattiaux swiftly tends to his customers, scooping his fresh products into a metal basket with his enormous hands. He chuckles good-naturedly in a sub-bass rumble, as he lifts bushels of potatoes, beets, crinkly-leaved cabbages, endives, *topinambourg*, and broad beans onto a long slanted table as if they weighed next to nothing. From tilling the land with his father on their farm in the Cergy-Pontoise region, the Cattiaux's bring the countryside to Paris with their seasonal crops. A few stands away, adjacent to the tiny office of the *placier,* there is always a line of patient shoppers waiting to be served by Claudine and Michel Tarry. They have a great selection of salads, herbs, artichokes, celery root, leeks, beets, cauliflower, apples, chestnuts, and pears that they pick every morning. While we were waiting our turn (not so patiently), we were entertained by the poultry vendor on the other side of the aisle who was thrilled to pose for a few pictures while plucking the feathers off a pheasant and cracking jokes with his co-workers.

Snuggled up against the back of the church, amidst a sea of fruit and vegetables, is the *fromagerie*, Maison Ventura, owned by an immaculately dressed *fromagère*. Clad in a frilly lace apron, she moves decisively along her stand, selecting from a wide array of cheeses. While one end of the table is stacked with trays of eggs, goat cheese, wedges of roquefort, *blue d'auvergne*, flat rounds of oozing *Brie*, pots of *fromage blanc*, and various hard cheeses are neatly displayed behind a glass countertop. She has a handful of helpers, among them Monsieur Dajot, a sprightly

CHAMPIGNONS DE PARIS

The cultivation of the world's best-known mushroom, the white and light-brown capped *champignon de Paris* (Agricus Hortensis), originated in the gardens of Louis XIV atop a pile of horse manure. The gardeners of Versailles were the first to make the discovery; from then on, this versatile mushroom has proceeded to conquer the planet. Eventually, the cultivation of mushrooms moved from the elaborate Royal gardens to more modest but very suitable surroundings, namely the abandoned underground quarries that crisscrossed the Montrouge area in the 14th arrondissement. Beneath the streets of Paris, in damp stone tunnels, these domed spores flourished, providing chefs with a firm, perfumed flesh with which they invented an endless variety of dishes. The little *champignon de Paris* was a grand source of inspiration: sautéed with thick cream and stuffed into *vol-au-vent* pastries; sliced raw into a light, crunchy salad; added to soups and stews; or preserved in oil, tinned, and dried. The *champignonnières* of Montrouge were employed up until the beginning of the 20th century, when the production was moved to the north and surrounding areas of Paris, the Val de Loire and Bordelais regions. France, being the third-largest producer after the United States and China, cultivates these delicious mushrooms all year-round.

STUFFED MUSHROOM CAPS

Nicole Denoit, the mushroom vendor at the Joinville market, rattled off this delicious and easy recipe one early market morning. The white- or brown-capped champignons de Paris are stuffed with a tasty mixture of parsley and garlic, and embellished with snails, which can be substituted by either ham or minced meat.

For four people, clean eight large mushrooms and pull off the stems. Scoop out the inside of the mushrooms with a spoon, and chop together with the stems, two shallots and a clove of garlic. In a skillet, heat 2 tablespoons of olive oil and 2 tablespoons of butter, and sauté the mixture for 4 minutes; do not brown. Add a cup (250g) of chopped snails (or meat of your choosing), 1/3 cup of parsley; and sauté for another 4 minutes. Pour in a dash of white wine, and salt and pepper to taste. Stuff the mixture into the mushroom caps. Wipe the skillet clean, and pour in 2 more tablespoons of olive oil. Over medium heat, sauté the mushroom caps, stuffed side up, for 8 minutes then place in an oven dish and bake for 20 minutes at 325 °F (160 °C). This makes an ideal side dish for a grilled steak or roast and touches perfection when accompanied by a round, spicy, red wine such as a Gigondas or Saint Emilion.

TESTUT
Old Amsterdammer

octogenarian who zips around ladling cream, slicing hunks of gruyère, pinching camemberts, and packing eggs ten times faster than the younger members of the crew. Having begun working at the open-air markets as far back as 1934, and at Joinville since 1969, this recently retired *fromager* seems to have a hard time leaving the thrill of market life. He is quite a character, always joking and grinning at everyone. His old customers trust only his expert eye to select their cheese and do not mind waiting to be served.

You can pick up an assortment of pistachios and olives from the stand across the way, where you will find an abundance of dried fruits, nuts, grains, spices, and condiments. Dressed in matching blue smocks, the vendors will readily give you tastings and suggest how to mix-and-match their different products: raisins, cinnamon, and ginger for the filling of flaky *pastillas*; almond powder, aniseed, and honey for Cornes de Gazelle; and green olives, saffron, and salt-cured lemons for a chicken *tagine*.

Towards the center of the market, you will come across a stand with dangling gold-and-bright-red-encased sausages, and a refrigerated display case crammed with yet even more of these plastic-skinned delicacies. Monsieur Bacha, a native of Algeria, purchases veal, turkey, beef, and chicken sausages from various suppliers. They are eaten cold, thinly sliced, in a sandwich or like any cold cut. If you would like to try, Monsieur Bacha will obligingly sell you a few *rondelles*. He makes traditional *merguez*, which accompany every bowl of steaming couscous, and also prepares fresh, spicy, beef sausages that are excellent grilled and savored with some olives and a crust of North African bread, called *khobs*.

At this point, you may want to climb the steps of the church to see the buzzing market from above, or make a last tour of the square and see what you might have missed. On the way out, we always like to pop into the Asian grocers along Rue Joinville for a knob of ginger root, a few stalks of lemon grass, a papaya, and a little bag of hotsy-totsy green chili peppers. They carry a small selection of fresh fish along with frozen squid and shrimp. The shelves are lined with exotic odds and ends, bottles of soy sauce, and cans with undecipherable labels. The Asian and Muslim butcher shops are slightly less compelling, but the cheese shop Aux Délices de Carole that opened its doors five years ago can be fun to step into, especially if your stomach is starting to grumble. The owner offers a nice selection of cheese and wine that you can take away and eat along the banks of the canal. Alternatively, you can drop your purchases and sit at one of the small tables for a *degustation* that the owner, Monsieur Rémond, will put together for you. He has some unusually named cheese which he buys from an *artisanal* cheese maker near Pont l'Eveque; for example, you might try *la vierge folle* (the crazy virgin) or *coup de pied au cul* (a kick in the behind).

You can continue your visit of the neighborhood with a walk through the picturesque mews and squares in the direction of the beautiful Buttes Chaumont park, where you can lounge on the grass or rent a rowboat at the lake. If you prefer to wander up the banks of the canal, make your way back past the market and up to the 19th-century church and beautiful drawbridge. Though the church is not especially spectacular, the drawbridge is the only functioning one of its kind in the city. If you have the time, wait for a boat to come by so that you can watch how gracefully the gigantic wheels lift up the bridge. The canal runs all the way to

Parc de la Villette, where you can spend the rest of the day pushing buttons at the science museum, watching a film on the spherical screen at the Géode cinema, or catching a concert at the striking new Cité de la Musique. There is always a lot going on in this complex, and it can be especially fun for children. If instead you want to sit down to a big Sunday lunch, go to the "temple of the steak," where meat-worshippers have been indulging in this Belle-Epoque setting since the days of the great abattoir. Au Boeuf Couronne, located at 188 avenue Jean Jaurès, stands true to its reputation of serving a good, if hefty, *pièce de bœuf*.

Left: Things are always hopping at the Maison Ventura cheese stand.
Above: Drawbridges and locks are still in use along the canal allowing barges to navigate the waterway.

PORTE BRUNET

Unfortunately, the bucolic setting of the Butte Chaumont mews does not overflow into the Porte Brunet market. Instead, approximately 20 vendors set up along the drab, lower end of Rue du Général Brunet, offering average-quality produce at reasonable prices. The market sets up in front of several food shops; the gem among them is a vintage *chevaline* butcher shop run by a smiling butcher who is just as charming as the store. Next door, there is a *rotisserie* that has plump chickens turning on a spit which seem to sell out faster than they can be cooked.

This is not a market worth coming out of your way for; but if you do find yourself in the area, pick up some items for a picnic and go to the little-known park, *Square de la Butte Chapeau Rouge*, just up the street.

VILLETTE

A block away from the Belleville métro stop, under a sheltering crown of trees, Marché Villette fills the central divider of Boulevard de la Villette. Approximately 40 vendors cater to the residents of the 18th and 19th arrondissements, offering a surprisingly inviting selection. You will come across tempting displays of fish and shellfish, *charcuterie*, flowers, fruit, and cheese. Among the offerings, there is a great array of wild and cultivated mushrooms at Françoise Chastang's stand; extra-plump, extra-delicious, free-range poultry at the Bourgeoise family's; and roast suckling pig at the *traiteur* down the way. Near the end of the long aisle, the smiling crew of La Boutique Creole can be found frying to a golden brown tasty *accras de morue*, which are perfect for taming your hunger.

RIQUET

Unfortunately most of Paris' covered markets are devoid of charm; and the Marché Riquet is the best example. Stuck on the ground level of an ugly modern building, a dozen vendors tend to the neighborhood clientele to the beat of piped Muzak and the chilling glow of neon lighting. In spite of the fact that the merchandise is of relatively decent quality, this market makes for a dreary outing.

SECRETAN

This beautiful, vintage, covered market is absolutely perfect from afar; but your hopes crumble as you step into the food hall. It has not suffered the overhaul to which most of these markets are subject, robbing them of all their charm; instead it has been robbed of its charm by merely standing sadly neglected. Only a handful of vendors occupy the enormous space, spreading out their displays and trying to do their utmost to keep the market running on a daily basis. One can find fruit and vegetables, cheeses, flowers, poultry, fish, and even organic products here; but sadly, Marché Secretan does not compare with the hurly-burly of times past.

JEAN-JAURES

This minuscule market, composed of a handful of stands, is unfortunately not worth a detour. A poultry vendor, a few sad fruit-and-vegetable merchants, and a couple of *marchands volants* selling the odd T-shirt or legging, make up the entire market that sets up along Avenue Jean-Jaurès.

If you are in the area, instead walk over to the other side of the picturesque Canal de l'Ourcq and do your shopping at the bustling Joinville market.

PLACE DES FETES

If you block out the modern apartment buildings surrounding the square Place des Fêtes, you might truly enjoy this tree-shaded market, which sets up here three times a week. Exiting from the métro station, you are directly brought to the hub of things, where approximately 60 stands line both sides of the sidewalk, forming a circle around a central playground. Some excellent *maraîchers* display mounds of garden-fresh vegetables; several fishmongers are in attendance, the most popular being Poissonier Gioia; *charcutiers*, poultry vendors, and butchers set up large displays; and a handful of *marchands volants*, selling such varied items as needles and thread, birdseed, candies, and socks, mix in with the lot. A rose farmer lines up buckets along the pavement, filled with fragrant buds.

Make sure you look for Escargots de la Butte (Snails of the Hill), where you will find wild snails that the vendor harvests himself in the south of France. Then try half a dozen of the *petit gris* and a half a dozen *bourgognes*, both deliciously prepared with garlic butter and ready to pop in the oven.

Left: Volaillers at Place des Fêtes. Right: Although fewer Parisians eat horse meat, this *chevaline* butcher at Porte Brunet has quite a following; spicy *merguez* sausages.

Les Volaillers

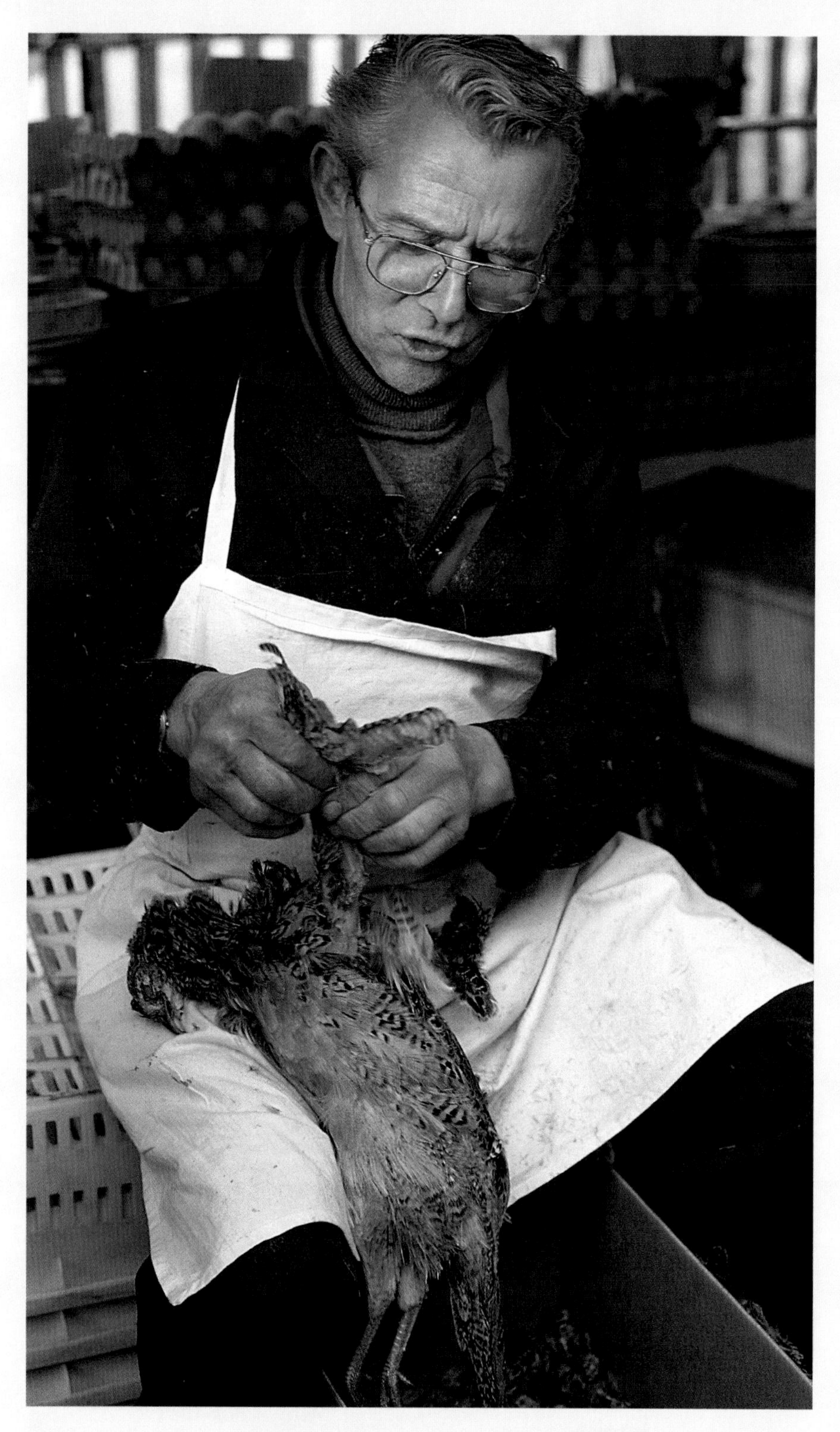

We came across the poultry vendor Daniel Letard sitting on top of an upturned crate, vigorously plucking the feathers of a pheasant, with a *Gauloise* cigarette hanging precariously from his lip, while his wife Monique was busy trimming a duck and giving cooking tips to a customer.

> "... always place the duck in a cold oven, never preheat it, as this hardens the meat... after salt and peppering it, you need to pierce the underside of the duck before placing it in the oven dish... you can make it with green olives, cherries, figs, or simply roast it... just place a bit of water or white wine in the pan with the olives or whatever you choose, and set the temperature at 200°C (375°F)... but remember never pre-heat the oven!!!"

She also mentioned that when cooking a pheasant, it is best to pick a female one as they are more tender; and one should always place a *petit suisse* (a farmer's cheese) in the cavity, as pheasants have a tendency to dry out.

A few days later, we visited the Letards at their house in the suburbs of Paris. Sitting in their neat living room, with a 25-year-old stuffed pheasant staring down from the mantelpiece and their white terrier rummaging at our feet, we inquired about how they came to be *volaillers*. Daniel's destiny was decided when, at the age of 18, he became an apprentice at his father's poultry shop. A few years later, when he and Monique married, they opened up a shop in the 14th arrondissement. They soon found it to be too costly and the hours restrictive; so they applied for a space at one of the open-air markets. Five years later, they were assigned to their current spot at Marché Brune, where they have been selling pheasant, capon, cock, pigeon, chicken, guinea hen, domestic and wild duck, quail, turkey, and rabbit for the past 30 years.

They are thinking of retiring in the near future, passing the reins on to their son, who is present with his wife at one of the covered markets in the suburbs of Paris. Although you may not have the opportunity to see the Letards for much longer at Marché Brune, you will always have the pleasure of enjoying Monique's scrumptious duck recipe.

The Letards are present at the Brune market.

FRITURE D'EPERLAN
Two-Minute Fish Fry

These delicate, finger-length fish are a real treat and are so simple to cook—they need virtually no preparation. Pop them in your mouth head and all, just like a French fry; their bones are so teeny you will not even notice them! If you cannot find *eperlan* fish, sweet or saltwater smelts will do just as well.

5 minutes   5 to 6 minutes

2 cups peanut oil
1 lb (500 g) *eperlan* fish (or smelts)
2 cups milk
1/2 tsp salt
1 cup (180 g) flour
Lemon, for garnish

1. Heat the oil in a high-sided pot, over a medium-high flame. **2.** Rinse the fish briefly under cold water, and put them in a bowl with the milk and salt. **3.** Put the flour in a large bowl. Remove the fish from the milk, and toss them gently in the flour. **4.** Shake off the excess flour, and deep-fry them in the oil, stirring occasionally so that they do not stick together. They should cook very quickly and be a light-golden color. Remove with a slotted spoon, and drain on a paper towel. Cook them in batches so they have ample space. Friture should be eaten as soon as possible—if not, they tend to get soggy. Sprinkle with salt and serve with a wedge of lemon. **Serves 4**.

Dry, citrusy whites: Touraine, Muscadet

CANARD AUX CERISES
Cherry Roast Duck

This scrumptious roast duck can be accompanied by anything you fancy; Madame Letard suggests you add cherries. If you are hesitant about cooking duck, follow her instructions, placing it in a cold oven and turning it once in a while. You will be sure to attain a delicious, moist roast with a golden-brown skin.

15 minutes | 1 1/2 hours

Salt and pepper, to taste
1 duck (4 to 5 lbs [2 to 2.5 kg])
Kitchen string
2 tbs butter
1 sprig rosemary
1/2 cup water
1/2 lb (250 g) stoned cherries

For the sauce:
1/2 to 1 cup white wine or water
1/4 cup kirsch (optional)

1. Salt and pepper the inside of the duck. Truss and rub the outside with butter, salt, and pepper. Prick the bottom with a fork, and place in a baking dish. Add the rosemary sprig and water, and place in a cold oven. Raise temperature to 375 °F (200 °C). **2.** After half an hour, turn the duck over and continue to cook, basting every once in a while. **3.** 30 minutes later, turn the duck over again, add the stoned cherries, and continue cooking, basting occasionally until done (1 1/2 hours total). **4.** When cooked, turn off the oven, open the oven door, and allow the duck to rest 10 minutes. **5.** Remove duck from the baking dish, place fruits in a bowl, and strain gravy into a measuring cup. Place the duck back on the dish and leave to rest in the oven with the door open. **6.** Remove as much fat from the gravy as possible. Measure how much gravy you are left with, pour it into a saucepan, and measure an equal amount of wine or water. Optionally, pour in the kirsch and cook over high heat a couple minutes so that the alcohol evaporates. Then add the wine or water and reduce to one half. **7.** Add the fruit, adjust seasoning, heat a couple of minutes, and place in a side dish. Carve the duck and serve. **Serves 4 to 6.**

Complex, aromatic reds: Pommard, Haut Medoc, Moulis

POULET AU RIESLING
Alsatian Style Chicken

This is a very simple recipe that one can whip together at any time of the year for a festive lunch or dinner. We made it with one of the free-range chickens that the Bourgeois family brings from their farm to the Joinville market and followed their cooking instructions.

15 minutes | 1 hour

1 chicken
Salt and pepper, to taste
16 baby onions
2 tbs peanut oil
2 cups (approximately 1/2 bottle) Riesling wine
1/2 cup chicken stock
1 bay leaf
1 tbs flour
1 tbs heavy cream
Chopped parsley, for garnish

1. Cut the chicken into pieces and rub with salt and pepper. Peel the onions. **2.** In a heavy-bottomed pot, heat the oil over medium-high heat; and brown the chicken parts and onions until golden. Remove, and place on a plate. **3.** Deglaze the bottom of the pot with the wine; add the stock and bay leaf; and return the chicken and onions. Cover and cook over medium-low heat for 45 minutes. **4.** When cooked, pour some of the sauce into a bowl with the flour, and whisk until smooth. Strain back into the pot, and cook for another 10 minutes. Stir in the cream, adjust the seasoning, remove from heat, sprinkle with chopped parsley, and serve. **Serves 4 to 6.**

Herbaceous whites: Riesling, Tokay, Pinot Gris

Right: Come autumn, quince make their appearance at the markets.

COINGS POCHES AU CASSIS
Autumn Quince Poached in Cassis

Whenever you come across Bernard Richaudeau's wooden bins at the Auteuil and Jeanne d'Arc markets, filled with apples, pears, and quinces, your mouth immediately starts watering, as you imagine baked apples, pear tarts, jams, and our favorite, poached quince. Slightly different from the more traditional poached pears, the texture is denser and the flavor fuller. Try this alternative with a touch of *cassis* to surprise your guests.

20 minutes   30 minutes

4 medium-sized quinces
2 lemons
4 cups (approximately 1 bottle) fruity red wine (Beaujolais)
1 cup water
3 tbs Crème de Cassis liqueur
1/2 cup (125 g) sugar
1 vanilla bean
4 cloves
4 black peppercorns
1/2 stick cinnamon

1. Peel the quinces, leaving the stems attached, and place them in a bowl of water with the juice of one lemon to stop them from discoloring. Do not discard the peels. **2.** In a high-sided saucepan, big enough to comfortably hold the quince, place the peel and juice of 1 lemon, along with the wine, water, cassis, sugar, vanilla, cloves, peppercorns, and cinnamon stick. Add the peels to the poaching liquid (they give a pretty pink color to the sauce, enhance the flavor, and thicken the sauce). Mix together and bring to a boil. **3.** Lower the heat to low, and place the quinces into the poaching liquid; they should be completely covered. Cook for approximately 30 minutes, depending on the size and ripeness of the quinces—you should be able to pierce the fruit easily. The poaching liquid can be reduced to obtain a more syrupy consistency by boiling at a high heat for about 15 minutes. **4.** Cool quinces in the poaching liquid for at least 2 hours before serving. They are even more delicious if prepared the day before. Remove fruit to serving bowl, and strain liquid on top. **Serves 4.**

Smooth, full-bodied wines

The 20th arrondissement does not reflect the sparkle of the ritzy *quartiers*; this is a tranquil corner of the city. Yet it happens to be one of the most frequented sections of Paris: streams of visitors come to the famous Pére Lachaise cemetery, to stroll through the beautiful park and pay homage to their idols. Few, however, think of exploring the other corners of the neighborhood, as it is on the periphery of the city without many known attractions. Most opt instead to head right back down the

XXe ARRONDISSEMENT

hill toward the Bastille or disappear into the métro to resurface in a more familiar locale. The 20th is quintessentially French in character: here is where the working class has settled for generations, holding onto the ideals of *Liberté, Egalité, Fraternité* at all costs; this is also the place from which emerged such icons as Edith Piaf and Maurice Chevalier. The amiable Réunion market brings a splash of life and animation to a peaceful square in the heart of this last arrondissement of Paris.

The quaint, residential neighborhood "La Campagne à Paris" is one of the city's best kept secrets.

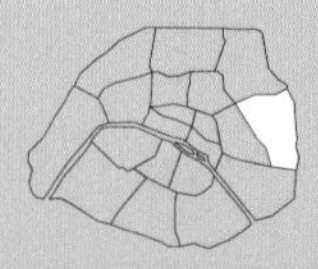

VIVE LA FRANCE
The Réunion Market

Come Sunday, Place de la Réunion bursts into life when what seems like the whole *quartier* converges on this square, to partake in the atmosphere of the convivial Réunion market. Sheltered under colorful awnings, over 40 vendors set up their stands, forming a maze of tempting displays. As the morning progresses, the narrow aisles fill up with shoppers peacefully checking off the items on their shopping lists, chatting with the vendors, and bantering with their neighbors as they stock up their baskets and shopping caddies.

The 20th arrondissement dates back to when the area was made up of four villages lying on the outskirts of the city. Residents subsisted off their crops and vineyards. Like other environs, the villages—Belleville, Menilmontant, Bagnolet, and Charonne—were highly valued by Parisians, who appreciated the clean air, beautiful vistas, and tax-free wine. There were as many as 100 taverns dotting the countryside, some of them reputed to be large enough to accommodate as many as 2,000 tipsy guests. One can imagine the melange of workmen, farmers, and city folk making merry while chickens pecked for insects in the next-door courtyards, and pigs grunted and squealed on country lanes. This lifestyle was disrupted when the four villages were haphazardly grouped together and annexed to the city in 1860, to form the 20th arrondissement. From one day to the next, the residents were no longer independent, subject to heavy city taxes, and found themselves grouped with the 500,000 citizens incorporated into the new city limits. Long avenues cut across villages, separating properties and families; the vineyards gradually disappeared and were converted into makeshift houses and workshops; farmers could no longer till their land and were forced to find employment for miserable pay; and the cost of living skyrocketed. Workmen and those looking for affordable housing flocked here. By the time the Industrial Revolution came into full swing, towards the end of the century, this had become one of the most populated areas of Paris, with hundreds of small workshops employing an army of laborers.

Nowadays, one finds only streets and avenues named after the villages, which are anything but reminiscent of their former rolling hills, streams, and cobblestone ways. Eventually, the sweatshops were torn down and replaced by modern housing complexes, which are quite an eyesore; many different architects had their hand in developing this *quartier*. The spirit and character of the inhabitants of the 20th arrondissement, though, has remained the same as when this working-class community strove for its rights in 1870; then, during the French Civil War, the groups referred to as "La Commune" valiantly fought against the conservative government. This is still one of the most socially conscious neighborhoods in Paris; you will often come across residents congregating at the market to discuss local issues and distribute pamphlets to the passers-by. The different sections of the 20th today each have their own character; as you cross the arrondissement, it may seem as if you are walking from one village to the next; but though the modern age has brought a diversity to this *quartier*, you will still find an overall unity and tranquility amongst the residents.

Despite being located in a remote section of the twentieth, the Réunion market truly embodies the spirit of this Parisian quartier.

The Réunion market is split into two sections by Rue Vitruve: the larger segment is more compact with a boisterous atmosphere, while the second is more spacious and less hurried. If you are arriving by métro, you will need to walk a couple of blocks. The market is set back from Boulevard Charonne, nestled on Place de la Réunion—so named in the mid-19th century as it united (*réunir*) the hamlets of Charonne and Bagnolet in the heart of this southern part of the arrondissement. The market has occupied this exact spot since 1856, when a small bronze fountain was built to grace the center of the square and was only turned on during market days (Thursdays and Sundays); it still gurgles and trickles, but is now hidden by a children's playground.

There are a couple of cafés on the square, but we like to have our coffee and *tartine beurée* at the funky Le Poisson Bleu a short block away. On the corner of Rue Vitruve and Rue des Orteaux, it lies alongside a lovely flower shop and popular bakery.

At the beginning of the market, *charcuterie* Grandjean sets up a sprawling stand with a gargantuan display of specialties. Four oversized skillets brimming with simmering stews are positioned at each corner. A variety of pâtés, hams, sausages, and pickled pork cuts known as *demi-sel* line the long tables. The mother-and-son team make the bulk of the goodies themselves. On market days, they are aided by a handful of young helpers who dart about serving customers, while joking with one another. They are a friendly welcome to this market.

The *volailler*, Michel Chamillard, sets up a bountiful stand of neatly trussed poultry and a row of *rôtisseries* with golden, crispy, brown birds rotating in the background. *Rôtisseries* date back to the Middle Ages, when the succulent smell of roasting goose, pheasant, venison, suckling pig, and grouse wafted through the streets of Paris. Though the preferences of the customers have changed (now you will mostly find chickens, turkeys, and rabbits on the spits), Parisians still love the convenience of perfectly seasoned, ready-to-go fowl and often reserve one before starting their shopping. Michel told us that in his younger years, he would drive in from the farm with his truck stacked with cages of clucking chickens, quacking ducks, and gobbling turkeys, as his customers preferred to buy them live and carry them flapping all the way home. Since this was forbidden by the government in 1980, the only place you can find a live chicken or rooster today is at the animal market along Quai de la Mégisserie by the Seine.

In former times, poultry and rabbits were sold live at the market. Nowadays, one often finds them already roasted for those who are not in the mood to cook.

Fruit and vegetable stands outnumber the rest of the offerings in this first section. Unfortunately, most of the quality is fairly mediocre (and extremely cheap); although there are some saviors, among them, Monsieur Mimouni who sells immaculate watercress, crunchy radishes, new-crop carrots, deep red beets, tasty lettuces, and a great selection of fresh herbs. He sets up a small table stacked high with his neat display and is often accompanied by his young son who seems to be just as shy as he is. The young team running Aux Délices Parmentier across the way offers over 15 different types of potatoes including the multipurpose *charlotte*, the nutty flavored *ratte*, and the reddish, new potato *francine*. All are meticulously identified by the names and cooking methods of each variety chalked on the blackboards hanging above. Pierrot and Henrique named their stand after the famous agronomist, Augustin Parmentier, who introduced the potato to France in 1787. They also carry onions, garlic, shallots, and *bouquets garnis*, which will spice up any *court bouillon* or *Hachis Parmentier*. The rest of the stands offer a large selection of Mediterranean-style fruits and vegetables. The vendors here are always calling at the top of their lungs to draw you to their pyramids of prickly pears, oranges, zucchinis, grapes, eggplants, clementines, tomatoes, broad beans, and bananas. This lively group is always good-humored, and their incessant commotion gets everyone going. As you pass by the stalls, from behind the tempting bunches of grapes dangling along the awnings, the vendors will briskly hand you an empty bag for you to pick and choose from the mounds of produce. If you are savvy, you can get a great deal; but if you are a novice, you might be disappointed with your non-refundable purchases.

At the far corner of this section, René Vigoureux graces the pavement with over a dozen buckets of colorful roses, which he brings from his small plot in the Val-de-Marne region. Monsieur Vigoureux has over

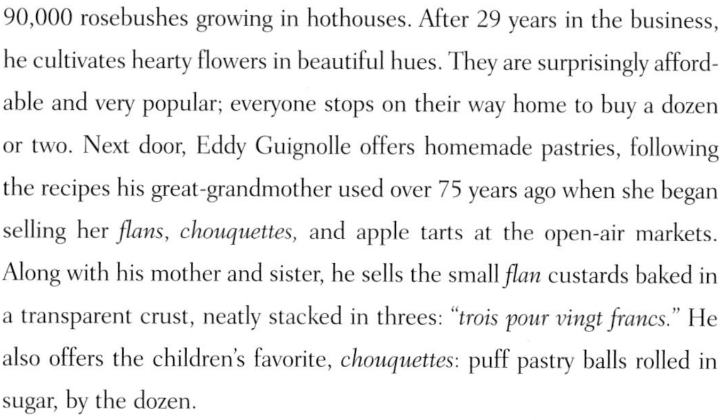

90,000 rosebushes growing in hothouses. After 29 years in the business, he cultivates hearty flowers in beautiful hues. They are surprisingly affordable and very popular; everyone stops on their way home to buy a dozen or two. Next door, Eddy Guignolle offers homemade pastries, following the recipes his great-grandmother used over 75 years ago when she began selling her *flans, chouquettes,* and apple tarts at the open-air markets. Along with his mother and sister, he sells the small *flan* custards baked in a transparent crust, neatly stacked in threes: *"trois pour vingt francs."* He also offers the children's favorite, *chouquettes*: puff pastry balls rolled in sugar, by the dozen.

This tranquil corner of the market might remind you of *La Campagne à Paris* (The Countryside of Paris), the only untouched section of the 20th, near Porte de Bagnolet. This network of small streets holds true to its name with its quaint houses and beautiful lush gardens that seem far removed from the city bustle. Built in 1927 atop a small hill, all you hear are chirping birds and meowing cats in this one-off attempt to make social housing agreeable—and what a jewel it is! The development was originally planned at the turn of the century by a philanthropic group that was not impressed with the miserable efforts made by the government to accommodate the working class. Believing that it was necessary to upgrade the living standards of the poor for the well-being of all, they envisioned this pocket-sized haven, which proved to be a great success. Unfortunately, their idealistic visions were not carried forth in the rest of Paris, as can be seen in the ghastly low-cost housing complexes that mar the skyline. Happen what may, these 89 idyllic cottages are now some of the most sought-after in the city—and way out of reach of any workman's budget! Crossing over to the next part of the market, you will most certainly be asked to sign a petition, be handed a few pamphlets, and maybe have a pin hooked onto your jacket by one of the dedicated volunteers from the

GAMA
AGUAMICH
AGUAMICH
AGUAMICH
AGUAMICH
AGUAMICH
AGUAMICH
AGUAMICH
Limones de
Tucumán
Producción

political, social, and neighborhood groups that congregate here. It is always interesting to find out about the different issues at hand; and if you are up to it, you can have a heated discussion which can be continued at the corner café. Instead, you may prefer to concern yourself with more important matters, such as which variety of potato to use to make the ultimate *purée*. Claude Ceccaldi is your man! With his 30 years experience, you can discuss at length the different qualities of the over 350 varieties grown in France (though thankfully he and his wife only bring a selection of 30). The potatoes are rolled onto a wooden trough, from which they are scooped up into metal bowls to be weighed, before being dumped into the bottom of your caddy. There is always a queue at their stand, as if potatoes were a rare commodity; this queue sometimes gets intertwined with the queue at the Portuguese and Italian specialty stand next door. There, although the owner Aderito Brito has a slightly brusk manner, you should not be deterred from perusing his excellent spread. Bottles of *Vinho Verde* and *Chianti Classico* line one end of the table, followed by olives, cheese, salamis, hams, breads, fresh pastas, and stacks of *bacalhau*. You may come across a bucket of salt codfish tongues, which are considered to be the tastiest part of the fish but quite a rarity as the fishermen are known to stash them away for themselves. They are prepared in the same manner as *bacalhau*; and combined with potatoes from the Ceccaldi's, you can make the perfect *brandade de morue*.

If you are not in the mood to spend hours desalting these fish, but still want to find out what *bacalhau* tastes like, ask Fahtim from La Calebasse to fry up a cod fish ball, *beignet de morue,* and eat it on the spot. This African *traiteur* has a whole array of cooked dishes, which vary from week-to-week; for example: *maffe*, a savory beef and peanut stew; *samousas*, deep-fried phyllo pastries filled with either vegetables or meat; and *colombo*, a chicken dish made with fiery green chili peppers. If you manage to get the recipe from her, buy the chicken across the way from Jacques Loquineau, who will most probably be chatting with his neighbors from the *charcuterie* Les Trois Frères. In their red-and-white striped jackets, the three brothers swiftly zip from one end of the stand to the other, cutting slabs of delicious pâté, thinly slicing smoked ham, and tying pork roasts. Next door, at Tan Ly Thong, eight vendors cramped between walls of greens and fruits tend to a swarm

Above: Potato vendors often bring as many as 30 different varieties to the market.

BACALHAU

Stacks of salt-encrusted *bacalhau* are omnipresent at the open-air markets of Paris. This air-dried codfish, flat and stiff as a board, will metamorphose after a bit of soaking into the basis of a deliciously moist stew. The Portuguese were among the first to appreciate this versatile fish, and the cod's popularity dates back to the discovery of the New World. When Portuguese galleons sailed up the Atlantic coast towards Canada, they were so amazed at the abundance of cod thrashing about in the cold waters that they baptized the new continent "Land of the Cod." By the end of the 16th century, they were braving the rough seas to haul up to 3,000 tons yearly. They shipped their salt-preserved catch back to Portugal, establishing *bacalhau* as a staple in the Portuguese diet. Years ago, a cod could weigh up to 220 pounds, but due to extensive fishing and modern techniques, today they rarely attain 50 pounds. Over the centuries, the tables have turned: Iceland has become the main exporter of codfish; in fact their economy so depends on the fishing industry that before their independence from Denmark, a golden-crowned codfish was their national emblem!

Morue, as this fish is called in France, has become anchored in French cuisine as well. The most famous dish is *brandade de morue*, made by desalting the dried cod for up to 24 hours, then cooking and mixing the lean, flakey meat with a potato purée, a drizzle of olive oil, and a touch of garlic. *Bon appétit!*

of customers. Here you can pick up a perfectly ripened pineapple or mango from Mexico, string beans from Senegal, asparagus from Chile, or clementines from Spain, as well as top quality, local, seasonal vegetables.

If you manage to squeeze past the crowd, take a rest at the secondhand book stall with the scent of flowers wafting from the adjacent florist; or grab a couple dozen oysters from Jean Claude Debotte, an *ostréiculteur* from the Oléron region, before checking out the catch-of-the-day at A Votre Service Poissonément. A few stands down, Crèmerie Bouvet has a large selection of cheese and dairy products; but if you are looking for a perfectly aged brie, a creamy sheep's milk cheese, or a pungent *tomme de Savoie*, you will have to return to the first section of the market and stop by Fromagerie Caillere. There Nali will readily help you make your choice. She has learned all the secrets of aging cheese from her father, André, who has been in the business for over 40 years. Nali will take over the reins when her parents retire. The only butcher at the market is Jean Pierre Retaud, who carries a selection of *Charolais* beef and veal from the Corrèze region, and lamb from Normandy. Having a shop nearby, where he also sells innards, offal, poultry, and homemade *charcuterie* products, he comes to the markets only on Sundays. He is an *artisan* butcher, which means that he buys whole carcasses from the slaughterhouse and prepares the different cuts himself. Each animal is registered and labeled with strict control on its origins and diet, especially since the outbreak of "mad cow" disease, and the meat is cut according to a long-established method that differs radically from those in other parts of the world. They remove whole muscles instead of cutting through them. Before receiving a license and being permitted to open shop, aspiring butchers must follow a two-year course at a butcher school in France, followed by an apprenticeship of a minimum of five years. They take their *métier* very seriously.

Round off your tour of the market with a peek at the large fish stand of Jean Pierre Bracke. Here you will often find live shrimp, spiny lobster, and from time to time spider crab, known as *araignée de mer.* This deep-orange-colored crab has a spiky round body, from which long spindly legs protrude. It is considered to have a more delicate-tasting meat than the rust-colored *tourteau.* Ask Marie Noële or Fredéric to select an active female for you, as they are by far the sweetest and have the much-prized roe. Make sure that it is alive and kicking, as you should never buy

Left: Jean Pierre Retaud and his helper take their *métier* very seriously while Nali serves her customers with a smile. Right: Fooling around at Jaques Loquineau's poultry stand.

CAILLE
15 00 F
POULET
JAUNE
1kg 41,80 F
Des Landes
Poulet Fermier
des Landes
41,80
Poulet Fermier des Landes
Poulet Fermier des Landes
Poulet Fermier des Landes

Cadran de Sologne

a dead crab! Mustering up a little courage, you can cook them yourself: bring a *court bouillon* to a boil, take a deep breath, and plunge the live crab into the pot and cover. Let it cook for 20 minutes, then remove it from the pot, and cool for the time it takes you to make a creamy mayonnaise. They are so delicious when they are freshly cooked that you will never want to order them in a restaurant again. Take a last look at the remaining stands to see if you come across something special, for example almond- or anchovy-stuffed olives, dried pistachio nuts, or toasted chickpeas for your *apéritif*. Do not forget to pick up your roses on the way out.

If your *araignée* is not jostling around too much in your basket, take a stroll through the Père Lachaise cemetery, and place a rose on Edith Piaf's grave; or walk a bit farther to admire the lovingly kept gardens adorning the houses in La Campagne à Paris; or venture even a few blocks further to Chinatown on Rue de Belleville, to buy some incense or have a quick wonton soup. If instead, a satisfying lunch is all you can envision, stop for a hearty *bœuf gros sel* at the restaurant of the same name or have some classic bistro food at Allobroges. Both are located a few blocks south of the market on Rue des Grands Champs. Contentedly sitting with your cognac in hand, think about your favorite markets, the charming characters, titillating smells, delicious tastes, and colorful sites that have led you to discover the many facets of this glorious city.

What once seemed to be a far-away neighborhood is now a familiar place that holds tempting treasures. It may no longer seem absurd to cross the city to fill your basket with olives and *coquilles Saint-Jacques* at Saxe-Breteuil, or apples and whole-wheat bread at Montrouge, organic crêpes and sweet marmalade at Batignolles, fresh raviolis and *côte de bœuf* at Saint Charles, *saucisson sec* and a *dorade royale* at Richard Lenoir, sinful brownies and bio-dynamic salads at Raspail, mushrooms and exotic spices at Joinville, flowers and caviar at Aguesseau, *chipolatas* and a bottle of Côtes du Rhône at Aligre, artichokes and fresh walnuts at Saint Quentin, fragrant mint and tapioca at Barbés, *accras de morue* and oysters at Maubert, roses and pomegranates at Réunion, strudel and roasted coffee at Rue Montorgueil, creamy brie and country pâté at Auguste Blanqui, and venison and *foie gras* at Président Wilson. The world of open-air markets has brought you to the heart of Paris and has enabled you to share in the passion that rules the soul of the French: food!

You will come across diverse and sundry offerings at the open-air markets.

Le Patatier

Claude Ceccaldi's stand cannot be mistaken for anything but what it is: a potato vendor's. Here a low, slanting table is partitioned to hold over 30 varieties of the tubers, along with a selection of onions, shallots, garlic, and herbs. It slopes towards the back, so that the potatoes can easily be scooped up into metal bowls for weighing. An expert in his trade, Claude is considered one of the last true patatiers.

When Claude originally started work in this métier at the age of 14, helping out his stepfather, his real aspiration was to become a maker of stained-glass windows. Soon, however, he was won over by the world of open-air markets: the early hours, the casse-croute (mid-morning snack), the intensity of the work, the camaraderie among the vendors, and the interaction with the shoppers took him under its spell. By the time he was 24, he found himself running his own potato business, having inherited a knowledge of the subtleties of the different varieties from his stepfather and a courteous sales manner from his mother.

Thirty years later, he is still going strong. With the help of his wife Catherine and their nephew, Claude will go to great lengths to make sure that you buy the potato with the exact flavor, texture, and color that you need. Potatoes vary dramatically at different times of the year, and Claude knows the taste and consistency of each. For example, in summer he recommends the berber for a light purée and the concurrent for a heavier one; in winter he suggests the *samba* and the *asterix*.

The Ceccaldis are present at the Richard Lenoir, Daumesnil, and Charonne markets.

THE POTATO

The potato arrived in France via Peru, Spain, and Ireland in 1540. It was first valued as an ornamental plant, and was only cultivated as a vegetable some 50 years later; soon, however, its harvesting was forbidden in the mistaken belief that the tuber caused leprosy. While England, Scotland, and the Netherlands adopted potatoes, at the time called *"batata,"* it took the love and understanding of the renowned agronomist Augustin Parmentier to ensure its breakthrough in France. During the famine of 1787, which weighed on the hearts and bellies of Parisians, Parmentier was allotted an arid parcel of land on the outskirts of the city. Here he plotted to convince the hungry populace and the disdaining royalty of the value of the lowly *batata*. He carefully planted row after row of potato seedlings, and guarded them with armed soldiers in the hope of arousing the interest of the neighboring farmers. His plan worked to perfection: come nightfall, the curious peasants plundered the field, making off with the young plants and promptly adding to their meager crops. He even swayed the regal resistance of Louis XVI, by charming him with a bouquet of potato flowers. Parmentier's initiative boosted the vegetable to the ranks of stardom, and a hearty potato-and-meat dish, known as *Hachis Parmentier,* has been baptized in his name.

These days, cross-cultivated and refined, over 350 different varieties can be found in France; among the most cherished are the *Rosa, Roseval,* and *Ratte*, as well as the new crop potatoes grown on the Ile de Ré and the Ile de Noirmoutier off the Atlantic coast. The characteristic flavor of these island potatoes, which are harvested before maturity at the beginning of Spring, is achieved by mixing the soil with seaweed. Favorite strains of these new potatoes include: *Amandine, Starlette, Alcmaria,* and *Charlotte*. Not yet having had time to form a hard, protective skin, these young potatoes are positively delicious simply boiled and savored with a bit of butter and sea salt. Their price can be quite steep, but they are well worth the extra francs; and Monsieur Parmentier would be proud of their great success!

LA PUREE

To make a perfect *purée* you should never use a machine to mash the potatoes, as this tends to over-beat them and your *purée* will come out heavy and pasty. The potatoes should be peeled, quartered, and boiled in salted water with a piece of onion thrown in for taste, then pushed through a ricer or smashed with a hand held masher. Pick your potato carefully, a good *purée* potato should hold its shape. If it begins to fall apart, it is full of water and of inferior quality. Add just a bit of butter, some fresh cream, a touch of nutmeg, and, if you want a rich yellow color, an egg yolk, to make a creamy *purée* fit for a king.

TELEGRAPHE

Marché Télégraphe offers a remarkably decent selection of products, considering its small size and out-of-the-way location. It is not necessarily worth a detour, but if you are in the neighborhood, come take a look at the handful of vendors who set up on both sides of Rue Télégraphe. The colorful displays of Clavière Ambroise and Yvonne Gervais are a warm welcome and always have a good array of seasonal and exotic produce; the *artisanal* butcher Yannick Lebert has excellent prime cuts; and La Ferme Normande has a good selection of cheese, free-range poultry, and homemade specialties. This section of the 20th arrondissement has very little to offer in terms of sightseeing; so after filling your basket and picking up a bouquet of flowers, venture back towards the heart of the city.

PYRENEES

During the week Marché Pyrénées is a sad sight, with only a handful of vendors showing up; but on Sundays, the square fills up and spills over onto Rue des Pyrénées. This large market is made up mainly of fruit-and-vegetable stands where the quality can fluctuate. Nevertheless, a few *maraîchers* stand out against the lot, among them Georges Planet, who arrives from his farm in the Seine et Marne region loaded down with crates of fresh greens, a basket or two of eggs, and a couple of chickens. The atmosphere is animated here, and along with a few fishmongers, *fromagers*, and butchers, you will find all that you need at Marché Pyrénées but nothing out of the ordinary.

BELGRAND

Situated in the easternmost quartier of Paris, the Marché Belgrand is a sprawling neighborhood market that reflects the traditional tastes and needs of this middle-class community. Over 60 vendors assemble on a quiet tree-lined back street; they wrap around Rue Belgrand, finally stopping at a small square named after France's most poignant singer, Edith Piaf. Among the extensive displays of fish, vegetables, and cheese, you will come across a number of *charcutiers*. Our favorite is run by a Spanish couple who besides the traditional selection of hams, *saucissons*, and pâtés, offers spicy *chorizo* and Salamanca sausages.

The atmosphere is convivial and the prices so reasonable at this market that you will find your basket filling up faster than you might expect. Make sure to leave a space for a baguette or two, which you should pick up on

your way out at number 226 Rue des Pyrenées. La Flûte de Gana bakery makes some of the best bread in the city and is renowned for its delicious, chewy *flûte*.

DAVOUT

Davout is a neighborhood market that sets up along one side of the long boulevard that skirts around the whole city. Although this market is an important place for the residents of this area, it lacks character and atmosphere; and it is quite out of the way. Near the métro stop, you will find a row of food shops that are reminiscent of former times and complement the market that sets up in front.

Some stands distinguish themselves from the more run-of-the-mill *charcutiers*, *fromagers*, *poissoniers*, and *marchands volants*. Jean Claude Bonneau brings fresh eggs, chickens, and goat cheeses from his farm in the Sartre region. Monsieur Boulemzahir offers a selection of fruits and vegetables that is rare to find at any market, including broccoli rabe, *topinambourg*, long-stemmed radicchio called *trevise*, fresh ginger, purple potatoes, pomegranates, raw olives, chilies, persimmons, and a basketful of greens.

MORTIER

Marché Mortier is located "a hop and a skip" away from the lovely area known as "La Campagne à Paris." Instead of being held here, amid the quaint gardens and houses, the market sets up on the wide and desolate Boulevard Mortier that hugs the edge of the city. Approximately 30 vendors offer a complete selection and bring a touch of color and life to the avenue.

The *tripier* Michel Sortais sells top-notch products to his faithful customers, who make it a point to take home a portion of his *tripoux d'Auvergne*, a hearty and savory dish made with rolled tripe. The fishmonger Philippe Yvernault tends single-handedly to his large display. Jean-Luc Bône stands behind mounds of garden-fresh vegetables which he and his family bring from their farm in the Essonne region. Le Boulanger du Marché offers a great selection of old-fashioned, country-style breads. Madame Genaoui has a lovely selection of fruits and vegetables. And to complete the list, there is a wine shop down the street where you can buy a bottle or two.

Above: Flowers and autumn vegetables at Marché Belgrand.

MARKET RECIPES

MOULES MARINIERES
Mussels Steamed with Shallots and Wine

"Simplicity is sophistication," says Jean Pierre, the owner of Poissonerie JPB. He insists that all you need to truly appreciate the delicate flavor of fresh fish is to steam, poach, or grill it; and drizzle a bit of olive oil and a twist of lemon over it before serving. Hold the sauce please! The same goes for mussels: he likes to just steam them with a sprig of thyme but decided to give us this slightly more elaborate recipe. It brings out the sweet taste of plump *bouchot* mussels from the bay of Mont Saint Michel. If *bouchots* are not at hand, use any small mussel for this recipe.

15 minutes   10 minutes

8 lbs (4 kg) mussels
2 tbs sweet butter
2 shallots, chopped
1 cup white wine
Twist of pepper
2 tbs chopped flat parsley
Chopped parsley, for garnish

1. Wash the mussels under running water and remove the beards. You would ordinarily estimate 2 pounds (1 kilo) of mussels per person, but depending on the appetites, an extra pound (1/2 kilo) can be added per serving. **2.** In a tall-sided pot, melt the butter over medium heat. Add the shallots to sweat, until translucent; they should not brown. **3.** Turn up the heat a notch, pour in the wine, and bring to a boil, so as to let the alcohol evaporate. **4.** Toss in the mussels, and shake and flip to mix with the wine and shallots. Cover and cook for 5 to 8 minutes, shaking the pot every once in a while. The mussels should pop open when cooked. If a few remain closed, they should not be eaten as they may not be fresh. **5.** Add the pepper, sprinkle with parsley, and remove from heat. The mussels can either be served in the cooking pot or transferred to a bowl or soup terrine with a cover (to keep them warm while you are enjoying your first serving). Do not forget to bring an extra bowl to the table for the shells and a fresh baguette to soak up the sauce. **Serves 4.**

Crisp, lively whites: Muscadet de Sèvres-et-Maine sur Lie, Pouilly Fuissé

Moules marinières

HACHIS PARMENTIER
Oven-Baked Meat and Potato Mash

Hachis parmentier is an old-fashioned, satisfying dish that is one of Claude Ceccaldi's favorites. He likes to prepare it with leftover stew and roast meat, but for this recipe, we chose to make it with fresh meat. The combination of pork, beef, and veal makes for a juicier and lighter dish.

30 minutes   30 minutes

For the purée:
2 lbs (1 kg) boiling potatoes
1/2 onion
2 tbs milk
3 tbs butter
Salt and pepper
1 egg yolk
For the meat filling:
1 tbs peanut oil
1 bay leaf
1 sprig thyme
1 onion, finely chopped
2 cloves garlic, finely chopped
4 oz (125 g) ground pork
10 oz (300 g) ground veal
10 oz (300 g) ground beef
Salt and pepper, to taste
3 tbs beef stock
2 tbs butter
1 tbs grated Swiss cheese

1. Peel and quarter the potatoes, and boil in salted water with half an onion, until tender. Strain, and return to pot to evaporate any remaining water. Remove from heat, place in a large bowl, and purée with a ricer or masher. Add the milk, butter, salt, and pepper, mix well, and stir in the egg yolk. The purée should have a smooth, dense consistency (not runny). Set aside. **2.** In a skillet, heat the oil, add the bay leaf and thyme, and sauté the onions and garlic until translucent. Add the ground meats, and sauté at medium heat very quickly, until just cooked—do not overcook, or it will become dry. Remove the bay leaf and thyme, add salt and pepper to taste, and moisten with the stock. **3.** Preheat the oven to 400 °F (205 °C), and butter an oval porcelain or glass baking dish. Line the bottom of the dish with half of the potato purée, make sure to cover the sides, cover with the meat mixture, and top with the remaining purée so as to seal the meat between two equal layers of potato. Dot with 2 tablespoons of butter, and sprinkle with grated cheese. **4.** Bake in the oven for 20 to 30 minutes, and then brown the top under the grill for 5 minutes. Remove and serve immediately accompanied by a green salad. **Serves 4.**

Light, fresh reds or rich, dominant reds: Chinon, Châteauneuf-du-Pape

BRANDADE DE MORUE
Southern Style Codfish and Potato Purée

Brandade de morue (puréed salt cod) is a southern French dish that is a classic—though there are many debates over how it should be prepared. Some use garlic, others omit the potato purée, use cream instead of milk, add a hint of nutmeg, or mix in a few slices of sophisticated truffle! This recipe calls for potatoes, garlic, and milk; but once you have your base, you can mix and match as you choose.

24 hours   45 minutes

1 1/2 lbs (750 g) *bacalhau* (salted codfish)
1 lb (500 g) boiling potatoes
1/2 onion
1/2 cup milk
1/4 cup olive oil
2 garlic cloves, minced and crushed
White pepper, to taste
Squeeze of lemon juice
Salt, to taste
1/2 a baguette, thinly sliced and basted with olive oil

1. Cut the salt cod fillets so that they fit easily into a large bowl. Wash under cold running water, and place in a bowl generously covered with water. Let the fish desalt for at least 24 hours, changing the water at least three times. **2.** Drain and cut into several even pieces, and place in a pot of cold water, skin-side up. At medium-low heat, bring to a boil, and then immediately lower heat so that the cod gently simmers. Cook for 8 minutes, skimming from time to time. Remove the pieces to a plate with a slotted spoon, and let them cool a bit. **3.** Peel and quarter the potatoes, add to a pot of water with half an onion, and boil until very tender. Drain, heat for one minute back in the pot to remove any excess water, and then crush with a fork and hold. **4.** Remove the skin and any remaining bones from the cod fillets, and shred with your fingers; then place in a dishcloth, and roll on top of the kitchen counter to mash the cod bits even more. **5.** In a small saucepan, scald the milk, and set aside. In a pot large enough to hold the cod and potatoes, heat the olive oil over a medium flame, toss in the garlic, and vigorously stir in the cod and potatoes. Add the milk, lower the heat, and continue stirring for about 10 minutes, until the mixture is smooth and light (be careful that it does not stick to the bottom of the pot and burn). If the mixture does not break down enough, give it a few pulses with an electric mixer or food processor. Add the ground white pepper to taste, a squeeze of lemon, and, if necessary, salt. **6.** Pop the basted baguette slices into a hot oven to brown for 2 to 3 minutes. **7.** Fill a warmed porcelain or ceramic baking dish with the brandade, smooth into a mound, and place under the grill of the oven for a few minutes to brown the top. Serve immediately in the baking dish accompanied by the warm, toasted baguette.
Serves 4 to 6.

Crisp, young, whites and rosés: Sancerre, Vinho Verde, Rosé de Loire

CLAFOUTI AUX CERISES
Cherry Clafouti

Monsieur and Madame Leveau from the Président Wilson market always have the sweetest cherries and love to prepare this traditional dessert at home. Ideally, clafoutis should be made in late summer, when the dark, sweet, ripe cherries are flowing over the sides of the displays; but canned cherries will do for this recipe—just strain and pit them before sautéing them in the butter.

20 minutes   1 hour

2 tbs butter
1 lb (500 g) stoned black cherries
2 tbs sugar
1/4 cup kirsch (optional)

5 tbs flour
5 tbs sugar
1 pinch salt
3 eggs
1 vanilla bean (or 1 tbs vanilla extract)
1 cup milk
Confectioners' sugar, for garnish

1 ceramic pie dish or a square, ovenproof dish

1. Preheat oven to 350 °F (180 °C). **2.** In a large frying pan, melt the butter, add the stoned cherries and the sugar, and sauté a few minutes until the cherries plump up. Optionally, add the kirsch; allow to warm a couple of minutes, then light with a match to flambé the cherries. Remove from heat and set aside. (Note: if fresh cherries are not in season use the canned stoned cherries, straining the liquid.) **3.** In a bowl, mix the flour, sugar, and salt together. Add the eggs, and mix using a wooden spoon. **4.** Split the vanilla bean in half lengthwise, and scrape the inside of the bean into the milk (or simply add the vanilla extract directly). Add the milk to the flour mixture, and stir well. If you find too many clumps, pass through a sieve. **5.** Butter the pie dish, and add a 1/4-inch (1 cm) layer of the batter to cover the bottom. Place in the oven for about 10 minutes, until it sets. Remove from the oven, add the cherries, and then pour the rest of the batter on top. Normally, the cherries will rise to the top. **6.** Place in the center of the oven, and bake for about 1 hour. Test for doneness by inserting a knife in the center and check if it comes out clean. **7.** When done, remove from oven and sprinkle with confectioners' sugar. Serve warm or cold. **Serves 6.**

Pink Champagne

Clafouti aux cerises

BAGUETTE
"BOULANGÈRE"
6f,50

CROTTIN FERMIER
Langres
18F90
St NICOLAS de BOURGUEIL
23F80
Bougon
SELLES-SUR-CHER
CHEVRE Long FERMIER
24F80
du PERCHE
14F80
EPOISSES
EPOISSES
BRIQUE de BRE
L'AVEYRON
CHAVIGNOL au Lait Cru
9F80
LE PETIT PERCHE
LE PETIT PERCHE

MARKET SCHEDULE

MONDAY

MARKETS CLOSED

TUESDAY

IIe
RUE MONTORGEUIL ★★★
IIIe
ENFANTS ROUGE
V^{e}
MAUBERT ★★★★
PORT ROYAL ★★★★
MOUFFETARD ★★★★
VIe
RASPAIL ★★★
SAINT-GERMAIN ★★★
RUE SEINE-BUCI ★★★
VIIe
RUE CLER ★★★★
VIIIe
AGUESSEAU ★★★★
EUROPE ★★
X^{e}
SAINT QUENTIN ★★★
SAINT MARTIN ★★
XIe
POPINCOURT ★★★
PERE LACHAISE ★★
BELLEVILLE ★★
XIIe
ALIGRE ★★★★
DAUMESNIL ★★★★★
XIIIe
AUGUSTE BLANQUI ★★★★★
SALPETRIERE ★★
BOBILLOT★★
XIVe
MONTROUGE ★★★★★
RUE DAGUERRE ★★★
XVe
SAINT CHARLES ★★★★★
CONVENTION ★★★★★
XVIe
PORTE MOLITOR ★★★
POINT DU JOUR ★★★
SAINT DIDIER ★★
PASSY ★★★★
GROS-LA-FONTAINE ★★
XVIIe
NAVIER ★★★
RUE LEVIS ★★★
BATIGNOLLES ★
RUE PONCELET ★★★★
TERNES ★
XVIIIe
ORNANO ★★
RUE LEPIC ★★★
LA CHAPELLE ★★★
XIXe
JEAN-JAURES ★
PLACE DES FETES ★★★
RIQUET ★
SECRETAN ★★
XXe
DAVOUT ★★

WEDNESDAY

IIe
RUE MONTORGEUIL ★★★
IIIe
ENFANTS ROUGE
V^{e}
MONGE ★★★★
MOUFFETARD ★★★★
VIe
SAINT-GERMAIN ★★★
RUE SEINE-BUCI ★★★
VIIe
RUE CLER ★★★★
VIIIe
EUROPE ★★
X^{e}
SAINT QUENTIN ★★★
SAINT MARTIN ★★
XIe
CHARONNE ★★★
XIIe
ALIGRE ★★★★
COURS DE VINCENNES ★★★★
XIIIe
VINCENT AURIOL ★★★
XIVe
ALESIA ★★★
VILLEMAIN ★★
EDGAR QUINET ★★★★
RUE DAGUERRE ★★★
XVe
CERVANTES ★
LEFEBVRE ★★
LECOURBE ★★
GRENELLE ★★★★
XVIe
PRESIDENT WILSON ★★★★★
AMIRAL BRUIX ★★
AUTEUIL ★★★★★
PASSY ★★★★
XVIIe
BERTHIER ★★
RUE LEVIS ★★★
BATIGNOLLES ★
RUE PONCELET ★★★★
TERNES ★
XVIIIe
BARBES ★★★★
CRIMEE ★
ORDENER ★★★★
RUE LEPIC ★★★
LA CHAPELLE ★★★
XIXe
PORTE BRUNET ★★
VILLETTE ★★★
RIQUET ★
SECRETAN ★★
XXe
TELEGRAPHE ★★
BELGRAND ★★★★

HOURS

All markets are open in the morning hours from 9 a.m. to 1 p.m. Covered markets and street markets are also open in the afternoon from 4 p.m. to 7 p.m., except on Sundays.

THURSDAY

IIe
RUE MONTORGEUIL ★★★
IIIe
ENFANTS ROUGE
V^{e}
MAUBERT ★★★★
PORT ROYAL ★★★★
MOUFFETARD ★★★★
VIe
SAINT-GERMAIN ★★★
RUE SEINE-BUCI ★★★
VIIe
SAXE BRETEUIL ★★★★★
RUE CLER ★★★★
VIIIe
EUROPE ★★
X^{e}
SAINT QUENTIN ★★★
SAINT MARTIN ★★
XIe
RICHARD LENOIR ★★★★★
XIIe
ALIGRE ★★★★
PONIATOWSKI ★★★
SAINT ELOI ★★★
LEDRU ROLLIN ★★
XIIIe
MAISON BLANCHE ★★
JEANNE D'ARC ★★★★
XIVe
BRUNE ★★★★
RUE DAGUERRE ★★★
XVe
CONVENTION ★★★★★
XVIe
POINT DU JOUR ★★★
PASSY ★★★★
XVIIe
RUE LEVIS ★★★
BATIGNOLLES ★
RUE PONCELET ★★★★
TERNES ★
XVIIIe
NEY ★
RUE LEPIC ★★★
LA CHAPELLE ★★★
XIXe
JOINVILLE ★★★★★
JEAN-JAURES ★
RIQUET ★
SECRETAN ★★
XXe
REUNION ★★★★
PYRENEES ★★
MORTIER ★★★

FRIDAY

IIe
RUE MONTORGEUIL ★★★
IIIe
ENFANTS ROUGE
V^{e}
MONGE ★★★★
MOUFFETARD ★★★★
VIe
RASPAIL ★★★
SAINT-GERMAIN ★★★
RUE SEINE-BUCI ★★★
VIIe
RUE CLER ★★★★
VIIIe
AGUESSEAU ★★★★
EUROPE ★★
X^{e}
SAINT QUENTIN ★★★
SAINT MARTIN ★★
XIe
POPINCOURT ★★★
PERE LACHAISE ★★
BELLEVILLE ★★
XIIe
ALIGRE ★★★★
DAUMESNIL ★★★★★
XIIIe
AUGUSTE BLANQUI ★★★★★
SALPETRIERE ★★
BOBILLOT ★★
XIVe
MONTROUGE ★★★★★
RUE DAGUERRE ★★★
XVe
SAINT CHARLES ★★★★★
XVIe
PORTE MOLITOR ★★★
GROS-LA-FONTAINE ★★
SAINT DIDIER ★★
PASSY ★★★★
XVIIe
NAVIER ★★★
RUE LEVIS ★★★
BATIGNOLLES ★
RUE PONCELET ★★★★
TERNES ★
XVIIIe
ORNANO ★★
RUE LEPIC ★★★
LA CHAPELLE ★★★
XIXe
PLACE DES FETES ★★★
RIQUET ★
SECRETAN ★★
XXe
DAVOUT ★★

SATURDAY

IIe
RUE MONTORGEUIL ★★★
IIIe
ENFANTS ROUGE
V^{e}
MAUBERT ★★★★
PORT ROYAL ★★★★
MOUFFETARD ★★★★
VIe
SAINT-GERMAIN ★★★
RUE SEINE-BUCI ★★★
VIIe
SAXE BRETEUIL ★★★★★
RUE CLER ★★★★
VIIIe
EUROPE ★★
X^{e}
SAINT QUENTIN ★★★
SAINT MARTIN ★★
XIe
CHARONNE ★★★
XIIe
ALIGRE ★★★★
COURS DE VINCENNES ★★★★
LEDRU ROLLIN ★★
XIIIe
VINCENT AURIOL ★★★
XIVe
BRANCUSI (BIOLOGIQUE) ★★★
EDGAR QUINET ★★★★
ALESIA ★★★
RUE DAGUERRE ★★★
XVe
LEFEBVRE ★★
LECOURBE ★★
CERVANTES ★
XVIe
PRESIDENT WILSON ★★★★★
AUTEUIL ★★★★★
PASSY ★★★★
AMIRAL BRUIX ★★
SAINT DIDIER ★★
XVIIe
BATIGNOLLES (BIOLOGIQUE) ★★★★★
RUE PONCELET ★★★★
RUE LEVIS ★★★
BERTHIER ★★
BATIGNOLLES ★
TERNES ★
XVIIIe
BARBES ★★★★
ORDENER ★★★★
RUE LEPIC ★★★
LA CHAPELLE ★★★
CRIMEE ★
XIXe
VILLETTE ★★★
PORTE BRUNET ★★
SECRETAN ★★
RIQUET ★
XXe
BELGRAND ★★★★
TELEGRAPHE ★★

SUNDAY

IIe
RUE MONTORGEUIL ★★★
IIIe
ENFANTS ROUGE
V^{e}
MONGE ★★★★
MOUFFETARD ★★★★
VIe
RASPAIL (BIOLOGIQUE) ★★★★★
SAINT-GERMAIN ★★★
RUE SEINE-BUCI ★★★
VIIe
RUE CLER ★★★★
VIIIe
EUROPE ★★
X^{e}
SAINT QUENTIN ★★★
SAINT MARTIN ★★
ALIBERT ★★
XIe
RICHARD LENOIR ★★★★★
XIIe
ALIGRE ★★★★
PONIATOWSKI ★★★
SAINT ELOI ★★★
XIIIe
AUGUSTE BLANQUI ★★★★★
MAISON BLANCHE ★★
JEANNE D'ARC ★★★★
XIVe
VILLEMAIN ★★
BRUNE ★★★★
RUE DAGUERRE ★★★
XVe
CONVENTION ★★★★★
GRENELLE ★★★★
XVIe
POINT DU JOUR ★★★
PASSY ★★★★
XVIIe
RUE LEVIS ★★★
BATIGNOLLES ★
RUE PONCELET ★★★★
TERNES ★
XVIIIe
NEY ★
ORNANO ★★
RUE LEPIC ★★★
LA CHAPELLE ★★★
XIXe
JOINVILLE ★★★★★
JEAN-JAURES ★
PLACE DES FETES ★★★
RIQUET ★
SECRETAN ★★
XXe
REUNION ★★★★
PYRENEES ★★
MORTIER ★★★

MARKET ADDRESSES

	MARKET	LOCATION	METRO STATION
	IIe		
33	* RUE MONTORGEUIL	On Rue Montorgeuil from Rue de Turbigo to the St Eustache church	Les Halles or Sentier
	IIIe		
33	• ENFANTS ROUGE	39 Rue de Bretagne	Filles du Calvaire
	Ve		
38	MAUBERT	Place Maubert just off Bd Saint Germain	Maubert Mutualité
56	MONGE	Place Monge	Place Monge
56	PORT ROYAL	Bd de Port Royal from Rue Saint Jacques to Rue Berthollet	RER Port Royal
53	* RUE MOUFFETARD	Rue Mouffetard from Place de la Contrescarpe to Square Saint Médard	Censier Daubenton
	VIe		
60	RASPAIL (BIOLOGIQUE)	Bd Raspail from Rue du Cherche Midi & Rue de Rennes	Sèvres-Babylone or Rennes
78	RASPAIL	Bd Raspail from Rue du Cherche Midi & Rue de Rennes	Sèvres-Babylone or Rennes
78	• SAINT-GERMAIN	3 Rue Mabillon from Bd Saint-Germain, make a right on Rue Montfaucon	Mabillon
78	* RUE DE SEINE-BUCI	Rue de Buci from Bd Saint-Germain to Rue Mazarine	Mabillon and Odéon
	VIIe		
82	SAXE BRETEUIL	Avenue de Saxe from Place de Breteuil to Avenue de Ségur	Ségur or Sèvres Lecourbe
99	* RUE CLER	Rue Cler between Avenue de la Motte Piquet and Rue de Grenelle	Ecole Militaire
	VIIIe		
104	AGUESSEAU	Place de la Madeleine	Madeleine
114	• EUROPE	1 Rue Corvetto, just off Rue de Lisbonne	Villiers or Miromesnil
	Xe		
120	• SAINT QUENTIN	85 Bd de Magenta between Rue des Petits Hôtels and Rue de Chabrol	Poissonnière or Gare de l'Est
129	• SAINT MARTIN	31 Rue du Château d'Eau, on the corner of Rue Buchardon	Château d'Eau or Jacques Bonsergent
129	ALIBERT	Beside the Saint Louis Hospital along Rue Alibert, off Avenue Claude Vellefaux	Colonel Fabien or Goncourt
	XIe		
134	RICHARD LENOIR	Bd Richard Lenoir from Place de la Bastille to Rue Saint Sabin	Bastille or Bréguet Sabin
150	CHARONNE	Bd de Charonne, on the corner of Rue de Charonne	Alexander Dumas
150	POPINCOURT	Intersection of Bd Richard Lenoir and Rue Oberkampf	Oberkampf
151	PERE LACHAISE	Bd Ménilmontant, beginning on the corner of Rue Oberkampf	Ménilmontant
150	BELLEVILLE	Bd de Belleville from Rue Jean Pierre Timbaud to Rue de Belleville	Couronnes or Belleville
	XIIe		
158	ALIGRE	Rue d'Aligre from Rue Saint Antoine to Rue de Charenton	Ledru Rollin
172	COURS DE VINCENNES	Cours de Vincennes from Place de Nation to Avenue Docteur Arnold Netter	Nation
173	PONIATOWSKI	Bd Poniatowski from Avenue Daumesnil to Rue de Picpus	Porte d'Orée
172	SAINT ELOI	36/38 Rue de Reuilly	Reuilly Diderot or Montgallet
172	DAUMESNIL	Bd de Reuilly from Place Félix Eboué to Rue de Charenton	Daumesnil or Dugommier
173	LEDRU ROLLIN	Avenue Ledru Rollin from Avenue Daumesnil to Rue de Lyon	Gare de Lyon & Ledru Rollin
	XIIIe		
178	AUGUSTE BLANQUI	Bd Auguste Blanqui from Place d'Italie to Rue Barrault	Place d'Italie or Corvisart
193	MAISON BLANCHE	Avenue d'Italie from Rue de Tolbiac to Rue Vandrezanne	Tolbiac
192	JEANNE D'ARC	Place Jeanne d'Arc	Nationale
192	SALPETRIERE	Under the métro pass along Bd de l'Hôpital	Gare d'Austerlitz or Saint Marcel
192	BOBILLOT	Rue Bobillot & Rue Rungis	Maison Blanche and bus 67 to Place Rungis
193	VINCENT AURIOL	Bd Vincent Auriol from Rue Nationale to Rue Dunois	Nationale
	XIVe		
198	MONTROUGE	Square located on the corner of Rue Brézin and Rue Saillard	Mouton Duvernet
212	VILLEMAIN	Place du Lieutenant Piobetta located on Rue Alésia and Avenue Villemain	Plaisance
212	ALESIA	Square situated where Rue d'Alesia ends and Rue Tolbiac begins	Glacier
212	EDGAR QUINET	Bd Edgar Quinet from Rue du Départ to Rue de la Gaîté	Edgar Quinet
212	BRUNE	33-73 Bd Brune from Avenue Jean Moulin to Rue Friant	Porte de Vanves
212	BRANCUSI (BIOLOGIQUE)	Place Brancusi, off Avenue du Maine along Rue de l'Ouest	Gaîté

	MARKET	LOCATION	METRO STATION
	XVᵉ		
216	SAINT CHARLES	Rue Saint Charles from Rue de Javel to Rue des Cévennes	Charles Michels
230	CONVENTION	Rue de la Convention from Rue de Vaugirard to Rue de Dantzig	Convention
231	CERVANTES	Rue Bargue between Rue Dutot and Rue Platon	Volontaires
231	LEFEBVRE	Bd Lefebvre corner Rue Vaugirard near Rue de Dantzig	Porte de Versailles
230	LECOURBE	Rue Lecourbe on the corner of Bd Victor	Balard or Lourmel
231	GRENELLE	Bd de Grenelle from Bd de la Motte-Piquet to Rue de Lourmel	La Motte-Piquet Grenelle or Dupleix
	XVIᵉ		
236	PRESIDENT WILSON	Avenue du Président Wilson from Rue Freycinet to Avenue d'Iéna	Alma Marceau or Iéna
252	AMIRAL BRUIX	Bd de l'Amiral Bruix & Rue Weber	Porte Maillot
252	AUTEUIL	Corner of Rue d'Auteuil and Rue La Fontaine	Michel-Ange Auteuil
253	PORTE MOLITOR	Place de la Porte Molitor and Bd Murat	Michel-Ange Molitor
252	POINT DU JOUR	Avenue de Versailles from Porte de Saint Cloud to Rue Murat	Porte de Saint Cloud
252 •	SAINT DIDIER	Located on the corner of Rue Saint Didier & Rue Mesnil	Victor Hugo
252 •	PASSY	Located on Place de Passy on Rue Duban just off Rue de Passy	La Muette
253	GROS-LA-FONTAINE	Corner of Rue La Fontaine and Rue Gros	Jasmin
	XVIIᵉ		
260	BATIGNOLLES ORGANIC	Bd de Batignolles from Rue Boursault to Rue des Batignolles	Rome
273 *	RUE LEVIS	Rue Levis off Bd de Courcelles	Villiers
273 •	BATIGNOLLES	24 Rue Brochant	Brochant
273 *	RUE PONCELET	Rue Poncelet and Rue Bayen off Avenue des Ternes	Ternes
273 •	TERNES	8 Rue Lebon	Ternes or Péreire
273	BERTHIER	Avenue Brunertière (behind Bd Berthier)	PC bus to Gourgaud-Paul Adam
273	NAVIER	Rue Navier just off Avenue de St Ouen	Porte St Ouen
	XVIIIᵉ		
278	BARBES	Bd de la Chapelle just off Bd Barbès	Barbès Rochechouart
291	CRIMÉE	Bd Ney next to Porte Aubervilliers	Porte de la Chapelle
291	ORDENER	Rue Ordener from Rue du Montcalm to Rue de Championnet	Jules Joffrin & Bus 31
291	NEY	Bd Ney and Porte de Clignancourt	Porte de Clignancourt
291	ORNANO	Bd Ornano between Place Albert Kahn and Rue Ordener	Simplon and Porte de Clignancourt
291 *	RUE LEPIC	Rue Lepic between Bd de Clichy and Rue des Abbesses	Blanche
291 •	LA CHAPELLE	10 Rue de l'Olive just off Rue Riquet	Marx Dormoy
	XIXᵉ		
296	JOINVILLE	Place de Joinville just off Rue de Joinville beside the canal	Crimée
308	PORTE BRUNET	Avenue de la Porte de Brunet just of Rue Sérurier	Danube
308	VILLETTE	Bd de la Villette	Belleville
309	JEAN JAURES	145-185 Avenue Jean Jaurès	Ourcq
309	PLACE DES FETES	Square located just of Rue Crimée and Rue Prés Saint-Gervais	Place des Fêtes
309 •	RIQUET	42 Rue Riquet	Riquet
309 •	SECRETAN	Crossing of Avenue de Secrétan and Rue de Meaux Bolivar	Bolivar
	XXᵉ		
314	REUNION	Place de la Réunion off Rue Alexandre Dumas	Alexandre Dumas
330	TELEGRAPHE	Rue du Télégraphe off Rue de Belleville	Télégraphe
330	BELGRAND	Along Rue de la Chine and Rue Belgrand	Gambetta or Porte de Bagnolet
330	PYRÉNÉES	Rue des Pyrénées from Rue du Jourdain to Rue de l'Hermitage	Pyrénées
331	MORTIER	Corner of Bd Mortier and Rue Capitaine Ferber	Porte de Bagnolet
331	DAVOUT	Bd Davout from Rue Paganini to Rue de Lagny	Porte de Montreuil

• Covered Market: food hall with individual stalls

* Street Market: pedestrian area where shops open up their displays onto the sidewalk

LES POISSONS ET LES FRUITS DE MER

TURBOT
Turbot

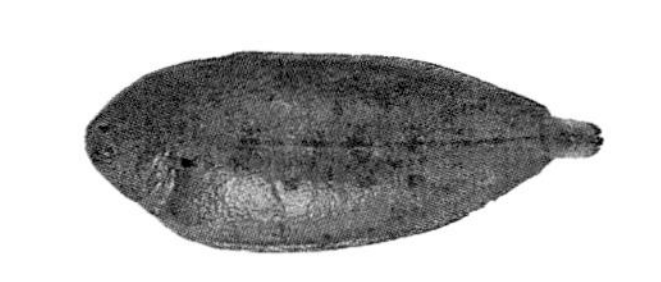

SOLE
Sole

CONGRE
Congre eel

RAIE
Skate

LOTTE
Monkfish

THON GERMON
Tuna

MERLAN
Whiting

MAQUERAU
Mackerel

CABILLAUD
Cod

MERLU
Hake

ANCHOIS
Anchovy

SARDINE
Sardine

DAURADE ROYAL
Gilt Head Bream

ROUGET / ROUGET-BARBET
Red Mullet

LOUP DE MER
Sea Bass

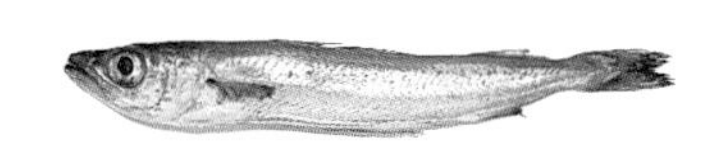

MULET
Mullet

PAGEOT
Pandora

RASCASSE ROUGE / CHAPON
Brown Sea Scorpion

SAINT-PIERRE
John Dory

POULPE
Octopus

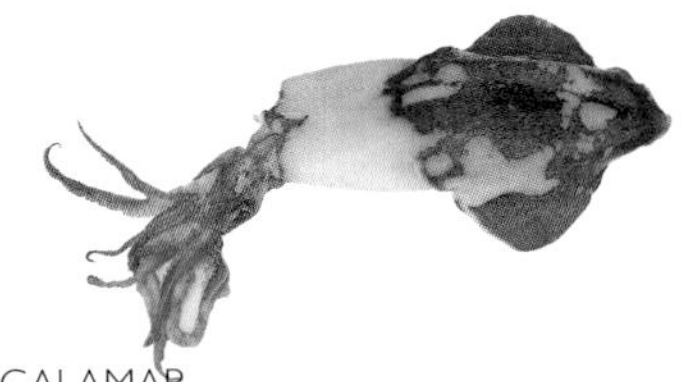

CALAMAR
Squid

CREVETTE ROSE / BOUQUET
Bouquet-Red Shrimp

CREVETTE GRISE
North Sea Prawn

LANGOUSTE
Spiny Lobster

HOMARD
Lobster

ECREVISSE
Crayfish

LANGOUSTINE
Dublin Bay Prawn

ARAIGNEE DE MER
Spider Crab

TOURTEAU
Edible Crab

OURSIN
Sea Urchin

BULOT
Whelk

HUITRE
Oyster

MOULE
Mussel

COQUILLE ST JACQUES
Sea Scallop

PETONCLE
Bay Scallop

PALOURDE / CLOVISSE
Venus Mussel

PRAIRE
Rough Venus Mussel

AMANDE DE MER
Dos Cockle

COQUE
Cockle

LES FROMAGES

COOKING GLOSSARY

Bain Marie — A hot water bath used to reduce the impact of heat on sensitive foods (like soufflés) or those requiring a long cooking time (like pâtés). This is done by immersing whatever you are cooking in a larger dish and filling it with hot water to the halfway point.

Beef Stock — To make a good beef stock, place 2 beef bones for stock (ask your butcher) in an oven-proof oven dish with 1 carrot, 1 peeled onion, and 1 celery stalk. Cook in a preheated oven at 450°F (230°C) and cook for about 20 minutes. Remove from oven and place ingredients in a large saucepan, cover with water, a teaspoon of salt, some parsley stalks, cover and bring to a simmer. Skim often and cook for at least 2 hours. This can be made ahead of time and frozen. When ready to use, skim off the hard fat on the top.

Bouquet Garni — A bouquet garni is a combination of different herbs that are tied together either in cheese cloth or in a leek leaf and added to a stew or baking dish. Normally the herbs used are parsley, bay leaf, and thyme, but any other herb can be added, including celery, garlic, rosemary, and black peppercorns depending on the recipe.

Chicken Stock — To make a good chicken stock, place the following ingredients in a large pot, cover with water and boil one hour: bones from 1 chicken, 1 carrot, 1 peeled onion, 1 celery stalk, peppercorns, parsley stalks, 1 teaspoon salt. Remove from heat, let cool. This can be made ahead of time and frozen. When ready to use, skim off the hard fat on the top.

Flambé — Flambéing is a very simple process that many of us fear as we have only seen it a grand restaurant done by a fancy waiter in a black tie. When it is time to flambé, just add the alcohol, move away from the pan, light a match and slowly lower it to the pan; it will ignite by itself. Turn the pan until the flame extinguishes.

How to peel a tomato — With a small knife make a cross on the bottom of the tomato. Bring a saucepan of water to a boil and immerse the tomato(es). After approximately 30 seconds, when the skin starts to pull away from the fruit, remove from water and run under cold water. When cool, peel the tomato, cut in half, remove seeds and slice as desired.

How to beat egg whites — Separate eggs and place whites in a large bowl. Add a pinch of salt to the bowl. Using a whisk or electric beater, beat the egg whites trying to incorporate as much air as possible. The mixture will begin to foam, and slightly hold its shape, this stage is called "soft peak." Continue beating until the mixture stiffens and the foam forms a peak when you withdraw the egg beater. The eggs are over-beaten when they start to become granular and separate. Using an unlined copper bowl speeds up the "peak" procedure but any glass or porcelain bowl will do.

How to blanch — Whether you are blanching vegetables, seafood, or beans, the process is the same. Basically you are boiling the item ever so slightly. All you need to do is plunge whatever you want to blanch into boiling water for about 1 minute. Remove from heat, strain, and run under cold water.

Parboil — To partially cook something in boiling water, most often vegetables, so that they can be finished off at a later stage in a sauté or roasting pan.

Salt and Pepper, to taste — Most of our recipes do not specify the amount of salt to be used as this is such a personal issue. We normally add salt and pepper at the beginning and then check to see that there is enough at the end, just before serving. Please note that the few that do specify amounts should be followed.

Scald — When you heat liquid (most often milk) nearly to a boil.

GLOSSARY

abbatoir **-** slaughterhouse
accras de morue **-** fried codfish balls
affinage - cheese aging process
affineur - person responsible for aging cheese
Amanites des Césars - type of mushroom
amuse-gueule - commonly refers to something that will whet your appetite before the meal, e.g. hors d'œuvre
andouillettes - sausage made from offal and innards such as tripe and intestines
antipasti - Italian starters
arrondissement - term used in Paris for neighborhood. The city is divided into 20 arrondissements or neighborhoods, which are numbered
artisanal - made according to tradition or homemade
auberge - family-run restaurant or bed-and-breakfast
bacalhau (aka morue or cabillaud) - salted codfish
baklava - Lebanese and Greek dessert made with phyllo pastry, walnuts, pistachios, and honey
ballon de rouge - colloquial for glass of red wine
barquettes - punnets or small baskets
belons - type of oyster (see oyster inset p. 29)
beurek - triangles of phyllo pastry filled with tasty meat, ricotta or spinach
bien cuit - well-done (a point=medium, rosé=rosé, saignant=rare)
bio / biologique - term used in France for organic
bleu de travail - overalls
blinis - Russian pancakes
bœuf Bourguignon - beef stew made with red wine (see recipe p. 258)
bœuf en daube - classic dish, beef in a brown sauce
bœuf gros-sel - classic dish, boiled beef (see *pot au feu* recipe p. 35)
bouché à la reine - classic dish, pastry filled with veal kidneys in a cream sauce
boucherie - butcher
bouillabaisse - fish stew
bouquetière - flower vendor
bouquinistes - secondhand bookseller
brandade de morue - puréed salted codfish (see recipe p. 334)
bresaola - Italian cured beef
brocante / brocanteur - bric-a-brac trade / trader
burma - Tunisian pastry made with angel hair dough filled with pistachios
café au lait - espresso with milk
cailles aux figues fraîches - roasted quails with fresh figs (see recipe p. 235)
canard croiser - crossed wild and domestic duck
casse-croute - mid-morning snack generally eaten at the workplace
cassoulet - stew made with a base of white beans and *confit de canard*, goose, lamb, sausage, or pork added
celeri remoulade - grated celery root mixed with mayonnaise
cèpes (aka porcini) - brown, umbrella shaped mushrooms with a smoky flavor
chabrot - habit in the country to add wine from the glasses to the bowls to finish off the remaining spoonfuls of soup or stew
champignons de Paris - button mushrooms
chanterelles (aka girolles) - trumpet shaped, mild flavored mushrooms
charcuterie / charcutier - pork-based products; also pork butcher shop or delicatessen counter / pork butcher or person tending delicatessen counter
Charolaises - breed of cow, white and stout, renowned to produce excellent quality meat
chevaline - horse meat
chevreuil - venison (see recipe p. 117)
chipolata - thin pork sausage
chorizo - spicy pork sausage originating in Spain
choucroute garnie - Alsatian dish made with a base of stewed pickled cabbage and a variety of pork meats and sausages added on top
chou farci - stuffed cabbage, usually with pork meat, onion, white wine, egg, and other spices
chouquettes - ball of fried batter, rolled in coarse sugar
clafoutis - a family dessert originating in the Limousin region (see recipe p. 334)
confit de canard - preserved duck, confit of duck
coq au vin - Burgundy-style chicken stew (see recipe p. 131)
coques - type of clam, white and small in size
cornes de cerf - delicate salad green ressembling deer antlers
cornichons - tiny, bite-sized pickles
côtes de bœuf - rib roast
coup de cœur - favorite thing
court bouillon - stock made with a lot of water, some wine, onion, garlic, and herbs, usually to cook fish
couscoussière - special steamer, recommended to prepare couscous
crème fraîche - thick cream with a butter content of at least 30%
cuisson - degree of doneness (for meat or poultry)
"dix balles" - "ten francs!"
dolma - stuffed vegetables (see recipe p. 103)
douzaine - a dozen
eau-de-vie - brandy or other high-percentage alcohol
epautre - old variety of wheat
éperlan - similar to smelts, a small silver fish that is fried and eaten whole
épicerie / épicier - grocery shop / grocer
escalope - thin slice of meat
escargots de Bourgogne - snails cooked in their shell with a parsley-garlic butter on top; typical of the region of Burgundy
fait maison - homemade
feuilletés - savory puff pastries
fez (pl. fezzes) - a skullcap used by men in Arabic countries
fines de claires - type of oyster
flan - rich custard
flûte - thin baguette
foie gras - a delicacy, fattened duck or goose liver that is normally prepared in a terrine (see recipe p. 118) or cooked fresh and served with a sweet sauce (inset p. 246)
fougasse - flat bread made in the south of France with olive oil and often flavored with herbs, or olives, or onions
fraises des bois - tiny wild strawberries
fricassée Auvergnat - dish made with sliced fresh sausages and potatoes cooked in duck or goose fat, from the region of Auvergne
friture - fish fry (see recipe p. 311)
fromagerie / fromager - cheese shop / cheese vendor
galette - crêpe or pancake
gare - train station
gariguette - elongated, slightly lemony-tasting strawberry
gelées - aspics, usually containing poultry, meats, and herbs
guinguettes - name given to outdoor wine and dance halls set up along the river banks during the late 1800s
hachis parmentier - oven-baked meat and potato mash (see recipe p. 333)
haricots verts - string beans
harissa - Maghrébine paste made with chilis, garlic, corinder seed, and oil

haut de gamme - top of the line
hôtel particuliers - private mansions
huîtres à la nage - oysters cooked in a light cream sauce (see recipe p. 57)
jambon - ham
jambon persillé - ham in aspic
La Vielle France - term used to depict France of olden days and its well-established traditions
lapin forestier - stew made with free-range rabbit and wild mushrooms
lentilles aux lardons - lentils and sautéed bacon
ligname - root from which a porridge is made
mâche - lambs lettuce
madeleine - French tea cake (see recipe p. 118)
magret de canard - breast of fattened duck
manioc - tapioca, cassava
maraîcher - garden farmer
marchand - vendor / merchant
marché - market
Martiniquaise - native women of the island of Martinique
merguez - spicy North African lamb sausage
métier - profession
mi-cuit - partially cooked
mollet - soft-boiled
morue (à la Provencale) - fresh codfish (cooked with tomatoes, garlic and herbs)
mousseron - small delicate purple or brown colored mushroom
museau de porc en vinaigre - pig snout in a vinaigrette sauce
natas - Portuguese custard-filled tarts
Nouvelle Cuisine - literally "New Cuisine," a way of cooking food in smaller portions, using reduced amounts of cream and butter; originated in France in the 1980s and took off all over the world
œuf à la coque - soft-boiled eggs
pain au chocolat - a croissant filled with chocolate
pain de campagne - country-style bread
parmigiano reggiano - parmesan
pastillas - North African dish, fried phyllo pastry stuffed with a meat, nut, and spice mixture (see recipe p. 294)
patatier - potato vendor
paupiettes - rolls of veal or turkey filled with a meat and vegetable stuffing
périphérique - the throughway that runs around the city of Paris
petit gris - small edible snail
petit salé aux lentilles - salt-cured pork, cooked with lentils
petit déjeuner - breakfast
pièce de bœuf - thick cut of meat, normally filet
pied de mouton - whitish mushroom with large, flat top and a delicate flavor
pissaladière - Provence-style onion tart (see recipe p. 232)
plat du jour - special of the day (at a restaurant)
plateau de fruit de mer - combination of oysters, clams, crabs, shrimps, langoustines, sea snails, mussels, and sea urchins served on an enormous metal platter lined with crushed ice and accompanied by rye bread, butter, lemons, shallot vinaigrette, and mayonnaise; typical in brasseries that have an oyster bar
Poilâne - a sourdough bread baked in a wood-burning oven. (The name originates from the famous baker, Monsieur Poilâne, who first put it on the market and whose sons continue the tradition.)
poivrade - baby artichokes from the south of France
pommes frites - French fries
pot au feu - savory boullion beef pot (see recipe p. 35)
poule au pot - literally "hen in a pot" - a chicken and vegetables stew cooked in stock
poulet de Bresse - prized chickens from the region of Bresse
poulet de Gers - same as above but from the region of Gers
prosciutto - an air-dried ham originating in Italy
provolone - an Italian cheese made from cow's milk
quartier - quarter or neighborhood
quenelles de brochet - light, oval shaped delicacy made with sweet water pike and served with a cream sauce
ragoût de marcassin - stew made of wild boar
rillettes - mixture of shredded pork meat and pork fat usually eaten on toasted bread with mustard and *cornichons*
rondelles - round slices
roquette - arugula, type of green used in salad
rosés - pink hued champignons de Paris
rôtisserie - roaster, stand or shop that sells spit roasted meat and fowl
salumeria - Italian term for delicatessen meat
sarrasin - buckwheat
saucisson - dried sausage
souper - supper
steak frites - typical French dish of grilled steak and French fries
steak tartare - typical French dish, of raw ground beef mixed with capers, onions, mustard, Tabasco, raw egg yolk, salt and pepper; served with French fries and salad
sur place - on the spot
taboulé - couscous salad with tomatoes, parsley, and mint
tagine - a North African stew (see recipe p. 294)
tapenade - olive caviar (see inset p. 90)
tarama (aka taramasalata) - spread made from smoked cod roe and heavy cream, olive oil, or mayonnaise
tarte aux pommes - apple tart
tartine beurrée - bread spread with butter
terrine - mixture of meat, poultry, fish, or vegetables, cooked and generally served in an earthenware baking dish (terrine)
teurgoul - a rice pudding, old-fashioned dessert from Normandy
topinambour - Jerusalem artichoke
tourteau - large, rust-colored, edible crab
Tout-Paris - literally "All of Paris," the chic and celebrities of Parisian society
traiteur - specialty shop selling prepared dishes
triperie / tripier - shop specializing in innards and offal / vendor selling innards and offal
trompettes-des-morts - black trumpet shaped mushroom with a deep nutty flavor
veau Printanier - dish of veal sautéed with spring vegetables
viticulteur - oenologist (winemaker)
volaille / volailler - poultry / poultry vendor
voyous - thugs

aka: also known as

ADDRESSES

Allobroges, 71 Rue des Grands-Champs, 75020 Paris
Au Bœuf Couronné, 188 Avenue Jean Jaurés, 75019 Paris
Au Cochon Rose, 137 Rue St. Charles, 75015 Paris
Aux Delices de Carol, 30 Rue de Joinville, 75019 Paris
Balajo, 8 Rue de Lappe, 75011 Paris
Bofinger, 5 Rue de la Bastille, 75004 Paris
Brasserie Lipp, 51 Bd St-Germain, 75006 Paris
Café de Flore, 172 Bd St-Germain, 75006 Paris
Café de France, 12 Place d'Italie, 75013 Paris
Carette, 4 Place du Trocadéro, 75016 Paris
Caves Péret, 6 Rue Daguerre, 75014 Paris
Caviar Kaspia, 17 Place de la Madeleine, 75008 Paris
Charcutier Lyonnais, 58 Rue des Martyrs, 75009 Paris
Cherche-Midi, 22 Rue du Cherche-Midi, 75006 Paris
Chez André, 12 Rue Marbeuf, 75008 Paris
Chez Gladines, 30 Rue des Cinq Diamants, 75013 Paris
"Chez Teil - Produits d'Auvergne", 6 Rue de Lappe, 75011 Paris
D'Chez Eux, 2 Avenue Lowendal, 75007 Paris
Daguerre Marée, 9 Rue Daguerre, 75014 Paris
4 Rue Bayen, 75017, Paris
Dominique Martino - La Truffe Noir Domaine de La Rabasse
04210 Valensole-en-Provence
Facchetti, 134 Rue Mouffetard, 75005 Paris
Fauchon, 30 Place de la Madeleine, 75008 Paris
Fouquet's, 99 Avenue Champs Elysées, 75008 Paris
Fromagerie Vacoux, 5 Rue Daguerre, 75014 Paris
Gremillet - Lafitte Foie Gras
20 Rue de l'Union, 78601 Maisons BP23
Laffitte Cedex web: www.sollers.fr/foie-gras
Hédiard, 21 Place de la Madeleine, 75008 Paris
Hotel Lutetia, 45 Bd. Raspail, 75006 Paris
Julien, 16 Rue du Faubourg St. Denis, 75010 Paris
L' Ebauchoir, 43-45 Rue de Cîteaux, 75012 Paris
L'Oiseaux de Passage, 7 Rue Barrault, 75013 Paris
La Galoche d'Aurillac, 41 Rue de Lappe, 75011 Paris
La Librairie des Gourmets, 98 Rue Monge, 75005 Paris
La Rôtisserie du Beaujolais, 19 Quai de la Tournelle, 75005 Paris
La Tour D'Argent, 15-17 Quai de la Tournelle, 75005 Paris
Ladurée, 16 Rue Royale, 75008 Paris
75 Avenue Champs Elysées, 75008 Paris
Le Baron Rouge, 1 Rue Theophile Roussel, 75012 Paris
Le Bœuf Gros Sel, 120 Rue des Grands-Champs, 75020 Paris
Le Celtique, 25 Bd Auguste Blanqui, 75013 Paris
Le Cochon à l'Oreille, 15 Rue Montmartre, 75001 Paris
Le Comptoir de la Gastronomie, 34 Rue Montmartre, 75001 Paris
Le Jardin d'Isa, 1 Charles Fillion, 75017 Paris
Le Moulin de la Vierge, 166 Avenue de Suffren, 75015 Paris
Le Moulin Rouge, 82 Bd de Clichy, 75018 Paris
Le Poisson Bleu, 12 Rue Vitruve, 75020 Paris
Le Raspail, 58 Bd Raspail, 75006 Paris
Le Tambourg, 41 Rue Montmartre, 75002 Paris
Le Viaduc Café, 43 Avenue Daumesnil, 75012 Paris
Les Vergers St. Eustache, 13 Rue Montorgeuil, 75001 Paris
Maison Maille, 6 Place de la Madeleine, 75008 Paris
Maison Molard, 48 Rue des Martyrs, 75009 Paris
Marius et Janette, 4 Avenue George V, 75008 Paris
Market Discoveries, 44 Fulham Road, London SW3 6HH (UK)
e-mail: markets@divertimenti.co.uk
Moisan Bakery (BIO), 5 Place Aligre, 75012 Paris
Museé de l' Erotisme, 72 Bd de Clichy, 75018 Paris
Noura, 12 Avenue Marceau, 75116 Paris
Parc André Citroën, Rue Saint Charles and Rue Balard, 75015 Paris
Parc de la Villette, 30 Avenue Corentin-Cariou, 75019 Paris
Parc des Buttes Chaumont, Rue Botzaris and Rue de Crimée, 75019 Paris
Parc Georges Brassens, Rue Brancion and Rue Morillons, 75015 Paris
Parc Montsouris, Métro: Cité Université, 75014 Paris
Printemps, 64 Bd Hausmann, 75009 Paris
Quatre Homme, 118 Rue Mouffetard, 75005 Paris
62 Rue de Sèvres, 75007 Paris
Quoniam, 107 Rue Mouffetard, 75005 Paris
Rendez-vous de la Nature, 96 Rue Mouffetard, 75005 Paris
Square Trousseau, 1 Rue Antoine Vollon, 75012 Paris

BIBLIOGRAPHY

Arcache, Jean: *Le Guide Hachette des Vins, 1998*
Paris: Hachette Livres, 1997.

Beck, Simone, Louisette Bertholde and Julia Child:
Mastering the Art of French Cooking.
New York: Alfred A. Knopf, Inc., 1961.

Christain, Glynn: *Edible France*
London: Grub Street, 1996.

Fierro, Alfred: *Histoire et Dictionnaire de Paris*
Paris: Robert Laffont, S.A., 1996.

Hillairet, Jacques: *Connaissance du Vieux Paris*
Paris: Payot et Rivages, 1993.

Hillairet, Jacques: *Dictionnaire Historique des Rues de Paris*
Paris: Ed. Minuit, 1991.

Larousse, Pierre: *Nouveau Dictionnaire Illustré*
Paris: Larousse, 1909.

Maureau, Andrée: *Recettes en Provences*
Aix-en-Provence: Edisud, 1991.

Vallois, Thirza: *Around and About Paris*
London: Illiad Books, 1997.

Varejka, Pascal: *Paris-brève histoire de la capitale*
Paris: Ed. Parigramme, 1995.

PHOTO CREDITS

All photographs taken by Nicolle Aimée Meyer and Amanda Pilar Smith except:

© AKG, Paris: pp. 20 (ills. 1, 2), 24 (ill. 2), 26 (ills. 2, 3), 27 (ills. 2, 3), 71 (ill. 1), 127, 139, 148, 288.

© AKG, Paris / Almasy: pp. 26 (ill.1), 224.

© Association Soleil, Paris: pp. 18, 21 (ills. 1, 2), 24 (ills. 1, 3), 25 (ill. 4), 27 (ill. 1), 111, 164 (ill. 1).

© Könemann Verlag GmbH, Köln / Studio für Landkartentechnik, Detlef Maiwald: endpapers.

Olaf Wipperfurth, Paris: pp. 36, 57, 59, 81, 116, 119, 133, 157, 197, 233, 257, 259, 276, 295, 311, 332, 335.

© Photo Disc, Hamburg: p. 265 (ill.2).

© Roger Viollet, Paris / Boyer: pp. 23, 208.

© Roger Viollet, Paris / Branger: p. 25 (ill. 1).

© Roger Viollet, Paris / Harlingue: pp. 22, 24 (ill. 4), 112 (ill. 2), 136, 166, 318.

© Roger Viollet, Paris / John-James Chalon: p. 2.

© Roger Viollet, Paris / LL: p. 25 (ill. 3).

© Roger Viollet, Paris: pp. 25 (ill. 2), 149.

© Tony Stone Images, Munich / Hulton Getty: p. 95 (ills. 1, 2, 3).

The publisher has not been able to trace all owners of rights to the images reproduced. Owners of such rights are requested to address any claims arising from them to the publisher.

NOTES ON ABBREVIATIONS AND QUANTITIES

1 inch	= 2.5 centimeters
1 oz	= 1 ounce = 28 grams
1 lb	= 1 pound = 16 ounces
1 cup	= 250 milliliters (liquids)
1 g	= 1 gram = 1/1000 kilogram
1 kg	= 1 kilogram = 1000 grams
125 ml	= 125 mililiters = approximately 8 tbs
1 tbs	= 1 level tablespoon = 15–20 g* / 15 ml (liquids)
1 tsp	= 1 level teaspoon = 3–5 g* / 5 ml (liquids)

* The weight of dry ingredients varies significantly depending on the density factor; e.g. 1 cup flour weighs less than 1 cup butter. The metric conversions for bigger quantities are given in the recipes.
Quantities in recipes have been rounded up or down for convenience, where appropriate. Metric conversions may, therefore, not correspond exactly.

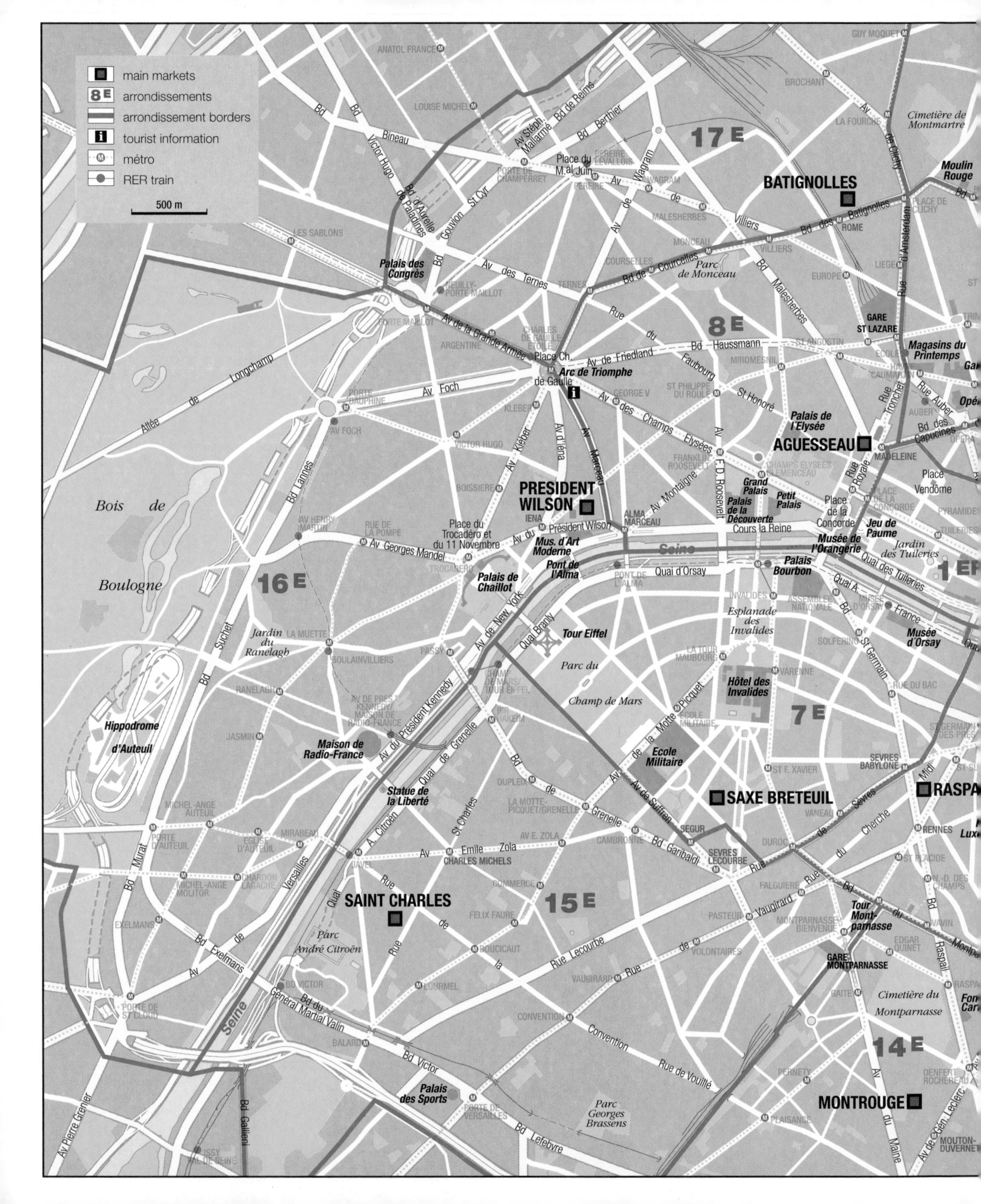
main markets
8E arrondissements
arrondissement borders
tourist information
métro
RER train
500 m
ANATOL FRANCE
GUY MOQUET
BROCHANT
LOUISE MICHEL
LA FOURCHE
Cimetière de Montmartre
17E
Bd Bineau
Bd Victor Hugo
Bd d'Aurelle de Paladines
Av Stéph. Mallarmé
Bd de Reims
Bd Berthier
Place du M.al Juin
PEREIRE LEVALLOIS
PORTE DE CHAMPERRET
PEREIRE
WAGRAM
Av de Wagram
Av de Villiers
MALESHERBES
BATIGNOLLES
Moulin Rouge
PLACE DE CLICHY
Av de Clichy
Bd des Batignolles
ROME
Rue d'Amsterdam
LES SABLONS
Gouvion St Cyr
MONCEAU
VILLIERS
COURCELLES
Bd de Courcelles
Parc de Monceau
LIEGE
EUROPE
Palais des Congrès
NEUILLY-PORTE MAILLOT
Av des Ternes
TERNES
Bd Malesherbes
GARE ST LAZARE
PORTE MAILLOT
Av de la Grande Armée
CHARLES DE GAULLE ETOILE
ARGENTINE
8E
Rue du Faubourg St Honoré
Bd Haussmann
ST AUGUSTIN
MIROMESNIL
Magasins du Printemps
Allée de Longchamp
Place Ch. de Gaulle
Av de Friedland
Arc de Triomphe
ST PHILIPPE DU ROULE
GEORGE V
Rue Tronchet
Rue Auber
AUBER
PORTE DAUPHINE
Av Foch
KLEBER
Av des Champs Elysées
Palais de l'Elysée
Bd des Capucines
OPERA
AV FOCH
VICTOR HUGO
Av Kléber
Av d'Iéna
Av Marceau
Av F.D. Roosevelt
AGUESSEAU
MADELEINE
FRANKLIN ROOSEVELT
CHAMPS ELYSEES CLEMENCEAU
Rue Royale
Place Vendôme
Bd Lannes
BOISSIERE
PRESIDENT WILSON
Av Montaigne
Grand Palais
Petit Palais
Palais de la Découverte
Place de la Concorde
PLACE DE LA CONCORDE
Bois de Boulogne
AV HENRY MARTIN
RUE DE LA POMPE
Place du Trocadéro et du 11 Novembre
IENA
Av du Président Wilson
ALMA MARCEAU
Cours la Reine
Jeu de Paume
TUILERIES
Av Georges Mandel
Mus. d'Art Moderne
Musée de l'Orangerie
Jardin des Tuileries
Seine
TROCADERO
Pont de l'Alma
PONT DE L'ALMA
Quai d'Orsay
Palais Bourbon
Quai des Tuileries
16E
Palais de Chaillot
Av de New York
INVALIDES
ASSEMBLEE NATIONALE
Quai A. France
MUSEE D'ORSAY
Esplanade des Invalides
Bd St Germain
Musée d'Orsay
Jardin du Ranelagh
LA MUETTE
Bd Suchet
Quai Branly
Tour Eiffel
SOLFERINO
LA TOUR MAUBOURG
BOULAINVILLIERS
PASSY
Parc du Champ de Mars
VARENNE
RANELAGH
CHAMP DE MARS/TOUR EIFFEL
Hôtel des Invalides
RUE DU BAC
AV DE PRES. KENNEDY/MAISON DE RADIO-FRANCE
Av du Président Kennedy
BIR HAKEIM
Av de la Motte Picquet
ECOLE MILITAIRE
7E
ST GERMAIN DES PRES
Hippodrome d'Auteuil
JASMIN
Maison de Radio-France
Quai de Grenelle
Ecole Militaire
SEVRES BABYLONE
ST F. XAVIER
Bd de Grenelle
Av de Suffren
RASPAIL
Statue de la Liberté
DUPLEIX
SAXE BRETEUIL
MICHEL-ANGE AUTEUIL
LA MOTTE-PICQUET/GRENELLE
VANEAU
Rue de Sèvres
Rue du Cherche Midi
RENNES
PORTE D'AUTEUIL
Bd Murat
MIRABEAU
EGLISE D'AUTEUIL
Quai A. Citroën
Rue St Charles
AV E. ZOLA
CAMBRONNE
Bd Garibaldi
SEGUR
DUROC
Av Emile Zola
CHARLES MICHELS
JAVEL
SEVRES LECOURBE
ST PLACIDE
N.-D. DES CHAMPS
MICHEL-ANGE MOLITOR
CHARDON LAGACHE
Av de Versailles
COMMERCE
FALGUIERE
Rue de Vaugirard
Bd du Montparnasse
SAINT CHARLES
15E
PASTEUR
MONTPARNASSE BIENVENUE
Tour Montparnasse
EXELMANS
FELIX FAURE
VAVIN
Bd Raspail
Parc André Citroën
Rue de la Convention
BOUCICAUT
Rue Lecourbe
VOLONTAIRES
EDGAR QUINET
Bd Exelmans
GARE MONTPARNASSE
BD VICTOR
VAUGIRARD
LOURMEL
GAITE
Cimetière du Montparnasse
PORTE DE ST CLOUD
Bd du Général Martial Valin
CONVENTION
BALARD
Bd Victor
Rue de Vouillé
14E
PERNETY
DENFERT ROCHEREAU
Palais des Sports
PORTE DE VERSAILLES
Parc Georges Brassens
MONTROUGE
PLAISANCE
Av du Maine
Av du Gén. Leclerc
Av Pierre Grenier
Bd Gallieni
Bd Lefebvre
ISSY VAL DE SEINE
MOUTON-DUVERNET

BIBLIOGRAPHY

Arcache, Jean: *Le Guide Hachette des Vins, 1998*
Paris: Hachette Livres, 1997.

Beck, Simone, Louisette Bertholde and Julia Child:
Mastering the Art of French Cooking.
New York: Alfred A. Knopf, Inc., 1961.

Christain, Glynn: *Edible France*
London: Grub Street, 1996.

Fierro, Alfred: *Histoire et Dictionnaire de Paris*
Paris: Robert Laffont, S.A., 1996.

Hillairet, Jacques: *Connaissance du Vieux Paris*
Paris: Payot et Rivages, 1993.

Hillairet, Jacques: *Dictionnaire Historique des Rues de Paris*
Paris: Ed. Minuit, 1991.

Larousse, Pierre: *Nouveau Dictionnaire Illustré*
Paris: Larousse, 1909.

Maureau, Andrée: *Recettes en Provences*
Aix-en-Provence: Edisud, 1991.

Vallois, Thirza: *Around and About Paris*
London: Illiad Books, 1997.

Varejka, Pascal: *Paris-brève histoire de la capitale*
Paris: Ed. Parigramme, 1995.

PHOTO CREDITS

All photographs taken by Nicolle Aimée Meyer and Amanda Pilar Smith except:

© AKG, Paris: pp. 20 (ills. 1, 2), 24 (ill. 2), 26 (ills. 2, 3), 27 (ills. 2, 3), 71 (ill. 1), 127, 139, 148, 288.

© AKG, Paris / Almasy: pp. 26 (ill.1), 224.

© Association Soleil, Paris: pp. 18, 21 (ills. 1, 2), 24 (ills. 1, 3), 25 (ill. 4), 27 (ill. 1), 111, 164 (ill. 1).

© Könemann Verlag GmbH, Köln / Studio für Landkartentechnik, Detlef Maiwald: endpapers.

Olaf Wipperfurth, Paris: pp. 36, 57, 59, 81, 116, 119, 133, 157, 197, 233, 257, 259, 276, 295, 311, 332, 335.

© Photo Disc, Hamburg: p. 265 (ill.2).

© Roger Viollet, Paris / Boyer: pp. 23, 208.

© Roger Viollet, Paris / Branger: p. 25 (ill. 1).

© Roger Viollet, Paris / Harlingue: pp. 22, 24 (ill. 4), 112 (ill. 2), 136, 166, 318.

© Roger Viollet, Paris / John-James Chalon: p. 2.

© Roger Viollet, Paris / LL: p. 25 (ill. 3).

© Roger Viollet, Paris: pp. 25 (ill. 2), 149.

© Tony Stone Images, Munich / Hulton Getty: p. 95 (ills. 1, 2, 3).

The publisher has not been able to trace all owners of rights to the images reproduced. Owners of such rights are requested to address any claims arising from them to the publisher.

NOTES ON ABBREVIATIONS AND QUANTITIES

1 inch	= 2.5 centimeters
1 oz	= 1 ounce = 28 grams
1 lb	= 1 pound = 16 ounces
1 cup	= 250 milliliters (liquids)
1g	= 1 gram = 1/1000 kilogram
1 kg	= 1 kilogram = 1000 grams
125 ml	= 125 mililiters = approximately 8 tbs
1 tbs	= 1 level tablespoon = 15–20 g* / 15 ml (liquids)
1 tsp	= 1 level teaspoon = 3–5 g* / 5 ml (liquids)

* The weight of dry ingredients varies significantly depending on the density factor; e.g. 1 cup flour weighs less than 1 cup butter. The metric conversions for bigger quantities are given in the recipes.
Quantities in recipes have been rounded up or down for convenience, where appropriate. Metric conversions may, therefore, not correspond exactly.

Propreté
de
Paris

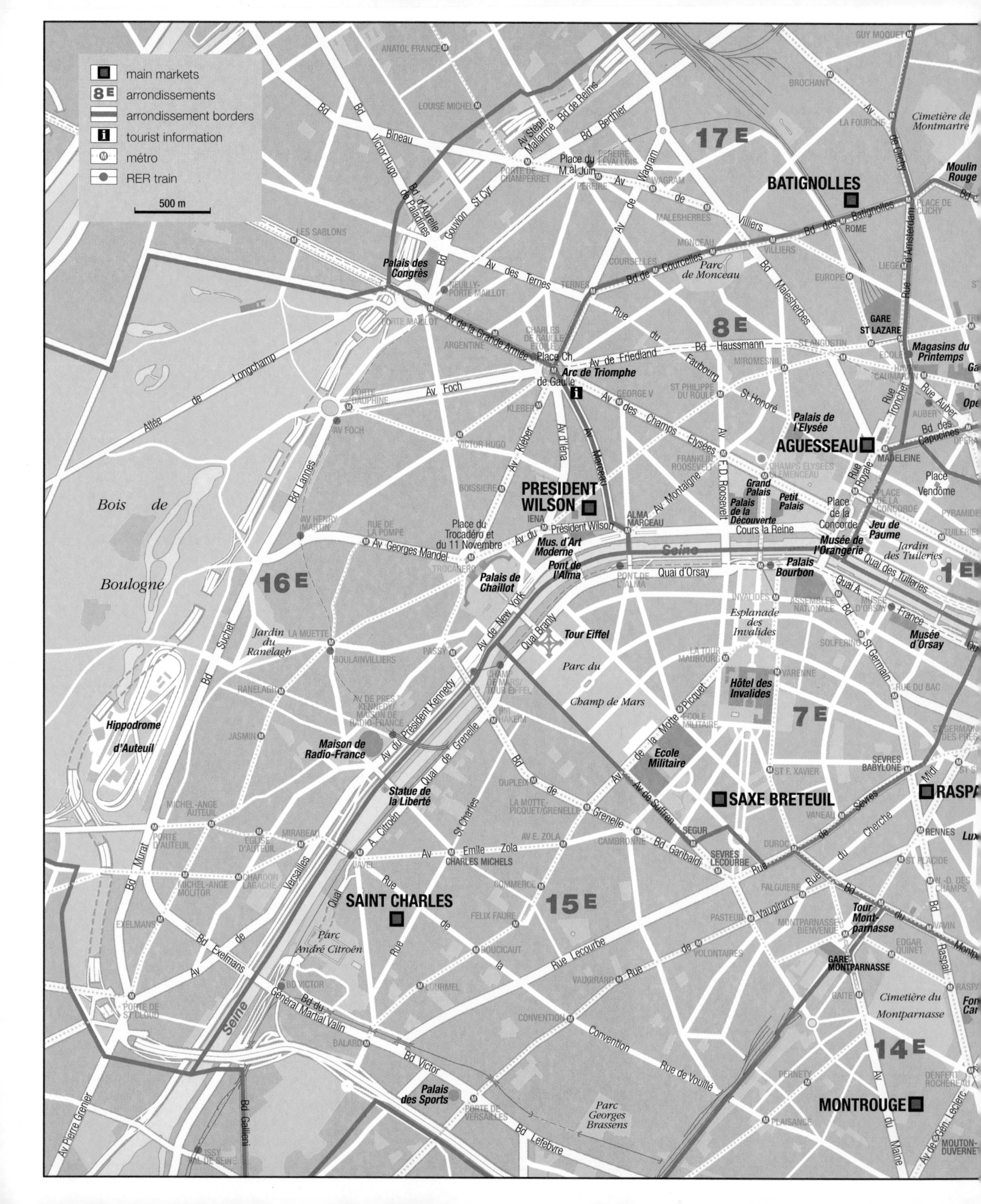

main markets
8E
arrondissements
arrondissement borders
tourist information
métro
RER train
500 m
17E
8E
16E
7E
15E
14E
BATIGNOLLES
AGUESSEAU
PRESIDENT WILSON
SAXE BRETEUIL
SAINT CHARLES
MONTROUGE
Cimetière de Montmartre
Moulin Rouge
Palais des Congrès
Arc de Triomphe
Place Ch. de Gaulle
Magasins du Printemps
Palais de l'Elysée
Parc de Monceau
Grand Palais
Petit Palais
Palais de la Découverte
Place de la Concorde
Place Vendôme
Jeu de Paume
Musée de l'Orangerie
Jardin des Tuileries
Palais Bourbon
Mus. d'Art Moderne
Pont de l'Alma
Palais de Chaillot
Place du Trocadéro et du 11 Novembre
Tour Eiffel
Parc du Champ de Mars
Esplanade des Invalides
Hôtel des Invalides
Musée d'Orsay
Ecole Militaire
Bois de Boulogne
Jardin du Ranelagh
Hippodrome d'Auteuil
Maison de Radio-France
Statue de la Liberté
Parc André Citroën
Tour Montparnasse
Gare Montparnasse
Cimetière du Montparnasse
Palais des Sports
Parc Georges Brassens
Gare St Lazare
Seine
Place du M.al Juin
Allée de Longchamp
Av Foch
Av de la Grande Armée
Av des Ternes
Bd de Courcelles
Bd des Batignolles
Av de Wagram
Bd Malesherbes
Bd Haussmann
Av de Friedland
Rue du Faubourg St Honoré
Av des Champs Elysées
Av Montaigne
Av Marceau
Av d'Iéna
Av Kléber
Av F.D. Roosevelt
Rue Royale
Av George Mandel
Av du Président Wilson
Av de New York
Quai Branly
Quai d'Orsay
Cours la Reine
Quai des Tuileries
Bd St Germain
Av de la Motte Picquet
Av de Suffren
Bd de Grenelle
Bd Garibaldi
Rue de Sèvres
Rue du Cherche Midi
Rue de Vaugirard
Rue Lecourbe
Rue de la Convention
Rue de Vouillé
Av Emile Zola
Quai de Grenelle
Av du Président Kennedy
Quai A. Citroën
Bd Exelmans
Bd Murat
Bd Suchet
Bd Lannes
Bd Victor
Bd du Général Martial Valin
Bd Lefebvre
Bd Raspail
Av du Maine
Av du Gén. Leclerc
Av Pierre Grenier
Bd Gallieni
Rue d'Amsterdam
Av de Clichy
Rue Tronchet
Rue Auber
Bd des Capucines
Bd Bineau
Bd Victor Hugo
Bd d'Aurelle de Paladines
Bd Gouvion St Cyr
Bd Berthier
Av Stéph. Mallarmé
Bd de Reims
Av de Villiers
Rue de Versailles